MUSLIM CULTURES OF THE INDIAN OCEAN

Based at the Aga Khan Centre in London, the Aga Khan University Institute for the Study of Muslim Civilisations is a higher education institution with a focus on research, publications, graduate studies and outreach. It promotes scholarship that opens up new perspectives on Muslim heritage, modernity, religion, culture and society. The Institute aims to create opportunities for interaction among academics and other professionals in an effort to deepen the understanding of pressing issues affecting Muslim societies today.

EXPLORING MUSLIM CONTEXTS

Series Editor: Farouk Topan

This series seeks to address salient and urgent issues faced by Muslim societies as they evolve in a rapidly globalising world. It brings together the scholarship of leading specialists from various academic fields, representing a wide range of theoretical and practical perspectives.

Development Models in Muslim Contexts: Chinese, 'Islamic' and Neo-liberal Alternatives
Edited by Robert Springborg

The Challenge of Pluralism: Paradigms from Muslim Contexts
Edited by Abdou Filali-Ansary and Sikeena Karmali Ahmed

Cosmopolitanisms in Muslim Contexts: Perspectives from the Past
Edited by Derryl MacLean and Sikeena Karmali Ahmed

Ethnographies of Islam: Ritual Performances and Everyday Practices
Edited by Badouin Dupret, Thomas Pierret, Paulo Pinto and Kathryn Spellman-Poots

Genealogy and Knowledge in Muslim Societies: Understanding the Past
Edited by Sarah Bowen Savant and Helena de Felipe

Contemporary Islamic Law in Indonesia: Sharia and Legal Pluralism
Arskal Salim

Shaping Global Islamic Discourses: The Role of Al-Azhar, Al-Madina and Al-Mustafa
Edited by Masooda Bano and Keiko Sakurai

Gender, Governance and Islam
Edited by Deniz Kandiyoti, Nadje Al-Ali and Kathryn Spellman Poots

What is Islamic Studies? European and North American Approaches to a Contested Field
Edited by Leif Stenberg and Philip Wood

Muslim Cultures of the Indian Ocean: Diversity and Pluralism, Past and Present
Edited by Stéphane Pradines and Farouk Topan

edinburghuniversitypress.com/series/ecmc

Muslim Cultures of the Indian Ocean

Diversity and Pluralism, Past and Present

Edited by Stéphane Pradines and Farouk Topan

EDINBURGH
University Press

IN ASSOCIATION WITH

THE AGA KHAN UNIVERSITY

Edinburgh University Press is one of the leading university presses in the UK. We publish academic books and journals in our selected subject areas across the humanities and social sciences, combining cutting-edge scholarship with high editorial and production values to produce academic works of lasting importance. For more information visit our website: edinburghuniversitypress.com

Edinburgh University Press Ltd
The Tun – Holyrood Road
12 (2f) Jackson's Entry
Edinburgh EH8 8PJ

Typeset in Goudy Oldstyle by
Cheshire Typesetting Ltd, Cuddington, Cheshire, and
printed and bound in Great Britain

A CIP record for this book is available from the British Library

ISBN 978 1 4744 8649 1 (hardback)
ISBN 978 1 4744 8651 4 (webready PDF)
ISBN 978 1 4744 8652 1 (epub)

Contents

Figures

Introduction

Stéphane Pradines and Farouk Topan

A Historiography of Indian Ocean Cultures

Over the past couple of decades, significant new research has been undertaken across East Africa, the Arabian Peninsula and the Indian subcontinent leading to fresh insights into several facets of Indian Ocean cultures. Scholars increasingly recognise the centrality of the Indian Ocean in the study of Muslim cultures. Some of these studies, written about the Indian Ocean in its *longue durée*, focused on local and regional histories. Cultural encounters across the Indian Ocean down the centuries have given rise to cities, towns, ports and other constructions and artefacts which, while remaining distinctive in themselves, also exhibit layers of shared features. Muslim participation in these transoceanic encounters has been diverse and significant, with links that created conduits for trade, commerce and exchange of ideas, beliefs, practices, scholarship and material goods. Recent publications highlight and theorise the interlinks, connections and networks across the region. These are discussed below as a prelude to engaging with the core premise of this volume: that interconnections and mobility among Muslim localities in the region have generated 'a cultural continuum' whose diversity is reflected in the exchange of knowledge, beliefs, practices, scholarship, trade, commerce and other endeavours. Several edited volumes examine the interconnectivity of the Indian Ocean World by using case studies,[1] a method also adopted in this volume.

Some previous books had explored the story of the Indian Ocean as a world system starting with the advent of complex societies between the Bronze Age

---

[1] Simpson and Kresse, 2007; Declich, 2018; Schottenhammer, 2019; Keller, 2019.

and late antiquity.[2] Most of the urbanisation, city-states and complex political systems emerged due to trade and mobility in the hinterland and along great rivers such as the Euphrates and the Tigris with the Mesopotamian Empires and the Harrapan civilisation along the Indus River.[3] At the beginning of the first millennium CE, the nautical revolution caused by using the monsoon winds of the Indian Ocean allowed for major water crossings. The Romans and the Axum kingdoms were the first to expand outside the Red Sea to Africa and India.[4] In the Gulf, the Sassanians expanded the maritime trade system first established in the Bronze Age to India and beyond.

During this early period, the Arabian Peninsula, the Red Sea and the Gulf played a major role in the Indian Ocean World system.[5] During the Abbasid Caliphate, Islam began to expand all over the Indian Ocean.[6] The Abbasid period was an age of exploration and discovery, as demonstrated most famously by the Sindbad the sailor stories. Merchants from the Gulf established a series of emporiums and caravanserais from East Africa to Southeast Asia.[7] Building on networks from late antiquity, this international trade was reinforced by the new religion, Islam, one of whose teachings required its followers to accomplish the Hajj or pilgrimage to Mecca.[8] Long-distance trade boosted the urbanisation and development of port cities and coastal and island cultures.[9] Several books have been published that explore the littoral societies, cultural exchanges and trading networks in Muslim contexts.[10]

Between the tenth and twelfth centuries, Shi'a traders and missionaries started to travel around the Indian Ocean. This period is also known as the Golden Age of the Shi'a caliphates, with the Fatimids in Egypt, the Qarmatians and the Buyid emirates in the Persian Gulf. Trading networks were also supported by non-Muslim communities such as the Jews in Yemen and Hindus and Buddhists in India and Southeast Asia.[11] The most important phenomenon was the fact that these travellers not only converted people from the places that they visited, but some settled in these distant places. These first migrations of non-indigenous communities heavily influenced local histories and traditions, including, for example, the emergence of the 'Shirazi' communities in East Africa.

---

[2] McLaughlin, 2018.
[3] Ray, 'Maritime archaeology of the Indian Ocean, recent trends and an overview', in Ray and Salles, 2012, pp. xiii–xxiv and 1–10; Beaujard, 2019, pp. 41–160.
[4] Power, 2012.
[5] Crone, 2004, pp. 51–83; Potts, D. T., 'The Archaeology and Early History of the Persian Gulf', in Potter, 2009, pp. 27–43.
[6] Hourani, 1995; Agius, 2008.
[7] 'Becoming an Islamic sea', in Alpers, 2014, pp. 40–68.
[8] Risso, 1995, pp. 99–106; Koehler, 2014.
[9] Toorawa, 2007; Schnepel and Sen, 2018.
[10] Chaudhuri, 1985; Risso, 1995, pp. 99–106.
[11] Goitein and Friedman, 2008, pp. 311–36; Lambourn, 2018, pp. 37–64.

Buddhism and Hinduism also played a very important role in the diffusion of Islam in the Indian Ocean World. Several kingdoms and religions in Southeast Asia from the seventh to the fifteenth century supported Muslim trading networks such as Anuradhapura in Sri Lanka, Majapahit in Java, Srivijaya in Sumatra and, of course, the kingdoms of Champa and Angkor in modern day Cambodia. Some of them, such as Majapahit and Srivijaya, were extremely powerful thalassocracies and they benefited from their strategic location between China and India.

Later, Sufi orders adapted themselves to pre-existing religious networks and gradually replaced them. These Sufi orders, such as the Naqshbandiyah and Kazaruniyya, became extremely powerful around the Indian Ocean. Sufi brotherhoods reinforced social links between maritime communities. Several articles and books explore the role of Sufi orders in Islamisation and the relationship with Buddhism in the Malay-Indonesian world within the sultanates of Malacca, Aceh and the Maldives.[12] In East Africa, contemporary practices in the Swahili world show how Sufi brotherhoods are reinforcing social links between maritime communities, as highlighted in several publications.[13]

The geography of the Indian Ocean World has also been explored through navigation and the monsoon wind system.[14] Some publications on the Indian Ocean focus specifically on the navigation, ships and sailors in Muslim contexts, such as Hourani's iconic reference work, *Arab Seafaring in the Indian Ocean in Ancient and Early Medieval Times* (1951); Dionisius Agius' *Classic Ships of Islam: from Mesopotamia to the Indian Ocean* (2008) and Abdul Sheriff's *Dhow Cultures of the Indian Ocean* (2010).

Several publications present a history of the Indian Ocean both as a world in itself and its role in world history.[15] These comparative studies on the *longue durée* discuss the political systems and modes of governance on the Indian Ocean coast, which were mainly thalassocracies. Swahili cities, for example Zanzibar and Kilwa, can be compared to those in the Mediterranean, such as Genoa and Venice.

The focus of some publications has been on specific regions and their cultural aspects: East Africa and the Swahili coast, South Arabia with Yemen and Oman[16] or India and the regions of Gujarat, Deccan and Kerala. The Yemen, in particular Aden and the port cities on the Hadramawt, were strategic locations in the Indian Ocean trade.[17] This monopoly at the crossroads between the

---

[12] Bang, 2003, ch. 1; Headley and Parkin, 2015; Ho, 2006.
[13] Eisenlohr, 2018; Headley and Parkin, 2015; Bang, 2014.
[14] Wink, 2002, pp. 416–45.
[15] Pearson, 2003; Alpers 2014; Sheriff, 2014.
[16] Freitag and Clarence-Smith, 1997; Nicolini and de Silva Jayasuriya, 2017; Kresse, in MacLean, 2018, pp. 31–50.
[17] Margariti, 2007.

Mediterranean worlds via the Red Sea and the Indian worlds was reinforced during the Rasulid and Mamluk dynasties, protecting not only the trade with Africa but also with India. Between the thirteenth and fifteenth centuries most of the city-states around the Indian Ocean reached their apogee. It was also during this period that the Red Sea took over most of the Gulf's maritime international trade via Cairo and Alexandria in Egypt. Finally, Sunni Islam (of the Shafiʿi persuasion) was propagated and adopted by most of the Muslim communities around the Indian Ocean.

The Indian Ocean got its name from the Indian subcontinent during the Greco-Roman period, when India played a major role in trade, politics and cultural relationships between all the regions around the Indian Ocean.[18] With early Roman ports such as Pattanam in Kerala and Banbhore in Sindh, which became the first Muslim port city in the Indus delta, India was connected to trade between China, Arabia and Africa. During the medieval period, Indian sailors and merchants travelled on both sides of the Indian Ocean, trading in imported products but also in Indian goods such as beads and textiles.[19] The main trading centres and cities were located around Kathiawar and Gujarat. Other regions involved in oceanic trade were the Deccan of the Bahmani Sultanate.[20] India played a major role in trade, politics and cultural relationships between all the regions around the Indian Ocean.[21] Indian cultures and tastes, ranging from architecture to gastronomy, strongly influenced Indian Ocean cultures from the Maldives to Yemen to Oman and the Swahili coast. Swahili civilisation expanded from Somalia, through Kenya, Tanzania, north Madagascar and the Comoros to Mozambique. The Swahili stand at the confluence of Muslim and African worlds, resulting in the development of a unique coastal culture based initially on long-distance trade.[22] The role of trade was crucial in the urbanisation and development of port cities and city-states.[23] On the Asian side, with the exception of the famous maritime expeditions of Admiral Zheng He in the fifteenth century, China never had direct contact with the Arabian Peninsula and Africa.[24] Nevertheless, trade with China in the Indian Ocean World economy was massive since, at least, the Abbasid period. Importing African ivory and trading Chinese stoneware and porcelain, China was a major player in the Indian Ocean trade called by Europeans the 'Spice Road' and by the Chinese

---

[18] Prange, 2005, pp. 1382–93.

[19] Risso, 1995, pp. 99–106; Machado, 2016, pp. 122–49.

[20] Green, 2011; Reese, 2018.

[21] Das Gupta and Pearson, 1987; Hawley, 2008; Kooria and Pearson, 2018; Keller, 2019.

[22] Pradines, 2017, pp. 211–36; Nicolini and de Silva Jayasuriya, 2017.

[23] Horton and Middleton, 2000, chs 1–2; Prestholdt, 2008.

[24] Nanji, 'A Chinese muse in the Caliph's court: the influence of Chinese ceramic technology across the Indian Ocean (eighth to fourteenth century CE)', in Keller, 2019, pp. 47–64.

the 'Maritime Silk Road', so named after the better known land route through Central Asia, the Silk Road.[25]

In 1498 the discovery by Vasco da Gama of a maritime route to Asia by way of Africa's Cape of Good Hope, the 'Carreira da India', completely changed the relationship between the different regions of the Indian Ocean World. During the sixteenth century the Portuguese built some fifty fortresses around the Indian Ocean, from Mozambique to Malacca. The idea was to protect and control European trade with India and to assure a monopoly for the Crown of Portugal. Piracy and violence, and attempts to protect maritime trade from them, had existed in the Indian Ocean a long time before the Europeans entered the Indian Ocean. But the advent of the Portuguese signals the beginning of the modern era for the Indian Ocean World, with the introduction of gunpowder and the establishment by Christian Europeans of new commercial networks with non-Muslim trading communities, such as the Hindus in Gujarat. Establishing Goa to the north of the Malabar coast as their headquarters, was also a strong political and economic choice for the Portuguese.[26] Following the Portuguese, Dutch, English and French traders also began to expand into the Indian Ocean, colonising coastal territories and islands for commercial profit. Through their trade in the Indian Ocean, the Europeans also came into direct contact with the Mughal empire. Across the Indian Ocean, from sub-Saharan Africa to Malacca, stock companies such as the Dutch and British East India companies attempted to control or get maximum benefits from the spice road.[27] The Indian Ocean World was transformed through the consumption of goods, intercultural connections, connectivity and circulation of new ideas coming from Europe,[28] and there are several publications that have explored this in detail.[29]

Writing about Indian Ocean diasporas was and is always connected to debates on race, citizenship and identity through forced migrations.[30] Hence several publications refer directly or indirectly to the creolisation of Indian Ocean societies.[31] Slavery in the Indian Ocean World can be traced back to at least the Abbasid period, when 500,000 revolting slaves besieged al-Basra in 869. Islamic legal traditions provided a legal framework to deal with slaves, directly inspired by late antiquity practices. Between the eighteenth and nineteenth centuries, the Omani became a mercantile superpower in the Indian Ocean, through their

---

[25] Schnepel and Sen, 2019.
[26] Silva, 2011; Prange, *Monsoon Islam: Trade and Faith on the Medieval Malabar Coast*, 2018.
[27] Chaudhuri, 1978, pp. 1–18 and 316–17.
[28] 'Cosmopolitanism contested: anthropology and history in the Indian Ocean', in Simpson, and Kresse, 2007, pp. 1–41.
[29] Chaudhuri, 1978; Satis, 1987; Bose, 2009.
[30] Ray, 2016.
[31] Shanti and Jamal, 2010; Moorthy, 2010.

clove plantations and their trade in ivory and slaves between India and Africa.[32] In 1832, the Sultan even transferred his capital from Muscat to Zanzibar in a unique instance of political shift between two continents, and demonstrating the great mobility of Indian Ocean cultures and people. During this period, slavery would be used by the French and Omanis to provide workers for plantations in Zanzibar, Mauritius and Réunion.[33]

MUSLIM CULTURES AND HERITAGE IN THE INDIAN OCEAN

A significant factor emerging from the historiographic survey given above has been the growing importance of the Indian Ocean as a field of study, and the role of Islam as a potent factor of change and transformation among the peoples of this vast region (Fig. I.1). The earlier perception of 'Islam is the desert', signifying the location of its origins, has been complemented by 'Islam is the ocean', an affirmation of its spread across the seas where Muslims have for centuries interacted with each other and with other peoples and cultures.[34] Islam not only provided the framework that facilitated cultural exchanges but was also the pivot for transforming local societies in this vast region. Some of the factors and facets, reflective of the diversity of Muslim cultures prevalent in the Indian Ocean region, are explored in this book, which developed from a conference organised in 2018 by the Aga Khan University's Institute for the Study of Muslim Civilisations (AKU-ISMC).

The papers in the book explore the role of Muslim communities through their evolving connections and mobilities across the Indian Ocean World. Spanning from the seventh century to the present day, the papers highlight different aspects of interconnectivity in relation to Islam. Analysing textual and material evidence, the book examines identities and diasporas, manuscripts and literature, as well as vernacular and religious architecture. It aims to explore networks and circulations of peoples, ideas and ideologies, as well as art, culture, religion and heritage. It focuses on both global interactions as well as local agencies in context.

The papers combine historical, archaeological and cultural approaches to the study of the Indian Ocean through a comparative study of Muslim societies within the context of three periods: the pre-colonial, the colonial and the modern. The case studies fulfil an heuristic function in terms of illustrating some of the points briefly that have been outlined above. Reflected is a dynamic

---

[32] Bose, 2009, pp. 193–282; Freitag and Clarence-Smith, 1997; Campbell, Gwynn, 'Slave Trade and the Indian Ocean World', in Hawley, 2008, pp. 17–51.

[33] Anderson, 2000.

[34] Bose, Sugata, 'Old Tides and New Waves in Indian Ocean History', in Keller, 2019, p. xxii, Bose references Braudel, 1995 and Jalal, 2000.

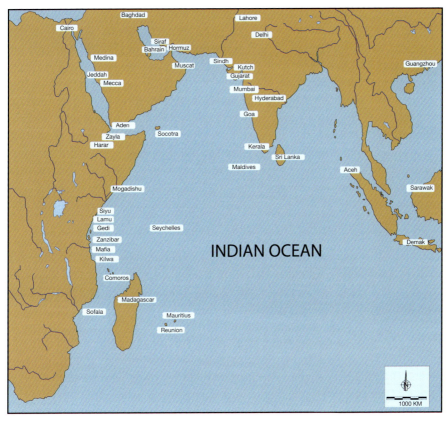

Figure I.1 Map of the Muslim cultures of the Indian Ocean.
Courtesy Stéphane Pradines.

expression of local agency in historical context, a continuous forging and reforging of identity, and a creative impulse generated through the interface of Islam and local cultures.[35] These factors are further explored in the papers dealing with Islamic architecture; intra-Muslim perceptions of belief; colonial interaction with Muslims/Islam; the travel of texts: Muslim attitudes to the Qur'an its preservation and transport; the intertwining of religion and ethnicity in identity; the impact of trade and maritime culture; and the role of women as actors within the Indian Ocean culture.

The papers are grouped in two sections. The first, Muslim Identities, Literature and Diasporas, explores the mobility of texts and manuscripts, and the forging of identity and its relation to religion, ethnicity, politics and trade.

---

[35] A process discussed in depth by many scholars, notably Geertz, 1968 and 1973; Eickelman, 1982; and, more recently, by Ahmed, 2016, 246–297.

The second, Monuments and Heritage in Muslim Contexts, focuses on the interaction between the local and the global in architecture. The case studies presented in the papers are drawn from Ethiopia, Tanzania, Oman, Gujarat, Kerala, the Maldives, the Malay-Indonesian archipelago and the Persianate cultural zone. The geography of the Indian Ocean as a maritime world is also explored through the specificities of the coastal natural resources, such as the mangrove and the coral reefs. Sites and monuments are looked at as parts of regional and national identities, and are presented through littoral political systems and coastal modes of governance: the thalassocracies and city-states. Finally, Indian Ocean heritage is presented through discussions about littoral societies and cultural exchanges.

Part I: Muslim Identities, Literature and Diasporas

The first two papers in this section relate to manuscripts of the Qur'an: their writing, production, illumination, transmission, preservation and the geographical interlinks across the Indian Ocean connecting Africa and the Indian subcontinent.

Sana Mirza's paper presents a major centre of Islamic learning, the city of Harar, which was a nexus of key trade routes linking the highlands of Ethiopia to the Red Sea and the Indian Ocean. Harar was also home to an extraordinary manuscript tradition that has so far remained largely unknown to historians. Produced between the seventeenth and nineteenth centuries, numerous Harari Qur'an manuscripts provide rich material with which to consider circuits of artistic interchange across the early modern Indian Ocean and their role in shaping local artistic idioms. The chapter argues for the development of a distinctive Harari calligraphic script and visual identity in the mid-eighteenth century, a time of increased transregional circulation around the Indian Ocean. This Harari style was formed by the active and selective participation by the city's artisans in long-distance artistic and religious networks, and their ability to synthesise from multiple sources while largely ignoring concurrent Ottoman trends. The manuscripts provide evidence not only of the mobility of artistic forms across the Indian Ocean, but also of Harar's position as an artistic centre within an interrelated constellation of centres of artistic production stretching from Egypt to Indonesia.

Walid Ghali introduces a rare Qur'anic manuscript from The Aga Khan Library that originated in East Africa. Despite the poor condition of the incomplete manuscript, it displayed two interesting features. The first is the calligraphy itself and the way the verses have been corrected and inserted. The second is the style of the illumination, which exhibits obvious South Asian features. Available historical information suggests three ways of establishing the manuscript's provenance: a) the manuscript could have been written by a South Asian calligrapher, who lived in East Africa; b) the manuscript could have been brought to East Africa from South Asia by traders or scholar(s); and c) the manuscript could have been copied from a similar copy by a calligrapher in East Africa. Ghali examines the manuscript from a codicological point of view to demonstrate the similarities of the style of illumination with South Asian practices in manuscript illumination.

Staying with the East African connection, the subsequent three papers explore dimensions of authority, power, identity, diplomacy and scholarship associated with the Omani Al Bu Said dynasty, which ruled Zanzibar and the East African coast during the nineteenth and twentieth centuries, ending with the Zanzibar Revolution of 1964. All three papers also reference European colonial rule, its power, authority and influence. Two papers – those of Valerie J. Hoffman and Farouk Topan – adopt a biographical approach in exploring their topics: Hoffman, through the diary of a scholar and judge from Zanzibar, and Topan, through two women prominent in modern Zanzibari history.

Beatrice Nicolini's chapter surveys various factors that first attracted the Al Bu Said Sultans to the East African coast, and then the strategy they employed to rule over a region with diverse populations with varied ethnic backgrounds and religious affiliations. The sultans exercised power through a delicate balance of military force, religious tolerance and different social groups. Omani rule during the nineteenth century operated through a devolution of its leadership among different groups: the Baloch mercenaries, the Asian religious and mercantile communities, and the African regional leaders (the Mwinyi Mkuu, for example). And it was during this period that sultans had also to negotiate with the colonial powers, principally the British, over their territories.

Valerie J. Hoffman analyses the relationships between religion, ethnicity and identity in the Zanzibar Sultanate. The sultanate ruled a singularly cosmopolitan but highly stratified population, including Arabs of Omani background (usually Ibāḍīs), scholars and labourers of Ḥaḍramī descent, Indians of diverse origins and religions, and Baloch and Persian mercenaries, in addition to people who self-identified as 'Shirazi', other people from the Banādir or Mrima coasts and large numbers of African slaves. Recent publications by John Wilkinson and Jonathon Glassman explore issues of religion, ethnicity and identity on the Swahili coast in new and interesting ways. Hoffman draws on their work while also analysing unpublished manuscript fragments by a Somali-born scholar, ʿAbd al-ʿAzīz al-Amawī, who served as a Shāfiʿī judge in Zanzibar and a counsellor and ambassador for its rulers. Sultan Barghash (r. 1870–88) sent Amawī on several exploratory and diplomatic missions to the African mainland. Amawī kept meticulous records, though unfortunately much of what he wrote is lost. Nonetheless, the remaining fragments of his diaries offer insights into his perspectives on religion, ethnicity and identity in the sultanate, which sometimes differ from those of British writers. Hoffman also explores the writings of nineteenth- and twentieth-century Ibāḍī scholars in Zanzibar, which adds an interesting dimension to our understanding of the relationships of different groups on the island.

The place of women in these coastal societies is discussed by Farouk Topan. His chapter explores aspects of the lives of two Zanzibari women – Emily Said-Ruete (1844–1924) and Siti binti Saad (1880–1950) – whose backgrounds and upbringing could not have been more different. Emily Said-Ruete was born as Salme, the daughter of the Sultan of Oman and the first Sultan of Zanzibar, Sayyid Said bin Sultan (d. 1856). She was raised as a royal princess in Zanzibar but had to flee the island in 1866 after falling in love with Heinrich Ruete, an official at the German Consulate. She converted to Christianity at Aden, married Ruete and settled in Germany. Her book, *Memoirs of an Arabian Princess*, was published in 1888. Siti binti Saad was born and raised in a village in Zanzibar and later became an accomplished singer; she was the first East African to be invited by gramophone companies – Columbia and His Master's Voice – to travel to Mumbai, India, in 1928 to record her songs. Her lyrics are about everyday life in Zanzibar, often referencing actual events. They contain social criticism, denouncing class oppression, corruption, the abuse of women by men and the shortcomings of the colonial legal system. The chapter examines the way the two women exercise their agency locally (Siti) and globally (Salme) within the cultural continuum of the East African coast, its links with Oman, and interaction with colonial powers (British and German).

Travel accounts in manuscripts by two scholars from India and Persia are discussed in the papers by Gulfishan Khan and Roghayeh Ebrahimi. The manuscripts not only display the vast extent of the regions covered by Jamali and Nishaburi, respectively, in their travels in the sixteenth and seventeenth centuries, but they also present valuable observations of the personalities, networks and architecture prevalent in those places at the time.

Gulfishan Khan depicts the travel experiences of the Indo-Persian Sufi-poet Hamid bin Fazl Allah, also known as Jamali (d. 1535), as embodied in his comprehensive biographical account of Muslim mystics entitled *Siyar al-arifin* (*The Biographies of the Gnostics*). A poet, literatus and a polymath, Jamali acquired experiences of the wider world through his extensive travels and social interactions in a variety of places, including Arabia (for the Hajj), Yemen, Jerusalem, Palestine, Turkey (Rum), Syria, Khurasan, Iraq-i-Arab and Iraq-i-Ajam, Azerbaijan, Gilan, Mazandaran, Khurasan and the lands of Maghrib. *Siyar al-arifin* offers strong evidence of lively networks of relationship between Suhrawardy Shaikhs of Delhi, Multan and Baghdad. It offers a personalised and multifaceted view of Sufi communities, their closely knit social networks, intellectual concerns, religious authority and the role of patronage and philanthropy. Jamali's views derive from his visits to mosques, *madrasahs* and Sufi-*khanqahs*, the cosmopolitan institutions of Islam. Jamali's activities demonstrate a dynamic process of cultural exchange at work in the Persianate cultural zone where people, ideas, goods, books and letters moved back and forth.

With the rise of the Safavid state in Iran and the expansion of Muslim trade through India, networks of Persian merchants became increasingly active in the eastern Indian Ocean maritime trade in the sixteenth and seventeenth centuries. Roghayeh Ebrahimi presents a Persian view of the maritime Muslim frontier in Southeast Asia, an unpublished Persian text of the period: the *Jām ʿa al-Bar wa ʾl-bahr* (*Compendium of the Land and Sea*). The author of the manuscript, Mahmud Ibn ʿAbdollah Nayshābūrī, was a textile merchant and a voyager with a life-long interest in commerce and navigation in India and beyond. In his account of the Indonesian archipelago, he presents a hierarchical view of civilisation in which Muslim merchants, and Persian traders in particular, are cast in the role of 'civilising agents' among the expanding Muslim communities of Southeast Asia. This included both the extension of participation in prosperous networks of exchange and the introduction of new cultural and literary traditions to local populations as part of their incorporation into a wider world of Islam. In this, it presents a striking comparative perspective on the accelerating processes of social transformation taking place during a period that was also marked by the arrival and intervention of new European powers in the region.

The final paper of this first section discusses the relevance of the Indian Ocean as an interregional arena by focusing on the status of Wahhabism in the Barelvi-Deobandi schism in South Asian Sunnism. In his discussion, Reza Pirbhai uses the *fatawa* literature to argue that the connections between South Asian and Arabian scholars over the last three centuries centred on the discursive hub of the Hijaz, and reveals that over time there were both a significant variety and significant shifts in the forms of Muslim cosmopolitanism and Islamic universalism connecting the Indian Ocean's littoral fringe. Changing relations of power promoted by colonial and post-colonial states have not just swept aside 'pre-modern' state formations such as the Ottomans, Safavids and Mughals, but also the pre-modern approach to Islamic doctrine and practice, ushering in a 'modern' brand of Islam that limits diversity and pluralism relative to the past.

PART II: MONUMENTS AND HERITAGE IN MUSLIM CONTEXTS

The paper by Eric Falt aptly opens the second part of the book as it posits a view of the Indian Ocean that straddles both sections. The Indian Ocean, to him, is one of the world's few regions where the concept of a 'maritime cultural landscape' is fully applicable. Indeed, Indian Ocean routes are characterised by unique architectural features and archaeological sites; local traditions of boat-building, travel and navigation; and narratives of the trans-local experiences of maritime communities. To put it another way, a maritime cultural landscape is a holistic idea that includes maritime communities' tangible and intangible cultural heritage. The importance of the Indian Ocean is multidimensional and vast. With at least forty nations bordering it and constituting a significant proportion of the global population, the Indian Ocean and its littoral states represent multiple ways of life, a plurality of traditions and a long history of social, cultural and economic exchange. The concept and definition of a 'heritage route' was recognized by UNESCO only in the 2000s, and public awareness about this new category of heritage is still at a nascent stage. The heritage of the Indian Ocean ought to constitute an 'Indian Ocean Maritime Heritage Route' and be studied and promoted as intensively as certain other famous routes such as the Silk Road or the Maritime Silk Route. Perceiving the Indian Ocean as a maritime cultural landscape and heritage route opens new possibilities for dialogue and international cooperation, and offers new perspectives to promote heritage development and sustainable tourism across the Indian Ocean region.

Following this, Stephen Battle and Pierre Blanchard introduce the reader to conservation and heritage on the Swahili coast. First, with a practitioner's experience in Zanzibar Old Town with the Aga Khan Trust for Culture project on the Old Dispensary building on the waterfront. Then the authors describe a practical case of conservation of an Indian Ocean World Heritage Site in Kilwa and how the Tanzanian Antiquities Authority, UNESCO and the World Monument Fund managed to protect and save the sites there with the help of local communities. Kilwa Kisiwani and Songo Mnara, situated in the Lindi region of the Kilwa district, are amongst the most important heritage sites in Tanzania. The structures that make up the sites constitute the exceptional oeuvre of 800 years of East African history. In Kilwa Kisiwani impressive remains of major Swahili monuments are conserved for their architectural achievement and their extent, notably an Omani fort, two palaces, large houses and several mosques, including the largest Swahili mosque still standing with significant parts of its domed roof remaining. Songo Mnara contains the ruins of mosques, cemeteries and forty stone houses dating from the fourteenth to the sixteenth centuries, some of which are better preserved and more archaeologically intact than any comparable medieval city in East Africa. More than a simple project of conservation, the article focuses on sustainable conservation, sea erosion, global warming and land use planning to manage heritage sites in Africa.

Still in the Swahili world, Stéphane Pradines explores the role of trade in the dissemination of mosque architecture and the process of Islamisation of the Indian Ocean communities. In sub-Saharan Africa, the first converts were among the elite, most often merchants and local leaders. Islamised cities and kingdoms quickly took advantage of this new religion by strengthening their administration and legitimacy using Arabic script. The dissemination of mosque architecture was done by the sea roads through the Indian Ocean migrations, diaspora and trading networks. There is a common denominator amongst the early mosques in sub-Saharan Africa: it is the preponderant role of what are now called the religious minorities of Islam, notably the Ibadis and the Ismailis. The legacy of the kharidjites and the shi'ites is immense in sub-Saharan Africa – they are at the origin of the Swahili mosques. After the thirteenth century Africans adopted Sunnism en masse, with Sunni shafi'ites in East Africa and Sunni Malikites in West Africa. From this period onward, the Sufi movements became extremely popular in sub-Saharan Africa, and Pradines claims that Sufism became a philosophical and moral substitute to the previous religious sectarian Ibadi and Ismaili movements. This observation is also supported by the permeability of symbolism between Sufism and Shi'a spirituality.

In her paper, Madhavi Desai explores the representation of Muslim diversity on the Indian subcontinent through a variety of rich architectural manifestations. Among these are inner-city dwellings of the Islamic community of the Bohras in Gujarat, who had converted from Hinduism in the seventh century. The dwellings are excellent living examples of traditional architecture rooted in urban landscapes. The Bohra neighbourhoods, Bohrwads, are morphologically well-knit, homogeneous and dense. They have a structural unity, an orderliness and a sense of visual surprise. Based on regional concepts and typologies, the houses in these neighbourhoods symbolise a unique and creative transformation generated by layers of decisive influences of their original (Hindu) and adopted (Islamic) religions, including the impact of colonial culture in the metropolises. This is expressed in the hybrid, eclectic aesthetics signifying the attempt to connect with the imperial British rulers.

Next, Miki Desai considers the issue of regionalism in religious architecture through a comparative study of mosques in Gujarat and Kerala. During the propagation of Islam across different regions and cultural traditions, a process of adoption and adaptation from local architecture occurred, giving rise to varying expressions of its built-form, especially in religious edifices. These forms became contemporaneous and akin to the architecture of the land where Islam entered. However, Islam as a syncretic religion adhered to the belief of orientation and the principles of plan-organisation of the necessary components of the mosque. The chapter focuses on drawing a comparison between the mosque architecture of Gujarat and Kerala, two distinct regions of India. The intention is to understand the cause of physical and philosophical differences and commonalities that shaped the mosques of these regions. The case of comparison stems from the fact that Muslims arrived in Kerala and Gujarat fairly early but not as a domineering power. In this comparison of mosque architecture, the location and circumstances are important. Both are coastal regions on the west side of India. Gujarat has the longest coastline and a hot, dry climate with ancient port towns and an entrepreneurial community that exported cotton, silk, fabrics, carpets and quilts, dyes, indigo, agate, beads and tobacco. Kerala, in contrast, has a shorter coastline with important ancient ports but is in a hot, humid region with spices and grains as its most valuable export commodities in the past.

In the following paper, Mohamed Mauroof Jameel evaluates the architecture of the coral stone mosques of the Maldives, providing an overview of the architecture and unifying features from the Indian Ocean region. Coral stone mosques of the Maldives are tropical mosques built from ornamental porite coral stone quarried from reefs, using dry construction with carpentry joinery so that the structures can be assembled and disassembled. They have features and decorations that illustrate a fusion and unification of architecture from the Indian Ocean regions of South Asia, East Africa, Southeast Asia and the Middle East. The chapter focuses on the eclectic nature of the architecture of the coral stone mosques of the Maldives, which was influenced by the regions of the Indian Ocean. It is based on surveys and studies of these mosques by the author from 2011 to the present.

Finally, the last paper is devoted to Southeast Asia in which Bernard O'Kane traces the development of early Islamic architecture and decoration in Nusantara (Indonesia). The kingdom of Melaka was founded by expatriate Javanese in the early fifteenth century, and evidence of the links of Muslims in Java with the broader trading community is shown in the tombstones made in Cambay in Gujarat that were used in Sumatra and Java. What is considered the earliest surviving mosque of Java is located at Demak on its north coast. The town and mosque are associated with many of the *wali sanga*, in particular with Raden Patah, the son of the ruler of the most powerful Hindu kingdom in Java, the Majapahit, who was instrumental in the downfall of the kingdom and who is credited with the founding of the mosque in 1488. It displays many features that are considered characteristic of the Javanese mosque: an enclosure containing a building of square plan with brick walls and four large columns supporting a multi-tiered roof made of shingles. The square plan with four main supports is also a feature of most early mosques in the Malay Peninsula. Where did these elements come from? The most thorough recent study, that of Budi, highlights the connections with earlier communal halls of square plan with multi-tiered roofs that are seen in the stone-carved reliefs of pre-Islamic Javanese temples. The original enclosure wall of Demak no longer survives, but in many other mosques the entrance to it is in the form of a *candi bentar*, a split gateway that is a direct borrowing from Javanese Hindu temple complexes. The use of brick for the walls and shingles for the roof, however, is more likely to be features derived from Chinese architecture. However, in the eclectic origins of mosques in the archipelago, what has not been looked at in sufficient detail is that the square room with four supports was one of the main mosque forms encountered on the entire Indian littoral, from Gujarat to Calicut to Bengal, an area also with many parallels in climate and building materials. The paper explores in detail the possibilities of links of the typical mosque plan of the archipelago with those of India, an area with which there was also the strongest possible links in trade.

This book is the first publication of the AKU-ISMC in its continuing programme on the Indian Ocean. We acknowledge with gratitude the support extended to us by the AKU-ISMC, particularly by the Dean, Professor Leif Stenberg, and by the present and former Publications Managers, Donald Dinwiddie and Charlotte Whiting.

BIBLIOGRAPHY

Agius, Dionisius. 2008. *Classic Ships of Islam: From Mesopotamia to the Indian Ocean.* Leiden: Brill.

Ahmed, Shahab. 2016. *What is Islam? The Importance of Being Islamic.* Princeton and Oxford: Princeton University Press.

Alpers, Edward. 2014. *The Indian Ocean in World History.* Oxford: Oxford University Press.

Anderson, C. 2000. *Convicts in the Indian Ocean. Transportation from South Asia to Mauritius, 1815–53.* New York: St Martin's Press.

Bang, Anne. 2003. *Sufis and Scholars of the Sea: Family Networks in East Africa, 1860–1925,* Indian Ocean series. New York: Routledge.

Beaujard, Philippe. 2019. *The Worlds of the Indian Ocean: A Global History,* 2 vols. Cambridge: Cambridge University Press.

Bose, Sugata. 2009. *A Hundred Horizons: The Indian Ocean in the Age of Global Empire.* Cambridge, MA: Harvard University Press.

Braudel Fernand. 1995. *The Mediterranean and the Mediterranean World in the Age of Philip II,* vol. I. Berkeley: University of California Press.

Chaudhuri, K. N. 2006. *The Trading World of Asia and the English East India Company, 1660–1760.* Cambridge: Cambridge University Press (first publication, 1978).

Chaudhuri, K. N. 1985. *Trade and Civilisation in the Indian Ocean: An Economic History from the Rise of Islam to 1750.* Cambridge: Cambridge University Press.

Crone, Patricia. 2020. *Meccan Trade and the Rise of Islam.* Piscataway, NJ: Gorgias Press (first publication, 1987).

Das Gupta, Ashin and Michael Pearson (eds). 1987. *India and the Indian Ocean, 1500–1800.* Calcutta and New York: Oxford University Press.

Declich, Francesca. 2018. *Translocal Connections across the Indian Ocean: Swahili Speaking Networks on the Move.* Leiden: Brill.

Eickleman, Dale F. 1982. 'The Study of Islam in Local Contexts', *Contributions to Asian Studies,* no. 17, pp. 1–16.

Eisenlohr, Patrick. 2018. *Sounding Islam: Voice, Media, and Sonic Atmospheres in an Indian Ocean World*. Oakland: University of California Press.

Feener, Michael (ed.). 2019. *Buddhist and Islamic Orders in Southern Asia Comparative Perspectives*. Honolulu: University of Hawaii Press.

Freitag, Ulrike and William G. Clarence Smith (eds). 1997. *Hadhrami Traders, Scholars, and Statesmen in the Indian Ocean, 1750s–1960s*. Leiden: Brill.

Geertz, Clifford. 1973. *The Interpretation of Cultures*. New York: Basic Books.

Geertz, Clifford. 1968. *Islam Observed: Religious Development in Morocco and Indonesia*. New Haven: Yale University Press.

Green, Nile. 2011. *Bombay Islam: The Religious Economy of the West Indian Ocean, 1840–1915*. Cambridge: Cambridge University Press.

Goitein S. D. and Mordechai Akiva Friedman. 2007. *India Traders of the Middle Ages: Documents from the Cairo Geniza 'India Book'*. Leiden: Brill.

Hawley, John (ed.). 2008. *India in Africa, Africa in India: Indian Ocean Cosmopolitanisms*. Bloomington: Indiana University Press.

Headley, Stephen and David Parkin. 2015. *Islamic Prayer Across the Indian Ocean: Inside and Outside the Mosque*, Indian Ocean series. New York: Routledge (first publication, 2000).

Ho, Engseng. 2006. *The Graves of Tarim: Genealogy and Mobility Across the Indian Ocean*. Berkeley: University of California Press.

Horton, Mark and John Middleton. 2000. *The Swahili: The Social Landscape of a Mercantile Society*. Oxford: Blackwell.

Hourani, George F. 1995. *Arab Seafaring in the Indian Ocean in Ancient and Early Medieval Times*. Princeton: Princeton University Press (original work published 1951).

Jalal, Ayesha. 2000. *Self and Sovereignty: Individual and Community in South Asian Islam Since 1850*. London: Routledge.

Keller, Sara (ed.). 2019. *Knowledge and the Indian Ocean: Intangible Networks of Western India and Beyond*. London: Palgrave Macmillan.

Koehler, Benedikt. 2014. *Early Islam and the Birth of Capitalism*. Lanham, MD: Lexington Books.

Kooria, Mahmood and Michael Pearson (eds). 2018. *Malabar in the Indian Ocean: Cosmopolitanism in a Maritime Historical Region*. New Delhi: Oxford University Press.

Lambourn, Elizabeth A. 2018. *Abraham's Luggage: A Social Life of Things in the Medieval Indian Ocean World*. Cambridge: Cambridge University Press.

Machado, Pedro. 2014. *Ocean of Trade: South Asian Merchants, Africa and the Indian Ocean, 1750–1850*. Cambridge: Cambridge University Press.

McLaughlin, Raoul. 2018. *The Roman Empire and the Indian Ocean: The Ancient World Economy and the Kingdoms of Africa, Arabia and India*. Barnsley: Pen and Swords.

MacLean, Derryl. 2009. *Cosmopolitanisms in Muslim Contexts: Perspectives from the Past*. Edinburgh: AKU-ISMC/Edinburgh University Press.

Margariti, Roxani Eleni. 2007. *Aden and the Indian Ocean Trade: 150 Years in the Life of a Medieval Arabian Port*. Chapel Hill: University of North Carolina Press.

Nicolini, Beatrice and Shihan de Silva Jayasuriya. 2017. *Land and Maritime Empires in the Indian Ocean*. Milan: EDUCatt.

Pearson, M. 2003. *The Indian Ocean*. London: Routledge.

Potter, Lawrence G. (ed.). 2009. *The Persian Gulf in History*. New York: Palgrave Macmillan.

Power, Timothy. 2012. *The Red Sea from Byzantium to the Caliphate: AD 500–1000*. Cairo: American University in Cairo Press.

Prestholdt, Jeremy. 2008. *Domesticating the World: African Consumerism and the Genealogies of Globalization*. Berkeley: University of California Press.

Pradines, Stéphane. 2017. 'Swahili Past in Peril. New Archaeology in East Africa', *Journal of Oriental and African Studies*, vol. 26, pp. 211–36.

Prange, Sebastian. 2018. *Monsoon Islam: Trade and Faith on the Medieval Malabar Coast*. New York: Cambridge University Press.

Prange, Sebastian. 2005. 'Scholars and the Sea: A Historiography of the Indian Ocean', *History Compass*, vol. 6, pp. 1382–93.

Ray, Himanshu Prabha (ed.). 2016. *Bridging the Gulf: Maritime Cultural Heritage of the Western Indian Ocean*. New Delhi: Manohar.

Ray, Himanshu Prabha and Jean-François Salles (eds). 2012. *Tradition and Archaeology: Early Maritime Contacts in the Indian Ocean*. New Delhi: Manohar (first published, 1996).

Reese, Scott. 2018. *Imperial Muslims: Islam, Community and Authority in the Indian Ocean, 1839–1937*. Edinburgh: Edinburgh University Press.

Risso, Patricia. 1995. *Merchants and Faith: Muslim Commerce and Culture in the Indian Ocean*. Boulder, CO: Westview Press.

Sanyal, Sanjeev. 2016. *The Ocean of Churn: How the Indian Ocean Shaped Human History*. Haryana: Penguin-Random House.

Satish, Chandra (ed.). 1987. *The Indian Ocean: Explorations in History, Commerce and Politics*. New Delhi: Sage Publications.

Schnepel, Burkhard and Edward Alpers (eds). 2018. *Connectivity in Motion: Island Hubs in the Indian Ocean World*. London: Palgrave Macmillan.

Schnepel, Burkhard and Tan Sen (eds). 2019. *Travelling Pasts: The Politics of Cultural Heritage in the Indian Ocean World*. Leiden: Brill.

Schottenhammer, A. (ed.). 2019. *Early Global Interconnectivity across the Indian Ocean World*, 2 vols. London: Palgrave Macmillan.

Shanti, Moorthy and Ashraf Jamal (eds). 2010. *Indian Ocean Studies: Cultural, Social, and Political Perspectives*. New York: Routledge.

Sheriff, Abdul. 2018. *Dhow Culture of the Indian Ocean: Cosmopolitanism, Commerce, and Islam*. Cambridge: Cambridge University Press (first published, 2010).

Sheriff, Abdul. 2014. 'Globalisation with a Difference. An Overview', in Abdul Sheriff and Ho Engseng (eds), *The Indian Ocean: Oceanic Connections and the Creation of New Societies*. London: Hurst, pp. 11–41.

Silva, Nuno Vassallo. 2011. *Goa and the Great Mughal*. London: Scala.

Simpson, Edward and Kai Kresse (eds). 2008. *Struggling with History: Islam and Cosmopolitanism in the Western Indian Ocean*. New York: Columbia University Press.

Toorawa, Shawkat. 2007. *The Western Indian Ocean: Essays on Islands and Islanders*. Port Louis: Hassam Toorawa Trust.

Wink, Andre. 2002. 'From the Mediterranean to the Indian Ocean: Medieval History in Geographic Perspective', *Comparative Studies in Society and History*, vol. 44, pp. 416–45.

PART I

Muslim Identities, Literature and Diasporas

CHAPTER I

Developing the Harari Muṣḥaf: The Indian Ocean Milieu of Ethiopian Scribes

SANA MIRZA[1]

In 2006, the fortified historic city of Harar was added to UNESCO's list of World Heritage Sites, bringing new attention to the long-standing religious centre in eastern Ethiopia.[2] Situated on a plateau, Harar overlooks deserts and savannahs, a strategic location that linked the coastal lowlands and central highlands of Ethiopia and Somalia. As a result, the city became an essential economic hub along trade routes leading to the Gulf of Aden. Its winding streets, mosques and shrines led Harar to be described as the 'Timbuktu of East Africa' – even before the recognition of the city's impressive manuscript culture, remarkable not only for its breadth but also its ability to illuminate the city's complex visual culture.[3]

Harar's rise is often linked with the relocation of Shaykh ʿAbādir ʿUmar al-Ridā, whose tomb still serves as a major monument in the city today.[4] According to local tradition, Shaykh ʿAbādir emigrated from Mecca to Harar in 1215 with 405 of his disciples.[5] In the following century, archaeological evidence indicates the main axis of Islamisation within Ethiopia moved westwards from the port city of Zayla to Harar as sedentary and agricultural town-dwelling populations adopted Islam.[6] Testifying to thriving trade in the region, excavations

---

[1] I wish to thank Professors Farouk Topan and Stéphane Pradines for organising this extraordinary conference and inviting me to participate in it. This paper was deeply enriched by the thoughtful feedback and suggestions of the other presenters, Finbarr Barry Flood, Annabel Gallop and Simon Rettig. I am very grateful to them all. My research has been kindly facilitated by the Barakat Trust.

[2] https://whc.unesco.org/en/list/1189/ (last accessed 17 March 2019).

[3] Burton, 1894, p. 1.

[4] Desplat. 2008, pp. 149–67; Gibb, 1999, pp. 88–90.

[5] However, some sources suggest Shaykh Abādir arrived in 405/1001 (*History of Harar and The Hararis*, 2015, pp. 41–2). The full account can be found in Yaḥya ibn Naṣr Allāh, *Legende und Geschichte der Fath madīnat Harar*, Ewald Wagner, trans., Mainz: Deutsche Morgenländischen Ges., 1978.

[6] Fauvelle-Aymar, Hirsch and Schiwangizaw, 2011, pp. 27–37.

in the nearby village of Harlaa reveal ceramics from China and Yemen as well as beads of glass, rock crystal, carnelian, coral and shell from the mid-twelfth to mid-thirteenth centuries.[7] Excavations in Harar have unsurprisingly recognised the importance of the sixteenth century for the city though future excavations may reveal earlier material.[8] The city would become the epicentre of the short-lived military campaigns led by Imam Aḥmad b. Ibrāhīm al-Ghāzī known as Grañ (d. 1543).[9] After his death, the city was briefly occupied by Solomonic Emperor Galāwdéwos (r.1540–1559) before re-emerging under the leadership of Amir Nur ibn Mujāhid (d. 1567), who is credited with building Harar's iconic walls. Afterwards, the city entered what is often called a 'dark period' as the capital of the Adal Sultanate (1415–1577) relocated and the city declined economically.[10]

A century later, Harar re-emerged as an independent emirate under the 'Ali b. Dāwūd dynasty.[11] This was a moment of rejuvenation: coins were minted, agriculture expanded and trade networks flourished – and it was a period of large-scale manuscript production.[12] Hundreds, if not thousands, of manuscripts were copied in the city between the seventeenth and nineteenth centuries. This corpus includes copies of the Qur'an, legal handbooks and praises of the Prophet Muhammad in Arabic and the local language, Harari. Some codices were kept within homes, but were taken to tombs and cemeteries to be read from on a regular basis.[13] Others were given to mosques and religious schools. Additionally, scholars and amirs were known for their private libraries.[14] These manuscripts are now scattered across the globe, with the largest collections being within the library of the Institute of Ethiopian Studies in Addis Ababa and the Sherif Harar Museum in Harar.[15] Many of these volumes contain colophons, endowment notices and other historical documentation, providing a rare opportunity for contextualised and historicised study of the Qur'an codex (muṣḥaf, pl. maṣāḥif) in sub-Saharan Africa.

This chapter will focus on one manuscript to illustrate a moment of experimentation and codification in the middle of the eighteenth century.[16]

---

[7] Insoll, Tesfaye and Mahmoud, 2014, pp. 100–9.
[8] Insoll, 2017, p. 210.
[9] Muth, 2003, pp. 156–7.
[10] Loimeier, 2013, p. 188; Zekaria 1998, p. 18.
[11] Braukämper, 2002, p. 32.
[12] Zekaria, 1998, p. 18; Zekaria, 1989, p. 26; Revault, 2004, p. 15.
[13] Gori, 2015, pp. 285–8.
[14] Drewes, 1983, pp. 68–70.
[15] Kawo, 2015, pp. 194–6; Gori et al., 2014. My thanks to Ahmed Zekaria, Hassen Kawo and Anne Regourd for their guidance and mentorship. I am incredibly grateful to the generosity of Abdullah Sherif and his family, the librarians of the Institute of Ethiopian Studies for facilitating my study of these manuscripts.
[16] This chapter presents an abridgement of the third chapter of my doctoral dissertation, which explores these manuscripts in greater detail.

The earliest Qur'an manuscripts produced in Harar possibly date to the late seventeenth century, though production seems to increase dramatically at the turn of the eighteenth century. In this early stage, Harari artisans drew upon older artistic repertoires, among them decorative elements rooted in the Mamluk arts of the book such as chapter headings, marginal vignettes and incipit page compositions. These resonances appear prominent in Yemeni manuscripts as well, suggesting an archaising southern Red Sea visual language that connected Egypt, western Arabia and eastern Ethiopia.[17] Yet in the second half of the eighteenth century, a definitive and distinctive Harari decorative and calligraphic style appears. In their formulation of this style, Harar's artisans revealed themselves as participants in multidirectional and nuanced circuits of artistic interchange that crisscrossed the Indian Ocean – circuits which, however paradoxically, informed the development of the city's unique visual culture.

A Harari Manuscript and its Transregional Connection

An example of Harar's multivalent manuscript culture is a single-volume Qur'an now at the Sherif Harar Museum. It was completed in *Dhu al-Qa'da* 1180/ March 1767 and signed by 'Umar b. Abd al-'Azīz b. al-Amir Hāshim (Fig. 1.1). The original binding no longer survives. On the first page of Qur'anic text, the main panel is framed by thin black rule-borders (*jadwal*) and divided into two sections. The upper portion contains information about the chapter (sura) below. For instance, on the right-hand page, the text mentions there are twenty-two names for the first sura, *al-Fatiha* (The Opening), and there are debates within the schools of recitation about whether the *basmala* is part of the sura or not. Therefore, there are different counts for the number of verses and words according to each tradition.

The lower portions, containing the text of sura *al-Fatiha* and the beginning of the second sura, *al-Baqara* (The Cow), are enclosed by four red panels containing twisted white designs. These decorative forms are almost buried beneath the numerous paratexts, which seem to visually dominate the page. In addition to the extended introduction text, the topmost annotation on each page discusses the benefits of reading the suras, drawing on hadith. The remaining notations explain the differences between the schools of recitation and how each suggests the text should be read. Starting in the 1730s, this distinctive format, combining the Qur'anic text with extensive glosses, appears increasingly popular in Harar. The overall impression of the page derives from the plethora of textual elements and their distinctive calligraphic script. Within it, there are stark

---

[17] Mirza, 2017.

Figure 1.1 Single-volume Qur'an, Harar, completed *Dhu al-Qa'da*
1180/March 1767 and signed by 'Umar b. Abd al-'Azīz b. al-Amir Hāshim.
Photo courtesy Finbarr Barry Flood.

juxtapositions between the thin vertical elements and the thick horizontal lines.
The wispy diacritics are horizontal rather than angled.

These calligraphic features, as well as the overall mise-en-page, find its closest
parallel in India in a unique cursive script know as *biḥārī* (Fig. 1.2). Rarely
seen outside of the subcontinent, the script is said to have been developed in
the region of Bihar in northeast India by the fourteenth century.[18] *Biḥārī* was
used only for religious texts, and almost exclusively for the Qur'an, a sign of its
prestige. The script has a distinctive visual rhythm with a stark juxtaposition
between thick extensions and thin verticals. The tails of final letters, such as
nūn, are shallow, stretching just below the baseline and broadening at the end
into a wedge-shape. Round forms, such as in *sād*, are particularly circular. The
letter *dāl* is wide and open, and the letter *mīm* has a short, oblique tail. The
diacritics are fine, thin and horizontal.[19]

---

[18] Blair, 2006, pp. 383–92; Brac de la Perrière, 2016 and 2003.
[19] Brac de la Perrière, 2003, p. 88; Brac de la Perrière, 2016, pp. 64–5.

Figure 1.2 Folio from a Qur'an, late 15th century, India, Ink, colour and gold on paper, Sackler Gallery of Art, S2003.9. Photo courtesy Freer | Sackler.

The script of the 1767 Harari manuscript has the same aura of *bihārī* though it lacks the wide spacing between words characteristic of Indian manuscripts. However, similar to *bihārī*, the extensions of sublinear letters are broad and slightly wedge shaped, particularly the final *nūn*. The final *kāf* and *lām* are also shallow, extending horizontally and thickening at the end. The thin connections between the letters furthers the juxtaposition of the thick and thin, of horizontal and vertical elements, providing a complementary rhythm to *bihārī*. The extended bases of final letters often sit right below the baseline. Similar to *bihārī*, letters are often slightly nested, fitting inside one another.[20]

Rather than incidental, these relationships between these two traditions are also found throughout the page layout. Indian Qur'ans in *bihārī* script often had zigzagging marginalia with *qirā'āt* (recitation) information. These glosses were written in a less angular script known as *naskhī-dīwānī*.[21] The Harari manuscript also juxtaposes two different scripts, a more stylised cursive for the Qur'anic text and a rounder one for the glosses (Fig. 1.3). This practice gives the Qur'anic text and glosses their own visual identity and perhaps helped prevent confusion between the two. In the Harari manuscript, there is a more consistent width in the script of the glosses but the final *lām*, *fā* and *yā* are wedged shaped, as is the tail of the final *'ayn*.

This similarity with Indian *bihārī* manuscripts can be felt from the second-half of the eighteenth century in different degrees in several Harari manuscripts, each of which serve as nodes for charting this moment of experimentation. The most obvious form is found in a manuscript in the Khalili Collection in London known as QUR706.[22] Completed in *Shawwāl* 1162/ September or October 1749, the Qur'an has long been attributed to East Africa, but codicological and stylistic similarity to the Harari manuscripts suggests it was produced in Harar.[23] The horizontal elements, such as the forms of the final *bā* and *dāl*, are thicker than the later Harari manuscript of 1767. The sublinear tails of letters like *nūn*, *yā*, *lām* and *sād* bear a closer relationship to *bihārī* and stretch just under the baseline. The enlarged first, middle and final lines also have parallels in Indian manuscripts. The strong *bihārī* features of this earlier manuscript are mirrored by other undated manuscripts within private collections in Harar. These imply a shared aesthetic conceptualisation between the Qur'an manuscripts of Harar and India yet also underscore a need to consider the possibility of long-distance artistic relationships more broadly.

Are the Harari artisans looking to Indian Qur'an manuscripts in formulating their own calligraphic style and manuscript formats? *Bihārī* appears to decline

[20] Brac de la Perrière, 2016, pp. 64–5.
[21] Brac de la Perrière, 2003, pp. 89–91.
[22] Stanley, 1999.
[23] Mirza, 2017.

Figure 1.3 Detail, Qur'an, completed *Dhu al-Qa'da* 1180/ March 1767 and signed by 'Umar b. Abd al-'Azīz b. al-Amir Hāshim. Photo courtesy Finbarr Barry Flood.

in India about two centuries earlier in the sixteenth century. However, Eloïse Brac de la Perrière has suggested that *bihārī* script continued in India into the nineteenth century, and the quality of execution indicates these later Indian manuscripts were likely produced for a market.[24] Therefore, they could have circulated widely within learning circles. The evidence is still too scattered to map the circulation of later Indian *bihārī* script manuscripts. However, several folios from such a manuscript were found in the ruins of the Great Mosque of Dawran in Yemen, which was established in 1638.[25] This could indicate that manuscripts in *bihārī* script were available in Southern Arabia in the mid-seventeenth century, if not later. One manuscript has been found in Ethiopia within a shrine, yet its history is still unknown.[26] However, Harar appears not

---

[24] Brac de la Perrière, 2016, pp. 70–1; 80–1.
[25] Witkam, 1989, pp. 157–8; Paluck and Saggar, 2002.
[26] My thanks to Hassen Muhammad Kawo for mentioning this manuscript to me.

to be alone in its crafting of scripts and formats related to Indian manuscripts in *biḥārī* script.

A *BIḤĀRĪ* HORIZON OR INDIAN OCEAN FORMS?

Harari calligraphers' experimentation with *biḥārī* script elements argues for positioning the city as a part of an interrelated long-distance artistic network. Jan Just Witkam noted several undated Qur'an folios in the Dawran ruins and a manuscript in the Leiden University library, which all appear to have been produced in Yemen but penned in a script related to *biḥārī*.[27] These works open the possibility that *biḥārī* was practised outside of India. Witkam also mentions it would not be surprising to find other connections between the manuscripts produced in the regions between Somalia and Pakistan – which would include Harar and Arabia – in terms of calligraphic relationships and shared scripts.[28] The dissimilarity between Harar's 'biḥārī-esque' script and classical *biḥārī* script from Indian examples in fact points to a similar conclusion: the existence of intertwined centres of manuscript production linked by calligraphic experimentation and formats within the Indian Ocean in the eighteenth century.

Biḥārī-esque scripts are found in a variety of manuscripts within this zone. Another Qur'an, attributed to the eighteenth- or nineteenth-century Indian Ocean regions, in the British Library also seems to be written by a scribe experimenting with *biḥārī* (Fig. 1.4). Much like the Harari manuscripts, the resulting script presents the same horizontal rhythm found in the *biḥārī* script. The scribe thickens these traditionally sublinear elements, which sit here just below or on the baseline. Within words, the jointures between letters are thicker for letters that could have horizontal extensions, like the letters *mīm* and *bā*. On the level of the mise-en-page, these features create the same sense of horizontal dynamism found in classical *biḥārī*. The decorative repertoire of the opening page seems to suggest an eastern Indian Ocean provenance, though it is difficult to locate with specificity. A similar script with exaggerated thick endings is found in a manuscript once in Pakistan completed in 1180/1766.[29] Additionally, an undated Indonesian manuscript also reveals *biḥārī* features (Fig 1.5).[30] However, the thick ends of forms like *'ayn*, which extends backwards, and *wā* are not found in classical *biḥārī* but seems instead to be characteristic features of these later

---

[27] Witkam, 1989, pp. 157–8.
[28] Witkam, 1989, pp. 157–8.
[29] This manuscript is now in a private collection, see http://abudervish.blogspot.com/2013/01/ancient-manuscript-review-100-antique.html. Annabel Gallop kindly mentioned both this and the BL manuscript to me.
[30] My thanks to Finbarr Barry Flood and Mirjam Shatanwai for kindly bringing my attention to this manuscript in the Museum Volkenkunde in Leiden. The manuscript is undated but must have been produced in the nineteenth century, if not earlier, as a later note is dated 1901.

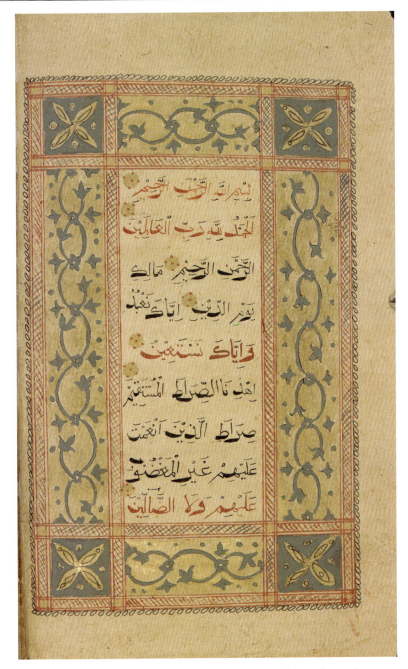

Figure 1.4 Qur'an, from India or Indian Ocean World, 18th–19th centuries,
British Library, Or. 16714, folio 1v. Reproduced courtesy of the
British Library Board.

Figure 1.5 Arabic Grammar, Aceh, Indonesia, Museum Volkenkunde, Leiden, TM-674-809. Photo courtesy Museum Volkenkunde, Leiden.

biḥārī-esque scripts. More broadly, Sheila Blair has noted a relationship between *biḥārī* style script and those of Southeast Asia due to the angularity of the forms and the flat baseline.[31] Seen against this wider context of calligraphic experimentations, the paleographic peculiarities of the Harari masahif and these wider Indian Qurʾan manuscripts appear to be the result of an eighteenth century moment. In this case, perhaps the Harari script is not truly evoking *biḥārī* but an Indian Ocean calligraphic tradition that may have been rooted in *biḥārī* but lost its connection to northern India by the eighteenth century.

The paratextual information within the 1767 Qurʾan provides another dimension for considering these wider connections. While glosses with commentary are not abnormal within Qurʾanic manuscripts, the extent of the Harari volumes' preoccupation with proper recitation (*tajwīd*) and *qirāʾāt* is significant. In the 1767 manuscript copied by ʿUmar b. Abd al-ʿAzīz b. al-Amir Hāshim, the Qurʾanic text is preceded by a twelve-page preface which includes the

---

[31] Blair, 2006, p. 563.

system of orthography canonised by ʿAbd al-Qāsim b. Firruh al-Shāṭibī, a major twelfth-century Andalusian authority on Qurʾan recitation. His didactic poem on the counting of Qurʾan verses and the seven canonical recitation styles was a central text for students for centuries.[32] The first occurrence of this type of text in Harar is found in a Qurʾan completed on 8 *Rabī al-Awwal* 1120/28 May 1708, which has a thirty-five-page introduction on these principles and verse counts.[33] However, the condensed text is found almost verbatim in at least twenty-three other Qurʾans copied in Harar between 1731 and 1874.[34] Each of these manuscripts contains a bipartite incipit page composition and the majority contain marginal glosses.

Several Indonesian manuscripts present similar texts in terms of content and layout. A Qurʾan from Southern Sulawesi in the Aga Khan Museum, completed in 1804, begins with six folios with notes on recitation and variant readings. Throughout the manuscript, diagonal annotations on the differences between the readings and hadith are copied in red and blue.[35] Annabel Gallop notes two other Qurʾan manuscripts with comparable, though not exact, marginal annotations and additional materials. She surmises these three volumes could be based on a prototype from the late seventeenth or early eighteenth century – the exact moment the Harari artisans were developing ways of presenting this same material.[36] Furthermore, Gallop has highlighted other Indian Ocean connections between artistic centres in Southeast Asia, particularly from Aceh and Penang, with those of East Africa and Oman, in the use of similar colours, geometric motifs and page layouts.[37] A likely nineteenth-century manuscript from Aceh, Indonesia also begins with a short tutorial on *tajwīd* in Malay and Achinese.[38] These almost simultaneous developments on opposite sides of the Indian Ocean appear to bear witness to artistic networks that connected the Indian Ocean, whether directly or indirectly, through shared interests and artistic forms.

The desire to incorporate *tajwīd* and *qirāʾāt* materials into the *muṣḥaf* may have shaped the distinctive incipit page of the 1767 Qurʾan. This layout organises the paratextual information to present the information about each chapter, hadith and *qirāʾāt* (recitation) along the Qurʾanic text. As mentioned earlier, there are over twenty-four known examples of this bipartite opening page from

---

[32] Neuwirth, 1997.
[33] This manuscript is in the Sherif Harar Museum in Harar known as AAShC 218. It is signed by hajj Khalif b. Kabir Hamid.
[34] These manuscripts are described in further detail in my forthcoming doctoral dissertation.
[35] Gallop, Graves and Junod, 2010, p. 171.
[36] Ibid., 173.
[37] Gallop, 2017, pp. 123–5.
[38] This manuscript is now in the library of the University of Leiden, Or.2064, and can be accessed online at https://catalogue.leidenuniv.nl/primo-explore/fulldisplay?docid=UBL_ALMA11321325430002711&context=L&vid=UBL_V1&lang=en_US.

Harar.[39] These manuscripts all incorporate an extended sura introduction into the decorative panels of the opening pages; each sura is preceded with a similar preface enumerating the differences in verse counts placed within the text. This compositional scheme, and related text, can be found in several Qur'ans associated with East Africa, some of which are preserved in Oman today.[40] One Qur'an linked to Siyu in the Fowler Museum at the University of California Los Angeles also presents diagonal glosses on the *qirā'āt*, the text itself differs slightly in its construction and framing (Fig. 1.6).[41] This could indicate the scribes copied from different textual models than the Harari calligraphers but were operating with the same decorative formats. The scripts of the manuscripts attributed to Siyu and Zanzibar are relatively uniform in width, with just a slight thickening at the end of each word. Diacritics are placed with thin, horizontal strokes. They have a clear relationship to those of Harar, but also indicate how the calligraphic styles of the Indian Ocean had been adapted into local scripts. The use of extended sura introductions and marginal annotations in Ethiopia, Kenya and Tanzania, points to the possibility of this decorative format having a greater popularity within East Africa and, perhaps, Oman.[42]

The eighteenth century has long been recognised as a moment of dramatic growth of Sufi networks and conversion to Islam in Ethiopia.[43] Against this backdrop, it is tempting to wonder if the phenomenon of '*bihārī*-esque' scripts and *qirā'āt* annotated Qur'ans may be intertwined, as they almost always appear together in Harar in the mid-eighteenth century. With the addition of recitation notations and hadiths, the manuscripts became not only the Word of God but also compendiums of scholarship on the Qur'an. They were essentially a tangible sign of the discursive networks of the Indian Ocean. Core texts consolidated Muslim scholars and communities across the Indian Ocean and these Qur'anic volumes consolidated several texts into a single manuscript that appealed to specific practical needs, which require more research.[44] These correspondences place Harari artisans within an extended network of interrelated manuscript

---

[39] I've been told there are many more volumes of this type within the libraries of the Abadier shrine and the mosques of Harar.

[40] Gaube and al Salimi, 2016, pp. 142–50.

[41] Another example of an East African Qur'an complied in 1245/1829 with similar but not exact additional textual material, see: https://elibrary.mara.gov.om/en/omani-library/imam-nour-al-din-al -salmi-s-library/book/?id=8#book/7 (last accessed 17 March 2019).

[42] More research might be needed to clarify the relationships between centres of manuscript production in East Africa and Oman. Many of these annotated manuscripts are found in Omani collections today. Additionally, some manuscripts attributed to Oman also have glosses with commentaries (Gaube and al Salimi, 2016, p. 143). Wider parallels between the Harari manuscripts and Omani ones can be found, such as the same colour palette of reds, greens and yellows, as well as twisted and vegetal decorative motifs.

[43] Trimingham, 2013, pp. 242–6.

[44] Bang, 2011, p. 91; Endress, 2016, pp. 203–4.

Figure 1.6 Qurʾan from Siyu, Kenya, early 19th century, Fowler Museum at UCLA, X90.184a, folio 245. Photo courtesy Fowler Museum.

centres. Yet, these resonances were tailored to Harar's local visual culture and religious milieu.

HARAR AS AN ARTISTIC CENTRE IN THE INDIAN OCEAN

There is a clear regional distinction between each manuscript, an overlay of similar concerns and scripts but a localised deployment of calligraphic and ornamental repertoires. For instance, within the manuscripts attributed to East Africa the *basmala* before each sura is often elevated into an interlacing calligraphic composition framed within concentric borders. A few place the sura title within elaborate frames with colourful, vegetal and floral borders. In Harar, the *basmala* is never treated in this way and the few decorated sura headings are much simpler and only found in manuscripts dating to the first half of the eighteenth century or earlier. Afterwards, sura titles are simply penned in red without any frames. In the same vein, each regional deployment of 'bihārī-esque' script is strikingly different, though they draw upon the most visually salient elements of *bihārī*. In Harar, these experiments solidify into a more uniform calligraphic style, fusing *bihārī* with elements of *muḥaqqaq* and *naskh*, two more common cursives, and creating a new script as a result. The early version of this script is found in the 1767 manuscript (see Fig. 1.1). It is characterised by rounder and less angular sublinear elements. It prefers the use of the *kāf mu'arran* (when the small s-like *kāf* is added to the top of the letter) form, which is not regularly found in *bihārī* or in the other Indian Ocean examples discussed above. This *kāf* form is found more widely in Harari manuscripts.[45] This specialised script would be used in Harar exclusively for the Qur'an until the end of the nineteenth century. The formation of this local script and format suggests the development of a distinctive visual culture in the mid-eighteenth century in Harar. This idiom looks less directly to transregional modes but selectively engages them to create a more rooted, local style.

These changes appear to coincide with a moment of increased regularisation, and the greater organisation of the mise-en-page, perhaps indications of a full book economy in Harar. Within the 1767 manuscript, the decorative panels compete with the paratexts in articulating the page layout. Ultimately, the stress is placed on the colourful calligraphy rather than the ornamental forms. This is in stark contrast to the earlier manuscripts, such as the manuscript completed in 1120/1708, where the text was penned in rough, individualistic *naskh* scripts, but bright decorative panels dominated the opening page (Fig. 1.7). However, by the mid-eighteenth century, artists appear to follow set conventions and templates.

The incipit page of the first *juz'* of a set endowed in the name of the Amir of Harar, Amir 'Abd al-Shakūr ibn amīr Yūsuf (1783–1794) to the Friday mosque in 1203/1789 illustrates the results of the greater standardisation (Fig. 1.8).[46] It draws upon the same basic forms of the 1708 manuscript. The page is divided into three zones: the rectangular registers at the top include the title of the sura, the number of ayat and its location of revelation. The sura text itself is penned within a circular panel, with twisted motifs on either side. The lower register includes verses from sura 56, *al-Wāqi'a* (The Inevitable) instructing readers to not touch the text except in a state of purity. Lines of red, yellow, green and white divide and embellish the panel, along with vegetal scrolls.

In the earlier manuscript, the lines waver, the large inscriptions lack a single baseline, and each leaf-like form is unique. Within the *juz'* volume, there is an order to the page: it is clear the artisan used the *mastara*, or ruling board, to guide the composition. The registers containing the verses from sura *al-Wāqi'a* are not only straight but also the height of two lines of text if compared with the following pages. The illuminated panel is also the same dimension of the text blocks. The multiple central rings were condensed to a single bold one; the vegetal scroll is carefully and more naturally rendered. The inscriptions are perfectly justified, so no words are squeezed in or were perhaps forgotten and

---

[45] Fani, 2017.
[46] Gori et al., 2014, p. 291.

Figure 1.7 Qur'an, copied by Ḥājji Khalīf b. Kabīr Ḥāmid, 1120/1708, Sherif Harar Museum, AAShC 218. Photo courtesy Sana Mirza.

added later. Whereas decorative elements, such as marginal medallions and chapter headings, were used to mark significant junctures such as *juz'* and *ḥizb* divisions, bold marginal inscriptions later replace them.

This same move towards standardisation is found in the paratextual information. There is a clear progression in the presentation of the additional textual content. In the first, dated to 1120/1708, the *qirā'āt* and numerological information is presented in a thirty-five-page preface and there are no interior glosses. By 1767, the introductory text has been reduced to twelve pages, but there is a multiplicity of glosses. This condensed format is present and sometimes shortened further in all later manuscripts with bipartite opening page compositions. The marginal glosses also reveal set programmes, which calligraphers drew upon. The red notations are found in every manuscript with glosses; the black ones are found in less. While the textual content is identical, the placement of the paratexts on the page, the orientation of each notation, and breaks within marginal notations are inconsistent with no discernable pattern, suggesting the artisans had freedom in how they employed the template. In their uniformity, the additional textual material, compositional regulation and calligraphic formulations reveal Harar had developed a local format for the *muṣḥaf*. Yet the individuality

Figure 1.8 Juz 1 of the Qur'an, Harar, endowed in 1203/October–November 1789 by Amir ʿAbd al-Shakūr ibn amīr Yūsuf, Institute of Ethiopian Studies IES 1850, folio 4r. Photo courtesy Marilyn Heldman.

of the manuscripts re-affirms how each must have reflected the concerns of its scribes and patrons, and the need to further study Harar's extraordinary book culture.

CONCLUSION

Ultimately, the calligraphic style of the 1767 manuscript, measured decorative panels and, often, the inclusion of paratextual material would shape the Harari form for the *muṣḥaf* into the nineteenth century. Additionally, manuscripts become increasingly unsigned, as they lose their personal, idiosyncratic style for a more streamlined one. Perhaps not coincidentally, these standardisations and fashionings of a distinctive Harari style coincide with the formalisation of Harar's manuscript culture. It would lead to the bureaucratic re-organisation of Amir ʿAbd al-Shakūr ibn amīr Yūsuf, who in 1200/1785–86 established the institution of formal legal and chancery record keeping.[47] In the preserved decree, this push appears rooted in a desire to reproduce the basic forms found in proper governance in the Islamic world. The amir's act reinforced his wish to see the city as one of the great centres of Islam in East Africa and evokes the heroic past of Harar. Perhaps due to these same motivations, he presented the elegant thirty-volume set to the city's Friday mosque (see Fig. 1.8). He also began to patronise religious institutions outside of Harar, including building a mosque for the shrine of Shakyh Husayn in Bale. This act of patronage asserted the re-conceptualisation of Harar as a sultanate and an important regional political power. He also nurtured long-distance networks by encouraging the expansion of the *Qādirīyya*, a Sufi order, in Harar.[48] In the following decades, the success of these transregional relationships and Harar's continued participation within an Indian Ocean artistic milieu would in fact further regularise the appearance of the Qurʾan manuscripts produced there in the decades before the rise of printed *maṣāḥif*.

BIBLIOGRAPHY

Bang, Anne K. 2011. 'Authority and Piety, Writing and Print: A Preliminary Study of the Circulation of Islamic Texts in Late Nineteenth- and Early Twentieth-Century Zanzibar', *Africa: Journal of the International African Institute* 81 (1), pp. 89–107.

Blair, Sheila. 2006. *Islamic Calligraphy*. Edinburgh: Edinburgh University Press.

Brac de la Perrière, Eloïse. 2016. 'Manuscripts in Bihari Calligraphy: Preliminary Remarks on a Little-Known Corpus', *Muqarnas* 33, pp. 63–90.

---

[47] Wagner, 1974, pp. 217–19.
[48] Zekaria, 1998, p. 23.

Brac de la Perrière, Eloïse. 2003. 'Bihârî et Naskhî-Dîwânî: Remarques Sur Deux Calligraphies de l'Inde Des Sultanats', *Studia Islamica*, no. 96, pp. 81–93. https://doi.org/10.2307/1596244.

Braukämper, Ulrich. 2002. *Islamic History and Culture in Southern Ethiopia: Collected Essays*. Münster: Lit Verlag.

Burton, Richard Francis. 1894. *First Footsteps in East Africa*. Gordon Waterfield (ed.). 2 vols. London: Tylston and Edwards.

Desplat, Patrick. 2008. 'The Making of a "Harari" City in Ethiopia: Constructing and Contesting Saintly Place in Harar', in Georg Stauth and Samuli Schielke (eds), *Dimensions of Locality: Muslim Saints, Their Places and Spaces*. Bielefeld: Transcript, pp. 149–67.

Drewes, A. J. 1983. 'The Library of Muḥammad b. ʿAlī b. ʿAbd Al-Shakūr, Sulṭān of Harar, 1272–92/1856–75', in R. L. Bidwell and G. R. Smith (eds), *Arabian and Islamic Studies: Articles Presented to R. B. Serjeant*. Boston: Addison-Wesley Longman Ltd, pp. 68–79.

Endress, Gerhard. 2016. '"One-Volume Libraries" and the Traditions of Learning in Medieval Arabic Islamic Culture', in Michael Friedrich and Cosima Schwarke (eds), *One-Volume Libraries: Composite and Multiple-Text Manuscripts*. Berlin: De Gruyter, pp. 171–205.

Fani, Sarah. 2017. 'Scribal Practices in Arabic Manuscripts from Ethiopia: The ʿAjamization of Scribal Practices in Fuṣḥā and ʿAjamī Manuscripts from Harar', *Islamic Africa* 8, pp. 144–70.

Fauvelle-Aymar, François-Xavier, Bertrand Hirsch and Addisu Schiwangizaw. 2011. *Espaces musulmans de la Corne de l'Afrique au Moyen Âge: études d'archéologie et d'histoire*. Paris: De Boccard.

Gallop, Annabel. 2017. 'Indian Ocean Connections: Illuminated Islamic Manuscripts from Penang', in Peter Zabielskis, Yeoh Seng Guan and Kat Fatland (eds), *Penang and Its Networks of Knowledge*. Penang: Areca Books, pp. 115–33.

Gallop, Annabel. 2010. 'The Boné Qurʾan from South Sulawesi', in Benoit Junod, Annabel Gallop and Margaret Graves (eds), *Treasures of the Aga Khan Museum: Arts of the Book and Calligraphy*. Istanbul: Aga Khan Trust for Culture and Sakip Sabanci University and Museum, pp. 162–73.

Gaube, Heinz and Abdulrahman al Salimi. 2016. *Illuminated Qurans From Oman*. Hildesheim: Goerg Olms Verlag.

Gibb, Camilla. 1999. 'Baraka without Borders: Integrating Communities in the City of Saints', *Journal of Religion in Africa* 29 (1), pp. 88–108. https://doi.org/10.2307/1581788.

Gori, Alessandro. 2015. 'Waqf Certificates of Qurʾans from Harar: A First Assessment', in Alessandro Gori, Alessandro Bausi and Denis Nosnitsin (eds), *Essays in Ethiopian Manuscript Studies. Proceedings of the International Conference Manuscripts and Texts, Languages and Contexts: The Transmission of Knowledge in the Horn of Africa. Hamburg, 17–19 July 2014*. Wiesbaden: Harrassowitz Verlag, pp. 281–96.

Gori, Alessandro, Anne Regourd, Steve Delamarter and Demeke Berhane. 2014. *A Handlist of the Manuscripts in the Institute of Ethiopian Studies. Volume Two: The Arabic Materials of the Ethiopian Islamic Tradition*. Eugene, OR: Pickwick Publications.

History of Harar and The Hararis. 2015. Harar: The Harari People Regional State Culture, Heritage and Tourism Bureau.

Insoll, Timothy. 2017. 'First Footsteps in the Archaeology of Harar, Ethiopia', *Journal of Islamic Archaeology* 4 (2), pp. 189–215.

Insoll, Timothy, Habtamu Tesfaye and Malik Saako Mahmoud. 2014. 'Archaeological Survey and Test Excavations, Harari Regional State, Ethiopia, July–August 2014. A Preliminary Fieldwork Report.' *Nyame Akuma* 82, pp. 100–9.

Kawo, Hassen Muhammad. 2015. 'Islamic Manuscript Collections in Ethiopia', *Islamic Africa* 6, pp. 192–200.

Loimeier, Roman. 2013. *Muslim Societies in Africa*. Bloomington, IN: Indiana University Press.

Mirza, Sana. 2017. 'The Visual Resonances of a Harari Qur'ān: An 18th-Century Ethiopian Manuscript and Its Indian Ocean Connections', *Afriques* 8: https://doi.org/10.4000/afriques.2052.

Muth, Franz-Christoph. 2003. 'Aḥmād b. Ibrāhīm Al-Ġazī', in Siegbert Uhlig (ed.), *Encyclopaedia Aethiopica*. Wiesbaden: Harrassowitz Verlag, vol. 1, pp. 155–8.

Neuwirth, Angelika. 1997. 'Al-Shāṭibī', in C. E. Bosworth, E. Van Donzel, W. P. Heinrichs and G. Lecomte (eds), *Encyclopaedia of Islam*. Leiden: Brill, Second Edition, vol. 9, pp. 365–6.

Paluck, Bruce and Rayya Saggar. 2002. *The Al-Hasan Bin Al-Qāsim Mosque Complex: An Architectural and Historical Overview of a Seventeenth Century Mosque in Ḍūrān, Yemen*. Paris: American Institute for Yemeni Studies and Le Centre Français d'Archéologie et de Sciences Sociales de Sanaa.

Revault, Philippe. 2004. *Harar: Une Cité Musulmane d'Éthiopie*. Paris: Maisonneuve et Larose.

Stanley, Tim. 1999. 'A Qur'an Once in Zanzibar: Connections between India, Arabia, and the Swahili Coast', in Manijeh Bayani, Anna Contadini and Tim Stanley (eds), *The Decorated Word: Qur'ans of the 17th to 19th Centuries*. London: Nour Foundation, pp. 26–31.

Trimingham, J. Spencer. 2013. *Islam in Ethiopia*. New York: Routledge.

Wagner, E. 1974. 'Arabic Documents on the History of Harar', *Journal of Ethiopian Studies* 12 (1), pp. 213–24.

Witkam, J. J. 1989. 'Qur'ān Fragments from Ḍawrān (Yemen)', *Manuscripts of the Middle East* 4, pp. 155–74.

Yaḥyá ibn Naṣr Allāh. 1978. *Legende und Geschichte der Fatḥ madīnat Harar*. Ewald Wagner, trans. Mainz: Deutsche Morgenländische Ges.

Zekaria, Ahmed. 1998. 'Some Notes on the Account-Book of Amīr ʿAbd Al-Shakūr b.Yūsuf (1783–1794) of Harar', *Sudanic Africa* 8, pp. 17–36.

Zekaria, Ahmed. 1989. *Harari Coins: A Preliminary Survey*. MA Thesis, Oxford: Oxford University.

CHAPTER 2

The Making of a Qur'ān Manuscript in Lamu Archipelago: The Indian Ocean Cross-cultural Influence

WALID GHALI[1]

INTRODUCTION

In 2016, the Aga Khan Library in London received a donation of a Qur'ānic manuscript that was added to the collection a year later due to its deteriorated physical condition. After a long restoration journey, the manuscript was fully restored and digitised. The examination of the object did not start until 2018 when the Aga Khan University organised the conference on *Muslim Cultures in the Indian Ocean*. It is worth mentioning that this donated copy, MS-QUR002 hereafter, is not the only Qur'ān manuscript in the library holdings.[2] Devotion to the Qur'ān by Muslims is exemplified by the way manuscripts of it have been devoutly and assiduously copied throughout the centuries, exhibiting diverse features of styles in calligraphy, illumination, the physical format and page layout, which often reflect their place of origin and date of production.[3]

From the late seventh to the nineteenth century, the writing of Qur'ān manuscripts was undertaken, as one would expect, in predominantly Islamic parts of the world and countries with Muslim majorities. Today, with the geographical spread of Islam covering Arabia and the Near and the Middle East, North Africa and Spain, sub-Saharan Africa, Iran and Central Asia, the Indian subcontinent, Southeast Asia and China, and with the availability of printed copies

---

[1] I would like to thank Professors Farouk Topan and Stéphane Pradines for inviting me to participate in the Indian Ocean Conference and their encouragement to develop my paper to be published in this volume. This paper has benefited from Dr Topan's feedback, suggestions and thoughtful guidance.
[2] The Aga Khan Library holdings include another Qur'ān manuscript (Ms Qur001) that was purchased from one of London's auction houses in 2007 by the Institute for the Study of Muslim Civilisations, AKU-ISMC. It was originally produced in Morocco in 1884.
[3] Baker, 2007, p. 13.

throughout all of these areas, the copying of the Qur'ān by hand is no longer necessary. However, it continues where traditional calligraphy is still practised.[4]

There are numerous Qur'ān manuscripts, complete and partial, dating from the first century AH onwards. Although there is no official count of Qur'ān manuscripts in existence today, Muhammad Mustafa Al-A'zami estimates the number at about 250,000.[5] They may be found in mosques, museums, libraries and institutions all over the world. Several early manuscripts have been published in facsimile editions in the past century, which reproduce as closely as possible the texts in their original manuscript forms. They may be purchased from specialised centres such as the Research Centre For Islamic History, Art and Culture (IRCICA) or borrowed from university libraries. Facsimile editions offer researchers in Qur'ānic studies and Arabic palaeography easy – if indirect – access to early Qur'ān manuscripts.[6]

The study of Islamic manuscripts, including Qur'ānic ones, has received noteworthy attention since the thirteenth century. However, according to Annabel Gallop, little was known of Qur'ān production outside the mainstream of the Islamic world until fairly recently. There have been great advances in the knowledge of Islamic manuscripts from most of these parts, not only from Southeast Asia but also from China, Caucasia and parts of Russian Central Asia and West Africa.[7]

Moreover, there is little doubt that Qur'ān manuscripts have been present in Southeast Asia since the earliest days of the establishment of Islam as the religion of state with the conversion of rulers, a process that appears to have commenced in North Sumatra in the thirteenth century. Copies of the Qur'ān were disseminated in the form of manuscripts, copied and recopied by scribes and, from the nineteenth century onwards, through printing, initially using the technology of lithography in Palembang in 1848 and then later by typesetting or photolithography.[8]

Similarly, the study of Islamic manuscripts in East Africa has not yet developed the full instrumentation for dealing with the written heritage in Arabic or Swahili, including the Qur'ān manuscripts from the eighteenth and nineteenth centuries. The establishment of Qur'ānic schools in East Africa started in centres such as Lamu, Malindi, Mombasa and Zanzibar. Islam encouraged literacy to enable the use of Qur'ān and hadith. By definition, Qur'ānic schools are the schools in which Muslims learn their religion and are generally found in mosques, private houses or premises set for that purpose.

---

[4] Ibid., p. 13.
[5] al-A'zami, 2003.
[6] Shaker, 2015.
[7] Gallop, 2017, p. 123.
[8] Ibid., p. 195.

The oldest Arabic manuscript that has been identified in East Africa is the *Kitab as-Sulwa fi Akhbar Kilwa* known as the Kilwa Chronicle, written in Arabic in the middle of the sixteenth century.[9] Of Qur'ān manuscripts, the oldest Qur'ān manuscript yet has been identified and described by Simon Digby, but there are possibly older, locally produced copies of Qur'āns that may still exist.[10] For instance, over the past thirty years, the Qur'ān manuscripts at the Royal Asiatic Society of Great Britain and Ireland and the Fowler Qur'ān at the Fowler Museum[11] have been regularly cited as examples of the coastal East African pre-modern tradition of Islamic learning and book production.[12]

This paper intends to examine the codicological Qur'ān manuscript MS-QUR002. In describing the manuscript, the paper aims to throw light on the characteristics of the manuscript in order to demonstrate its transregional connection and circulation within different cultures.

PROVENANCE AND PHYSICAL REMARKS

The manuscript was originally purchased from an auction in Mombasa, Kenya more than fifty years ago. It was kept in an elephant skin cover in a private collection of books of an Ismaili family until they decided to have it examined. Despite the deteriorating condition, it is clear how heavily this copy was used in teaching and recitation, evidenced in finger marks on the edges of each folio. It is worth repeating that the establishment of Qur'ānic schools in East Africa started in centres such as Lamu, Malindi, Mombasa and Zanzibar, and Islam encouraged literacy to enable the use of the Qur'ān and hadith.[13] Consequently, this chapter assumes that this copy was initially created for a madrasa (Islamic school) in Lamu or Mombasa to be used in teaching the recitation of the Qur'ān with variant readings.

The manuscript was received unbound with two stab stitches; however, evidence of a previous sewing structure was traced throughout the volume. Four sewing stations are evident on some folios, and previous threads remain. The volume did not have any cover or case, and there was no evidence of what the previous binding that had been in place was like. Full of mould stains and worm traces, the manuscript required significant restoration work by a specialist in paper preservation.[14]

---

[9] Samsom, 2012, p. 5.
[10] Digby, 1975.
[11] RAS Arabic 12a and FMCH90.1840AB, respectively.
[12] Hirji, 2019, p. 432.
[13] Komba, 2015, p. 2.
[14] On behalf of the Aga Khan Library, I would like to acknowledge the help of Mr Firoz Rasul, the President of the Aga Khan University, who donated the manuscript to the library, and sponsored the

Consisting of 260 folios (32.8 × 26 cm) with text area size (20 × 10 cm) that displays twelve lines of text separated by three dots in a triangle shape with occasional use of one dot in red; the Qur'ānic text is framed by double red lines surrounded by a single black line. The text is written in black ink, except the word *Allah* and the beginnings of each part (*Juz'*) that are written in red across the entire manuscript. The vocalisation is in black and recitation marks are in red. (Fig. 2.1). The sura titles are written in a rectangular frame in red; the catchwords exist on the verso of each folio written slightly in the middle of the bottom margin. The manuscript is on European paper with watermarks featuring three crescent moons and imposed initials, possibly reading 'AM', that is visible on some pages.

MS-QUR002 has several lacunae probably because of the previous poor conditions in which it was kept.[15] As a result, it was hard to confirm if the manuscript was produced as a single volume or in two volumes. In addition, without the colophon, it was difficult to confirm the name of the scribe, date of completion and any information about where it was produced. However, with its close resemblance to script, style and decoration between MS-QUR002 and the Flower Qur'ān, MS-QUR002 was likely produced in one volume.

SCRIPT AND DECORATIVE FEATURES

There is a dearth of palaeographic research on East Africa's script due to the lack of different examples. In his study of three Qur'āns from East Africa, Zulfikar Hirji argues that the script appears to have no exact regional or classical counterpart but is comparable to scripts in other pre-modern manuscripts produced in the Lamu Archipelago, some of which were used in a teaching-learning context. If determined to be local, then the style of the script would add to the repertoire of Arabic scripts developed in sub-Saharan Africa that hitherto have been interpreted as idiosyncratic versions of classical styles.[16]

The text in QUR002 is written in large *Naskh* with variant readings written in the smaller script in the margin. In some respects, it resembles the script of the Bihari Qur'āns produced in India in the late fourteenth to the early seventeenth centuries, especially its angular letterforms, the horizontal vowel signs and the combination of large and small scripts. Comparing this with Hirji's study of the three-illuminated Qur'āns from Siyu, QUR002 shares the same palaeographic features where the execution of the medial *kāf* and the tails of the *nūn* below the baseline (Figs 2.2 and 2.3).

restoration and digitisation project that helped us to make this valuable resource available for a wide range of scholars.
[15] The lacunae are Q1–Q19: 9; Q19: 21–Q19: 65; Q30: 54–31: 5 and Q95: 5–Q114.
[16] Hirji, 2019, p. 441.

Figure 2.1 The page layout and chapter title in MS QUR002, Aga Khan
Library. Photo courtesy Aga Khan Library.

Figure 2.2 AKL-QUR002, Naskh script at Sūrat Taha (Q. 20), fol. 7v, Aga Khan Library. Photo courtesy Aga Khan Library.

Figure 2.3 RAS Arabic 12a, Naskh script at Sūrat Taha (Q. 20), fol. 9r.
Reproduced courtesy of the Royal Asiatic Society of Great Britain and Ireland.

Moreover, looking at highly respected texts copied in 1792 known as
Hamziyya,[17] the poem in the praise of the Prophet, would evidence an enduring
and sophisticated scribal tradition on the East African coast. In my opinion,
using such script in Qur'ān manuscripts and other texts such as Hamziyya,
confirm two facts: the script was recognised amongst the scribes and scholars as

---

17 SOAS MS 53823a. This manuscript contains a very old copy of the famous religious poem, given to
Hichens by Muhammad Kijumwa. The Swahili translation of the poem dates from 1792 (1207 AH)
and was done by Sayyid Idarus bin Athman. The Hamziyya, as it is known among the Swahili, is
written in Arabic and Swahili and it is an ode in praise of the Prophet Muhammad. The first line of
each verse is in Arabic and the second line is the Swahili translation of the first line. The Arabic part
of the poem in known as 'Ummul-Kura' and was written by Sheikh Muhammad bin Said, known as
Albusiry, a prominent Egyptian poet. The name Hamziyya, which refers to the poem that combines
the Arabic and Swahili lines, originated from the fact that in Arabic prosody every poem rhyming in
'Hamza' is called Hamziyya. However, this is not a concern for the Swahili community who knows the
poem as Hamziyya per se, without any reference to the rhyming pattern. The main linguistic characteristic of the poem is that it is written in Kingov(z)i, archaic Swahili, and the translation from Arabic
to Swahili is very literal. A typical stanza contains thirty mizani (syllabic measures) in each baiti. The
number of syllables in each line varies between fourteen and fifteen. The poem used to be recited by
professional singers from Pate, Siu and Bajuni. They learned the poem by heart and performed it in
coastal towns. Available at: https://digital.soas.ac.uk/LOAA000084/00001/pdf?search=hamziyya.

prestigious, and that this script received influences from all cultures in the east coast such as Maghribi, Sudani and Bihari to name but a few.

The most outstanding feature of MS-QUR002 are the decorative elements that can be divided into two different areas (Fig. 2.4). The first is the chapters' headings that are written inside a rectangle framed by red lines and include the name of the chapter, place of revelation and number of verses. Two chapters have received particular attention where the names of the chapters were written inside a decorative cartouche on a black background, Sura Yāsīn (Q36) and Sura al-Muzzamil (Q73), where the Basmala was written inside a similar cartouche. In addition, the Basmala in most of the chapters is written in a slightly thickened decorated style.

The second instance of decoration are the marginal ornaments that mark the beginning of *Juz'* (parts), *Ḥizb* (groups) and every quarter (*Rub'*) (Fig. 2.5). A roundel marks each *Juz's* beginning in an intense palette dominated by yellow, red and brown. There are thirteen of these circles – marking the start of each *Juz'*.[18]

It should be noted that the artists who illuminated the Qur'āns came from different ethnic, artistic and historical backgrounds, which nurtured what became distinct Islamic civilisations and distinct Islamic art traditions. Next to the uniqueness of the text, these backgrounds were the source of the formation and development of Qur'ān illuminations as we can follow them up chronologically and regionally. These sources were primarily Arabic and Persian.

Although calligraphically and structurally MS QUR002 offers a few visual congruencies with Southeast Asian manuscripts – the earthy palette of red, brown ochre, black and white does resonate with Malay-world preferences. Very similar illuminations are found in the opening pages of the first volume of a thirty-volume Qur'ān said to be from Ethiopia, held in a private collection.

To conclude, it is worth mentioning that despite the significance of the decorative programme of MS-QUR002, it seems that different artisans might have done them in different periods, or MS-QUR002 was a work in progress. Both claims are supported by the alterations in size, shape and colours of all decorations, and the incomplete sole attempt to mark the prostration *Aya* (Q32: 15) without illumination, as it is a common feature in Qur'ān manuscripts from coastal East Africa and Southeast Asia. In addition there are the missed-out verses that were corrected or inserted in margins, as will be discussed later. With that having been said, the decoration of MS-QUR002 would benefit from a separate detailed study in the future.

---

[18] The Qur'ān is divided into thirty chapters (*Juz'*), each *Juz'* is divided into two groups (*Ḥizb*) with a total of sixty *Ḥizb*, and each *Ḥizb* is divided into four quarters (*Rub'*).

Figure 2.4 Ornament and illumination in QUR002. Clockwise from top left: Decorated Basmalla (ff.240), Elevated Basmalla (ff.237) and Yāsīn Ṣal'am (PBUH) Thamanun wa-thalāth āyah, Makkīyyah. Photo courtesy the author.

CORRECTIONS AND VARIANT READINGS GLOSSES

In addition to the significant ornamentation elements in the margins of MS-QUR002, it also includes some textual features such as variant readings or corrections. The variant readings, known as *Qirā'āt*, are mentioned in the margins.[19] In MS QUR002, variant readings are given in marginal glosses in red and black *Naskh*, with their authorised transmitter mentioned at the beginning

---

[19] It means the changes which occur in the words of the Qur'ān about the extension (*madd*), shortening (*qaṣr*), punctuation or written text, the order of the words in the text and the reading accordingly (*I'rāb*). Dogan, Recep. 2016. *Uṣūl al-Tafsīr: The Sciences and Methodology of the Quran*, Clifton, NJ: Tughra Books, p. 243.

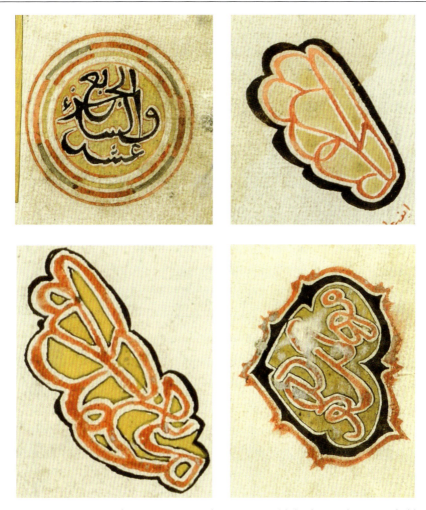

Figure 2.5 Marginal ornaments marking parts of (clockwise from top left)
a *juz'*, Hizb, Nisf and Rub'. Photo courtesy the author.

of each line in red ink. The zigzagging commentary is often linked to the Indian
manuscript culture.

Another interesting feature in this manuscript is that the copyist occasionally missed some words, phrases or even a whole verse (Fig. 2.6). The verses
missed out have been inserted in the margins, some of which are in a different
hand. The majority of corrections or insertions are followed by the word *Ṣaḥḥa*
(correct) to confirm the corrections. It should be noted that this is a common
practice in Islamic manuscripts, including Qur'ānic manuscripts, mainly if the
manuscript was produced in low economic circumstances.

Figure 2.6 MS-QUR002 (Q48: 19) insertion of part of the verse that was missed out in the writing. Photo courtesy the author.

This above confirms my previous claim that MS-QUR002 was likely a work in progress manuscript or meant to be produced for daily use, which explains the lack of binding. It is hard, however, to speculate whether these corrections were completed during the writing process or after completion in the process of collation (muqābala), one of the many incidents where the scribe missed out a verse or word from a verse and corrected it in the margin. Moreover, there are three incidents where the names of suras are translated into Gujarati in the margin but in a more recent pen. Comparing the QUR002 with the RAS Qur'ān, in the latter more attention was given to the script, vocalisation and decoration (see Fig. 2.3), and this can shed more light on the scribal traditions and its connection to the cultural and social milieu in East Africa.

It is believed that the manuscripts from Africa share certain physical attributes. Some of these manuscripts were produced for use in the mosque or library and some were produced for daily use and for travelling with their owners. Because of this, they have their own unique character and structure. They were also passed between members of the learned community who would also take them on their travels for teaching purposes. They were obviously much used, show signs of wear and tear, and often have a somewhat battered appearance. Examples of such texts from earlier centuries would be unlikely to have survived the climatic conditions and such heavy use.[20]

Another observation, which is common in North and East African and Indian manuscripts, is using the less canonised names of the chapters. The scribe used al-Malā'ikah (Angels) for Q35 instead of Fāṭir (The Creator), al-Mu'min (The Believer) for Q40 instead of Ghāfir (The Forgiving), Hā Mīm al-Sajdah for Q41 instead of Fuṣṣilat (Revelations Well Expounded), and finally he used al-Dahr (Period of Time) for Q76 instead of al-Insān (Man).

BETWEEN SOUTH ARABIA AND SOUTHEAST ASIA

The focus of this section is to trace the cross-cultural influences from the Indian Ocean regions on MS-QUR002. This Indian Ocean culture stretches from Cape Town in South Africa upwards along the eastern coast of Africa in the west, across the southern tip of the Arabian Peninsula, through the scattered islands of the Indian Ocean, including the Maldives, Comoros and Sri Lanka, along the southern coasts of India, up to Bengal and down via coastal Burma to the Malay Peninsula.[21] As Hirji argues, these connections happened through the movement of Ḥaḍramī merchants and religious scholars in the twelfth/

---

[20] Ansorge, 2020.
[21] Gallop, 2017, p. 123.

eighteenth and nineteenth centuries.[22] It is worth mentioning, however, that the emphasis will be three distinct geographical areas: South Arabia, East Africa and Southeast Asia.

Until recently, the two studies by Simon Digby (1975) and James de Vere Allen (1981) were the most cited studies about East African Qur'ān manuscripts. The two studies discuss the well-known Qur'ān manuscripts RAS Arabic 12a and Fowler Qur'ān FMCH90.1840A-B. In 1989, Witkam argued that it is not strange to find Indian materials, be it Qur'ān manuscripts or any product of human manufacture, in South Arabia because of the close connection with the Indian subcontinent. Examining three manuscripts named Ḍawrān fragments from Yemen, he confirms some resemblance of East African and stylistic relations to the Bihari Qur'ān.[23]

In 2017 Sana Mirza suggested that the Qur'ān manuscript in the Khalili Collection in the School of Oriental and African Studies (QUR706) is connected to the Harari manuscript culture. Her study provided '[an] opportunity to consider long-distance artistic circulations and encounters in the early modern Indian Ocean.'[24] A recent study by Zulfikar Hirji in his edited work[25] provided a comprehensive comparison between RAS, Fowler and Hinawy Qur'ān manuscripts.[26] He argues that they were all produced in Siyu between the seventeenth and nineteenth centuries. Hirji's significant study means that we have a new Qur'ān manuscript (Hinawy) to be added to the corpus.[27] It is hoped that the MS-QUR002 also adds a new object and perspective to the current corpus of manuscripts that belong to coastal East Africa.

Several striking facts emerge from the study of Qur'ān manuscripts from Oman and its accompanying illustrations, suggesting a surprising connection between the known Qur'ān manuscript in Oman and those of the Indian Ocean, especially the Malay world, and with other Ibadi communities beyond Oman.[28] In their study of the illuminated Qur'ān manuscripts in Oman, Gaube and al-Salimi connect the illumination in MH149, dated 1245/1829, to East Africa and India. They argue that these fascinating styles do not have matching

---

[22] Hirji, 2019, p. 444.

[23] Witkam, 1989, pp. 157–8.

[24] Mirza, 2017.

[25] *Approaches to the Qur'an in Sub-Saharan Africa* is an edited volume by Zulifikar Hirji, published by Oxford University Press in association with the Institute of Ismaili Studies in 2019. The volume covers a wide range of topics concerning the study of Qur'ān and manuscript culture in sub-Saharan Africa.

[26] Sheikh-Sir Mbarak al-Hinawy (1896–1959) served as Liwali (governor) for the Coast under the Sultanate of Zanzibar from 1940 to 1949. He witnessed the final decades of the British imperial era, colonialism and the rise of African nationalism from the port-city of Mombasa, the coastal capital of present-day Kenya (Hirji, 2012).

[27] Hirji, 2019.

[28] Gallop, 2017, p. 124; King, 2011, p. 218.

patterns in manuscripts that were produced in Arabia.[29] Al-Salimi and Hafyan's study of the illuminated Qur'ān manuscripts in the holdings of the Ministry of Heritage and the Library of Sayyid Mohammed Bin Al Busaidi in Oman suggested that the Qur'ānic manuscripts in Oman represent an unstudied field of research.[30]

The connection of MS-QUR002 to other manuscripts in Oman (MH149 and No.2220) is evidenced in their script and decoration's resonance. The MH149 exists in the Ministry of Heritage collection (Fig. 2.7), the stylised Basmala inside a coloured cartouche resonates with the one in ff.240 (see Fig. 2.3). The manuscript No.2220 exists in the Ministry of Religious Affairs collection, and it shares similar features with both manuscripts in script and decoration. However, the Basmala in MH149 and No.2220 is written in black ink on a yellow background, while in MS-QUR002, Basmala is reversed white on a black background. Still, the compositional schema, colour patterns and the script in the three manuscripts would support the argument made by Hirji that they were all produced in East Africa and preserved in Oman.[31]

Similar to Oman, East Africa has been the central point connecting many cultures. Muslim areas of East Africa have traditionally been the coastal strip that extends for over 1,000 miles and includes Somalia, Kenya, Tanzania (including Zanzibar) and northern Mozambique. This area has a homogenous culture, known as Swahili, which is distinct from but related to the Arabic Islamic world and the Bantu-speaking peoples of the interior. For instance, showing the importance of the Lamu Archipelago as a religious centre for the Swahili between 1750 and 1820, Pradines argues that twenty-two mosques were built in Lamu and twelve mosques for the city of Pate. Siyu itself was a recognised centre for producing many Qur'ān manuscripts.[32] This is exemplified in work undertaken by Hirji comparing three manuscripts from Siyu. He drew his conclusions based on the similarities in the decoration and script in these manuscripts. Moreover, he linked these features, mainly the red and black ink, to the nineteenth-century Swahili language manuscripts written in Arabic script in the SOAS collection.[33]

The third cultural impulse on MS-QUR002 comes from the South Asian region. Although there have been many studies of Islamic manuscripts from India, most have focused on the Mughal and other court traditions of the north; almost nothing is known of Islamic manuscript art of the southern Tamil-speaking coastal regions. One of the few published contributions towards lifting

---

[29] Gaube and al-Salimi, 2016.
[30] al-Salimi and al-Hafyan, 2008, p. 108.
[31] Hirji, 2019.
[32] Pradines, 2022, p. 276.
[33] MS 45022a, MS 45022b, MS 45022c. Hirji, 2019, p. 444.

Figure 2.7 No.2220, Ministry of Endowments and Religious Affairs, Sultanate of Oman. Courtesy Ministry of Endowments and Religious Affairs, Sultanate of Oman.

the veil from the artistic traditions of these little-known areas is the study by Tim Stanley on Qurʾān manuscript and its connection to Zanzibar.[34]

In her study about the Harari Qurʾān manuscript, Sana Mirza concluded that Indian Qurʾān manuscripts with *bihārī* script often included marginal glosses, which contain variant readings and hadith in another, less angular cursive script, *nashī-dīwānī*. In her paper published in this volume, Mirza argues that the Harari artisans developed a distinctive Harari decorative and calligraphic style through their participation in multidirectional artistic interchange across the Indian Ocean circuits.[35]

The MS-QUR002 shares many similarities with the majority of the manuscripts mentioned above. The decoration of the sura headings, the page layout, marginal variant readings in red and black ink and an approximate number of lines on one page indicate that MS-QUR002 belongs to the same corpus of

---

[34] Stanley, 1999, cited in Gallop, 2017, p. 123.
[35] This study is included in this volume titled: *Developing the Harari Muṣḥaf: The Indian Ocean Milieu of Ethiopian Scribes*.

Qur'ān manuscripts with Indian Ocean connections. More importantly, the decorative programme and script in MS-QUR002 are similar to those in the Fowler Qur'ān and the Royal Asiatic Society item. It is likely that MS-QUR002 was produced in Lamu sometime between 1800 and 1900. We also see the same rectangular form of decorated frames, with the circle as the central decorative motif and a predilection for hatched lines. Also notable is that within the decorated frames, each line of text is set within ruled frames, just as in the Penang Qur'ān.

Conclusion

The present chapter intended to show the similarities between the QUR002 manuscript and the other manuscripts belonging to the cultural milieu of the Indian Ocean. The codicological analysis concerning the script, decoration and text structure resonate those features existing in some Qur'ān manuscripts from Oman, Kenya and India as evidence of various cultural influences. These similarities cannot be coincidences, but it reflects a strong tradition that possibly flourished in the eighteenth century. We should be grateful for the recent discoveries of Qur'ān manuscripts from East Africa and the associated comparative studies by researchers such as Annabel Gallop, Zulfikar Hirji and Sana Mirza.[36] One could easily confirm that the tradition of producing manuscripts in this extended geography and culture was unique in some features such as illumination and script.

In my opinion, it might be reasonable to confirm that the QUR002 was originally produced in the Lamu Archipelago region, most probably Pate Island and the town of Siyu in particular. This means that it can be added to the corpus of the manuscripts from the same period and provenance. That said, there are still questions that require answers, such as who the scribe was and whether the decoration and writing took place at the same time or whether the illumination happened much later. Also, the question of patronage and the reasons for producing these manuscripts. Some manuscripts were produced for daily use (such as QUR002) and some were elegant enough to be deposited in private libraries or mosques (such as the Hinawy Qur'an).

The cultural heritage in East Africa is a rich corpus that has yet to be discovered, and it is not limited to its oral traditions. This insight led to a general acceptance of the fact that the analysis of manuscripts offers essential information about the societies and cultures in which they were used. Nevertheless, there is a need to focus on collaborative research to contextualise manuscript studies pertaining to the Indian Ocean region. The codicology of Swahili manuscripts

---

[36] Gallop, 2004, 2005, 2010, 2015 and 2017; Hirji, 2019 and Mirza, 2017.

written in Arabic or one of the vernacular languages is an important field that requires further attention.

BIBLIOGRAPHY

Ansorge, Catherine. 2020. 'Some Islamic manuscripts from Africa'. https://specialcollec tions-blog.lib.cam.ac.uk/?p=20276.

'Antique Ethiopia Quran (18th Century CE)'. 2013. Abu Dervish Blog, review no.105. http://abudervish.blogspot.com/2013/02/ancient-manuscript-review-105-antique. html.

al-Azami, M. M. 2003. *The History of the Qur'anic Text from Revelation to Compilation: A Comparative Study with the Old and New Testaments*. Leicester: UK Islamic Academy.

Baker, Colin. 2019. 'Calligraphy of the Qur'an – The British Library'. https://www.bl.uk /sacred-texts/articles/illumination-of-the-quran.

Baker, Colin. 2007. *Qur'an Manuscripts: Calligraphy, Illumination, Design*. London: British Library.

Blair, Sheila. 2006. *Islamic Calligraphy*. Edinburgh: Edinburgh University Press.

Digby, Simon. 1975. 'A Qur'an from the East African coast'. *Art and archaeology research papers*, 7, pp. 49–55.

Gallop, Annabel. 2017. 'Indian Ocean Connections: Illuminated Islamic Manuscripts from Penang', in Peter Zabielskis, Yeoh Seng Guan and Kat Fatland (eds), *Penang and Its Networks of Knowledge*. Penang: Areca Books, pp. 115–33.

Gallop, Annabel. 2015. 'The appreciation and study of Qur'an manuscripts from Southeast Asia: past, present, and future', *Heritage of Nusantara: International Journal of Religious Literature and Heritage*, Dec., Vol.2, No.2, pp. 195–212.

Gallop, Annabel. 2010. 'The Boné Qur'an from South Sulawesi', in Benoit Junod, Annabel Gallop and Margaret Graves (eds), *Treasures of the Aga Khan Museum: Arts of the Book and Calligraphy*. Istanbul: Aga Khan Trust for Culture and Sakip Sabanci University and Museum, pp. 162–73.

Gallop, Anabel. 2005. 'Islamic manuscript art of Southeast Asia', in James Bennett (ed.), *Crescent Moon: Islamic art and civilisation in Southeast Asia / Bulan sabit: seni dan peradaban Islam di Asia Tenggara*. Adelaide: Art Gallery of South Australia, pp. 158–83.

Gallop, Annabel. 2004a. 'A remarkable Penang Qur'an manuscript', *Heritage Asia* 1, no. 2, pp. 39–41.

Gallop, Annabel. 2004b. 'An Acehnese style of manuscript illumination'. *Archipel* 68, pp. 193–240.

Gaube, Heinz and Abdulrahman al Salimi. 2016. *Illuminated Qurans from Oman*. Hildesheim: Georg Olms Verlag.

Hirji, Zulfikar, 2019. 'The Siyu Qur'ans: three illuminated Qur'an Manuscripts from Coastal East Africa', in Zulfikar Hirji (ed.), *Approaches to the Qur'an in sub-Saharan Africa*. Oxford: Oxford University Press, pp. 431–71.

Hirji, Zulfikar. 2012. *Between Empires: Sheikh-Sir Mbarak al-Hinawy, 1896–1959*, London: Azimuth Editions.

King, Geoffrey. 2011. 'Review of: Islamic Art in Oman. By Abdulrahman al-Salimi, Heinz Gaube and Lorenz Korn. Muscat: Ministry of Heritage and Culture and Ministry of Endowments and Religious Affairs, 2010', *Journal of the Royal Asiatic Society*, 21:2, pp. 218–21.

Komba, Stanislaus Clemence. 2015. 'The Beginnings and Development of Islam and Quranic Schools in East Africa', *Journal of Philosophy, Culture and Religion*, 6.

Mirza, Sana. 2017. 'The Visual Resonances of a Harari Qur'ān: An 18th-Century Ethiopian Manuscript and Its Indian Ocean Connections.' *Afriques* 8: https://doi.org/10.4000/afriques.2052.

Pradines, Stéphane. 2022. *Historic Mosques in Sub-Saharan Africa, from Timbuktu to Zanzibar*. Leiden: Brill.

Qur'ān from Khalili Collection. SOAS Digital Collection: https://digital.soas.ac.uk/LOAA003338/00001/41?search=quran.

al-Salimi, Abdulrahman and Faysal al-Hafiyan. 2008. 'Omani Quranic manuscripts: the tradition of writing and artistic design', in Heinz Gaube and Lorenz Korn (eds), *Islamic art in Oman*. Muscat: Mazoon, pp. 106–17.

Samsom, Ridder H. 2012. 'Swahili Manuscripts: Looking in East African Collections for Swahili Manuscripts in Arabic Script.' Unpublished extended English version of a paper presented at '50 Years of Kiswahili as a Language of African Liberation, Unification and Renaissance, Dar-es-Salam, 4–6 October 2012, http://www.academia.edu/26313364/SWAHILI_MANUSCRIPTS_Looking_in_East_African_Collections_for_Swahili_Manuscripts_in_Arabic_Script_1.

Shaker, Ahmad, 2015. Facsimile Editions of Early Qur'an Manuscripts. https://iqsaweb.wordpress.com/2015/10/26/shaker_facsimile-editions/.

Stanley, Tim. 1999. 'A Qur'an Once in Zanzibar: Connections between India, Arabia, and the Swahili Coast', in Manijeh Bayani, Anna Contadini and Tim Stanley (eds), *The Decorated Word: Qur'ans of the 17th to 19th Centuries*. London: Nour Foundation, pp. 26–31.

Witkam, J. J. 1989. 'Qur'ān Fragments from Ḍawrān (Yemen)', *Manuscripts of the Middle East*, 4, pp. 155–74.

CHAPTER 3

Muslim Identities of the Indian Ocean: the Ibadi Al Bu Sa'id of Oman during the Eighteenth and Nineteenth Centuries

BEATRICE NICOLINI

INTRODUCTION

Since the end of the eighteenth century the Ibadi Al Bu Sa'id of Oman were recognised as the protagonists of an important empowering process towards the mercantile expansion on the oceanic coasts of Africa; therefore, there developed within the Indian Ocean cultural and religious connections represented by continuous migratory flows. The present study aims to re-read Asian groups movements and presences along the Swahili coast as well as their potential influences on local cultures, religions and societies. It should be noted that ethnocentric views – especially Eurocentric ones – have informed numerous studies for a long time, and sometimes still do. In this regard, most of the Western-orientated studies and analysis on the role of Afro-Asian littorals and of their people throughout history often focused on external menaces, interests and priorities. Accordingly, within an interlinked cluster like the Swahili littorals, could we have been so sure on the effects of early globalisation in this vast area? Moreover, could we have been sure about a series of enthusiastic and lyrical images of a sea-life full of different people, ideas, goods and religions, exchanging and living together in a sort of peaceful liquid world before the Europeans? During the nineteenth century the dominions of Muscat consisted of the island of Bahrain, the coast of Makran, some areas along the Persian coast such as Chah Bahar, the island of Socotra, the islands of Kuria Muria, the islands of Zanzibar and Pemba and adjacent ports of the East African coast from Cabo Delgado to Cape Guardafui. And it was in this very period that the presence of many challenges on the East African littorals was a potent factor that led the Omanis more and more towards Zanzibar. The power of the Al Bu Sa'id sultans of Oman was widely known as being based on a delicate balance of forces and social groups among them. In fact, the elements that composed the nineteenth-century Omani leadership were, and had always been, inevitably shared amongst diversified groups such as the Baloch, the Asian religious and mercantile communities, and the African regional leaders (such as the Mwinyi Mkuu).

MUSLIM IDENTITIES ON THE SWAHILI COAST

Along the Swahili coast of East Africa, the relationships between spirit possession, Islam and the new presence of European powers soon developed local societies where economic and political inequalities were inevitably destined to increase along with the economic expansion in the Indian Ocean.[1] The fluid space of the Swahili coast was influenced by different forces of capital and by the knowledge–power nexus during and after the colonial period. During the nineteenth century, gradual processes of osmosis occurred. Local cults and magical practices interchanged with the precepts of the Qur'ān,[2] resulting in a social and political interpretation of Arab powers on the East African coast that reflected a multiplicity of cultural and religious roots.

COMMUNITIES AND PRESENCES

Islamic presence created Arabian traditions for Arabians in East Africa to replace the indigenous structures of power. Moreover, the vast network of international trade links and the presence of various mercantile communities were progressively consolidated, stretching from Africa, Arabia, the Gulf and India as far as Southeast Asia, Indonesia and even China, regarding Zanzibar (Unguja) as a polarising new centre. In fact, the choice of Zanzibar Island was a winning one due to numerous elements that made the new Omani capital the centre of a new Indian Ocean world. A vital atmosphere in Zanzibar soon led a small fishing village to develop into a very profitable entrepôt.[3] The variety of regional forms of political organisation of the Swahili coast has been eclipsed by the colonial imposition of the European nation-state model. The British colonial necessity to connect the multiple local realities with the appearance of continuity of Western rule was shown by how these appositions were tools for the colonial administrators. The sea voyages – as well as the land ones – were wider than we suppose: the ports of western India were connected to the Arabian Peninsula and to the Horn of Africa, and beyond. During the period

---

[1] Hardinge, 1899, pp. 5–6.
[2] Olsson, 2019, pp. 27–9; Bang, 2019, p. 1033.
[3] Bishara and Wint, 2020, pp. 1–21.

that saw the rise of Europe in East Africa, there were many revolutions, and new protagonists emerged along the Asian, Arabian and East African coasts. Against these backdrops, the emergence of Arab dynasties was supposed to arise from polarisations that followed the struggle against the Portuguese presence in the Indian Ocean. In East Africa we have essential distinctions between cultural and geographical areas. Since notable geo-morphological differences and cultural, historical, political and social peculiarities result in numerous and often contrasting considerations concerning precise geographical definitions, we prefer here the definition of cultural crossbow that relates to the coastal strip of sub-tropical East Africa, the Mrima coast, and to the Indian Ocean islands, Pate, Lamu, Pemba, Zanzibar and Mafia, where the Swahili civilisation flourished. The Swahili coast has always nurtured contacts with the outside world, constituting that western part of the Indian Ocean so indissolubly linked to other shores and inserted in the context of a far wider theatre. One of the natural causes for this difference consists of the wooded belt surrounding the Eastern African coast to the west.

THE EAST AFRICAN LITTORALS

Poor and with limited rainfall, the wooded belt is known in Kiswahili as *nyika* (bush, wild). This strip running from modern-day Kenya, through valleys and rivers towards the south, forms a natural barrier to contacts between the shore and the interior. For centuries the East African interior was afflicted by the presence of the tsetse fly and made inhospitable by long periods of drought and malarial infection. On the contrary, the coastal area of modern-day Tanzania (Mrima), with its humid and temperate climate, encouraged settlements and agricultural activity. The influence of the environmental ecosystem and the subsequent settlement patterns of populations along the coast on the one hand, and of the savannah of the East African interior on the other, led to the development of different cultures. Lying at the very edge of the monsoon area that ends at the Mozambique Channel, an area of extremely unstable mari-time climes, where the winds from the southeast begin to blow and favourable conditions cease, the Swahili coast benefited from the ecosystem of the Indian Ocean.[4] Its strategic position eased links between East Africa, the Red Sea, the Gulf, the Arabian Peninsula and western India. The regularity and force of the monsoons contributed to making the East African littoral a fringe of the great navigation system of the Indian Ocean. Mogadishu, Malindi, Mombasa, Zanzibar, Kilwa and Sofala were the most flourishing cities. The progressive homogenisation between Arab-Islamic culture and Swahili traditions – also

---

[4] Agius, 2018.

caused by inter-marriages due to the monsoon sailing periods that obliged long months of men's stay in Africa – stimulated the creation of new Islamic identities along the coasts of East Africa. Kilwa exported copper, Malindi and Mombasa iron, and Mogadishu cloth. Copper coins symbolised power and were used in trade activities. Mosques reflected the influence of their diverse origins: early Shi'a Sirafi, Indian and Ibadi Omani during the sultanate.[5] The Swahili who lived on the islands and along the coasts of East Africa were comprised of urban-based merchants who dealt in short- as well as long-distance inter-continental trade.[6] They belonged to a sophisticated society that spoke the same language, a society that represented a central rather than some form of peripheral entity. Swahili language, culture, literature and poetry have always represented an important source for any attempt to understand the history of the coast and islands of East Africa. In regard to socio-economic relationships, numerous Swahili families – especially on the littorals where they lived in mud and straw huts as fishermen and farmers – developed different exchange and trade patterns; here the traditional definitions of a middlemen society have been analysed by T. Vernet through articulated, flexible, dynamic and diversified lenses.[7] The towns hosted numerous foreign merchants and life was lively and vibrant and the connections were wide, based on imports and exports, moneylending, ship-building and repairs. This was an interchanged world where the Swahili coast was an active protagonist as well as the Indian Ocean.

IBADI IDENTITIES ALONG THE INDIAN OCEAN

Land and maritime realities before and after the Arab and the European presence did constitute crucial issues throughout the history of the Swahili coast. As already stated above, we are aware of the role of external influences in this region, as well as of the ethnocentric views of numerous studies for a long time, and sometimes still do; there are now no serious scholars who suggest external origins or significant Arab or Persian colonisation as the starting point for coastal settlement.[8] Such links and relationships were to be sought in those elements that constituted the equilibrium of the Indian Ocean, that is, in the monsoons, in the presence of thalassocracies, in the presence of different traditions and religions, and in the many exchanges of people and goods. Starting from the sixteenth century onwards, the European conflicts for conquest of commercial monopolies contributed to the consolidation of new threads that interconnected three continents: Europe, Asia and Africa. Two main political

---

[5] Rhodes, Breen and Forsythe, 2015, 339; Pradines, 2009.
[6] Walker, 2018.
[7] Vernet, 2015.
[8] Wilkinson, 2015.

realities were destined to co-exist along the Swahili coast: the kaleidoscopic societies of the coasts, and the tribal, pastoral societies of the interior where, from time to time, the former succeeded in prevailing and imposing its laws. The Arab powers thus created new markets between the ports of southwestern Asia and the Arabian, western Indian and East African coasts.

The balance created by the monsoons was achieved over the space of a year with the following rhythm: from December to March the monsoon blows from Arabia and the western coasts of India in the northeast, pushing as far as Mogadishu. The term derives from the Arabic *mawsin* (pl. *mawasin*) season, from the Portuguese *monção*. The winds are light and constant, the climate hot and dry. In April the monsoon starts to blow from the southwest, from eastern Africa towards the coasts of the Gulf, the climate cooler but much more humid. The rains are mainly in April and May, while the driest months are November and December. Moreover, along the East African coasts and in the islands of the Indian Ocean, the tropical climate is always tempered by sea breezes. Until the introduction of the steam ship during the second half of the nineteenth century, sailing from Arabia in November in a south-south-westerly direction took thirty to forty days in ideal weather conditions. In December, thanks to the stabilisation of the monsoon, the voyage took only twenty to twenty-five days. Consequently, thanks to the monsoons, the international trade relations of Arabia had been historically through the sea; although we must remember that Arabian trading was pervasive via land as well. Maritime coastal trades, as well as long-distance trades, constituted the expressions of an economy that was sophisticated and organised; therefore, the necessity of control of these sea trade routes represented a crucial element: a political element.

Near the coast of equatorial Africa, separated from the continent by thirty-one miles, lies the island of Zanzibar. It is the largest coral island of East Africa and forms part of a coral reef that stretches from the island of Pemba in the north to the island of Mafia in the south, creating a kind of coastline detached from the continent itself. Zanzibar is twelve to eighteen miles wide and roughly fifty-two miles long. The city of the same name lies on the western side of the island and its port, one of the best in Africa, provided good anchorage for deep-sea fishing vessels. The island of Pemba (Djazira Al-Khadra, the green or the emerald island) is roughly twenty-eight miles long and twelve miles wide – an area of approximately 611 square miles – and is found thirty-four miles from Zanzibar. Consisting mainly of coralline rock, it is hillier than its sister island, Zanzibar. Pemba was well known for its cloves, still the main source of income today. Despite the extremely heterogeneous nature of its population, Pemba's original inhabitants are the Wapemba – a Bantu group who take their name from the island. The largest town on the island, Wete, in the west, has an imposing square-plan fortress built by the Portuguese that looms over a bay of mangroves.

In the past Pemba had no harbour suitable for large ships. With its shallow waters and dense vegetation, the island had limited reserves of drinking water. Pemba supplied to Zanzibar a little excellent ghee and poor rice: cloves were cultivated and, in common with all the coast, exported cowries, while coconuts were grown where soils were unsuitable for the clove trees.[9] However, since the reef protects their coasts, Zanzibar and Pemba were the only islands of strategic predominance thanks to two variables of fundamental importance: the monsoon winds and their proximity to the African continent. The islands offered better services compared to other cities of the East African coast. In addition to its traditional commerce of ivory, beeswax and tortoise shells, Zanzibar emerged as a main trade hub for the whole region. Here traditional cults mixed with new people coming from the hinterlands of East Africa supplying the growing demand of goods on the coast. The Sultan of Oman expanded the clove plantations and extended them to the island of Pemba, dominating eighty per cent of the world production. After spices and ivory, cloves became the third source of exports. The fleets of the eighteenth- and nineteenth-century Omani rulers, moreover, defended the merchants' ships, taxes were low and, not least, Zanzibar had drinking water. The traditional thalassocratic system that had developed along the shores of the Swahili coast was altered by the Europeans, who started to extend their mercantile and territorial ambitions, pursued from land (terra firma) to the seas.

Since the end of the eighteenth century, the Ibadi Al Bu Sa'id of Oman – according to available sources – energised the mercantile expansion towards the oceanic coasts of Africa;[10] therefore, within the Swahili coast developed cultural connections represented by continuous migratory flows. And it was in this period that the presence of many opportunities on the East African littorals became a potent factor that led the Omanis more and more towards Zanzibar. The dynasty of the Al Bu Sa'id (1749 to the present day) – Ibadi – emerged at the end of the eighteenth century along the Swahili coast, with its wide range of links and connections and enjoying the mediating roles and receiving loans from the various Indian communities present in Zanzibar.[11] In 1832, Sayyid Sa'id bin Sulṭan Al Bu Sa'id decided to move the capital of the sultanate from Muscat to Zanzibar.[12] The traditional mercantile relationships between the Indian communities and the Omanis were destined to develop new trade patterns. Consequently, during the nineteenth century the growth in the volume of trade managed by the Indian mercantile communities led to a gradual but progressive weakening of the Swahili groups. They experienced the decrease in their trade, and their most deeply rooted social and cultural traditions underwent

---

[9] Croucher, 2015, p. 349.
[10] Gaube, 2013; Hoffman, 2018.
[11] Bishara, 2017.
[12] Nicolini, 2016.

traumatic changes. Among them the supernatural elements, the traditional cults and aggregation ceremonies were deprived of their forcefulness in the political and social fields.[13] On Zanzibar, instead, processes of osmosis occurred that often linked magical practices with the precepts of the Qur'ān, resulting in a politic-socio mix and management of power that reflected a multiplicity of cultural and religious roots. Unlike nearly all other parts of the Islamic world of the epoch, Islam was not spread on the Swahili coast by military conquest. It was a voluntary development. This intermingling also gave impetus to commercial activity, and during the second half of the nineteenth century the connections between the Swahili coast and its hinterland were innumerable.

Starting from the first half of the nineteenth century this network began to feel the effects of the European impact, the European ships – for example, the East Indiamen – before this time being inferior in both size and capital investments compared to the Arab dhows of the Indian Ocean. Since the siege of Fort Jesus of Mombasa in December 1698, Oman started exercising its power from Muscat over the formerly wealthy cities of the Swahili coast, north of Cabo Delgado (Mozambique). However, the ports of East Africa failed to recover the splendour they achieved in the past, since the new metropolis exerted identical control on traffic along the Swahili coastal commercial routes. This, together with the presence of the Omani governors (liwali) in the coastal cities, drove an uprising in Mombasa and Pate, where the representatives were murdered and the citizens refused to pay taxes to Oman. Hence started a period of conflicts between the cities still under the control of Oman and those in which the rebels had seized power and declared independence.

An attempt to solve the revolts was to hand out the ruling of the cities to Swahili families who remained loyal to Oman. In Mombasa, the Mazrui dynasty was appointed to govern the island in 1741. However, the operation was not as successful as expected: after the murder of the ruler of Oman, Saif ibn Sultan (1692–1711), the first Mazrui governor of Mombasa, Muhammad ibn Uthman al-Mazrui (1755–1773) refused to be subordinate to the new Omani ruler.[14] The new ruler resolved to terminate the insurrection in Mombasa, then commissioned a fleet to murder Al-Mazrui and take Fort Jesus. But one year later, one of Al-Mazrui's brothers murdered the new governor and reconquered the fort. The effect of rebellion spread to other Swahili coastal cities and the island of Pemba. Internal clashes in the ruling dynasty in Muscat also affected the stability of the Swahili coast. In 1784, a brother of the Al Bu Sa'id ruler seized the southern strip of the shoreline, taking Kilwa and Zanzibar, with the aim of creating his own sultanate. The ruler reacted rapidly and conquered the possessions of his

---

[13] Larsen, 2014, p. 26.
[14] Maurizi, 1819.

rebel brother, an operation that allowed him to retrieve the rest of the revolting cities. Thus started a short peaceful period under the Omani government, until the early 1800s when the Mazruis attacked back. They launched a campaign to seize the coastal cities, from Pangani to Malindi. At the same time a new sultan came to power in Oman in 1806: Sa'id bin Sultan Al Bu Sa'id.

Meanwhile, the two emerging European powers, Britain and France, were in contention regarding the trading routes with India. France dominated the Isle de France, Bourbon, Seychelles and the Rodriguez Islands. In order to supply slaves to the sugar cane plantations in their Indian colonies, the French were supposed to control the slave trade on the south coast, with Kilwa, once in Oman's hands, as their main supply centre. The defeat of Napoleon in 1815 allowed the British to expand their power to the Seychelles and to the Isle de France. Isle de France, now Mauritius, was discovered by the Portuguese in 1507 and was later occupied by the Dutch from 1598 until 1710. In 1715 it came into the possession of the East India Company and, in 1767, of King Louis XV of France, who christened it 'Isle de France'. Captured by the British in 1810 and then acknowledged by the Treaty of Paris in 1814, the British allowed the French settlers to use their language and their civil code. Sa'id bin Sultan Al Bu Sa'id's father had signed an alliance with the victors, of which the sultan took advantage to request their help in an operation to re-conquer the Swahili coast. An important conflict clouded the alliance between Oman and Great Britain: the British wished to abolish the slave trade. The Omanis benefited from slave trade centres in Kilwa, Bagamoyo and Zanzibar, the latter to supply India and the Arab countries. In 1822 the Ibadi ruler was convinced by the governor of Mauritius to sign a treaty abolishing the human trade. Actually, this agreement had political intentions: it did not affect the slave trade with Arabia, which could transfer the supply of slaves from the Omani possessions to the French colonies.

The Mazruis did not remain silent for long. In view of their expansionist ambitions, other coastal ports felt themselves threatened. In 1822, the Pate governors requested help from the Sultan of Oman, who sent his troops against Mombasa. The Mazruis had already applied for British favours, being rejected twice by virtue of the British–Omani alliance. But in 1824 Captain Fitzwilliam Owen (1754–1857), in command of the ship HMS *Leven*, docked at the Mombasa port right at the time when Oman's navy assaulted Fort Jesus. With a unilateral decision, Owen resolved to support the Mazruis, feeling that the establishment of a British base in Mombasa could promote abolition of the slave trade in the region. A twenty-one-year-old Lieutenant Reitz disembarked with a small contingent and set the British flag in Mombasa, declaring the first British protectorate. Later, in 1826, the Oman ruler's pressures obliged Great Britain to abjure. The first attempt of the Omani ruler to retrieve Mombasa was followed by a second one, until finally Sa'id bin Sultan Al Bu Sa'id's son conquered the city for his father.

In 1832, the capital of the new Omani leadership became Zanzibar. Although Sayyid Sa'id and his successors in Zanzibar appointed governors along the coast and had agents as far inland as the Congo, actual control was weak. Regarding the relationships with the Asian community, it was a fleet belonging to a Bhattia mercantile family of India that brought the Omani ruler from Muscat to Zanzibar and provided extra armed ships and manpower in his wars with Mombasa and feuds which arose in Zanzibar. This Bhattia family was none other than that of Shivji Topan (b. 1792 Mundra, Kutch), which, together with the Gopal Bhimani family at Muscat, were the two most prominent Indian families whose roles were vital for the nineteenth-century commercial expansion of Oman at Muscat and Zanzibar. These families originated from the Kutch region of northwestern India.[15]

In 1840, the European perception – or strong political will – was that the whole Swahili coast was finally in the Omani sultan's hands. The resolution was also economy-driven: as above described, besides ivory, beeswax and tortoise shells, the traditional commerce in the island, it was emerging as a slave trade centre.[16] Here traditional cults mixed with new people coming from the hinterland of East Africa for the growing demand of slaves on the coast. The Ibadi ruler expanded the clove plantations and extended them to the island of Pemba, dominating eighty per cent of the world production. After slaves and ivory, cloves became the third source of exports. On political grounds, Sa'id bin Sultan Al Bu Sa'id defeated the Mazruis, whose major leaders had been arrested and deported in 1837. The key factors in the strategy adopted by Britain were the need to establish a juridical-international order for British subjects on the Swahili coast to achieve abolition of the slave trade. In 1837 Saiyid Sa'id bin Sultan Al Bu Sa'id requested a British advisor to his personal assistance. The Court of Directors of the East India Company agreed. On 4 May 1841, Captain Atkins Hamerton (1804–56) of the 15th Native Infantry of the Calcutta Government was nominated British Consul and Political Agent to Zanzibar.[17] Hamerton was the only consul who spoke Arabic. Based on an agreement between the East India Company and the Foreign Office, Captain Hamerton was given the task of overseeing the commercial interests of the company, a task that was given the understanding between the wealthy Indian merchant, Jairam Topan, and the American consul, Edmund Roberts. He was also to communicate directly with the Secretary of State for Foreign Affairs in

---

[15] Larsen, 2004, pp. 121–45.
[16] Machado, 2014.
[17] Crofton, 1935.

London, as well as with the government in Bombay, referring to them any intelligence of a political nature that it may be interesting to the British government to be made acquainted with.[18]

THE AL BU SA'ID OF OMAN

The Omani rulers could not possess the same kind of political and territorial control of the East African islands and of the East African littorals as the Western powers of the time expected to maintain. With Omani powers established on Zanzibar, the leaders of the Hadimu and the Tumbatu swore allegiance to the sultan and, with the spread of the Omani possessions, the Tumbatu moved towards the village of Dunga, in the more sheltered and protected interior. The western part of Zanzibar, north of the port of the same name, was instead included in the ever-growing territories occupied by the Omani. Saiyid Sa'id bin Sultan Al Bu Sa'id favoured the occupation and exploitation of the forests and more fertile areas of the islands, distributed amongst his followers to be used for cultivating cloves and coconuts, activities that were labour intensive. These political actions altered the prosecution of local cults and the use of the Swahili territory as a sacred space for ceremonies.[19] Under constant pressure from Atkins Hamerton to abolish slavery throughout his dominions, Saiyid Sa'id bin Sultan Al Bu Sa'id ordered his subjects to pray in the mosques and made every effort to convince the British official of the good inherent in this ancient custom, which he presented as being anything but damaging but, on the contrary, as essential to the collective well-being of local societies.

On 2 October 1845 Saiyid Sa'id bin Sultan Al Bu Sa'id signed a treaty with Great Britain for the abolition of the slave trade, to enter into effect on 1 January 1847. This also foresaw the seizure and confiscation of any ship belonging to the sultan found to be transporting slaves, except for any in the Swahili ports of Lamu, Kilwa, Pemba, Zanzibar and Mafia.[20] Moreover, British subjects would also be prohibited from trading in slaves and this, included the Asian merchants. Thus, the fundamental question arose of the juridical status of the Asian community resident in East Africa, who refused to agree to such orders. And yet the articles of the treaty were expressed quite differently in the Arabic and English versions. This discrepancy would enable Lord Palmerston (1784–1865) to send a dispatch where he claimed that the slave trade was prohibited throughout East Africa. The profit margin was, however, too great. A slave bought on Zanzibar for 5–10 pure silver Maria Theresa thalers could be

---

[18] Hamerton Papers, 1841–54.
[19] Fair, 2001; Nicolini, 2019, pp. 237–49.
[20] Burton, 1858.

sold in Muscat for 25 and, at Bushire or Basra, for 40.[21] The reality was such that Hamerton's treaty was totally ineffective.

The power of the Al Bu Sa'id sultans of Oman along the Swahili coast was believed to be based on a balance of forces and social groups. In fact, the elements of nineteenth-century Omani leadership were generally supposed to be distributed between groups: the Baloch soldiers, the Asian merchant communities and the African regional leaders (Mwinyi Mkuu). The role played by European powers, particularly by the treaties signed between the sultans of Oman and the East India Company for abolishing slavery and by the arms trade, was crucial for the development of the Gulf and the Indian Ocean international networks. They contributed to the change of the Omanis from the slave trade to clove and spice cultivation – the major economic source of Zanzibar Island – along the coastal areas of sub-Saharan East Africa. Saiyid Sa'id bin Sultan Al Bu Sa'id (1804–6–1856) was believed to be the first sultan who did vitalise along the Swahili coast an important mercantile empire. The main factors of the spread of a maritime trade network were constituted by the expansion of the spice trade, especially by the cultivation of cloves in Zanzibar and the Pemba islands, by the slave trade, by ivory exportation and by their relations with the European powers of the nineteenth century. Saiyid Sa'id bin Sultan Al Bu Sa'id spoke Arabic, Hindi, Persian and Swahili;[22] he had seen the island of Zanzibar for the first time in 1802, when he was only eleven years old, and he had remained enchanted. He represented the major exponent of the evaluation of the spice trade as a means of creating a new Arab power elite, through a significant expansion of the cultivation of cloves in Zanzibar. This highlighted one of the first major steps towards the importance of spice. At the end of the eighteenth century the introduction of cloves (*Eugenia caryophyllata*, from the Myrtaceae family, *karafuu* in Kiswahili) onto this tropical island determined a new perception of economic-commercial potential in the eyes of the Al Bu Sa'id. The creation of a new niche of agricultural exploitation in Zanzibar itself and in Pemba was destined to transform Zanzibar and Pemba islands into new centres of global mercantile interests. In order to control the population, the influence on Swahili spirit possession cults was high.

In October 1856, Saiyid Sa'id bin Sultan Al Bu Sa'id died off the Seychelles on a ship named *Victoria* that was taking him from Muscat to Zanzibar. The struggle and the intrigues that followed his death were intense among his heirs. The Al Bu Sa'id dominions in Muscat and in Zanzibar were divided under the terms of the settlement of May 1861 – with Zanzibar having to pay 40,000 Maria Theresa thalers to Muscat annually – and formalised by the Canning Award,

---

[21] Semple, 2005; Perkins, 2015.
[22] Lorimer, 1915, p. 440.

confirmed by the Anglo-French Agreement of 1862. With this division, the possessions were assigned to the sons of Saiyid Sa'id bin Sultan Al Bu Sa'id, Majid Bin Sa'id Al Bu Sa'id (1856–70), from a Circassian second wife on Zanzibar, and Thuwayni bin Sa'id Al Bu Sa'id (r. October 1856–February 1866), from a Georgian second wife in Muscat.[23]

CONCLUSION

On the Swahili coast the gradual and progressive political process of eroding Arab power in East Africa started, and British predominance was to increase still further. In this context, external powers and trade, once established from the Gulf to the Indian Ocean with wider scenarios and different economies, contributed to modify the identities within regional and international leaderships. They were inevitably subjected to future substantial changes of this seaboard region. Concerning the working hypothesis, the variety of regional forms of political and social organisation of Zanzibar has been often eclipsed by the colonial imposition of the European nation-state model. The British colonial necessity to connect the local realities with the appearance of continuity of Western rule was shown by how these appositions were tools for the colonial administrators for 're-inventing' Arabian traditions for Arabians in Africa to replace the existing ones. In this regard, starting from 1842 onwards, the presence of Omani political leaders on the East African coasts led to new intersections between regional and international interests. Britain often played a role of turning realities into new political scenarios. After World War I, when the British took control over Tanganyika, the role of Muslim political leaderships gradually diminished. The British indirect rule did not ease the development of the Muslim identities from the coast. It was a struggle for identities, for power as well as a series of territorial and political claims of control, especially Arab control, and dominance upon a vast, as well as indefinable, liquid area such as the western Indian Ocean.

BIBLIOGRAPHY

Documents

Public Record Office (P.R.O.).

Hamerton Papers. 1841–54. F.O. 54/4 P.R.O. 1841–42; F.O. 54/5 P.R.O. 1843–44; F.O. 54/6 P.R.O. 1844–45; F.O. 54/7 P.R.O. 1845–46; F.O. 54/10 P.R.O. 1846–48; F.O. 54/12 P.R.O. 1848–50; F.O. 54/13 P.R.O. 1850–54.

Admiralty Records. 1824–1826. Journal of Lt Emery, who was in Mombasa from 1824 to 1826, f. 52/3940.

---

[23] Lorimer, 1915.

References

Agius, Dionisius. 2018. *The Life of the Red Sea Dhow: A Cultural History of Seaborne Exploration in the Islamic World*. London: I. B. Tauris.

Bang, Anne K. 2019. 'Islamic Incantations in a Colonial Notebook. A Case from Interwar Zanzibar', *Cahiers d'Études Africaines*, LIX/4, 236, pp. 1025–46.

Bennett, Norman Robert. 1973. 'France and Zanzibar, 1844 to the 1860s', *The International Journal of African Historical Studies*, 6/4, pp. 602–32.

Bhacker, Muhammad Reda. 1992. *Trade and Empire in Muscat and Zanzibar: Roots of British Domination*. London: Routledge.

Bishara, Fahad. 2017. *A Sea of Debt: Law and Economic Life in the Western Indian Ocean 1780–1950*. Cambridge: Cambridge University Press.

Bishara, Fahad and Hollian Wint. 2020. 'Into the Bazaar: Indian Ocean Vernaculars in the Age of Global Capitalism', *Journal of Global History*, 13/1, pp. 1–21.

Broome, Robert M. 1972. 'The 1780 Restrike Thalers of Maria Theresa', Doris Stockwell Memorial Papers 1, reprinted in *Numismatic Chronicle*, Series 7, London, pp. 221–53.

Burgess, G. Thomas. 2018. 'The Zanzibar Revolution and Its Aftermath', in Thomas Spear et al. (eds), *Oxford Research Encyclopedia of African History*, pp. 1–24.

Burton, Richard Francis and John H. Speke. 1858. 'A Coasting Voyage from Mombasa to the Pangani River; Visit to Sultan Kimwere; And Progress of the Expedition into the Interior', *The Journal of the Royal Geographical Society of London*, 28, pp. 188–226.

Crofton, Richard. 1935. *The Old Consulate at Zanzibar*. Oxford University Press: London.

Croucher, Sara K. 2015. 'Visible People, Invisible Slavery Plantation Archaeology in East Africa', in L. Wilson Marshall (ed.), *The Archeology of Slavery: A Comparative Approach to Captivity and Coercion*. Occasional Paper, 41, Southern Illinois University, pp. 347–74.

Declich, Francesca (ed.). 2017. *Translocal Connections across the Indian Ocean: Swahili Speaking Networks on the Move*, Leiden: Brill.

Fair, Laura. 2001. *Pastimes and Politics: Culture, Community, and Identity in Post-Abolition Urban Zanzibar, 1890–1945*. Oxford: J. Currey.

Farsi, Abdallah Saleh. 1986. *Seyyid Said Bin Sultan. The Joint Ruler of Oman and Zanzibar (1804–1856)*. New Dehli: Indological Book Corporation.

Gaube, Heinz (ed.). 2013. *The Ibadis in the Region of the Indian Ocean. Section One: East Africa, With contributions of A. Al Salimi*. Hildesheim: Olms.

Ghazal, Amal. 2014. 'Transcending Area Studies: Piecing Together the Cross-Regional Networks of Ibadi Islam', *Comparative Studies of South Asia, Africa and the Middle East*, 34/3, pp. 582–9.

Graham, Gerald. 1967. *Great Britain in the Indian Ocean. A Study of Maritime Enterprise 1810–1850*. Oxford: Clarendon Press.

Hardinge, Arthur H. 1899. 'Legislative Methods in the Zanzibar and East African Protectorates', *Journal of the Society of Comparative Legislation*, 1/1, pp. 1–10.

Hoffman, Valerie. 2018. 'Ibadis in Zanzibar and the Nahda', in A. Al-Salimi and R. Eisener (eds), *Oman, Ibadism and Modernity*. Hildesheim: Olms, pp. 129–40.

Hopwood, Derek (ed.). 2015. *The Arabian Peninsula: Society and Politics*. London: Routledge.

Kingdon, Zachary. 2012. *A Host of Devils. The History and Context of the Making of Makonde Spirit Sculpture*. London: Routledge.

Larsen, Kjersti. 2014. 'Possessing Spirits and Bodily Transformation in Zanzibar Reflections on Rituals, Performance and Aesthetics', *Journal of Ritual Studies*, 28/1, pp. 15–29.

Larsen, Kjersti. 2004. 'Change, Continuity and Contestation: the Politics of Modern Identities in Zanzibar', in P. Caplan and Farouk Topan (eds), *Swahili Modernities. Culture, Politics and Identity on the East Coast of Africa*. Asmara: Africa World Press, pp. 121–45.

Lewis, Ioan Myrddin. 2017. *Islam in Tropical Africa*. London: Routledge.

Lorimer, John G. 1915. *Gazetteer of the Persian Gulf, Oman and Central Arabia*. Calcutta: Superintendent Government Printing, vol. 1, pp. 440–69.

Machado, Pedro. 2014. *Ocean of Trade: South Asian Merchants, Africa and the Indian Ocean, c. 1750–1850*. Cambridge: Cambridge University Press.

Makris, Gerasimos. 2019. 'Devotees and Clients: The Ṭumbura Cult, Spirit Possession and Magic in the Sudan', in E. Montgomery (ed.), *Shackled Sentiments: Slaves, Spirits, and Memories in the African Diaspora*. New York: Lexington Books.

Maurizi, Vincenzo. 1819. *History of Seyd Said, Sultan of Muscat*. London (new edition Cambridge, 1984): Oleander Press.

Montgomery, Eric (ed.). 2019. *Shackled Sentiments: Slave, Spirits, and Memories in the African Diaspora*. New York: Lexington Books.

Nesbitt, Frederick. 2018. 'Swahili Creolization and Postcolonial Identity in East Africa', in J. Knörr and W. T. Filho (eds), *Creolization and Pidginization in Context of Postcolonial Diversity*. Leiden: Brill.

Nichols, Christine. 1971. *The Swahili Coast. Politics, Diplomacy and Trade on the East African Littoral 1798–1856*. London: Africana Publishing.

Nicolini, Beatrice. 2019. 'The Swahili Coast: Spirit Possession, Islam and European Power', in E. Montgomery (ed.), *Shackled Sentiments: Slaves, Spirits, and Memories in the African Diaspora*. Lanham: Lexington Books, pp. 237–59.

Nicolini, Beatrice. 2018. *The Historical Relationships between Balochistan and Oman in the Indian Ocean*. Milan: Educatt.

Nicolini, Beatrice. 2016. 'A Maritime History: Maritime Activities in Oman throughout the Indian Ocean 1650–1856 CE', in E. Staples and A. Al-Salimi (eds), *Maritime Oman*. Hildesheim: Olms, pp. 139–57.

Olsson, Hans. 2019. *Jesus for Zanzibar: Narratives of Pentecostal (Non-) Belonging Islam and Nation*. Leiden: Brill.

Perkins, John. 2015. 'The Indian Ocean and Swahili Coast Coins, international networks and local developments', *Afriques*, 6. http://afriques.revues.org/1769.

Pollard, Edward and Okeny Charles Kinyera. 2017. 'The Swahili Coast and the Indian Ocean Trade Patterns in the 7th–10th Centuries CE', *Journal of Southern African Studies*, 43/5, pp. 927–47.

Pradines, Stéphane. 2009. 'L'île de Sanjé ya Kati (Kilwa, Tanzanie): un mythe Shirâzi bien reel', *Azania: Archaeological Research in Africa*, 44:1, pp. 49–73.

Rhodes, Daniel, Colin Breen and Wes Forsythe. 2015. 'Zanzibar: A Nineteenth-Century Landscape of the Omani Elite', *International Journal of Historical Archaeology*, 19/2, pp. 334–55.

Ruete, Emily (Sayyidda Salme). 1993. *An Arabian Princess between Two Worlds: Memoirs, Letters Home, Sequels to the Memoirs, and Syrian Customs and Usages*, E. van Donzel (ed.). New York: Brill.

Seland, Eivind Heldaas. 2010. *Ports and Political Power in the Peryplus: Complex Societies and Maritime Trade in the Indian Ocean in the first century* A.D. Oxford: B.A.R.

Semple, Clara. 2005. *A Silver Legend: The Story of the Maria Theresa Thaler*. Manchester: Barzan Publishing Ltd.

Staples, Eric. 2018. *Indian Ocean Navigation in Islamic Sources 850–1650* CE. History Compass: Wiley Online Library.

Thompson, Katrina Daly. 2011. 'How to be a Good Muslim Wife: Women's Performance of Islamic Authority during Swahili Weddings', *Journal of Religion in Africa*, 41, pp. 427–48.

Vernet, Thomas. 2015. 'East African Travellers and Traders in the Indian Ocean: Swahili Ships, Swahili Mobilities c. 1500–1800', in M. Pearson (ed.), *Trade, Circulation and Flow in the Indian Ocean World*. London: Palgrave, pp. 169–202.

Walker, Ian (ed.). 2018. *Contemporary Issues in Swahili Ethnography*. London: Routledge.

Wilkinson, John. 2015. *The Arabs and the Scramble for Africa*. Sheffield: Equinox.

CHAPTER 4

Religion, Ethnicity and Identity in the Zanzibar Sultanate

Valerie J. Hoffman

Memories of the Zanzibar Sultanate

The Zanzibar sultanate (1832–1964) ruled a singularly cosmopolitan but highly stratified population, including Arabs of Omani background (usually members of the Ibadi sect), Sunni Muslim scholars and labourers of Hadrami descent, Indians of diverse origins and religions, and Baluchi and Persian mercenaries, in addition to locals who self-identified as 'Shirazi', natives of the Mrima and Banadir coasts, and large numbers of African slaves.

African history is a politically charged subject. College textbooks on the history of Africa in the 1980s presented the continent as largely free of conflict until the advent of the Europeans. Although the violence of the Atlantic slave trade and the European colonialist project in Africa cannot be denied, the image of an idyllic, peaceful pre-colonial Africa is a product of wishful imagination. The reasons for such a presentation are self-evident: no one, especially a Western scholar, wishes to understate the violence of European imperialism.

But if such problems exist in scholarship on Africa, they are doubly so for scholarship on the Zanzibar sultanate. Should the Omani sultanate on the Swahili coast be seen as a colonial project, or was the sultanate a haven of racial, ethnic and religious equality, where Omanis were so well integrated into Swahili society over the course of generations that they were no longer alien to it? Was the East African slave trade as horrible as its depictions in the writings of David Livingstone, or was slavery in East Africa so benign that slaves were treated as part of the family, owning their own property and even their own slaves, and frequently manumitted upon the death of the master? Was the lot of slaves in East Africa better than that of those who lived in grinding poverty after slavery's abolition? This favourable perspective on East African slavery may seem far-fetched, but it is affirmed repeatedly by Omanis who lived in East Africa or whose ancestors lived there. Al-Ismaily, for example, claims that images circulated by European abolitionists alleging to depict maltreatment of slaves in East Africa actually depicted Portuguese enslavement of Africans.[1] In 1950 a Zanzibari of Omani descent, Sa'id al-Mughayri, wrote that Omanis had good relations with local rulers because the Ibadi sect and the Omani spirit make no distinction based on race or religion.

> The Omani Arabs did not dominate or mistreat the indigenous people in any way, and did not impose humility or servility, but rather strove to release them from the oppression of others *of their race* [emphasis mine] who abducted them and drove them like cattle. They taught them literacy and agriculture and shared all matters of life with them. By the grace of God, the blacks and the Arabs became brothers.[2]

Towards the end of the book he writes, 'I asked one of the old former slaves whether he was more at ease now or in the days of slavery. He said, "Sir, we were beaten on the back with sticks, and now hunger beats us on the stomach with hunger. Which is better? Judge for yourself".[3] A Facebook group dedicated to Zanzibar and Oman has evolved into a nostalgic forum in which former residents of Zanzibar lament the loss of an idyllic culture that was viciously exterminated in the Zanzibar Revolution of 1964.

Jonathon Glassman argues against the near consensus that the genocidal violence of 1964 was the product of over two millennia of tensions created by Arab racial domination.[4] He dismisses as far-fetched the notion that Arabs had been living in East Africa as a distinct racial elite for over two millennia, though this view was propagated by both Arab and African nationalists. He points out that this model of deeply rooted divisions between Arabs and Africans directly contradicts another common representation of this part of East Africa: that Swahili culture is a synthesis of African and Middle Eastern elements and that its society is the epitome of ethnic fluidity and racial indeterminacy, that Swahili-speakers simultaneously perceive themselves as Arab, Persian and/or Indian, as well as African. Mazrui and Shariff describe the identity of many African communities, including the Swahili, as 'assimilative and flexible', veering toward 'a concept

---

[1] Al-Ismaily, 1999.
[2] Mughayri, 1986, pp. 17–18.
[3] Ibid., p. 540.
[4] Glassman, 2011.

of belonging that is truly liberal'.[5] The authors contrast this African model of identity to rigid, racially orientated European identity paradigms.

Throughout the colonial era, both indigenous and British elites represented Zanzibar as islands of racial harmony. Glassman dismisses this representation as a myth informed by overlapping sets of paternalistic ideals and belied by many instances of tension that punctuated the sultanate's public life. Yet, he says, 'it contained a kernel of truth, for Zanzibaris had not, as a rule, organised themselves into ethnically discrete communities, and, despite occasional tension, few thought of ethnic divisions with the kind of exclusionary rigidity that informed the pogroms of the early 1960s'.[6]

Many scholars in African studies rely heavily on oral sources, but such reliance is seriously problematic when historical memories are extremely polarised, as is the case with regard to Zanzibari history. Written sources, on the other hand, may be difficult to locate: the revolutionary government that came to power in Zanzibar in 1964 did its utmost to destroy the legacy of the Zanzibar sultanate by destroying or hiding its written records. When R. S. O'Fahey was working on a catalogue of Arabic manuscripts in East Africa, the managers of the Zanzibar National Archives told him that they had no Arabic manuscripts – despite 150 years of rule by an Omani dynasty.[7] Ultimately, O'Fahey was permitted to search the Archives' storage rooms, where he found boxes containing hundreds of Arabic documents.[8] Unfortunately, most of them had been vandalised, leaving mere fragments, some of them so eaten away by insects and humidity that they disintegrated at the slightest touch. They were often missing the first and last pages as well as large chunks of text, leaving the title, author and date of the manuscripts unknown without careful research. The suppression of the sultanate's written documents allowed the government of Zanzibar to construct an entirely new narrative of its history, one that villainised the sultanate and emphasised the cruelties of the slave trade.

This chapter offers some insights into aspects of religion, ethnicity and identity in the Zanzibar sultanate in the nineteenth century. These observations are not intended to provide a complete description of this vast topic, but are based on two sources: (1) the writings of Ibadi scholars in Zanzibar in the nineteenth and early twentieth centuries; and (2) manuscript fragments written by a Brava-born Shafi'i scholar, 'Abd al-'Aziz al-Amawi (1834–96), who served as a qadi, counsellor and ambassador for several of the sultans of Zanzibar.

---

[5] Mazrui and Shariff, 1994, p. 9.
[6] Glassman, 2011, pp. 4–5.
[7] Hunwick, O'Fahey and Stewart, 1994–present.
[8] Personal communication. Also, Declich, 2006, pp. 10–11. Declich provides a rather different narrative that makes it sound as if an 'Arabic Books and Manuscripts Fond [Fund]' remained in continuous known possession of the Archives since the revolution.

RELIGION AND IDENTITY IN IBADI PERSPECTIVE

The Ibadi sect of Islam is neither Sunni nor Shiʿite but emerged out of the Kharijite secession, which occurred at the battle of Siffin in June 657. According to legend, the Kharijites divided into three main branches in 684, after their leaders went together to Mecca to question ʿAbdallah ibn al-Zubayr, who had made a counterclaim to the caliphate in opposition to the Umayyads. The Ibadis are often called 'moderate Kharijites', although Ibadis deny they are Kharijites at all, because of the term's association with the violence of the Azraqi branch.

Ibadis survived years of persecution by moving to the geographical margins of the Umayyad and ʿAbbasid empires. They live today in the Sultanate of Oman (the only country in the world that claims that a majority of its Muslims are Ibadi), in small pockets in the Mzab valley of Algeria, the Nafusa mountains of Libya and the island of Djerba in Tunisia, and in very small numbers among people of Omani background in East Africa. As Wilkinson points out, the Omanis who dominated the Zanzibar sultanate and pioneered the expansion of trade into the African mainland were nearly all Ibadis whose families originated in Oman's mountainous interior.[9] This mountainous interior was Oman's cultural heartland, and indeed is the portion of today's sultanate that was called 'Oman' (in contradistinction to 'Muscat') during the period from 1913 to the mid-1950s, when 'Oman' was ruled by a religiously legitimated Ibadi imamate, and 'Muscat' meant the rest of the country, which was ruled by a dynastically legitimated sultan. To be Omani was to be Ibadi, and in the context of the Zanzibar sultanate, says Wilkinson, only Omanis could be Ibadi.[10] Unlike Sunnis, Ismaʿilis[11] and Ahmadis in East Africa, Ibadis made no effort to convert other people to their sect. British observers in Zanzibar praised the tolerant policies of the sultanate; Sayyid Saʿid, for example, prohibited the slaughter of cows in Hindu quarters, out of deference to their religious sensitivities,[12] and he instructed his governors to judge each person according to the precepts of his or her religion. Based on his personal experiences in Zanzibar and Yemen, one British official wrote that Ibadis are the most tolerant of Muslims.[13] It may therefore come as a surprise to learn that, until the mid-twentieth century, Ibadis did not believe that non-Ibadi Muslims should be called 'believers' or 'Muslims'; they could only be called 'monotheists', 'people of the *qibla*', or members of the

---

[9] Wilkinson, 2015, p. 5.

[10] Ibid., p. 9.

[11] Mughayri wrote, 'Sultan Agha Khan and the family of Karmaji Jiyunji al-Bohori are very active in charitable deeds to set up Islamic schools, so that the number of Muslims in the African interior has increased by means of the missionaries of the Agha Khan. May God reward them for this'. Mughayri, 1986, p. 472.

[12] Al Barwani, 1997, p. 33.

[13] Ingrams, 1931, pp. 191–2.

umma of the Prophet Muhammad. Unlike the radical Azraqis, Ibadis did not deem non-Ibadi Muslims to be *mushrikun* (unbelievers or polytheists); they were guilty of a lesser degree of unfaithfulness called *kufr ni'ma* (ingratitude for or denial of God's blessings) or *kufr nifaq* (the unfaithfulness of hypocrisy). Such *kuffar* will suffer eternal punishment in hellfire; unlike the Sunnis, Ibadis do not believe that the Prophet will intercede for grave sinners.

Like the Shi'a, Ibadis lay great emphasis on association or affiliation (*walaya*) with true believers and dissociation (*bara'a*) from those who are unfaithful due to faulty doctrine or lack of strict adherence to the rules of the Shari'a; hence, unrepentant, sinning Ibadis were also subject to dissociation. Questions regarding how to determine who deserves affiliation and who deserves dissoci-ation, and the implications of this determination, have filled volumes. It is a matter of such importance that an Ibadi scholar of Zanzibar wrote in 1920, 'It is necessary to deem an unbeliever anyone who is ignorant of the necessity of affiliation and dissociation in general, or anyone who affiliates with all people or dissociates from all people or suspends judgment concerning all people'.[14] Ibadi scholars define *bara'a* as a duty to 'hate' those who are unfaithful to God. Nonetheless, non-Ibadi members of the *umma* share the privileges of all Muslims, including the greeting of peace, being visited when sick, intermar-riage, mutual inheritance, burial in a Muslim cemetery and having Muslim prayers done at their funerals. The property of non-Ibadi Muslims may not be plundered, and their wives and children may not be enslaved. So despite the notion that one should separate from and 'hate' non-Ibadi Muslims, in fact one interacts with them in a way similar to the way one interacts with affiliates. An important early Ibadi theologian, 'Abdallah al-Fazari, was a business partner and inseparable companion of an important early Shi'ite theologian, Hisham ibn al-Hakam.[15] Although Ibadis categorise Jews and Christians as *mushrikun* (polytheists), they follow the standard practices of imposing *jizya* and allowing them to practise their religion. In practice, the sultanates in Oman and Zanzibar granted respect to followers of all religions, both during the nineteenth century and in Oman today, where Sultan Qaboos has granted lands to the Hindu com-munity for the building of temples, the Ministry of Religious Affairs publishes a journal titled *Al-Tafahum* (*Mutual Understanding*) that promotes interfaith dialogue and cooperation, and the minister of that body, Shaykh 'Abdullah bin Mohammed Al Salmi, has published a book titled *Religious Tolerance: A Vision for a New World*, that, in Arabic, English, German, Hebrew and Chinese, argues that all religions are based on a common foundation of values such as freedom, equality and tolerance, that there can be no peace between nations

---

[14] Hoffman, 2012, p. 158; Bahlani, 2004, p. 248.
[15] Madelung 1979, p. 127.

without peace between religions, and there can be no peace between religions without dialogue, which must go beyond the Abrahamic religions.[16] I mention this contemporary setting, which is clearly tangential to a paper on the Zanzibar sultanate, in order to stress the discrepancy between Ibadism's strict doctrine and actual Ibadi practice.

In East Africa, even during the sultanate, Ibadis were a small minority among the Muslims of the coast, who were mainly Sunnis of the Shafiʻi school. When Sayyid Saʻid made Zanzibar the capital of the Omani empire (the date of this event is variously given as 1828, 1832 and 1840), he invited Shafiʻi as well as Ibadi scholars to come to Zanzibar, where they were appointed as qadis and became part of court life. After Sayyid Saʻid's death in 1856, Zanzibar and Oman were ruled separately by two of his sons. The Al Bu Saʻid dynasty remained in power in Zanzibar until the violent revolution of 1964; in Oman, it remains in power to this day.

The relationship of Ibadism to the sultans of Oman and Zanzibar is complicated. On the one hand, the sultans have always been Ibadi, and Ibadi scholarship is a revered part of the cultural heritage. This is evident by the fact that nearly all the works published by Oman's Ministry of Culture and Heritage are by Ibadis. In 1880 Sultan Barghash bin Saʻid of Zanzibar established a printing press that issued the first-ever publications of Ibadi works and was entirely devoted to Ibadi scholarship. Nonetheless, although the sultans sponsored Ibadi scholarship, Ibadi religious zeal was a great threat to them, because Ibadism is founded on a religious imperative to establish a righteous imamate and insists that political leadership should not be granted based on lineage. The nineteenth and early twentieth centuries were a time of great political turmoil in Oman that included not only the alienation of land to Wahhabi invaders to whom the Omani government was forced to pay tribute, but also a series of rebellions led by Ibadi religious scholars following the religious imperative to overthrow tyrants and establish justice. One of these rebellions was spectacularly successful, overthrowing the government of Sultan Salim bin Thuwayni in 1868, establishing the government of Imam ʻAzzan b. Qays, and even managing to expel the Wahhabis. This imamate was defeated in early 1871 through funding from Zanzibar, Wahhabi assistance and British complicity. Even after it was overthrown, its supporters continued to launch attacks against Muscat. In 1913 a new rebellion led by the blind scholar Nur al-Din al-Salimi (grandfather of the current Minister of Religious Affairs) was only partially successful: it conquered the Ibadi heartland but not the rest of the country, which led to the split between 'Muscat' and 'Oman'.

---

[16] Al Salmi, 2016.

The sultan who made Zanzibar the capital of the Omani empire, Sayyid Saʿid, had regarded the leading Ibadi scholar of Oman, Abu Nabhan Jaʿid ibn Khamis al-Kharusi, as a danger to his government, but refrained from harming him out of fear of the man's occult powers. After Abu Nabhan's death in 1822, Sayyid Saʿid launched an attack on the scholar's family compound, only to learn that Abu Nabhan's son Nasir was likewise gifted with talismanic powers. A shrewd leader, Sayyid Saʿid decided that the best way to protect himself from Nasir's potential malevolence was to keep him by his side. Whereas other scholars of Zanzibar had their own homes, Nasir lived in Sayyid Saʿid's Mtoni Palace, and when he died in 1847 his head was resting on Sayyid Saʿid's lap.

It was inevitable that friendships would develop between Ibadis and Shafiʿis in East Africa. This caused Ibadis some anxiety: an unidentified man wrote to the aforementioned Abu Nabhan asking whether a Shafiʿi who had been a good Muslim all his life could be admitted into paradise. Abu Nabhan's response was categorically negative: by definition, a Shafiʿi adhered to such errors in doctrine and religious practice that he could not be defined as a good Muslim. In the above-mentioned Ibadi theological textbook written in Zanzibar in 1920 in the form of a dialogue between a teacher and a student, the hypothetical student asks what he should do if a non-Ibadi is so kind to him that he begins to feel affection for that person. The teacher replies that this is not a problem; Muslims should show courtesy to all people, and feelings of affection are not a problem as long as one knows in one's heart that this person is not a religious affiliate. Hatred was thus removed from the concept of 'dissociation', despite centuries of Ibadi scholarship to the contrary. (The current mufti of the Sultanate of Oman actually denies that Ibadis dissociate from non-Ibadi Muslims.)

More problematic to Ibadi scholars was the conversion of many Ibadis to Sunni Islam. The Ibadis of Zanzibar did not have Friday congregational prayer because of a long-standing doctrine that such prayers should be done only under the rule of a pious imam. Given the lack of such an imamate in Zanzibar, the congregational prayer with its customary sermons that included prayers of blessing on the ruler was deemed inappropriate. It seems that many Ibadis began to attend Sunni mosques for Friday prayers. Sunni doctrine might have seemed less harsh to many Ibadis, with its guarantee of salvation even for sinners, thanks to the intercession of the Prophet, and its prohibition against labelling professing Muslims as infidels. The activities of Sufi orders among the Sunnis were also attractive to many Ibadis. Ibadism is not inherently hostile to Sufism; in fact, many of the leading Ibadi scholars of Oman in the nineteenth and twentieth centuries were distinctly Sufi in their spiritual orientation, including Abu Nabhan, his son Nasir and the great poet Abu Muslim Nasir b. Salim al-Bahlani al-Rawahi, who was also the author of the aforementioned theological text.

But Ibadis do not have Sufi orders, nor do they practise group *dhikr* with ecstasy-inducing music and movements.

Ibadi scholars of Zanzibar in the nineteenth century produced works that attacked Sunni doctrines, especially the possibility of seeing God in the after-life, and aimed at undermining the appeal of Sunnism to Ibadi youth. Most of Zanzibar's sultans were untroubled by such conversions – Majid allegedly arranged for one scholarly convert to defend the vision of God in the afterlife[17] – but Barghash, who ruled from 1870 to 1888, imprisoned leading converts.[18] In light of Wilkinson's comments about the linkage between Ibadism and Omani identity, such conversions could have been perceived as nothing less than treasonous.

Nasir ibn Abi Nabhan, the scholar whom Sayyid Saʿid kept by his side, wrote a massive multi-volume work analysing Sunni doctrine and critiquing it. Nonetheless, it was standard practice among Ibadis not to insult Sunni doctrines publicly; indeed, the doctrine of *kitman* (hiding) allowed Ibadis to keep their beliefs secret in hostile circumstances. Thus, at one point in his massive work, Nasir recounts a gathering of scholars from different sects in Zanzibar in which 'a foolish, weak-minded' Ibadi brought a copy of a highly polemical Ibadi work[19] and showed it to a Sunni scholar, who scanned its contents and cursed the Ibadis. A Shiʿi scholar who believed in the obligation of *taqiyya* (hiding one's true beliefs in a hostile environment) returned it to its owner and ordered him to leave the assembly, threatening that if he found him in any Sunni or Shiʿi scholarly gathering he would have him arrested – something he could do, says Nasir, because he had influence with the sultan. Then the Shiʿi rebuked the Sunni who had cursed the Ibadis, asking, 'What good is it to say such things? You will lose either in this world or the next – wouldn't silence be better for a person who is wise and discerning?' Nasir, it seems, kept silent, but clearly approved of the Shiʿi scholar's words.[20]

What these different examples reveal is that, although Ibadis in the Zanzibar sultanate in the nineteenth and early twentieth centuries maintained a theo-retical dissociation from non-Ibadis, reality on the ground was very different. Ibadis socialised freely with people of other sects and generally avoided open controversy, although Ibadi scholars devoted works to defending Ibadi doctrine and attacking Sunni doctrine. Ibadism remained linked to Omani identity, but this did not prevent defections to the Sunni camp and, with the exception of Sayyid Barghash, the rulers of Zanzibar were untroubled by these defections.

---

[17] Farsy, 1989, p. 32.
[18] Ibid., pp. 20–2, 32.
[19] Qalhāti, 1980. Written in the seventeenth century, this work is so insulting to its theological oppo-nents that it has been banned by Sultan Qaboos.
[20] Nasir ibn Abi Nabhan, n.d., p. 415.

The Ibadi perspective that only pious members of their sect were true believers could more readily be maintained in the relative isolation of Oman's mountainous interior than in the highly cosmopolitan environment of Zanzibar, where Ibadis were a small minority and traditional notions of exclusion and separation appear to have eroded. Dissociation continued to be affirmed in normative texts, but as we saw, Rawahi's theological textbook dislocated its meaning from actual separation and excommunication to internal recognition of religious difference, to some extent reconciling the distinction between Ibadi theory and lived reality. On the other hand, Rawahi's book, like most Ibadi works, maintained traditional attitudes and doctrines that were far removed from the author's own experience: he discusses at length the necessity of and rules for imposing the *jizya* tax on non-Muslims, although Zanzibar had been a British protectorate since 1890.

RELIGION, ETHNICITY AND IDENTITY IN THE WRITINGS OF ABD AL-AZIZ AL-AMAWI

The Shafi'i scholar and Qadiri Sufi shaykh Abd al-Aziz al-Amawi (1834–96), born and raised in Brava, Somalia, was accomplished in all the Islamic sciences and did most of his writing in the form of poetry with commentaries. He moved to Zanzibar in his early teens to study with the Bravan scholar Muhyiddin al-Qahtani, the chief Shafi'i qadi of Zanzibar. Amawi was appointed qadi in Kilwa at the tender age of eighteen. He was soon transferred to Zanzibar, where he served a succession of sultans until 1891, when his son Burhan took his place as chief Shafi'i qadi. In addition to his scholarship, Amawi served as a political advisor, ambassador and diplomat on behalf of sultans Majid (r. 1856–70) and Barghash (r. 1870–88) in Somalia, the Comoro islands, the Rovuma River region and other places on the mainland. Abdullah Salih Farsy, author of a short book on the Shafi'i scholars of the Swahili coast, wrote that Amawi was the most effective anti-Christian polemicist. He also wrote that although Amawi was a Sufi shaykh, he had written a poem attacking the practice of 'doing *dhikr* with bursting noises', and became a virtual prime minister during the reign of Sayyid Khalifa (1888–90), who tried to impose Islamic law. Despite Amawi's prolific scholarly production, Farsy reported that nearly all his works had been lost.[21] Thus Farsy, a scholar of a strict reformist orientation, paints Amawi as a defender of Islam against Christians, a reformer critical of popular Sufi practices, and an advocate of the imposition of Islamic law. This depiction receives further elaboration in Randall Pouwels' book, *Horn and Crescent*, which relies on Farsy's book (which Pouwels translated) and on interviews with Farsy

---

[21] Farsy, 1989, pp. 44–8.

in Mombasa. According to Pouwels, Amawi was a thorn in the side of Sayyid Barghash because his popularity as a Sufi shaykh won many converts to Sunni Islam, including, according to rumour, Barghash's brother Khalifa, who came to power after Barghash's death. Pouwels writes that Barghash removed Amawi from his position as qadi and tried to prevent his followers from saying their Friday prayers, which led Amawi to defy him by going to Friday prayers armed, in the company of his students. Under Khalifa's rule, Pouwels writes, Amawi was a reactionary zealot who advised Khalifa to execute all the criminals in Zanzibar prison and to restore the island completely to the letter of Islamic law.[22]

Fortunately, we no longer need to rely on this oral history based on a single source, with all the problems of reliability alluded to earlier, because some of Amawi's writings have indeed been found. Some fragments were found by Muhammad Idris Muhammad Saleh of Zanzibar (1934–2012) among the papers left by Mohammed Burhan Mkelle, a Zanzibar-born scholar in Dar Es Salaam. Mkelle published an article about Amawi in which he credits him with innovating the use of Swahili *tenzi* verse 'to introduce and popularise Islamic themes along local people'. Mkelle describes Amawi as a palace favourite, especially during the reigns of Khalifa (1888–90), Ali bin Sa'id (1890–3) and Hamad bin Thuwayni (1893–6), and says that as early as the reign of Majid (1856–70) he was known as 'wisest of all the wise people' of the age.[23]

Even more significant than the fragments found in Mkelle's possession are large portions of Amawi's works that I discovered in the private library of Sayyid Muhammad bin Ahmad Al Bu Sa'id in Seeb, Oman.[24] These include parts of his travelogues from two of the seven journeys he undertook on behalf of Sultan Barghash in the region of the Rovuma River, which today marks the boundary between Tanzania and Mozambique. Although incomplete, these manuscripts, written in Amawi's own hand, are substantial and provide a rare glimpse of East Africa in the second half of the nineteenth century from the perspective of an agent of the sultan at the time, without any European mediation.

Significantly, there is nothing in any of the manuscripts in Oman or the fragments found in Dar es Salaam that indicates that Amawi's relationship with Sayyid Barghash was anything but deferential. In one fragment he summarises his career, beginning with his first appointment as qadi in 1853 under Sayyid Sa'id. After Sa'id's death, his son and successor Majid made Amawi one of his closest advisers and an assistant to his roving ambassador and minister, Sayyid Hamad bin Sulayman Al Bu Sa'id, a member of the royal family. Amawi and Sayyid Hamad travelled on ambassadorial missions to the

[22] Pouwels, 1987, p. 169.
[23] Mkelle, 1992.
[24] Hoffman, 2006.

Comoro Islands (1866) and London (1867). In 1868 Amawi was sent as an envoy to Kilwa Kivinje, 300 miles south of Dar es Salaam, on the coast of present-day Tanzania, when it was attacked by the Mviti.[25] Amawi wrote that Sayyid Hamad 'exaggerated in his praise of me', and from that point Amawi's reputation for cleverness was sealed. When Barghash first came to power in 1870, he dismissed most of the Sunni qadis, including Amawi. During that time Amawi travelled to many places along the coast, especially the islands off the southern coast of Kenya, until Barghash summoned him back to Zanzibar to resume his judgeship and become a member of his council. In spring 1879 Barghash sent him on the first of his seven journeys to the Rovuma River region, in the company of Sayyid Hamad, with horses and an armed contingent consisting of 'Arabs and Persians', in the company of the chiefs of the Mrima coast. Their mission was to follow the Rovuma to a rumoured coalfield and verify its existence. But when the journey became difficult, Sayyid Hamad turned the leadership of the expedition over to Amawi. Amawi says he divided the company into two halves, one to travel by land and the other by boat. He explored the rivers with the group that travelled by water, entered the lands of the Mviti and the Zunuj, and held counsels with them.[26] It seems that they were not successful in finding the coalfield, however, as the sultan sent a second expedition with the same mission in November that year. In addition to finding the coalfield and ascertaining its value, they were told to scout out the terrain between Tungi Bay and Lake Nyasa (today Lake Malawi) to see if it would be worthwhile to build a railroad there. They were additionally charged with settling any disputes among the people and with making a record of everything they encountered along the way.[27]

For this mission, the overall leader was Bakil bin Katim, a native of Mtawanya, a village near Mtwara, a town on Mikindani Bay, about 350 miles south of Dar es Salaam. Bakil knew the use of the astrolabe, had studied navigation and had travelled to India and Arabia,[28] but it seems he was illiterate. Amawi had travelled with Bakil on the first journey to the region on behalf of Barghash,

---

[25] A *Handbook of Portuguese Nyasaland* (1920, p. 48) says : 'The Mviti [also called the Mvita, Mviti or Mavita] are a tribe of raiders who have crossed the Rovuma into the north-east portion of the colony. The name means Zulu, but is only correctly applied to this people in the sense that they have copied the Zulu mode of warfare; they are really Waninde, and are variously known as Wandonde, Wagindo, Wangindo, Mazitu, Mwangoni. They owe their origin as a raiding tribe to a great Zulu raid which swept over their country, and inspired them with a desire to abandon their peaceful agricultural pursuits for buccaneering. They adopted therefore the head-dress and war cry of the Zulu, and inspired similar terror along the Rufiji and Rovuma and farther south where they came in 1878. Their principal abodes are the plateau country east of the confluence of the Rovuma and Lujenda, and the islands of the latter river.'

[26] Amawi, 1880, p. 23.

[27] Ibid., p. 25.

[28] Ibid., p. 40.

during which Bakil had put down a rebellion with such ferocity that he had incurred the hatred of many people.[29] As Bakil continued to use bad judgement on this journey, Amawi tried to reason with him, reminding him that he was the only one who had defended Bakil after the first journey and managed to keep him out of prison. Besides Amawi and Bakil, the third leader was Muhammad Kidhahabu, a native of Brava whose maternal relatives belonged to the Makua, the largest ethnic group of southern Tanzania and northern Mozambique. Interestingly, Amawi frequently refers to himself as a son of the coast and assumes that, since he grew up on the mainland, he is capable of understanding the mainland better than any of the 'Arabs', meaning those of Omani descent. So Barghash's selected envoys for an exploration of the Rovuma River region were three natives of the mainland; there were no Omanis in the company.

Amawi was second in command at the beginning of the second expedition, but when Bakil refused to move forward without clearing a path through the jungle, which Amawi said would take years even if the labour of an entire army were devoted to the project,[30] Barghash had Bakil thrown into prison and made Amawi leader of the expedition. In his travelogue, Amawi writes that he had acquired such a reputation in the region that his presence was sufficient to bring peace between warring peoples.[31] Nonetheless, and despite his descent from the tribe of Quraysh and the Banu Umayya clan (one of his ancestors was the great Umayyad caliph Abd al-Malik ibn Marwan, r. 685–705), Amawi frequently refers to his lowly status. He tells Bakil that Barghash sent him with him to advise him, knowing of their friendship. 'Why else would he send me,' he asks Bakil, 'when he has all the leading Arabs with all their cunning? I don't even come up to the fingertip of any of them!' When Bakil chafes under Barghash's wrath, Amawi tells him, 'Our lord the Sayyid speaks against the mightiest of his subjects in his assembly in the presence of the honoured Arabs, and no one gets angry over it. On the contrary, they humble themselves before him', with the implication that someone of Bakil's stature should be even more humble.[32] Amawi also notes at one point that none of the 'Arabs' could read or write Swahili.[33] Clearly, an 'Arab' here is not someone of Arab ancestry, for that would include Amawi himself; it means someone of Omani background.

By the time of Amawi's sixth journey in the Rovuma region, conducted in 1885, Barghash had consigned to him the full authority to issue orders in his name, an authority of which Amawi made good use, dismissing governors he described as 'unfit to rule their own households, let alone the realm of

---

[29] Ibid., pp. 48, 63–4, 77.
[30] Ibid., p. 81.
[31] Ibid., pp. 57–64.
[32] Ibid., p. 91.
[33] Amawi, 1885, p. 19.

the sultan', and appointing new ones from the same family, not upsetting the established social order.[34] Towards the end of his reign, Barghash sent Amawi with Hamad Al Bu Sa'idi on missions to settle disputes in southern Somalia and the Comoro Islands. As Amawi records himself telling a close adviser of Sayyid Hamad bin Thuwayni (r. 1893–6), 'I don't think there is a single town in the entire realm that I did not visit to solve a problem during the reign of Sayyid Barghash bin Sa'id'.

The sultan and Amawi himself took great care to show respect to all the chieftains ('sultans') of the non-Muslim peoples of the region, whom Amawi categorised as the Mviti (the earlier-mentioned marauders) and the Zunuj, who included the Makua. Zunuj literally means 'blacks', but Amawi uses the term only for non-Muslims. In Amawi's account of his second journey, he refers to the Zunuj as 'ignorant of human rights (ghafilin bi- 'l-huquq al-insaniyya) because of their animalistic natures',[35] so the honour with which he treated the Zunuj undoubtedly stemmed from prudence rather than genuine respect. By the time of Amawi's sixth journey, the Mviti had settled into particular villages, but their fierce reputation remained, to the extent that when the Mviti came to see him upon hearing he was in Meningini, at the mouth of Tungi Bay south of the Rovuma River, the Makua were alarmed.[36] When two of the now-deceased Bakil's relatives refused to let agents of the sultan pass through their land to access the coalfield, the Mviti offered to attack them and hand them over to the sultan for imprisonment.[37] Amawi was not above agreeing to take them up on this offer if necessary, but he prided himself in his ability to settle things amicably. Hamad bin Sulayman had tried to persuade Sayyid Barghash to send an army against them, but Amawi persuaded Barghash that he could avoid conflict by merely sending him, without any armed escort.[38]

Despite his earlier description of the Zunuj as ignorant of human rights because of their animalistic natures, and despite his status as a judge of Islamic law and Pouwels' description of him as a rigid legalist, there is no hint whatsoever of criticism of any of the cultures he encounters in his chronicles. He freely criticises people he deems untrustworthy or oppressive to others, but he seems unoffended by un-Islamic customs, commenting on such differences by quoting lines from a famous seventh-century poem to the effect that every people has customs it has received from its forebears.[39] Barghash had asked him to explore the border between his domain and that of Portugal in Mozambique

---

[34] Ibid., pp. 15–16.
[35] Amawi, 1880, p. 12.
[36] Amawi, 1885, p. 33.
[37] Ibid., p. 33.
[38] Ibid., pp. 4–9.
[39] Amawi, 1885, p. 24.

and to ascertain its precise location. This was, of course, shortly after the Berlin conference of 1884–5, where the European powers divided the African continent among themselves. Furthermore, Germans had begun to make agreements with chieftains in East Africa designed to launch their eventual colony in Tanganyika. The German East Africa Company was founded in February 1885, and the German emperor promised protection to any territory acquired by the Society for German Colonisation. European encroachment led Amawi to suggest that they guard the by-then discovered coalfield against European invaders, and this was the impetus for this sixth journey. Only two months later Britain would conspire with Germany and France to restrict the sultan's domains to a coastal strip only ten nautical miles in width. My point for this chapter, however, is that Amawi and other leading servants of the sultan in the region ventured into Portuguese territory on this expedition, and Amawi describes both Christian and pagan shrines with simple curiosity, devoid of the sort of revulsion one might expect from a stern legalist.[40]

Amawi clearly admired the strength and courage of a female chieftain among a matrilineal people that had always had a female chieftain. Amawi says that she commanded six thousand armed men and had a higher status than most of the chiefs he met along the way. Amawi says the men of other groups always ask for the hands of these female chieftains in marriage, but they refused, lest their power be alienated to a different group.[41] Amawi also speaks of a male Makua chieftain who brought a retinue of serving women, who sat around him as he drank wine, congratulating him on the drink. Despite the prohibition against wine in Islamic law, Amawi made no criticism of this practice, and the chieftain and his retinue were put up in the house where Amawi was staying in Meningini. The chieftain spoke nostalgically with Amawi about their joint adventures in earlier years and said he had missed him and was glad Amawi had returned. One day the chieftain asked Amawi for permission to let the women dance in the traditional manner of their people. Amawi replied, 'They're your servant women; they may do as you please.' The women danced all night and the following day, which, Amawi says, was a source of great pleasure in the town.[42] There is no indication that Amawi found anything inappropriate in this entertainment.

The markers of ethnicity and histories of conflict play an important part in Amawi's story, and he clearly lived in a highly stratified society. Among the different types of people Amawi mentions are the Arabs, by which he means Omanis, Mrimans, by which he means natives of the mainland coast, the Zunuj,

---

[40] Ibid., pp. 40–1.
[41] Ibid., p. 31.
[42] Ibid., pp. 35–6.

by which he means non-Muslim Africans of the region, including tribal groups such as the Makua and the Yao, and the fearsome Mviti, marauders who had settled in the region. Sayyid Barghash is depicted as intelligent and authoritarian, and throughout Amawi's accounts the various chieftains affirm their love of the sultanate and their loyalty to the sultan. We also see evidence of interactions across ethnic and religious lines that are truly fascinating, including apparent friendships formed between the esteemed scholar and non-Muslim African chieftains. Amawi was no ordinary man, of course, and his mission forced him to interact with people he might otherwise have avoided, but the frequency of his travels and his non-judgemental curiosity about the customs of the various peoples on the African mainland are noteworthy.

It is also noteworthy that, in contrast to Farsy's description of Amawi as legalistic and reformist in outlook, Amawi describes himself as having entered into a trance-like state while performing Sufi *dhikr*.[43] Elsewhere, in the Dar es Salaam fragments, he writes of his experience of the Sufi state of *jadhba*, in which the rational mind is overcome by the ecstasy of divine illumination, something he regarded as a fundamental part of the experience of all truly accomplished Sufis. He also wrote that he was so enamoured of his fiancée, Dédé, daughter of the famed Sufi master Uways al-Barawi (1847–1909), that he had visions of her walking on the trail ahead of him as he travelled in the Rovuma River region, and that he saw her serving as his imam whenever he bowed in prayer. 'It is permissible,' he wrote, 'in the law of desire (*shar' al-hawa*) for a man to follow a woman' – hardly the sort of statement one would expect from someone zealous to enforce a harsh version of Islamic law.

There are also indications in the Dar es Salaam fragments, as well as in Bishop Edward Steere's own writings[44] and in Steere's acknowledgement of Amawi's assistance in translating portions of the Bible into Swahili,[45] that Amawi's relationship with Christians in Zanzibar was not adversarial, in contrast to Farsy's depiction of him as devastating the Christians with his arguments. The cumulative evidence of Barghash's pleasure with and reliance on Amawi, and of Amawi's broadmindedness, diplomatic skill and mysticism that emerges from his writings raises questions about the accuracy of Farsy's depiction of him, and whether that depiction was not, perhaps, a projection of Farsy's own zeal for a reformed society orientated towards a puritanical version of Islam. Pouwels discusses Amawi and his relationship with Barghash in *Horn and Crescent* with great authority, despite the fact that his only source is Farsy's book and interviews with Farsy. As indispensable as oral sources are

---

[43] Ibid., p. 38.
[44] Heanley, 1888, p. 309.
[45] Steere, 1883; Steere, 1884, pp. vi–vii.

in African studies, the discrepancy between Farsy's account and the evidence of written sources should serve as a caution against excessive reliance on oral tradition as conveyed through a single individual. This is not to deny that written sources can be just as biased as oral sources, and there is no doubt that Amawi's depiction of his shrewd management style and diplomatic skills, not to mention Barghash's pleasure with him, are undoubtedly self-serving and even self-inflating. Nonetheless, his writings offer a perspective on his personality that offers a significant enough contrast to Farsy's description of him as to warrant scepticism over the latter.

CONCLUSION

How can we situate these observations within the debate over the meaning of Zanzibar's cosmopolitanism, Omani colonialism and slaving, and allegations of racism? The cumulative evidence of this limited sample cannot lead to a clear conclusion, but it provides evidence of all of the above.

The Zanzibar sultanate's cosmopolitanism is evident in the intermingling of religious and ethnic groups, both on the island of Zanzibar and on the mainland. Sectarian affiliation among Muslims in Zanzibar was not unimportant, especially to Ibadis, as is evident in the writings of Ibadi scholars and in the punishment Barghash inflicted on Ibadi converts to Sunni Islam. Nonetheless, it is evident in Nasir ibn Abi Nabhan's anecdote that Muslim scholars of different sects met together, and that it was considered bad form – as well as politically dangerous – to discuss religiously divisive issues.

There is no question that Omanis perceived themselves as superior to the inhabitants of the coast. Academics have engaged in lengthy discussions of Swahili identity, but I am inclined to agree with Wilkinson that Omani families who were established on the coast did not consider themselves Swahili, despite allegations to the contrary.[46] Wealthy Omanis rarely married non-Omani women, but they had many concubines of various origins. In the patriarchal society that pertained among them, the offspring of such concubines were considered Omani; it was only patrilineality that mattered. Hence Amawi's co-leader in the 1879 expedition, Muhammad Kidhahabu, called himself al-Barawi, a native of Brava, a distinguished scholarly town of Somalia, and spoke disparagingly of the competence of the people of Mrima, although his own mother belonged to the Makua, a people of the Mrima coast.

Omani rule on the Swahili coast could certainly be seen as colonialism, although, like British colonial rulers in many of their domains, Sayyid Saʿid came to terms with the Mwinyi Mkuu, the native ruler of Zanzibar island, as well

---

[46] Wilkinson, 2015, p. 5.

as with other chieftains who accepted him as overlord. Scholars have discussed whether the sultanate should really be seen as a state, given the unevenness of its power and reach on the mainland. Amawi's writings indicate broad acknowledgment of the sultan's authority and power, and it is of historical interest to know that Barghash, who had done so much to modernise Zanzibar town by introducing piped water and electricity, was interested in constructing a railway from the port to Lake Nyasa and in discovering and protecting a coalfield in the Rovuma region. At the same time, the sultan's need for clarification of the boundary between his domains and those of Portugal and of an account of the different people groups and customs on the mainland indicate that the sultanate's penetration of the region was somewhat superficial.

The slave trade doesn't figure as such in Amawi's writings, but he does say that the porters in his caravan were slaves. There is some evidence of racism in Amawi's 1880 account, both in his description of the Zunuj as heedless of human rights and in Muhammad Kidhahabu's disparaging remark about Mrimans, but in most of his accounts race is not mentioned at all, beyond the use of what Westerners would interpret as a racial term (Zunuj) to refer to non-Muslim Africans. It is evident that, despite racial, religious and cultural differences, Amawi respected many of the non-Muslim chieftains he met, and his 1885 account provides glimpses of apparently close relationships formed with some over the years.

Ultimately, the evidence offered by this chapter supports neither the notion that the Zanzibar sultanate was excessively oppressive and racist, nor that it was a society in which the different ethnic groups lived in such harmony that ethnic and religious differences were irrelevant. This modest conclusion is scarcely surprising, but in light of the contemporary battle over what the sultanate was like and how it should be depicted, the texts discussed here provide valuable insights into a fascinating and understudied period in the history of East Africa and the Indian Ocean.

Bibliography

Amawī, ʿAbd al-ʿAzīz b. ʿAbd al-Ghanī. 1885. *Tārīkh al-riḥla ilā barr al-Tanj li- 'l-dawla 'l- ʿaliyya 'l- ʿarabiyya 'l-saʿidiyya*, Bū Saʿīdī Library ms. 1346mīm, Seeb, Oman.

Amawī, ʿAbd al-ʿAzīz b. ʿAbd al-Ghanī. 1880. *Tārīkh Rovuma*, Bū Saʿīdī Library ms. 1345mīm, Seeb, Oman.

Bahlānī, Nāṣir b. Sālim b. ʿUdayyim. 2004. *Al-ʿAqīda 'l-Wahbiyya*, Ṣāliḥ b. Saʿīd al-Qunūbī and ʿAbdallāh b. Saʿīd al-Qunūbī (eds). Muscat: Maktabat Musqaṭ.

al Barwani, Ali Muhsin. 1997. *Conflicts and Harmony in Zanzibar*. n.p.

Declich, Lorenzo. 2006. *The Arabic Manuscripts of the Zanzibar National Archives: A Checklist*, supplement no. 2 alla Rivista Degli Studi Orientali, nuova serie, vol. 78. Pisa and Rome: Istituti Editoriali e Poligrafici Internazionali.

Farsy, Abdallah Salih. 1989. *The Shafiʿi Ulama of East Africa, ca. 1830–1970: A Hagiographic Account*, Randall L. Pouwels, trans. and ed. Madison, WI: University of Wisconsin African Studies Program.

Glassman, Jonathon. 2011. *War of Words, War of Stones: Racial Thought and Violence in Colonial Zanzibar*. Bloomington, IN: Indiana University Press.

A Handbook of Portuguese Nyasaland. 1920. London: His Majesty's Stationery Office.

Heanley, Robert Marshall. 1888. *A Memoir of Edward Steere, D.D., L.L.D., Third Missionary Bishop in Central Africa*. London: George Bell and Sons.

Hoffman, Valerie J. 2012. *The Essentials of Ibāḍī Islam*. New York: Syracuse University Press.

Hoffman, Valerie J. 2006. 'In His (Arab) Majesty's Service: The Career of a Somali Scholar and Diplomat in Nineteenth-Century Zanzibar', in Roman Loimeier and Rüdiger Seesemann (eds), *The Global Worlds of the Swahili: Interfaces of Islam, Identity and Space in 19th and 20th-Century East Africa*. Berlin: LIT Verlag, pp. 251–72.

Hunwick, John O., R. S. O'Fahey and C. C. Stewart (eds). 1994–present. *Arabic Literature of Africa*, 6 vols, Leiden: Brill.

Ingrams, W. H. 1931. *Zanzibar: Its History and Its People*. London: H. F. G. Witherby.

al-Ismaily, Issa Nasser Issa. 1999. *Zanzibar: kinyanʾanyiro na utumwa*, Ibrahim Noor (ed.). Ruwi, Oman: I.N.I. Al-Ismaily.

Madelung, Wilferd. 1979. 'The Shiʿite and Khārijite Contribution to Pre-Ashʿarite *Kalām*', in P. Morewedge (ed.), *Islamic Philosophical Theology*. Albany, NY: State University of New York Press, pp. 120–39.

Mazrui, Alamin M. and Ibrahim Noor Shariff. 1994. *The Swahili: Idiom and Identity of an African People*. Trenton, NJ: Africa World Press.

Mkelle, Mohammed Burhan. 1992. 'A Scholar for All Seasons: Sheikh Abdul Aziz Al Amani [*sic*] of Zanzibar', *Journal of the Institute of Muslim Minority Affairs*, vol. 13, no. 1, pp. 116–121.

Mughayri, Saʿīd b. ʿAlī. 1986. *Juhaynat al-akhbār fī tārīkh Zinjibār*, Muḥammad ʿAlī al-Ṣulaybī (ed.). Muscat: Wizārat al-Turāth al-Qawmī wa-ʾl-Thaqāfa, 2nd edition.

Nāṣir ibn Abī Nabhān. n.d. *Al-Ḥaqq al-mubīn wa-ʾl-ʿilm al-yaqīn*, vol. 1., Bū Saʿīdī Library ms. 1883h, Seeb, Oman.

Pouwels, Randall L. 1987. *Horn and Crescent: Cultural Change and Traditional Islam on the East African Coast, 800–1900*, Cambridge: Cambridge University Press.

al-Qalhātī, Abū ʿAbdallāh Muḥammad b. Saʿīd. 1980. *Al-Kashf wa-ʾl-bayān*, Sayyida Ismāʿīl Kāshif (ed.), 2 vols. Muscat: Wizārat al-Turāth al-Qawmī wa-ʾl-Thaqāfa.

al-Salmi, Shaikh Abdullah bin Mohammed. 2016. *Religious Tolerance: A Vision for a New World*. Hildesheim, Zurich, New York: Georg Olms Verlag.

Steere, Edward. 1884. *A Handbook of the Swahili Language as Spoken at Zanzibar*. London: Society for the Promotion of Christian Knowledge.

Steere, Edward. 1883. *Kitabu cha Agano Jipya la bwana na mwokozi wetu Isa Masiya: kimefasirika katika maneno ya kwanza ya kiyonani*. London: British and Foreign Bible Society.

Wilkinson, John C. 2015. *The Arabs and the Scramble for Africa*. Sheffield and Bristol, CT: Equinox.

CHAPTER 5

Transcending Boundaries: Sayyida Salme/Emily Ruete and Siti binti Saad

FAROUK TOPAN

INTRODUCTION

Much has been written about Sayyida Salme/Emily Ruete (d. 1924) and Siti binti Saad (d. 1950), the two women whose thoughts, activities and achievements we explore in this paper. Salme/Emily has left an autobiography and other texts that have provided scholars with ample material for a continual assessment of her life, status and legacy.[1] Likewise, the life of Siti binti Saad has been narrated by Tanzania's national poet, Shaaban Robert (d. 1962), in a biography that has featured periodically over the years on the Swahili school curriculum in Tanzania;[2] there is also an in-depth study of Siti's life by Laura Fair both in Swahili and in English;[3] and a compilation of some of her songs in an anthology edited by Matola, Shabaan and Whiteley.[4] By drawing on these sources, this paper attempts to consider the lives of Salme/Emily and Siti as women exercising their agency by responding to personal and national issues and events on a continuum that stretches for almost a century, from the 1850s, when Salme was turning into an independent teenager, to Siti's death in 1950. Their decisions and actions – with favourable or adverse consequences for themselves – show agency 'as a capacity for action that historically specific relations of subordination enable and create'.[5] Their narratives continually exhibit a

---

[1] Van Donzel, 1993; Prestholdt, 2014; Maxwell, 2015; Oruc, 2019; et al.
[2] Robert, 1967 [1958].
[3] Fair, 2001, pp. 169–225; Fair, 2013.
[4] Matola, Shabaan and Whiteley, 1966.
[5] Mahmood, 2001, p. 203.

going beyond what is expected of girls and women, a transcending of boundaries both soft and hard.

As modern scholarship has accorded high prominence to the achievements of Salme/Emily and Siti, it is worthwhile to explore the conditions that enabled the women to make their choices and effect their agency. These conditions would have evolved through the *long durée* of East African history, with diverse formative factors operating at varying times and spaces along the coast.[6] The following section identifies such factors at play in the development of Swahili women's status on the coast, particularly in the nineteenth and twentieth centuries.

SWAHILI WOMEN

History gives us glimpses of women of status, authority and influence who have existed on the East African coast since at least the 1550s. Not much is known about them and, as Askew notes, even the women who had ruled as queens of some city-states on the East African coast, such as Pate, Mombasa and Zanzibar, are generally mentioned in 'incidental footnotes' in historical accounts of the coast.[7] The first known queen was Mwana Mkisi who ruled Kongowea, an older name for Mombasa, around 1500;[8] the last was Sabani binti Ngumi who, 'as late as 1886 ... was recognised as the chieftainess of Mikindani [on the southern coast of Tanzania] and her daughter was recognised as her successor'.[9] Askew has collated references to a total of twenty-five female rulers in between the periods of Mwana Mkisi in the sixteenth century and Sani Ngumi and her daughter in the late nineteenth century.[10]

Accounts about the Swahili queens during the two centuries of Portuguese rule (1500s–1700s) deal, unsurprisingly, with engagement with the European power regarding their authority and status as queens. The Portuguese had the capacity to engineer or force their enthronement and, more significantly, their dethronement. While some of the queens submitted to Portuguese demands – one reportedly converting to Christianity – others could be rebellious and defiant, choosing their allies in accordance with their interests (sometimes siding with other foreign powers in an attempt to oust the Portuguese from the coast). Biographies or information about the queens would have given us some insight into the nature and social organisation of Swahili society as affected by coastal

---

[6] See Pouwels, 1987, for an example of a study and analysis of such formative factors affecting Swahili culture vis-à-vis Islam through the centuries (800–1900).
[7] Askew, 1999, p. 81.
[8] Ibid., p. 82; Berg, 1968, pp. 42–3
[9] Gray, 1961, p. 129, cited in Askew, 1999, p. 84.
[10] Ibid., p. 102.

encounters with other peoples, faiths and cultures across the Indian Ocean. Some of the questions that interest us today – were the Swahili matrilineal in the past? did the Arabs impose a patriarchal system? how did women negotiate their space in society? to what extent was female agency effective? – might have received firmer answers. As Strobel has remarked: 'To write about women on the Swahili coast is to probe the history of the inarticulate and invisible. Evidence written by women themselves is scarce.'[11]

The outcome of Strobel's own research was the first book-length historical account and analysis of Muslim women in Mombasa during the period 1890–1975. She drew from three main sources: documentary evidence, extensive interviews with both men and women, and works of scholars of previous decades on various aspects of women's status in coastal (and some mainland) societies. She has shown that women's development during this period was impacted by four interlinked factors. The foremost was colonialism, with its ideology, institutions and practices; associated with colonialism was the process of 'Westernisation' as well as the presence and activities of Christian missionaries on the East African coast. The second factor was the impact of colonial policies on the economic system and balance of the Swahili of Mombasa (and elsewhere). The abolition of slavery in the earlier period and the progressive introduction of wage labour in various enterprises during the early to mid-twentieth century transformed the gender pattern of the labour market. Initially, the professions open to women after completing school (and further training) were those which they were expected to enter – teaching, nursing, midwifery and various domestic works – but, during the 1950s, quite a few women and girls also sought work in offices, thus competing directly with men. A third factor – religious precepts and ethical behaviour – was invoked in debates on this issue: for instance, was it proper for women and girls to work in proximity to men in offices? The plea of an 'Arab girl', published in the *Mombasa Times* of 9 July 1957, gave her answer:

> Why should Arab girls learn only housework and religion? It is due to our parents' ideas that for a long time we have not been expected to take up any other form of employment . . . I do not think there are rules in our religion that stop us working . . . So, please, parents, try to let us take higher studies, and let us work like other people and do not try to give us only lessons in domestic science, because the time has changed and we cannot depend on cooking for a living.[12]

---

[11] Strobel, 1979, p. 4.
[12] Strobel, 1979, p. 122.

Further on in her letter, she counters the argument against girls working in offices by stating bluntly that she 'would rather risk the temptation of an office than . . . sin because of hunger'.

The fourth factor, implied in the letter, was the overarching patriarchy that permeated traditional Swahili life on the coast. A text from the pre-colonial era, written by a woman, demonstrates this factor with apparent clarity. It sheds some light on the way women responded to patriarchal customs and conventions in the nineteenth century. The text – a poem – was written by Mwana Kupona bint Msham, two years before her death in 1860. Mwana Kupona was a woman of high status, the wife of the governor of Siyu, a member of the nobility. The principal theme of this well-known poem is an ailing mother's advice to her teenage daughter, Mwana Hashima bint Sheikh (d. 1933) on the way she should behave and conduct herself in life, especially in relation to her husband. Mwana Kupona viewed the husband as the fifth being/person to have claim on her obedience: the first being God, then the Prophet, followed by her parents, and then the husband. A woman's admittance to Paradise in the next world depends upon the will and choice of her husband. Thus, a prima facie reading of the poem displays a text which has not only been written by a woman operating within the bounds of patriarchy but decidedly upholding its customs, conventions and mores. That is how it has been judged for years, evoking both praise for the text and vitriol against its author (and her society).[13]

A rather different reading, however, has been suggested by Ann Biersteker, a scholar of Swahili studies.[14] In her analysis of the text, Biersteker draws attention to the sub-text which Mwana Kupona seems to have weaved into her poem deliberately, even if surreptitiously. She highlights the way Mwana Kupona used irony, metaphor and structure to project the other deeper message. One telling example relates to the use of speech. In Swahili society, as in many others, speech is deemed to be an index of one's personality, upbringing, good manners, status and intelligence, all as manifestations of human worth (*utu*). Mwana Kupona labours this point to her daughter, even using herself as an example in the way she has related to her husband in her own marriage. Yet her advice to the young Mwana Hashima, with more than a hint of irony, is that she should treat her (future) husband as 'a youth who cannot speak' (verse 35)[15] – a phrase usually used of a baby than a person of strength and ample sense

---

[13] Those who praised the text also sought its dissemination by including it as part of the trousseau of a newly-wed girl. Those vehemently opposed to the poem could not believe that a woman could give such advice to her own daughter; therefore, they argued – against historical fact – that Mwana Kupona may not have been a woman (Decker, 2014, p. 198, note 35).

[14] Biersteker, 1991, pp. 59–77.

[15] Ibid., pp. 69–70; Allen, 1971, p. 62.

(*kijana*, a youth).[16] This advice is followed, in the very next verse (verse 36), by a line which again is ambiguous in its interpretation – *Mpumbaze apumbae*: 'Amuse him so that he may relax',[17] or, lexically closer to the meaning of the verb: 'Render him stupid/speechless so that he remains stupid/speechless' or 'Delude him so that he remains deluded'.[18] It is recognised that this is not the only message of the poem, nor was it intended to be. But it counters the predominance of male power and, as Decker points out, it foregrounds Biersteker's argument that Mwana Kupona's 'obsequious tone advising her daughter to please her husband mocked patriarchal expectations'.[19]

Be that as it may, Mwana Kupona served as a useful point of reference for Strobel in comparing the poet's message, conduct and worldview to those of the Swahili women of Mombasa (and the coast) a century or so later. The four factors mentioned earlier – patriarchy, religious and moral precepts, colonialism, the economy – working in combination to various degrees, shifted the position of women through the decades from one of expected dependence in a patriarchal society to one of limited freedom in the colonial period. The parameters depended upon one's education, class status, the extent of one's control over inherited or acquired wealth, and the courage and will to transcend what were perceived to be religious and moral boundaries. Colonialism (in the mid-twentieth century) had loosened the hold of patriarchy, but it had also deepened class differences. Women who had no husbands, or wished to be less dependent on them, struggled in the new economic system, particularly if they did not belong to the upper class or whose level of education was inadequate to serve their needs. As Strobel observed: 'The farther the women were from the upper tier of society, the more distant was the voice of Mwana Kupona and the Qur'ān prescribing wifely obedience and seclusion'.[20]

---

[16] Cf Youth in the classical Arabic and Persian sense, respectively, of *fata* and *javanmard*. It may be worthwhile to quote verse 35 in full as the remaining lines also contain their own message:

Mtunde kama kijana	Tend him like a youth
asiyoyua kunena	who cannot speak
kitu changalie sana	And take particular care
kitokacho na kungia	of the thing which goes out and in.

Scholars have interpreted the 'thing' generally as household expenses or food but, as Biersteker points out, since the verse occurs in the context of other verses which describe wifely actions for her husband in the privacy of their bedroom, it is not difficult to infer what 'thing' refers to.

[17] Allen, 1971, p. 63.

[18] Biersteker, 1991, p. 71.

[19] Decker, 2014, ch. 3, note 35. Cf. a similar practice of coded messaging among German women authors of children's stories in the nineteenth century: 'These stories provide a window, not into the minds of male writers as they adjusted tales to fit nineteenth-century patriarchal values but into the minds of women writers, the rightful heirs of female storytelling, sometimes expressing the same patriarchal values we see in the work of male writers, on one level, yet engaging in a subversive rebellion against patriarchal traditions, on another' (Koehler, 2016, p. 9).

[20] Strobel, 1979, p. 149.

The four factors mentioned above had a significant and varied impact upon the lives of the two women, some of whose activities, thoughts, and agency we explore here. Their backgrounds could not have been more different: Sayyida Salme was born a princess in 1844 (thus a contemporary of Mwana Kupona), a daughter of the first sultan of Zanzibar, Sayyid Said bin Sultan (d. 1856). Siti was born in the mid-1880s in Fumba, a village not far from Zanzibar Town where she became a street hawker selling clay pots and wares; her given name was Mtumwa, 'slave'. Thus, between them, Salme and Siti traversed the class hierarchy, and their combined lifespan straddled the pre-colonial and colonial periods: Salme, 1844–1924, and Siti, mid-1880s–1950.[21]

SALME/EMILY

Salme's life became a focus of attention beyond Zanzibar from 1866 onwards when she left the island 'in secret' in a British ship bound for Aden. The events that had led to her departure have been described since then by various writers and scholars, but principally by herself in her *Memoirs of an Arabian Princess*, first published in German in Berlin in 1886. The *Memoirs*, together with three of her other works – *Letters Home*, *Sequels to My Memoirs* and *Syrian Customs and Usages* – have been published in one volume by E. Van Donzel as *An Arabian Princess Between Two Worlds*.[22] Van Donzel provides a comprehensive introduction to the volume, which places in historical and social perspective both the life of Salme/Emily and her works. Although he mentions various major English translations of the *Memoirs*, the version in the volume is Van Donzel's own, which he supplements and annotates with copious notes. References to the *Memoirs* in this paper are to Van Donzel's translation.

Salme lived in Zanzibar from birth for a period of twenty-two years. During her father's reign and, later, during those of her brothers Majid (r. 1856–70) and Barghash (r. 1870–88), Zanzibar attained a status of prime importance in the political, commercial and religious activities of the East African coast. European presence in Zanzibar in the latter half of the nineteenth century was manifest in three-fold ways: first, through political and diplomatic activities of the consulates (mainly British, German and French); second, through trading companies and the commodities they sold and exchanged; and, third, through missionary activities, including the construction of two grand churches which endure as

---

[21] It is interesting to note that both women, albeit very briefly for Siti, were contemporaries of female queens; when Siti was born, a female queen was still ruling at Mikindani. I follow Fair (2001, p. 179) in indicating Siti's birth to have been in the mid-1880s as there are no records of the exact year of her birth (although most sources posit 1880).

[22] Ruete, 1993.

historical buildings to this day.[23] European engagement with the sultanate, with merchants and traders and with the people, was starkly different – at least in the second half of the nineteenth century (that is, prior to the establishment of Zanzibar as a British Protectorate in 1895) – from the earlier approach and attitude of the Portuguese as an occupying military power. There was now commercial, professional and social interaction between Europeans and the people, which, though limited in extent (to particular levels of society), nonetheless added to the already cosmopolitan dimension of Zanzibar as a dynamic hub and entrepôt of commerce and knowledge in the Indian Ocean. For Zanzibar, like some other towns and cities along the coast, had been for centuries a cultural and commercial node in a network that had extended to the Arab countries, Iran, and across the ocean to India and beyond.[24] Verne provides an ethnographic account of the network in contemporary times extending far across the Indian Ocean.[25]

Despite being raised in a palace, Salme's account of her childhood and youth reflects a cosmopolitan atmosphere and influence, even within the bounded space of a royal harem (from which she often ventured out, riding horses with her brothers although the princesses were generally meant to ride donkeys).[26] Her father had one official wife and several *sarari*, unofficial wives. Among the latter was Jilfidan, Salme's mother, a Circassian woman who 'had come into my father's possession, probably at the tender age of seven or eight, as she lost her first baby tooth in our house'.[27] Status, rank, order and knowing

---

[23] The first is Christ Church, the Anglican cathedral at Mkunazini, which was opened in 1879 and whose construction was inspired by the vision of the third Anglican Bishop at Zanzibar at the time, Edward Steere (1828–82), himself a pioneer scholar of Swahili; his body is buried behind the altar. See Liebst (2014) for Steere's role in the building of the cathedral; Steere's comments on Princess Salme are given below. The other is St Joseph's Cathedral, a Roman Catholic church in the Baghani area of the town; it was built between 1893 and 1898 by French missionaries who adopted the design of Marseilles Cathedral with its twin spires (*minara miwili* in Swahili, a phrase used locally to refer to St Joseph's Cathedral).

[24] Pouwels, 1987; Prestholdt, 2019, pp. 318–19. Prestholdt aptly captures the status of Zanzibar in the nineteenth century: 'Between the 1830s and the early twentieth century the island of Zanzibar (Unguja) was the primary node of linkage among eastern African, Indian Ocean and Atlantic basin economic systems. More precisely, the seat of the Sultanate of Zanzibar and Oman was a *nexus*, a critical point of economic and social interrelation that reflected diverse interests and broadcasted shifting sociocultural trends. Few ports in the world have commanded a relationship with such a vast hinterland as Zanzibar in the nineteenth century. The island capital acted as an interface between the greater eastern African region – stretching from Malawi to the Congo and southern Somalia – and ports as distant as Boston, Cape Town and Canton. Zanzibar City thus became a metropolis in the latter nineteenth century, one that embodied the dividends and tensions of eastern Africa's economic growth.'

[25] Verne, 2012.

[26] Ruete, 1993, p. 149.

[27] Ibid., p. 152 and footnote 8. According to the information supplied by Freeman-Grenville to Van Donzel, 'Circassian slaves were recruited in the Ottoman Empire from villages near the Russian border. The women are of striking appearance, black-haired, blue-eyed for the most part, with very pale, ivory complexion (Fr. –Gr.).'

one's place formed a staple constituent of palace protocol. Salme describes various facets of rules and etiquette that governed different actions expected of family members – for example, when to visit the sultan, who should do so, who could and could not dine with him, that one should only speak in Arabic in his presence, and so on – but, interestingly, she also states that the unofficial wives had 'introduced a classification among themselves' whereby the 'beautiful and expensive Circassians, well aware of their particular value, did not want to take their meals with the coffee-coloured Abyssinians'.[28] Each race, she tells us, took its meals by itself, but immediately adds that there was no such separation among the children. The presence of diverse ethnicities also meant a multiplicity of languages was spoken at the palace, a 'babel of languages' as Salme describes them, listing Persian, Turkish, Circassian, Swahili, Nubian and Abyssinian. She herself spoke Arabic and Swahili, a fact that seems to have demeaned Zanzibari Omanis in the eyes of their brothers and sisters in Oman.[29] When European ladies visited the palace they were usually met by Salme and her elder sister, Chole ('Khole' in Swahili, 'Khawla' in Arabic). According to the Anglican minister Edward Steere (later Bishop of Zanzibar and a pioneer scholar of Swahili), Salme 'knows a little English, is very anxious to get to Europe and to Europeanise in every possible way'.[30]

The death of Salme's father in 1856 en route back to Zanzibar from Oman was a decisive moment not only for the two countries but for Salme and her siblings as well. Oman and Zanzibar became separate kingdoms, each with its own sultan. The eldest son of Sayyid Said, Thuwayn, became the ruler of Oman, and Majid, the eldest in Zanzibar, became its first sultan. Salme, though barely twelve, was declared of age and given her inheritance (mainly a plantation and some slaves) and was expected to be independent in her livelihood.

Three events, occurring sequentially, led Salme to the decision to leave Zanzibar. The first was the death of her mother in 1859, a victim of the cholera epidemic that had afflicted the island that year. Losing her mother at that age was a deep loss, and bereft of her mother's guidance, Salme compared herself to a rudderless ship in a stormy sea. The metaphor was apt, as she then found herself not long afterwards embroiled in a conspiracy to remove Majid and install his younger brother, Barghash, as sultan. Majid had been very kind to her, and it seems from her account that he was fond of his little sister with

---

[28] Ruete, 1993, p. 174.

[29] According to Salme: 'Not many of us cared much about going to Omân; the proud Omani ladies treat those of Zanzibar as uncivilized creatures. This arrogance even prevailed among our brothers and sisters; a member of our family born in Omân felt and imagined herself particularly aristocratic vis-à-vis us "Africans". . . . Our greatest uncouthness, they think, is that we (how awful!), speak another language besides Arabic.' (Ruete, 1993, p. 230).

[30] Van Donzel, citing from a letter written by Steere on 26 August 1866, that is, the day after Salme's departure. Ruete, 1993, pp. 11–12.

whom he used to go riding. But after her mother's death, Salme placed herself under the wing of her elder sister, Khawla (known as 'the bright star' because of her striking beauty and personality) whom she loved and adored. Khawla strongly supported Barghash's insurgence, and Salme went along with her, despite her feelings for 'the noble Majid'. But once she was in the conspirators' group, Salme found herself playing an active role since she could both read and write.[31] At only fifteen, she became the secretary of the group, corresponding with Arab chiefs and ordering weapons and ammunition in preparation for the coup. With the help of the British, however, the insurrection was quashed, Barghash was exiled to India, and Salme, shunned by the supporters of Majid, retreated to her plantation outside the town. But Majid seems to have forgiven her, for he re-established contact with her and in time normalised their relationship. She was now in turn shunned by her beloved Khawla, by some of her other brothers and sisters and, most significantly by Bargash, who felt betrayed by her renewed friendship with Majid. It was during this period, when Salme had moved to town and was living as a young twenty-two-year-old independent woman, that the final event occurred. Unlike the previous acrimonious episode of her teenage years, however, this was an act of her own choice. She became friends with her neighbour, a young German businessman named Heinrich Ruete, and the two fell in love. It was clear to Salme that their relationship could not be accepted as normal in Zanzibar, and that therefore she had to leave the island if she wished for 'the union with the beloved'.[32] Helped by Emily Seward, the wife of a British doctor and acting consul, Salme left the island in secret in August 1866 on board the British ship *Highflyer*, bound for Aden.

The trip, south to north along the western rim of the Indian Ocean, metaphorically transcended that part of Salme's life bounded by upper class Arab patriarchal traditions underpinned by Islamic tenets and Muslim conventions that operated in an Arabo-Swahili culture in a dynamic cosmopolitan setting. Salme stayed in Aden for nine months, the in-between place on her passage to Europe where she attempted to shed one identity (or at least parts of it) and to assume another. She converted to Christianity at Aden and chose to be baptised as Emily, the name of Mrs Seward.[33] Heinrich joined her in May 1867 when they got married in church and set out for Marseilles and thence to Hamburg, which she made her adopted home. But their marriage was short-lived as Heinrich

---

[31] While boys' education at the palace included both reading and writing, that of girls only focused on the ability to read. Salme taught herself how to write: she 'then paid one of our so-called educated servants the rare honour of appointing him as my master' to guide her through calligraphy after she had mastered the basics of writing by copying letters from the Qur'an (Ruete, 1993, p. 187).

[32] Ruete, 1993, p. 371.

[33] According to Van Donzel, Salme gave birth to a baby boy in Aden on 7 December 1866; he was named Heinrich but died before the couple left for Europe in May 1867 (1993:20).

died in a tram accident in August 1870. Now aged twenty-six, Salme/Emily 'became a widow with three small children in a strange land, a declining fortune, and an inability to speak German'.[34] Yet she remained in Germany (travelling outside it for short stays) for a period nearly thrice longer than she had lived in Zanzibar. She had considered returning home but she felt that she had to keep her promise to her husband to raise and educate the children in Europe. More specifically, she speaks of a suggestion from her sister Chole (Khawla): 'In 1871, after my husband's death, she had a letter written to me – she was unversed in writing – that I could send her one of my children, whom she wanted to adopt. As the child would have had to embrace Islam, I could not accede to that'.[35] She explains further in the *Letters Home* the agonising decision she had to take of remaining in Europe for the sake of her children's upbringing, education and welfare. Salme/Emily viewed this as an act of moral obligation on her part, even a logical one – 'And so, simply and purely, I followed piety's voice'[36] – a fulfilment of an unspoken promise to her late husband. But there might also have been an additional dimension to this decision, one which has not been specifically mentioned by her as such: this is Salme/Emily's intellectual attachment to the ways of the north (an affirmation and extension, perhaps, of Steere's observations mentioned above).

The decision not to return to Zanzibar after her husband's death would have been particularly difficult for Salme as she was then a young woman (close to her twenty-seventh birthday), with three small children, very limited knowledge of German, and an uncertain income at her disposal. Barghash's refusal to grant Salme her inheritance and allowance, the mishandling and even misappropriation of her husband's investments by the agents of the German company in Zanzibar, and the mismanagement and embezzlement of his assets and investments in Germany (particularly by a rogue lawyer who was meant to protect Salme's interests) gradually pushed Salme into a state of dire financial need and insecurity. She moved from Hamburg to other towns and smaller residences in Germany to enable her to live within her means[37]; she pawned and sold pieces of her jewellery; and even taught Arabic and Swahili to select individuals.[38] Yet, through all the difficult years, she never wavered from her

---

[34] Maxwell, 2015, p. 41.
[35] Ruete, 1993, p. 247.
[36] From *Letters Home*, Ibid., p. 455.
[37] Salme moved from a villa to a house within Hamburg itself, thence to Dresden, to Rudolstadt, to Berlin and finally back to Hamburg. She had also lived in the Levant just before World War II when her circumstances had changed for the better.
[38] It is interesting to note her views on the teaching of the two languages, an activity which engaged her in what was to her a new experience of employment: '. . . for the first time I had to earn money by the sweat of my brow' (Ibid., p. 498). On her method of teaching Arabic: 'Often I had to pronounce one single word five to seven times before they were able to repeat it more or less correctly. You have no idea what kind of difficulties the riches in words of our language cause to Europeans. They do not call

decision to raise her children in Germany in the ways of their father. (Though she later muses in hindsight in *Letters Home*: 'If I had been able to foresee the miserable years which lay ahead of me here, I scarcely would have had enough courage to carry out my intention.')[39]

The education and welfare of her children became the most dominant goal of Salme's life after Heinrich's death, and linked to this was her struggle to obtain her inheritance and allowance both from Zanzibar and Germany. Oruc even suggests that Salme's motivation for writing the *Memoirs* was, at least partially, monetary in view of her circumstances especially at a time when 'extravagant and salacious tales of the "Orient" already enjoyed wide readership and were lucrative topics for authors'.[40]

While Salme might well have written the *Memoirs* partly for material gain, it was undoubtedly for her a platform for projecting her thoughts, teachings and personality, a reaching out to her new compatriots of 'the North' both as Salme and Emily. She started writing the *Memoirs* in 1877 (when she was thirty-three, and weak of health) as 'some sketches of my life for my children, who until that time knew little more about my origin than that I was an Arab woman and a native of Zanzibar'.[41] However, by the time the book was published nine years later, its tone and voice had transcended the simple notion of being just a bequest; it was now a statement of beliefs, values, views, a narrative and even a questioning of self-identity (a theme expressed more reflectively and extensively in the *Letters*). It is not surprising that, given the author's status, circumstances, forthright views and legacy, the *Memoirs* should have received wide-ranging attention when it was published in 1886.[42]

The *Memoirs* may be divided in two parts in relation to Salme's own develop-ment as an individual. The first part, mainly a description of her life in Zanzibar, reflects a growing intellectual curiosity, a sense of independence, a desire to explore and achieve, and to develop oneself as an individual, expressed initially in acts such as riding a horse (and not a donkey, as girls were expected to do)

---

to mind any other European language, and our guttural sounds reduce many to sheer despair' (Ibid., p. 499).

On Swahili: 'Unfortunately, Arabic lessons were not in much demand, probably because at that time there yet was little interest for the Orient in Germany. Later, I also taught Swahili, which is much easier for Europeans to learn. I had to give to my pupils lectures on every conceivable item, like for instance inhabitants, flora and fauna, climatic conditions, means of subsistence, religion and other such questions. But the main theme was slavery. The good people were usually openly astonished when I answered with a quite natural yes, when they asked whether I personally had kept many slaves.' (Ibid., p. 500).

[39] Ibid., p. 455.

[40] Oruc, 2019, p. 5.

[41] Ruite, 1993, p. 144.

[42] 'Though published in German, *Memoirs* was translated into several other languages. As a measure of the book's success, the Parisian newspaper *Le Figaro* dubbed Ruete "Author of the World"' (Prestholdt, 2018, p. 148). See also Oruc, 2019, pp. 1–2.

and learning how to write, and later, living on her own on her plantation, joining the rebellion against the reigning sultan and being socially independent. I believe her independence of mind and intellectual courage underpins the major decisions she had to take in her adopted home, especially after her husband's death in 1870 when she had to rely on her own judgement. It also underlies her comments, observations and criticism of certain European habits and behaviour; these form the second dimension of the *Memoirs*. These, however, are not limited to the *Memoirs* but blend into views expressed in *Letters Home*. I draw on both to convey three areas of concern to her (among several others): the imposition of the North on the East/South, slavery and foreign 'experts'. I have chosen these as, in one way or another, they are still relevant and topical today.

Salme's impressions of Europe proved to be different from the ones she might have nurtured in Zanzibar. Whereas there, her views would have been formed through her friendship and association with the small expatriate community on the island, here she was living as a citizen amidst the stark realities of European society, with its own values (which she had to accommodate), social organisation, educational aspirations, political systems, class structures, economic stratifications and even some disagreeable attitudes of superiority towards the East (which she also called the Orient or the South). These attitudes, she felt, were based on misconceptions and misrepresentations based largely on ignorance; hence her attempts in the *Memoirs* to describe, analyse and translate the true East to the North. She gives the example of the way harems are perceived in the North: the stories were transmitted by European ladies who had only paid brief visits to women at the palace and were not, in any case, given access to the harem itself but were received in the anteroom. Similarly, she was dubious of 'experts' whose opinions of the women of the Orient were based on flimsy and superficial anecdotes:

> A tourist goes for a couple of weeks to Constantinople, to Syria, Egypt, Tunisia or Morocco, and then writes a bulky book on life, customs, habits in the Orient. He himself is never able to get an insight into real family life. He contents himself with writing down the stories which circulate – and thus gradually become more and more distorted – as he heard them told by a French or German waiter at his hotel, by sailors, or donkey-drivers, and forms his opinion accordingly![43]

Another irritation for Salme was the North's engagements in postures of teaching civilisational values to others when, in her view, its own educational system – at least in Germany – failed to impart useful education to the majority

---

[43] Ruite, 1993, p. 259.

of its people. Instead, the race to the top of the educational hierarchy benefited the minority at the top, while the 'majority's needs and just and unjust claims to life increase[d] of course with the superficial knowledge thus attained.'[44]

Slavery was another topic Salme tackled in the *Memoirs*. She was conscious of the highly controversial nature of the topic, and that she would 'not make many friends by my opinion, but I consider it my duty to express it'.[45] Her views were formed by her own – and her family's – experiences of owning slaves in Zanzibar, and the relationship the slaves had with their owners. From her point of view, it was a symbiotic relationship of benefit to both parties, with the owners undoubtedly possessing power of coercion (to be applied when necessary). Besides, it was not unusual for slaves to earn their freedom, and the children of slave women married to free men were born free. Salme contrasted this with the brutal treatment slaves received from their Northern owners. And although she herself was not in favour of abolishing 'at one stroke a so deeply-rooted institution',[46] she felt that a pragmatic and humane way of bringing an end to slavery would be through a two-pronged approach: to implement the abolition gradually over time while preparing the conditions that would mitigate the adverse effects of this act (on both parties).

Salme's written works have been a focus of analysis by scholars as conduit for knowledge and understanding through translation. Maxwell neatly posits the *Memoirs* and *Letters Home* on a geographical compass of 'knowledge flows' where the former speaks to the North and the latter to the South.[47] Oruc focuses on the *Memoirs* as a platform through which Salme/Reute is able to wield her agency of translating the Orient to the North in a context where she was considered simultaneously as an exotic princess and an outsider/insider. He goes further: translation 'is not simply a linguistic and cultural endeavour; more important, it is an embodied act.'[48] Thus, Salme/Emily engages in the process of translation as she moves through certain spaces with her multiple identities and is 'able to claim several social bodies, without having to renounce one for the other.'[49]

Salme's other work, *Letters Home*, was first published in 1993 in English as part of the volume edited by Van Donzel. The *Memoirs* attributes the beginnings of *Letters Home* to notes made by Salme to record her initial impressions of

---

[44] '. . . I have no desire to judge European education as a whole, for I am not able to do so; I only wished to express some of my observations, which convinced me that school and education here have many bad sides. At any event, it must seem understandable after this, that for me it always is and will remain an open question, whether it is indeed justified for Europeans to deplore a people as "unenlightened", and whether they are allowed to forcibly impart their enlightenment on such a people' (Ibid., p. 214).

[45] Ibid., p. 327.

[46] Ibid., p. 333.

[47] Maxwell, 2015, pp. 42–4.

[48] Oruc, 2019, p. 8.

[49] Ibid.

Europe and of life and customs in Germany.[50] They are addressed to an uniden-tified woman in Zanzibar whom she addresses as 'sister' (who might not have been a member of the royal family). As such, the tone is familiar, frank and, at times, critical (as we have seen above); it conveys a more intimate reflection of her thoughts, a sharing of her inner feelings with a sister in the country of her birth and youth. There are also periods of introspection and self-reflection, especially about her identity and religion. It is clear throughout her writings that Salme thought of herself, first and foremost, as Arab; other identities got built on that bedrock. A similar assertion could perhaps be made to a degree about Islam, the faith of her upbringing. Christianity did not replace Islam in her; the two seem to have co-existed in an interface that allowed Salme to draw on both (though she confesses of her poor knowledge of Christianity as, she says, she had not been provided with a systematic teaching of her adopted religion). But, as Oruc notes, Salme several times in the *Memoirs* includes herself in the usage of the plural pronoun, 'we Muslims'.[51] She brings religion and identity together in a rhetorical question she poses about herself and her life:

> The events of my life are all too manifold, and my feelings and sentiments are geared to them. For a great part the human being is only what life, experience and the commanding circumstances make of him: I left my home a complete Arab woman and a good Muslim and what am I now?[52]

It has not been an easy question to answer, not then nor now[53]. But Salme does move on in her perceptions and mentality after the earlier phase (in 1886) of intense introspection. For, after leaving Zanzibar on her second visit to the island in 1888, she travelled to the Middle East where she lived intermittently first in Jaffa, and then in Beirut, for a total of twenty-five years. She felt at home there, as she could dress as a European woman (as did some of the local ladies) and speak Arabic naturally as the 'vernacular' language. In Beirut, as Prestholdt observes, Salme/Emily 'did not have to choose to be either European or Arab;

---

[50] 'I soon accustomed myself to the strange circumstances and eagerly learned everything that was necessary for my new life. My unforgettable husband followed the various stages of my development with vivid interest, and it was a particular joy to him to observe the first impressions which European life and the customs of the civilized world made on me. I have noted down these [impressions] in devout memory, and I shall perhaps avail myself of a later opportunity to report on these too' (Ruete, 1993, p. 372)

[51] Oruc, 2019, p. 8.

[52] Ruite, 1993, p. 389.

[53] An even deeper reflection of her situation and inner conflict relating to her decision to convert to Christianity is offered in *Letters Home*; she tells her sister to 'beware of changing your religion without true conviction' (Ibid., pp. 410–12). To Van Donzel, the account in these pages 'sounds like a *cri de coeur*' (Ibid., pp. 31–2).

she believed she could be both.'[54] Here, too, she continued her writings. She wrote *Sequels to My Memoirs* and, ever observant, she wrote a four-page document entitled *Syrian Customs and Usages* which gives her descriptions and views of life in Beirut. Both form part of the volume edited by Van Donzel.[55]

SITI

Although Salme and Siti were born with widely differing backgrounds of status and wealth, they shared similar strands of personality and character. Like Salme, Siti had ambition, resolve, a keen sense of justice and fair play, and a desire to speak and to be heard. While Salme projected her voice through her writing, Siti broadcast it through her songs and the *taarab* music of Zanzibar.

Fair provides us with a useful sketch of Siti's – or Mtumwa's – early life in Fumba: she had a childhood and youth similar to the other girls of the village, was married at an early age and had her only child (Mariamu), got divorced and, most importantly, besides farming, she was also initiated and trained in the art and skill of pottery by her mother and other women of the village. She used to make regular trips to town to sell her pottery, especially in the Swahili side of Zanzibar Town called 'Ng'ambo', literally 'the other side'.[56] It was so called because it was located across the creek that then ran between it and Zanzibar Stone Town. The division was not simply geographic but it was also demographically political, economic and cultural.

The population of Ng'ambo was made up of lower and middle class Swahili, of immigrants from the mainland and other islands along the East African coast, of Arab (mainly Hadhrami) recent migrants and generations of settlers, of Asian petty traders and shopkeepers – the *dukawalas* – who sold groceries, textiles and general commodities. The majority of the residents were working class Swahili and mainland African individuals and families and, probably for that reason, the colonial authorities had designated Ng'ambo as 'Native Quarters', distinguishing it from the Stone Town's status of being 'European, Arab and Asian Quarters'.[57] After gaining familiarity with Ng'ambo and its residents, Siti settled there in 1911 to seek new opportunities of bettering her life. The timing was opportune, as it was around this period that *taarab* music and performance were beginning to gain popularity in the public sphere.

The introduction of *taarab* to Zanzibar is attributed to Salme's brother, Sultan Barghash, who was exiled after the failed coup of 1859 (described above). Barghash travelled widely while abroad, and during his stay in Egypt he would

---

[54] Prestholdt, 2014, p. 219
[55] Ruete, 1993, pp. 511–22 and 523–6, respectively.
[56] Fair, 2001, p. 179.
[57] Folkers and Perzyna, 2019, p. 10.

have attended *taarab* performances. After becoming sultan in 1870, he initiated the practice of *taarab* performance at the palace by groups of musicians and singers from Egypt. They performed in Arabic, and their repertoires 'consisted largely of songs praising the sultan or other members of the royal family'.[58] Gradually, upper and middle class Arabs adopted the practice of having *taarab* performed for entertainment, weddings and other celebrations. By the time of Siti's 'migration' to Ng'ambo in 1911, *taarab* had spread even further in the society of Stone Town to the extent that two bands had been formed by then: Nadi Ikhwanu Safaa in 1905 and Nadi Shuub in 1910[59]. Both continued the practice of singing in Arabic.

Interestingly, Siti's entry into *taarab* as an accomplished singer was facilitated by her grasp of Arabic pronunciation and intonation. After Siti moved to Ng'ambo, it did not take long before her melodious voice brought her to the attention of the reciters of the Qur'ān and other devotional performances who offered to train her as a reciter. Siti was accordingly instructed in *tajwid*, a way of reciting the Qur'ān that appeals to the hearts of the believers; it required Siti to learn the rules of its recitation and their application with skill, to undergo vocal training, and to place due emphasis on 'correct pronunciation, breathing techniques that allow phrases to remain intact' and to appreciate 'the importance of tone and timbre to the conveyance of textual meaning'.[60] If we consider her earlier trips to Ng'ambo and consequent move to the area as the first phase of Siti's path to success, then her role as a skilled reciter of Islamic and Muslim texts formed the second. The third and most significant phase was her role in a *taarab* band, which has since been referred to as Siti's band.

Besides Siti, the band had four male accomplished performers who, between them, were skilled in poetry, recitation of Arabic texts and in music; they also possessed respectable knowledge of Islam. The Stone Town elite thus accepted the members of the band not only as bona fide artistes, but they acknowledged that, in Siti ('the Lady'), they had the most gifted and skillful female *taarab* singer of Zanzibar, if not of the whole of East Africa. Her rise to fame, however, had not been smooth. When, earlier in her career, Siti had gained a foothold in *taarab* and was beginning to get recognised, her rivals maligned her looks and lowly origins in a vain attempt to humiliate her and stifle her popularity. They had sung:

---

[58] Fair, 2001, p. 171.
[59] Nadi Ikhwanu Safaa, renamed 'Malindi Musical Club' after the Zanzibar Revolution of 1964, celebrated its centenary in 2005. Like the genre of *taarab* itself, the club has gone through various changes to accommodate newer tastes and innovations, most notably the use – traditionalists might say overuse – of electronic musical instruments.
[60] Fair, 2001, p. 180.

Siti binti Saad ulikuwa mtu lini?
Ulitoka shamba, na kaniki mbili chini.
Kama si sauti, ungekula nini?

Siti binti Saad, since when have you become a (civilized) person?
You had come from the countryside, wrapped (only) in two pieces of coarse
    cloth
Had it not been for your voice, you'd have gone around hungry [lit. what
    would you have eaten?]

The implication is cruelly palpable: she would go hungry as no man would touch
a woman with such awful looks. Siti noted their insults, transcended their
inhumanity and allowed her talent to bloom. In her 'reply', Siti shifted the
focus from beauty and good looks to possession of intelligence (akili).[61] She
reasoned that a person without beauty and good looks could still earn respect
for herself and her family; however, a person devoid of intelligence is in great
loss.

The band also had another audience whose appreciation of their performance
was much warmer. All the band's members lived on 'the other side' and, as such,
they also performed in and for Ng'ambo. Its performance in Ng'ambo generated
a different orientation to the one experienced in Stone Town. The absence of
a rigidity imposed by class divisions produced an atmosphere in which a taarab
performance was informal, relaxed and easy-going; the replacement of Arabic
by Swahili enabled the band to reach a wider audience and, more significantly,
to render the songs meaningful to them as reflective of their daily lived experiences. This rendering, however, seems to have been the outcome of a symbiotic
relationship through which Ng'ambo residents narrated their stories, and Siti
and her band weaved them into their songs.

Siti and her colleagues understood well, and shared in, the challenges faced
by the residents of Ng'ambo as a working-class community. Class divisions on
the island festered inequalities that were, in turn, reinforced by the colonial
administrative system. To Ng'ambo dwellers, it seemed the system almost always
favoured the wealthy, leaving the poor exposed to acts of greed and injustice.
Women were even more disadvantaged as, generally, their social and economic
status made them vulnerable to exploitation and abuse by unscrupulous men
from both sides of the town. Even Siti herself had not been spared the attention

---

[61] Possibly drawing on the Swahili saying, Akili mali, 'intelligence is wealth'. Siti's reply (my translation):

Si hoja uzuri na sura jamali	It's not vital to have beauty and good looks
Kuwa mtukufu na jadi kubeli	to be a respected person from a noble family: to
Hasara ya mtu kukosa akili	being devoid of intelligence is a greater loss.

of a stalker who only stopped following her when he could not resist the strong pressure of disapproval from the community. Siti and members of her band were thus well placed to air the concerns and grievances of ordinary people, and they did so both openly and at times covertly through metaphors and *mafumbo*, inner layers of meaning.[62]

It is worth observing three aspects that Fair mentions about the conception and composition of Siti's songs, about the ambience of their production, and what they meant to the residents of Ng'ambo.[63] The first is in relation to the engagement of the audience with the political and economic realities of the time. Although largely illiterate (especially in the Latin alphabet), Siti's audience in Ng'ambo were keenly aware of the changes occurring on the island, particularly the gradual consolidation of British power (after the establishment of the Zanzibar Protectorate just over two or so decades earlier in 1895).[64] Current political and social issues were discussed at what seems to have been Siti's *baraza* – her home as a place of regular gatherings for her friends and fans[65] – where Siti and her band also performed for them. One of the more serious issues discussed during the mid-1920s would have been the exorbitant increase in the ground rent of most of the residents of Ng'ambo. Three Asian landlords, between them, owned almost half of the land in Ng'ambo and, seemingly unchecked by the colonial administrators and even the judiciary, they felt unfettered in their bold actions, raising rents 300 to 400 per cent. Eviction notices were served on those who would not pay. As the situation worsened during mid-1928, with rents rising steeply, the residents decided to go on strike and totally stop paying rent. It was a collective action, and through debates, public rallies and even 'rescuing' their compatriots from jails, they managed to get the colonial administration to see their point of view. A decree was passed in November 1928 which reduced rent across the board and made evictions more difficult.[66] Siti's band is recognised as having 'played a critical, if indirect, role in bringing the strike to fruition, as the band's music helped to craft the

---

[62] Texts of Siti's songs and those of her colleagues – Maalim Shaaban, Mbaruku Effandi Talsam, Budda Swedi – are given in Matola, Shaaban and Whiteley (1966) and in Fair (2013, pp. 76–108); the latter contains details of the gramophone recordings of Siti and her colleagues, Maalim Shaaban, Subeti Ambar and Budda Swedi (from the 'Black Label' records of His Master's Voice Swahili releases of 1929 and 1930; a list of songs released in 1928–30 is given in Appendix 2, Ibid., pp. 185–225).

[63] Ibid., pp. 179–90.

[64] One of Siti's songs – *Ela kafa ndugu zangu* – speaks of the *mzungu* (the white man, in this context, the British) as *maliki wa duniyani*, 'ruler of the world' (Fair 2001, p. 193).

[65] A common practice among the Swahili is for friends to meet regularly (often daily) at a particular place, the *baraza*, for chats, discussions, gossip and even for board games. On the definition, function and case study of *baraza*, see Kresse, 2007, pp. 72–80 and Loimeier, 2009, pp. 177–97.

[66] See Chapter 3, 'The Land is Ours! Why Should We Pay Rent?' in Fair, 2001, pp. 110–68. It gives a detailed account of the Ground Rent Strike of 1928 and its aftermath.

community and mould the class consciousness that were at the root of the strike.'[67]

The second aspect is related to a reassertion of societal and personal values. The songs of Siti and her colleagues became a medium through which social norms were highlighted, broadcast and their breaches critiqued. As in all *taarab* bands, love in its various expressions and manifestations was the principal subject of attention: on true love and its uneven, meandering course, on longing and the pain of separation, on unrequited and nostalgic love, on rivalry in love, on the beauty and virtues of the beloved, the cheats for whom love is only a game, and so on. But the band also sang about errant individuals who transgressed normative boundaries, for example: the habitual drunkard who infringed upon the space and freedom of others; an abusive husband; a nefarious womaniser; corrupt officials, particularly those who defraud the poor, and so on. In a relatively small face-to-face Ng'ambo community, the people would have known the identity of the rebuked individuals.

The third aspect concerned the position of women in society and the way they were treated by the colonial system, especially in relation to their legal rights as individuals. While the colonial enterprise might have loosened the hold of patriarchy by the 1950s (as discussed above), the situation was rather different earlier in the century. For Fair's study clearly demonstrates the bias of the judges and magistrates in favour of men, especially wealthy men, in cases involving women as victims or appellants.[68] For instance, in the case of a young man who had raped a pre-pubescent girl, the judge focused more on the parental responsibility of the mother (for leaving the daughter on her own) than on the young man's criminal act. The mother had asked her daughter to sleep at one of her relative's place; the daughter was on her way there after going to see a dance when she was abducted and raped. The judge ruled that the girl had not been taken out of custody as, at that time, she was not in custody; and the young man had not committed rape, but intercourse. He was thus sentenced to a caning of ten strokes with a light cane.

Siti and her colleagues sang about such affronts to women, drawing attention not only to the miscarriage of justice in the courts, but also to the behaviour of men within and outside of Ng'ambo. One of Siti's songs, which is still sung today, narrates the true story of a man named Kijiti (literally, 'a little stick', possibly a derogatory euphemism) who raped and murdered a woman. She had come over from Dar es Salaam to visit her friends in Zanzibar. She went for a night out with some of her friends, among them Sumaili and binti Subeiti who

---

[67] Ibid.

[68] Ibid., pp. 195–209. And not just in Zanzibar: 'During the colonial era, women and the poor became increasingly alienated from religious, customary, and civil courts throughout the British African colonies.' Ibid., p. 196.

had organised the party and had brought along some alcohol. The woman was raped and murdered by Kijiti who was then taken into custody by the police but managed to escape and flee to Dar es Salaam. When the case went to court, Sumaili and binti Subeiti testified against Kijiti as witnesses. The judge, however, ruled that the two women who had organised the party and served alcohol were guilty of the murder of their friend and should be imprisoned. Siti and her band composed the song, *Kijiti*, as a response to the judge's gender bias and a patronising attitude of treating women like children who need to be controlled and taught manners. A stanza states (my translation):[69]

> These are amazing actions:
>   the more we consider them, the more incredible they seem –
> Kijiti has murdered a human being
>   who carried another in her womb –
> Yet he has safely crossed the river:
>   it's the witnesses who have drowned.

It is extremely unlikely – given the class, linguistic and geographic divide – that the colonial officials and administrators were aware of Siti's comments about their judiciary. However, that is a moot point, as of far greater significance was the role that Siti's band played in reinforcing Ng'ambo identity through its songs, discussions and even the sharing of narratives and stories about the townspeople themselves. The latter's grievances were channelled through songs and ways of facing the challenges of their reality aired. Siti's popularity and fame grew through the 1920s, culminating in the band's journey across the ocean to Mumbai (Bombay) in March 1928 (coincidentally, at the height of the Ground Rent Strike in Zanzibar) to make gramophone records of her songs under the label of His Master's Voice (HMV). The distribution and sale of the records made Siti famous well beyond Zanzibar, enabling her to achieve what Sanga terms a 'stardom status' internationally. The recording project 'made her music circulate throughout East Africa and this fame increased exponentially with the resulting invitations, visits and live performances in these other places.'[70]

---

[69] Mambo haya ni ajabu kila tukiyatazama
Kijiti kauwa mtu na tumboni mna mwana
Kijiti kavuka mto mashahidi wamezama

The song has been sung by various artistes in recent times, the most famous being Bi Kidude (d. 2013), a contemporary of Siti. Bi Kidude's rendition of *Kijiti* is available on YouTube.

[70] Sanga, 2016, pp. 34, 41.

CONCLUSION

A dominant trait that comes through the biographies of Siti and Salme is their willingness to seize opportunities to improve the quality of their lives and of those close to them. For Salme, living in a foreign land, her children were her closest family; for Siti, living in her own country (but under colonial control) those close to her were her family but also her friends, neighbours and the community in Ng'ambo. It is telling that, despite her fame, Siti continued to live in Ng'ambo out of choice, whereas Salme had to move from town to town in Germany (at least during the first two decades) to enable her to provide for the welfare of her children. In the process of fulfilling their goals, each employed her agency to engage with social, economic and political factors affecting them and their people. Each transcended expectations: Siti, in being the first woman singer south of the Sahara to sing her songs on gramophone records; Salme, as the first Arab woman in the nineteenth century to publish her memoirs in Europe. Behind each of these twin accolades lay resolve, determination and sacrifice, probably doubly so for them as women. This is reflected in Robert's perception of Siti's personality given in his fulsome biography (my translation):

> If Siti had taken seriously [her rivals' smears about] her appearance, she would have considered herself incapable of any action; she would not have done a single good deed if she had looked at her black skin and thought that she deserved to be forgotten; she would not have been remembered by anyone if she had considered herself inferior; she would not have gained in stature; and if she had not attempted to face life's challenges, she would never have received answers to her (own) questions.[71]

And, as already noted, similar sentiments could be expressed about Salme's crucial decision not to return to Zanzibar after her husband's death. Her writings and subsequent stature flow from that decision. Both women exercised their agency as – to borrow McNay's words – 'the capacity for autonomous action in the face of often overwhelming cultural sanctions and structural inequalities'.[72]

The legacy of Salme and Siti is observable through their families, their works, their influence. Both have left descendants who are now at least in their fourth, if not the fifth and sixth generations. The lives of Salme's own children have been documented, particularly that of her son, Rudolph Said-Ruete.[73] Interestingly,

---

[71] Robert, 1967, pp. 49–50.
[72] McNay, 2000, p. 10, cited in Burke, 2012, p. 122.
[73] Ruite, 1993, pp. 109–40. Her descendants are said to reside in Germany, Holland, Brazil and Zanzibar: '. . . further evidence of her global legacy' (Maxwell, 2015, p. 45).

one of Siti's descendants – her great grandson, Muharam Mohammed – is a *taarab* singer in Zanzibar.

Inevitably, Salme's and Siti's respective historical periods and spheres of residence have shaped the nature of their works and legacy. Salme wrote mainly for the North (or the West, as we might say today) while also permitting some direct insight into her personality, thoughts and struggles; Siti focused on the challenges of local realities, created and abetted, to a large extent, by the colonial administration and a class system which favoured the wealthier segment of society at the expense of the others, especially the poor. The texts of both women – the prose writings of Salme and the songs of Siti – have enabled scholars to understand the issues of their respective periods and, more importantly, to recognise the value of their status and struggles as women. They show Salme as a single mother raising three children in a foreign land, and opting to do so on a matter of principle; Siti as a village woman who navigates through a class conscious, partly colonial and partly patriarchal society, to rise to a unique position of acclaim and fame for a woman as a recording artiste in sub-Saharan Africa.

The legacy of the two women in their country of birth has moved at different paces. Although Barghash is said to have been quietly pleased with his sister's autobiography[74] there was little sign of reconciliation from him nor from his immediate successors. It was not until 1929 – five years after her mother's death – that Salme's son, Rudolph Said-Ruete, was awarded the Brilliant Star of Zanzibar (second class) by the Sultan of Zanzibar, Sayyid Khalifa ibn Harub ibn Thuwayn (d. 1960), who, in 1932, also conferred on Rupert the title of 'Sayyid'.[75] Both these acts took place abroad during the sultan's visit to Europe. Despite these and other gestures, however, Sayyid Khalifa seemed incapable of accepting Salme's action and of forgiving her, even posthumously. For the acting British Resident had reported in 1941 to have been told by the sultan 'that the elopement of Mr Ruete's mother was and still is regarded by the Arabs as a shameful affair and that they prefer not to be reminded of it.'[76] Nonetheless, Salme as a historical figure had begun to re-enter Zanzibar through her personal objects and artefacts. In 1937, Rudolph had donated to the Zanzibar Museum a shawl worn by Salme when she had left Zanzibar for the first time in 1866, as well as a gold signet ring; the museum had also acknowledged in its annual report for 1937 receiving other personal artefacts of the princess for display.[77] Decades later, when the Al Bu Said dynasty itself had been overthrown in the Zanzibar Revolution of 1964, and the former sultan's palace was renamed the People's

---

[74] Ruite, 1993, p. 521.
[75] Ibid., p. 131.
[76] Ibid., p. 140.
[77] Ibid., p. 133.

Palace, a 'Princess Salme Room' was created in 1994 to exhibit even more of Salme's personal possessions and artefacts. This has now been superseded, since 2015, by a small but vibrant 'Princess Salme Museum' at Hurumzi in Zanzibar Stone Town that exhibits a more in-depth narrative of Salme's life in videos, a range of artefacts, documents and a display of books (the *Memoirs* among them); the curator, Said el-Gheithy, also organises periodic public lectures on the life of Princess Salme.

Unlike Salme, Siti always remained 'a home player' throughout her life. Her legacy is thus more tangibly woven into the *taarab* music of East Africa in general, and of the islands, in particular. Her songs have continued to be sung by generations of *taarab* artistes, most notably by her then younger contemporary Bi Kidude (d. 2013) and by Siti's own great grandson. Since her death, Siti has gradually grown into an icon symbolising not only female artistry, but also a feminism underlined by principles and courage. According to Sanga, Robert characterises Siti as 'a symbol of East African identity (and African identity more generally), a role model for subverting traditional and oppressive gender roles, and an exemplar of ethical life in East African colonial context.'[78] Nearly four decades after her death, members of the Tanzania Media Women's Association paid tribute (in 1988) to Siti's advocacy of improving women's position in society by naming their newsletter, *Sauti ya Siti* ('The Voice of Siti'), which is now only available online.

BIBLIOGRAPHY

Allen, J. W. T. 1971. *Tendi: six examples of a Swahili classical verse form with translations and notes*. London: Heinemann Educational.

Askew, Kelly M. 1999. 'Female Circles and Male Lines: Gender Dynamics along the Swahili Coast', *Africa Today*, 46, nos. 3–4, Islam in Africa (Summer–Autumn 1999), pp. 67–102.

Biersteker, Ann. 1991. 'Language, Poetry, and Power: A Reconsideration of "Utendi wa Mwana Kupona"', in Kenneth W. Harrow (ed.), *Faces of Islam in African Literature*. Portsmouth, NH: Heinemann, pp. 59–77.

Burke, Kelsy C. 2012. 'Women's Agency in Gender-Traditional Religions: A Review of Four Approaches', *Sociology Compass*, 6:2, pp. 122–33, 10.1111/j.1751-9020. 2011.00439.x.

Decker, Corrie. 2014. *Mobilizing Zanzibari Women: The Struggle for Respectability and Self-reliance in Colonial East Africa*. New York: Palgrave Macmillan.

Fair, Laura. 2013. *Historia ya Jamii ya Zanzibar na Nyimbo za Siti binti Saad* [A Social History of Zanzibar and the Songs of Siti binti Saad], Kimani Njogu, trans. Nairobi: Twaweza Communications.

---

[78] Robert, 2016, p. 34.

Fair, Laura. 2001. *Pastimes and Politics. Culture, Community, and Identity in Post-Abolition Urban Zanzibar, 1890–1945*. Athens, OH: Ohio State University Press.

Folkers, Antoni and Iga Perzyna. 2019. *Ng'ambo Atlas. Historic Urban Landscape of Zanzibar Town*. Zanzibar: Department of Rural and Urban Planning Zanzibar.

Gray, Sir John Milner. 1961. 'Zanzibar Local Histories, Part II', *Swahili* 31, pp. 11–139.

Koehler, Julia. 2016. 'Kind Girls, Evil Sisters, And Wise Women: Coded Gender Discourse in Literary Tales by German Women in the Nineteenth Century'. Wayne State University Dissertation Paper 1402.

Kresse, Kai. 2007. *Philosophising in Mombasa. Knowledge, Islam and Intellectual Practice on the Swahili Coast*. Edinburgh: Edinburgh University Press for the International African Institute, London.

Liebst, Michelle. 2014. 'African workers and the Universities' Mission to Central Africa in Zanzibar, 1864–1900', *Journal of Eastern African Studies*, 8:3, pp. 366–81, DOI: 10.1080/17531055.2014.922279.

Loimeier, Roman. 2009. '*Baraza* as Markers of Time in Zanzibar', in Kjersti Larsen (ed.), *Knowledge, Renewal and Religion. Repositioning and changing ideological and material circumstances among the Swahili on the East African coast*. Uppsala: Nordiska Afrikainstitutet.

McNay, Lois. 2000. *Gender and Agency: Reconfiguring the Subject in Feminist and Social Theory*. Malden, MA: Polity Press.

Matola, S. M. Shabaan and W. H. Whiteley. 1966. *Waimbaji wa juzi*. Dar es Salaam: Chuo cha Uchunguzi wa Lugha va Kiswahili.

Maxwell, Katherine. 2015. 'Sayyida Salme/Emily Ruete: Knowledge Flows in an Age of Steam, Print and Empire', *Global Societies Journal*, 3, pp. 37–48.

Oruc, Firat. 2019. 'Transoceanic Orientalism and Embodied Translation in Sayyida Salme/Emily Ruete's Memoirs', *Journal of Women of the Middle East and the Islamic World*, 17, pp. 1–20.

Pouwels, Randall L. 1987. *Horn and Crescent. Cultural Change and Traditional Islam on the East African Coast, 800–1900*. Cambridge: Cambridge University Press.

Prestholdt, Jeremy. 2019. 'The Island as Nexus: Zanzibar in the Nineteenth Century' in Toyin Falola, Joseph Parrott and Danielle Porter Sanchez (eds), *African Islands: Leading Edges of Empire and Globalization*. Rochester, NY: University of Rochester Press.

Prestholdt, Jeremy. 2018. 'Zanzibar, the Indian Ocean, and Nineteenth-Century Global Interface', in Burkhard Schnepel and E. A. Alpers (eds), *Connectivity in Motion: Island Hubs in the Indian Ocean World*. London: Palgrave (Palgrave Series in Indian Ocean World Studies).

Prestholdt, Jeremy. 2014. 'From Zanzibar to Beirut: Sayyida Salme bint Said and the Tensions of Cosmopolitanism', in James L. Gelvin and Nile Green (eds), *Global Muslims in the Age of Steam and Print*. Berkeley: University of California Press.

Robert, Shaaban bin. 1967 [1958]. *Wasifu wa Siti binti Saad* [The Biography of Siti binti Saad]. Nelson: Nairobi. First published as supplement to No. 28/1 of *East African Swahili Committee Journal*, 1958.

Ruete, Sayyida Salme/Emily. 1993. *An Arabian Princess between Two Worlds: Memoirs, Letters Home, Sequels to the Memoirs, and Syrian Customs and Usages*, E. van Donzel, ed. New York: Brill.

Sanga, Imani. 2016. 'The Archiving of Siti binti Saad and her Engagement with the Music Industry in Shaaban Robert's *Wasifu wa Siti binti Saad*', *Eastern African Literary and Cultural Studies*, vol. 1–2, pp. 34–44.

Strobel, Margaret. 1979. *Muslim Women in Mombasa, 1890–1975*. New Haven and London: Yale University Press.

Verne, Julia. 2012. *Living Translocality. Space, Culture and Economy in Contemporary Swahili Trade*. Stuttgart: Franz Steiner Verlag.

CHAPTER 6

Exploring the Geographies and Locales in Shaykh Jamali Dehlawi's Siyar al-'ārifīn (The Virtues of Gnostics)

GULFISHAN KHAN

INTRODUCTION: CONTEXTUALISING ḤĀMID B. FAḌL ALLĀH DEHLAWI AS AN INDO-PERSIAN SUFI POET

This chapter aims to present the travel experiences of Ḥāmid b. Faḍl Allāh, an Indo-Persian poet, traveller and a Sufi biographer of early modern South Asia who visited a number of countries of Asia and Africa during the last quarter of the fifteenth century. To later generations of Indian historians and scholars he became known as Shaykh Jamali Dehlawi, sometimes Shaykh Jamali Kanboh or, more often, simply as Shaykh Jamali. A scholar and a Sufi shaykh, Jamali referred to himself most of the time as a dervish ('*derwish*'), an appellation considered synonymous with a Sufi shaykh in the contemporary historical and hagiographical literature.

Jamali's fame rests on his two accomplishments: one literary, the other architectural; the former as a distinguished Sufi poet and the latter through his self-constructed *Khānaqāh*-cum-tomb along with a mosque, known as the Jamali Kamali mosque, standing in the Mehrauli Archaeological Park, adjacent to the Quṭb Minar World Heritage Site Complex in New Delhi.[1] Perhaps of

---

[1] The main primary sources used in the first part of the essay are 'Abd al-Qādir Badā'ūni's *Muntakhab al-tawārikh*, *Tārikh-i Khān-i-jahāni wa Makhzan-i-Afghāni* of Afghan historian Ni'mat Allah ibn Habib Allah Harawi, *Tārikh-i-Shāhi* (*Tārikh-i-Salātin-i-Afāghina*) of another Afghan historian Ahmad Yadgar and *Akhbār al-akhyār* of Shaykh 'Abd al-Haqq Muhaddith Dihlawi completed in 1618, *Kalimāt al-Sādiqain* (Discourses of the Truthful) and *Ṭabaqāt-i-Shāhjahāni* of Muhammad Sadiq Hamadani Dehlawi Kashmiri compiled in 1023/1614 and early1630s respectively. The first part is a revised version of my paper 'Shaikh Jamali Dehlawi: The Indo-Persian Sufi Poet,' M. Sundriyal and Juan Manuel E. Baztan eds. *Lo divino y lo humano: poetas misticos de India y de Espana en la modernidad temprana*, Jawaharlal Nehru University, New Delhi, 2017 pp. 41–56. The second part is based on *Siyar al-'ārifīn* (The Virtues of Gnostics) supplemented by contemporary account called *Bāburnāma*

equal significance was the composition of an autobiographical memoir-cum-hagiographical account entitled *Siyar al-ʿārifīn* (The Virtues of Gnostics) a 'spiritual journey of a mystic', which he has bequeathed to posterity as a record of his thoughts, observations, experiences and aspirations of an educated elite in the early modern era.[2] Thus, a premier literary figure of the period, he was also one of the earliest Sufi hagiographers. While Shaykh Jamali's literary fame comes from his poetry, it also rests upon his comprehensive biographical account, namely the above-mentioned *Siyar al-ʿārifīn*, which remains his central critical production in Persian, the then language of political administration, commerce, literature, belles-lettres and polite social intercourse. The work, composed in the 1530s, in the twilight years of the author's life, is dedicated to Nāṣir al-Dīn Muḥammad Humāyūn Padishah (d. 963/1556), the second Mughal emperor, who ruled intermittently in India and (modern) Afghanistan from 937/1531 to 947/1540, and from 952/1545 to 963/1556. It is a memoir of Indian mystics and an authentic source for the biography of the representative Sufi saints of India, later identified as Chishtiyya and Suhrawardiyya saints of India. Thus, Jamali wrote about the most venerable saints who lived in the historical period when the main Sufi orders called *silsila* (orders, literally, 'chain'), as a principle of legitimising Sufi activity and teaching, were formed.

A study of Shaykh Jamali's literary and architectural contribution should show that he must be regarded a harbinger of the Perso-Islamic culture which witnessed its full flowering in the high Mughal era. A perusal of the *tazkira*, *Siyar al-ʿārifīn* provides strong evidence of lively transregional Sufi networks of intellectual and social relationship between the Sufi shaykhs, *ʿulamāʾ* (Islamic religious scholars), and bureaucrats of Delhi, Multan, Shiraz, Baghdad, Herat and Hijaz as well as other parts of the Indian Ocean World. Jamali's comprehensive biographical account, though a personalised one, offers a highly complex and multifaceted view of Sufi communities of the Indian Ocean, with their closely knit social networks, intellectual concerns, religious authority and the crucial role of patronage and philanthropy. A careful appraisal of Jamali's multifarious religious, social and intellectual activities shows a dynamic process of cultural exchange at work in the Persianate and Arabic cultural zone where people, ideas, goods, books and letters moved back and forth in the entire zone.

memoirs of Zahīr al-Dīn Muḥammad Babur (886–937/1483–1530), the founder of the Timurid-Mughal Empire of India. Brown, 1968, p. 29; Khan, 2016; Zaweed, 2015; Asher, 2017.

[2] There exist various manuscripts as well as printed editions of the *Siyar al-ʿārifīn*, For details, Storey, 1953, pp. 969–71. For the present article I have utilised the following two manuscripts: Shaykh Jamali, *Siyar al-ʿārifīn*, *Farsiya Tazkirat al-Awliya*, 22/11, Habib Ganj Collection, Maulana Azad Library, Aligarh Muslim University. Another manuscript Number 115 dated 964 A.H./dated 1556-7 preserved in the John Rylands University Library, University of Manchester, UK., of which a rotograph number 173, is available in the Seminar Library of the Department of History, Aligarh Muslim University. In this article all the references are to the same Rotorograph Number 173.

However, in this respect an important aspect to be noted is that while migration from the Islamic world to India was a regular feature of medieval Indian life, Shaykh Jamali remains an exception in that he travelled outside India in the opposite direction, again not in search of patronage and employment but boundless intellectual curiosity and devotion to the Almighty.

He was a progenitor of the Indo-Islamic culture that flourished later; therefore, Jamali's intellectual contribution and literary attainments must be viewed against the backdrop of dynamic socio-cultural milieux of contemporary India. Ideally, what is required is to construct a geographical and historical landscape behind Jamali's life in Delhi and beyond. Since the purpose of the paper is not to assess him as a poet and litterateur, only a broad profile of the life of the poet and his literary works is presented in an attempt to appreciate Jamali's worldview as embodied in his *Siyar al-'ārifīn*. Until now published scholarship on Jamali is confined mainly to Persian and Urdu.[3]

A Sufi poet and a polymath, Jamali was a widely travelled man of his age who had acquired vast experience of the wider world through extensive travelling and social interaction with scholars (*ulama*), Sufi shaykhs, poets and men of learning and letters. He was a man endowed with a sharp intellectual curiosity, spiritual quest and an irresistible desire to see and experience the world. He was a prolific writer and a Sufi thinker of great standing and most of the biographical information about the author-poet is embodied in his own writings, which are available in elegant poetry and his mostly unexplored prose works. He is described in the most effusive terms by the sixteenth-century scholar and historian at the court of Akbar, 'Abd al-Qādir Badā'ūnī (1540–1615), as well as by the Afghan historians Ahmad Yādgar and Ni'mat Allah ibn Habib Allāh Harawi, the authors of *Tārikh-i-Shāhi* and *Tārikh-i Khān-i-jahāni wa Makhzan-i-Afghāni* respectively. They portrayed him as a literary genius whose literary fame, in their perception, was linked to his Sufi stature as well. Shaykh 'Abd al-Ḥaqq Muḥaddith Dihlawī (958–1052/1551–1642), a well-known hadith scholar and Sufi of Akbar and Jahangir's reign and Muḥammad Ṣādiq Kashmiri Hamadāni, a seventeenth-century Sufi scholar, who enjoys a rare distinction of being a prosopographer as well as a topographer of Delhi, also described Jamali in the most fulsome terms. They considered Jamali a talented writer and poet whose writings were rich and multifaceted.

Later commentators report on Jamali's wide-ranging transnational travels in the Islamic world with snippets of his memorable encounters with prominent Sufi shaykhs, learned men and influential elites. They noted that he embarked on his journey for the two holy cities of Mecca and Medina (*Ḥaramayn Sharifayn*) to

---

[3] Qadiri and Rashidi, 1976, pp. 19–138. H. S. Rashidi also presents a comprehensive study of the Sufi poet and his literary contribution and historical background of the period.

perform the Hajj pilgrimage through the land route and from there he proceeded to the lands of Maghreb as well as other destinations. On his homebound journey he visited Bait al-Muqaddas (Jerusalem), Turkey, Baghdad and thence Shiraz and Herat. Sultan Husayn Mirza of Herat and his learned minister and state figure Mir Niẓām al-Dīn ʿAlī Shīr Navāʾī (844–906/1441–1501), also known as Mīr ʿAlī Shīr, also showed great regard for him. Clearly, Jamali became a legend whose peregrinations continued to be narrated and more specifically his stay in the Timurid cosmopolis and meeting with Jami entered the realm of popular memory in Mughal India. Modern scholar Anna Suvorora describes a popular anecdote related by a sixteenth-century Afghan historian Muḥammad Kabir bin Shah Ismāʿīl in his book *Fasāna-i-Shāhān-Hind* that Jamali was dressed as a wandering ascetic, his head was shaved and his body was smeared with ashes. He was taken for an ordinary cadging *qalandar* (a wandering ecstatic dervish) and he was mocked for his appearance and rather impolitely asked what the difference was between him, Jamali, and a donkey. The guest replied with a joke that the difference was in the skin, because the donkey wore it all its life and the *qalandar* in order to sit on it. Then Jamali, bearing in mind that the guise of a *qalandar* conceals the piety and intensity of mystic experience, recited his celebrated line: 'The dust of thy lane has settled on my body like a garment' ('*Mara zi khak-i kuyat pirahan ast bar tan*'). Here Jami at last understood that his visitor was Jamali himself, and treated him with great respect, asking him to explain some Hindi words in the verses of Amir Khusrow and Amir Hasan.[4] Later authors continued to relate several anecdotes about his worldwide travels and global and local experiences; in particular they recounted his meeting and intellectual interaction with Jami. Jami's literary reputation as an extraordinary and outstanding scholar and his high stature as a Sufi thinker granted him a celebrity status in Central Asia, Transoxiana and India at the same time. Jami's persona and his erudite mystical and didactic works had become an integral part of Indo-Muslim elite's cultural, devotional and religious discourses which became manifest in varied forms of literary and artistic expression as well.[5]

Delhi, Jamali's City

The lifestory of Shaykh Jamali belongs to the last quarter of the fifteenth century and first three-and-a-half decades of the sixteenth century. The centre of Jamali's spiritual and literary activities was Delhi. He described Delhi as his

---

[4] Suvorora, 2004, p. 193.
[5] Topsfield, 2012, p 103. Jami's *Bahāristān* (Garden of Spring) composed in 1487, was illustrated for Emperor Akbar (r. 1556–1605) at Lahore in 1595, and is described by the art historian Andrew Topsfield as 'the high point of Mughal luxury manuscript production achieved towards the end of his reign'.

beloved homeland as well as a place of his permanent residence (*watan-i-ma'lūf*) and reverentially called it *Ḥaḍrat-i-Dehli* meaning majestic or exalted, a joyous city, an 'abode of happiness' and a 'city of light, famous far and wide'. Delhi was the city where he grew up, studied, flourished and produced a variety of prose and poetry. He was probably born there around 1460, but the exact date and place of birth cannot be determined as Shaykh Jamali did not mention anything about his early life and parentage. Later biographers like 'Abd al-Ḥaqq and Ṣādiq Dehlawi wrote that he lost his father early in his childhood. After the death of his father Jamali sought guidance from the Multan-born Shaykh Sama' al-din, an erudite and learned Sufi saint. He was one of the most important factors in shaping Jamali's Sufi and poetic personality, and for his Sufi shaykh and mentor Jamali entertained a profound reverence and deepest regard throughout his life.[6] Like Amīr Khusraw Dihlavī (651–725/1253–1325), Jamali began his *Siyar al-'arifin* with prayers for the safety, security and continued prosperity of its citizens. He implores Omnipotent thus in the brief prologue: 'May the Almighty Allah protect its foundations. May Allah the Most Beneficent keep its citizens safe from calamities forever.' He cited Amīr Khusraw's literary productions in the course of his narrative while describing the urban architectural landmarks of Delhi. In his description of a public water tank called Hauz-i-Shamsi, built by Sultan Shams al-Dīn Iltutmish, Jamali cited *Qiranus Sa'dayn* (Conjunction of the Two Auspicious Planets), which is Khusraw's long narrative poem called *mathnawi* wherein the versatile poet lavishly praises Delhi's architectural monuments. Like Khusraw he was an eyewitness to the reigns of five kings, three Lodi sultans and the two early Mughals. The personality of the fourteenth-century Sufi poet and his fertile thoughts as expressed in his literary and historical works would have served as a great source of inspiration and hence to be emulated. Khusraw, the greatest Indo-Persian poet of the sultanate period, was an exemplar of close interaction between royal courts, Sufi circles and the vigorous intellectual climate of the city, and therefore a source of creativity for Jamali.[7]

The historic city had been the seat of the sultanate of Delhi for more than three centuries (thirteenth to fifteenth) when Jamali was recording his reminiscences; therefore Jamali called it *dār al khilāfā-i-Hindustān*, India's 'seat of Caliphate'. Under the aegis of sultans, Delhi, with its flourishing educational institutions, burgeoning royal courts which offered patronage to scholars and men of letters and learning, and a vibrant economy and court, generated

---

[6] On the life of Shaykh Sama' al-Din see the detailed biographical account *Siyar al-'arifin* folios 141–150; Dehlawi 1988, pp. 104–6. Dehlawi, 2013, vol. 2, pp. 10–11. For more information on Muhammad Sadiq Dehlawi Kashmiri Hamadani, see Khan, 2017.

[7] Abū l-Ḥasan Amīr Khusraw Dihlawi (651–725/1253–1325) was the greatest Indo-Persian poet of the sultanate period. He was widely known among the contemporary Sufi circles for his devotion to his Chishti Ṣūfi-Shaykh Niẓām al-Dīn Awliyā'. A classical work on him remains Wahid, 1974; Dehlawi Amir Khusrau, 1918.

commerce and had become an established metropolis par excellence.[8] It is to be noted that in this period the monarchs of the Pashtun-descended Lodi dynasty (855/1451–932/1526) and Sūri rulers (947/1540–962/1555) made vigorous efforts to revive the city's status as they commenced extensive building activities in Delhi. Architectural projects sponsored by the sultans and their ambitious nobles included palaces, marketplaces, strong forts, pleasure gardens, baolis, tombs and mosques which proliferated throughout the landscape of the historic city (Fig. 6.1). The period is noted for its impressive funerary architecture such as the garden-tombs of Sayyid and Lodi sultans, Bahlul and his son and successor Sikandar, and a series of mosques such as the Masjid-i-nau at Bara Gumbad, Moth ki Masjid, Jamala Mosque and Qila-i-Kuhna Mosque. Percy Brown, the art historian, thought very highly of the striking uniqueness of the designs of the above-mentioned mosques, especially the mosque of Miʾān Bhuʾa, now known as Moth ki Masjid, and remarked that, 'There was evidently a very talented group of craftsmen engaged in this art during the fifteenth century, reminiscent of that much greater school of artists who, at about at the same time were perpetuating wonders in similar technique on the walls of Alhambra in Spain.'[9]

The court of Sikandar Lodi was a major centre of literary production in Persian, encompassing works of poetry, art, music, medical treatises, Sufi manuals, lexicons, biographical accounts and historical works.[10] The revival of Delhi was accelerated under the reigns of the first two Mughal rulers, Emperor Babur and Humāyūn. Delhi had become a foremost Sufi centre as well as a seat of political power. Out of the thirteen Sufi shaykhs discussed by Jamali, six of them lived and preached in Delhi, such as Shaykh Quṭb al-Dīn Bakhtiyār Kaki Ushi (d. 1235), Shaykh Niẓām al-Dīn Muḥammad Badaʾūnī (636/1238–725/1325) and Naṣīr al-Dīn Maḥmūd 'Chirāgh-i Dihlī' (d. 757/1356), and thus shaped much of the religious life and intellectual culture of the city. Therefore, in his self-view Jamali's spiritual and literary activities were expressions of the effervescent cultural life of the celebrated city.[11]

'JAMALI: A MAN OF LETTERS'

As a poet and a religious savant Jamali enjoyed close association with the Lodi Afghans (1451–1526) who ruled over northern India from the middle of the fifteenth century until the first quarter of the sixteenth century. Due to his literary fame he was invited by Sultan Sikandar Shah Lodi (r. 1489–1517) who

---

[8] Siddiqui, 2012, pp. 28 and 70–100; Aquil, 2008.
[9] Brown, 1968, p. 29; Digby, 1975.
[10] Husaini, 1988.
[11] Some of his poems expressing his love for Delhi are found in *Mathnawi-yi Mihr-u-Mah* (The Sun and the Moon). Dehlawi, 1974. One such poem is also quoted in Pello, 2014, p 167.

Figure 6.1 An 1860 view by Colonel Robert Smith of the ruins of the Qutb complex of ancient Dehli with the Jamali Kamali Mosque in the distance. Digital image courtesy of Harvard Fine Arts Library's Digital Images and Slides Collection.

appointed Jamali to the high position of poet-laureate of his court. Jamali too reciprocated and appreciated Sikandar Lodi, for providing a charismatic leadership to the Afghans and described him as a man of cultivated manners, amicable nature and literary taste. On the death of his benefactor in 923/1517, the poet paid rich emotional tribute to his patron-king expressing his gratitude in the form of touching elegies. Describing the amiable qualities of the personality of the erstwhile Afghan despot, Jamali wrote that he was gifted with exceptional qualities and a noble disposition and above all, he was also favourably inclined towards men of learning and piety. At the same time, Jamali also offered serious reflections on the Afghan polity after the death of a capable ruler like Sikandar. In his view Sultan Sikandar's son and successor Sultan Ibrahim Lodi (r. 1517–1526) lacked those character traits of his father and, being misled by his own flattering courtiers, set aside a highly accomplished prime minister like Masnad-i-ʿAli ibn Khawwāṣ Khan whom he referred to by his popular name Miʾān Bhuʾā (d. 958/1551). He lamented deeply the dismissal of Miʾān Bhuʾā by Ibrahim Lodi, which was an impolitic decision as he committed no breach of conduct.

On the other hand, in Jamali's considered opinion Miʾān Bhuʾā was an immense source of stability in the disorderly Afghan polity. Miʾān Bhuʾā was a prime minister (Wazir and Ṣadr) who was also adept in learning and scholarship, and enjoyed prestige for his administrative talent, strong sense of justice and patronage of learning and men of piety. Disunity among the Afghan chiefs after the demise of a benevolent ruler like Sikandar, disgrace and humiliation of a first-rate administrator Wazir Mi'ān Bhu'ā, in view of the observer, led to the ultimate ruin and the end of Indo-Afghan polity.[12] Later, following the defeat of Ibrahim Lodi, Jamali joined the court of Zaḥīr al-Dīn Muḥammad Babur Padishah (r. 932–7/1526–30), the founder of the Mughal Empire with whom he enjoyed intimacy and cordial relations and dedicated many of his poetic compositions. Perhaps Jamali was a man who was skilled in accomplishments that mattered most to the Persianised Islamised Turco-Mongol aristocrat as were the Mughals: poetry, religion and war. Therefore, it was only natural that Jamali was entertained lavishly by the first two Mughal emperors as well. It was during Humāyūn's Gujarat campaigns that Jamali, who accompanied him on the expedition, died at Ahmadabad on 10, Dhū l-Qa'da 942/1 May 1536.

The event of the sad demise of Jamali at Ahmadabad was noted by the Indo-Persian historian 'Abd al-Qādir Badā'ūnī (1540–1615): 'And in this year Shaikh Jamali Kanbawi of Delhi left this transitory world for the kingdom of eternity. A chronogram has been invented to commemorate this in the words *Khusrau-i-Hind buda* (He was the Khusrau of Hindustan).'[13] His mortal remains were brought to Delhi where the body was laid to rest in the chamber he had previously built in 1528–9. His residence along with the mosque was commissioned by the poet during his lifetime. Shaikh 'Abd al-Ḥaqq Muḥaddith Dihlawī, the biographer of saints of Mughal India wrote:

> His tomb (*maqbara*) is located in the premises of Khwaja Bakhtiyar Kaki [Shaykh Quṭb al-Din Bakhtiyār Kaki Ushi, d. 1235]. May his grave be hallowed. It is a pleasant and graceful building which the saint got constructed (*ba-huzur-i-khud*, lit. in his presence) himself. The [square] chamber (*khana*) in which his grave is located was his dwelling place (*maskan*) during his life time. (*Akhbār al-Akhyār*, 1914, 221–2)[14] (Fig. 6.2)

The present square-chamber-tomb would have served as his *aramgah* and *khwabgah* both, that is where the poet-saint would have worked and rested. The mosque was meant for offering prayers while some part of the large complex would have been used as *Khānaqāh* for some spiritual and literary activities of his poetic friends and his Sufi circles. (Figs 6.3 and 6.4) The entire tomb complex would have served as a residential centre for his intellectual and mystical activities as well as for the comforts of his family members. For Shaykh Jamali was a family man and a dedicated father who had three sons whom he provided with

---

[12] *Siyar al-'ārifin* folio 79. Masnad-i-'Āli called Mian Bhua (d. 958/1551) was the eldest son of Masnad-i-'Āli Khawwās Khan both Wazirs in succession. For details see, Mushtaqi, 2002, pp. 79–80. Siddiqui, 1993, pp. 81–4.
[13] *Badā'ūnī*, 1868, p. 347.
[14] 'Dehlawi, 1914, pp. 221–2; Yādgār, 1939, pp. 47–8; Harawi, 1960, vol. 1, pp. 210–11.

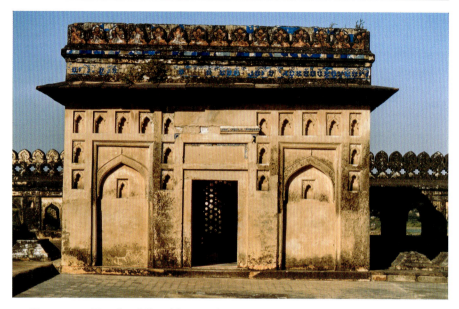

Figure 6.2 Tomb of Shaykh Jamali, exterior view. Courtesy: Stuart Cary Welch Islamic and South Asian Photograph Collection, Special Collections, Fine Arts Library, Harvard University.

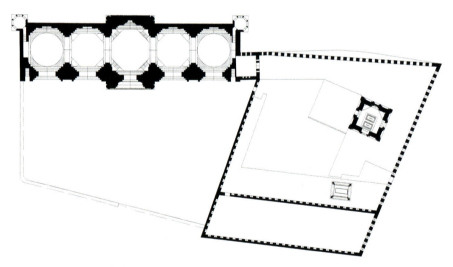

Figure 6.3 Ground plan of the mosque and the tomb of Shaykh Jamali Kanbuh (after the Archaeological Survey of India). Courtesy Merklinger Collection, Special Collections, Fine Arts Library, Harvard University.

Figure 6.4 Mosque of Shaykh Jamali, exterior view, 1885. Photography by Henry Hardy Cole.

an excellent education suitable for aristocratic gentlemen, and in their youth they distinguished themselves as men of letters and learning. One of them, named Shaykh Hasan, died at a young age, for whom the poet wrote a poignant elegy (*marthiya*). His other son ʿAbd al-Ḥayy Ḥayatī (d. 959/1551–2), who was also his successor at his *Khanaqah* (*sahib-i-sajjada*), was 'adorned with the excellences of knowledge and poetics'.[15] He was a courtier and a boon companion of Islam Shah (r. 1545–54) and wrote a history of the reign of Islam Shah, which unfortunately has not survived. He is lying buried in the precincts of his father's tomb-complex. His eldest son Shaykh Gadai (d. 976/1568–69) is more famous as he was a well-known bureaucrat who occupied the influential position of *Sadr al-Sudur* (the controller of land grants and stipends for religious purposes), under the Mughal Emperor Akbar (r. 1556–1605).[16]

A Sufi Poet: 'Khusraw the Second'

It is to be noted that the cultivation of letters, especially the art of poetics, was one of the major preoccupations of the Sufi saints who were also men of learning and knowledge. Jamali also combined in his person poetic talent with a dervish bent of mind. Unlike his prose, his poetry tells much about his emotional life. He left a wide-ranging collection of his poems called *dīwān*, which contains his lyrics called *ghazals* and odes (*qasidah*). Historian Badāʾūnī (1540–1615) also mentioned his voluminous *diwan*, which contained more than eight or nine thousand verses. Badāʾūnī considered him one of the distinguished court poets of Sultan Sikandar, who also showed his literary compositions to him. In view of

---

[15] *Badauni*, 1868, p. 410; Dehlawi,1914, p. 229
[16] Dehlawi, 1914, p. 229

Badā'ūnī, Jamali was a distinguished man of his age. He possessed many merits, as he alone had undertaken extensive travels. Badā'ūnī specifically pointed out that Jamali was also privileged person who is said to have enjoyed a fellowship (ṣuḥbat) marked with the literary and intellectual exchanges with the exalted Sufi and renowned figure Jami. He also presented his verses to his illustrious host while at Herat and the historian also provided chosen verses (bayt) of such a poem, which is cited by later writers as well.

ما را خاک کویت پیراهنی است بر تن
آن هم ز آب دیده صد چاک تا بدامن

The dust of thy lane has settled on my body like a garment
And that too is torn from top to bottom due to my tears

طال شوقی الی منازلکم
فاسئلو عن خیالکم خبری
روز و شب مونس خیال شماست
ای با الغائبون عن نظری

The language of love decides in seconds, what words cannot convey in
 centuries.
A friend speaks to a friend in the twinkling of an eye.

It seems that Jamali's literary influence was not confined to the portals of royal courts alone; his lyrics were popular in his lifetime and were recited by the elite as well as common Indian masses. Badā'ūnī cited a beautiful bilingual (Arabic and Persian) verse of the *ghazal* that the historian noted was exceptionally popular in those days. Badā'ūnī wrote that that the following *ghazal*, which the lyricist had set to Indian music, is marvellously inspiring and popular.

طال شوقی الی منازلکمفاسئلو عن خیالکم خبری
روز و شب مونس خیال شماستایها الغائبون عن نظری

My heart's desire is fixed on thy abode
Oh thou that art long absent from my sight;
By day and night the thought of thee alone
My constant partner is, ask then thy thought.
Should'st thou desire, to bring thee news of me.[17]

It is to be noted that Jamali is one of the outstanding Indian poets, who has been styled *Khusraw-i-Sani*, 'Khusraw the Second'. It was his talent in poetics

---

[17] Badauni, 1868, p. 325; Dehlawi, 1988, pp.122–3. Dehlawi, 2013,vol. 2, pp. 58–9

that made him famous in his lifetime. Initially he composed poetry with 'Jalal' meaning 'wrath' as his nom de plume, but later he changed his pen name to 'Jamali', meaning 'splendour', on the advice of his spiritual mentor. As a poet of the Persian language, Jamali followed the rich tradition of Persian mystical poetry, a mature expression of *tasawwuf*, the mystical dimension of Islam. A scholar by temperament, he also possessed a profound knowledge of the Holy Qurʾān and hadith (traditions), and his poetry is replete with allusions to the Qurʾānic figures, events and phrases and terms. One of his verses composed in praise of the Prophet Muhammad (Peace be on him) became very popular among the elite poetic circles.

موسی ز هوش رفت به یک پرتو صفات
تو عین ذات می نگری در تبسمی

Moses lost his consciousness even at the first glance at the reflection of your attributes, O you who behold His Existence but smiled.[18]

His poetic collection (*dīwān*) comprises 9,000 lines. His poetic oeuvre consists of almost all the traditional genres of classical poetry such as *qaṣīdah* (ode) long narrative poem of internally rhyming distiches, didactic or narrative in nature (*mathnawi*), lyrics (*ghazal*), *rubāʿīyāt* (quatrain, verses having four hemistiches), *qitʿa* (*qitʿa* lit., fragment) – all forms are represented. Noteworthy among his verses is a heartfelt elegy for his son, Shaykh Hasan, who died while still young, and the other poignant elegy in the form of a *marthiya* written on the death of his liberal patron Sultan Sikandar Lodi. Apart from a *dīwān* he composed two *mathnawi* poems. One is entitled *Mirʾāt al-maʿānī* (The Mirror of Meanings) which is considered to be the finest expression of Sufi thought, and it made him immensely popular in India, Iran, Afghanistan and Central Asia, a cultural zone that could be defined as the Persianate. Written in the figurative and metaphorical language of Sufis it explains in thirty-eight chapters their ecstatic experiences, their exertions in the path of love and their union with the divine beloved concentrating on the spiritual symbolism of the beloved's body, the meaning of wine, wine-seller, and cup-bearer. In this poem Jamali shows how the mystical could be united with the Beloved through Gnostic knowledge of the formal body. It is a journey from phenomenal world into one's real self which is the Truth.[19] The other long poem is an allegorical romance entitled *Mehr wa mah* (The Sun and the Moon), and it was this same poem that was eagerly sought by Sultan Sikandar.[20] His literary works, strongly imbued with

---

[18] Dehlawi, 1914, pp. 228–9, Dehlawi, 1988, pp. 122, The above popular *ghazal* is also reproduced by Dehlawi, 2013, vol. 2, p. 59. For Shaikh Jamali, see Dehlawi, 2013, vol. II, pp. 58–9, 122

[19] Dehlawi, 2002; *Mathnawi Mirʾāt al-maʿānī*, 21/137.

[20] Dehlawi, 1974; *Badauni*, 1868, p. 323

Sufi themes and inner meanings, would have influenced the distinct literary style called Sabk-i-Hindi (Ahmad, A., 1965, 420–1).[21]

SIYAR AL-'ĀRIFĪN: NARRATING THE SUFI SHAYKHS, SCHOLARS, NETWORKS AND LOCALES

For Jamali, the poet-saint, travel (safar, a sanctified passion of Sufi shaykhs), cultivation of letters and composition of poetry, for which he possessed a versatile and vigorous talent, remained major preoccupations. Pilgrimage and migration in Islamic societies are forms of political and social activism as well. Jamali travelled all over the Muslim world in search of knowledge and for intercourse with the spiritual fraternity. He briefly mentions a visit to Sri Lanka undertaken by him during the reign of Sultan Bahlul Lodi (r. 1451–89) with the purpose of seeing Prophet Adam's sacred footprint in the rock, as Ibn Baṭṭūṭa (d. 770/1368–9), the celebrated traveller of pre-modern times had done, but the above-mentioned Moroccan traveller, he did not mention by name. The main journey undertaken by the poet-saint was to Mecca and Medina to perform Ḥajj, the annual pilgrimage, one of the five pillars of Islam and therefore of paramount importance. According to his own statement, during the course of the voyage en route to the Hijaz and in the course of the homebound journey, he visited the lands of Maghreb (Zamin-i-Maghrib), Yemen, Jerusalem, Turkey, Syria (Rum wa Sham), Iraq-i-Arab and Iraq-i-Ajam, Azerbaijan, Gilan, Mazandaran and Khurasan. It seems that he travelled in the last quarter of the fifteenth century. The precise chronology of his travels and stay at different places remain uncertain as he provides no specific dates of his travels. Whether he undertook such a journey once or twice is not clear, but he returned to the city with which he was to be associated for the rest of his life, sometime during the reign of Sikandar Lodi and before the death of his revered mentor Shaykh Sama' al-Din (d. 17 Jumādā I 901/2 February 1496). According to his own account, having returned safely from his long and arduous travels, he was looking after the ailing murshid (teacher) and also participated in the last rituals of his saintly preceptor to his utmost inner satisfaction. On his return to Delhi, the reigning Sultan Sikandar Lodi invited him to his court at Sambhal with a specific request to provide a copy of his latest composition Mehr wa Mah and sent the following poem:

Oh Jamali! The store house of eternal wealth,
The wayfarer in the path of faith,

---

[21] See, Ahmad, 1965.

You went round the world,
And have come back happy to your home.[22]

Initially, Jamali had little inclination to join the imperial court; however, on the advice of his spiritual guide, Shaykh Samā' al-Din, who is also regarded patron-saint of Lodi Sultans, he responded positively to the imperial summons. He was warmly welcomed by the sultan. Gradually both came to have a dervish-king or philosopher-king relationship, in which the king respected the dervish/philosopher for his high spiritual status and consulted him on matters spiritual and temporal. As a companion and confidant of the sultan, Jamali also commanded immense respect among his contemporaries. In the fifteenth and sixteenth centuries the Indo-Afghan elite are said to have become deeply intertwined with the Sufi orders and institutions that by this time flourished throughout the region wherever the Indo-Afghans lived and ruled. The Sufi shaykhs in turn also contributed immensely to the refashioning of the nascent Afghan polity and influenced their cultural outlook and ethos, serving them as religious leaders, scholars, judges and Sufi shaykhs (Aquil, 2007).[23]

Poetics as well as biographical accounts called *tazkira* for the educated elite in general and poets and Sufis in particular were forms of self-representation and worldview. *Tadhkira/tazkira* and *malfūzāt* have been the major genres of hagiography in South Asia. *Tazkira* describes the saintly lives of Sufis in the tradition of works written in the Middle East and Central Asia, whereas *malfūzāt*, the recorded discourses of a Sufi master, evolved in India. The Sufi biographical accounts are considered to be 'one of the most powerful processes of cultural production at any point in the history of Islamicate South Asia',[24] and are an invaluable supplement to the standard historical sources. The *Siyar al-'ārifīn*, though a Sufi *tazkira*, is a skilled combination of what are considered three primary literary modes of expression, being defined as *tārikh* or history, biography called *siyar* or *tazkira* and the didactic conversations of shaykhs *malfūzāt/majālis*. The Oxford historian Zeynep Yürekli has commented upon their historical value, saying, 'at first glance they may seem to be composed of anachronistic legends, but those elements can still tell us a great deal about the historical consciousness, political opinions and group identities of their authors and readership.'[25] Evidently, Jamali utilised both historical works as well as Sufi sources in the composition of his Sufi biographical compendium. Amongst the historical

---

[22] For close relations with Sikandar see Harawi, 1960–62. Nimatullah writing in 1613 wrote that the letter of Sultan Sikandar inviting Jamali to join his court was still in the possession of the shaykh's descendants. See Roy, 1958, pp. 103–4.

[23] For the political role of Sufis in the Afghan polity see Aquil, 2007, pp. 171–99; Digby, 1965; Green, 2006; and Green, 2008.

[24] Cf. Hermansen and Lawrence, 2002, p. 160.

[25] Yürekli, 2012.

works cited by him are *Ṭabaqāt i-Nasiri*, a universal history written by Minhāj-i Sīrāj-i Jūzjānī (d. after 657–8/1259–60) and *Tarikh-i-Fīrūz Shāhi* (Chronicles of Firuz Shah) of Ziya al-Din Barani (1285–1357), a dynastic history of the sultans of Delhi from *Ghiyāth al-Dīn* Ulugh Khān Balban (d. 686/1287/r. 1266–87) to the sixth regnal year of Fīrūz Shāh Tughluq (r. 752–90/1351–88). He made extensive use of Sufi memoirs of the Delhi-born famous Sufi author Sayyid Muḥammad Mubārak ʿAlawī Kirmānī (d. 770/1368-9), called Amīr Khurd entitled *Siyar al-awliyāʾ dar aḥvāl va malfūẓāt-i mashāyikh-i Chisht* ('Biographies of the Ṣūfīs and the states and conversations of the Chishtī Ṣūfī masters'), shortened to *Siyar al-awliyāʾ*, an extensive hagiographical account compiled between 1351 and 1382, and *Fawaʾiduʾl-Fʾuad* (Morals for the Heart) of Amir Najm al-Din Ḥasan Sijzī (b. 652/1254), the Badaun-born distinguished poet-disciple of Shaykh Niẓām al-Dīn Awliya constituted another major source of information. Indo-Persian *malfūẓ* (lit., conversation, pl. *malfūẓāt*) *Khayr al-Majālis* ('The best of assemblies') of Ḥamīd al-Dīn Dihlawī (d. 768/1366-7), called Ḥamīd Qalandar which are records of the assemblies of the renowned Chishtī Ṣūfī, Naṣīr al-Dīn Maḥmūd 'Chirāgh-i Dilhī' (d.757/1356) and multifaceted writings of Amīr Khusraw are frequently cited.[26]

Giving the reason for composing his classic work, the *Siyar al-ʿārifīn*, Jamali says that on his return home his friends requested him to record his observations and experiences of his wide-ranging visits to the shrines and tombs of the prophets and saints and his meeting and interactions with the scholars and pious men of those places. Thus he was asked by his friends and wellwishers, men of learning and piety, to record his experiences both physical and spiritual, in a book form for the benefit of a much larger circle of readers, both scholars and laymen. However, instead of writing a detailed travelogue containing an account of the wonders and curiosities, writing a Sufi *tazkira* of Indian Sufi shaykhs in the high tradition of biographical account was the literary choice of the author. Chronologically, it is the last and perhaps the only prose work but a magnum opus of the author, which contains a brief introduction and thirteen chapters devoted to Sufi shaykhs whose life stories the author chose to narrate.[27]

Suhrawardiyya along with the Chishtiyya were the two prominent orders in Khurasan and Transoxiana in the fourteenth and fifteenth centuries. The Chishti *silsila* was the most widely spread and popular order, which had its origin in the eastern Khurasan, a region rich in Sufi tradition and visited by the author. But there is no mention of the Chishti and Suhrawardi in the entire account of the author in specific sense of the terms to denote these Sufi orders, which

---

[26] Lawrence, 1992; Qalandar, 1959; Khwurd, 1884-5.
[27] *Siyar al-arifin*, folios 1–4.

shows that institutionalised forms of Sufi orders did not yet exist. Perhaps the transregional *ṭarīqa* (spiritual path) lineages were in formative stage. It was not until the age of the gunpowder empires that the Sufi groups began to coalesce into the *ṭarīqa*-based units. Nonetheless, out of the thirteen Sufi shaykhs, seven came to be associated as Suhrawardiyya at least in the modern historiography of Sufism and the remaining six are the eminent Chishtiyya masters of South Asia. The author provided an account of their early lives and youth, education and travel in search of knowledge and preceptors, people and mainly the Sufi shaykhs (*mashāikh*) they encountered, mystical experiences, places visited, and finally many anecdotes and miracles associated with them. It is therefore, in the course of the narrative, that the author relates personal experiences and observations on many places mostly as part of his wide-ranging travels and sojourn at the famous tombs and shrines.

He dwelt on the pre-Indian past of the Sufi shaykhs and mainly highlighted their congregation in Baghdad. The first detailed biography is of Khwaja Muʿīn al-Dīn Ḥasan Sijzī (536/1142–633/1236), the founder of the Chishtiyya Sufi community in India, called Sultan al-Mashāyikh (King of the Shaykhs). It was specifically noted that he was born in Sijistan or Sīstān (an area of eastern Iran and southwestern Afghanistan), and grew up in Khurasan. He received his *khirqa* (Sufi cloak/frock of successor ship) from Shaikh Usman Harwani (d. 1211). The other mystic Shaykh Quṭb al-Din Bakhtiyār Kaki Ushi (d. 1235) entitled Sultan al-ʿĀrifin (King of the Gnostics) is chiefly remembered for his ecstatic and contemplative life. The chapter on Farīd al-Dīn Masʿūd called Shaikh al-*mashāyikh* 'Ganj-i Shakar' (lit., treasure of sugar) (b. c. 569/1174, d. c. 670/1271) is very comprehensive with details of his early life: birth in Kohwal, a small town near Multan, where his father Jamāl al-Dīn Sulaymān served as the qadi. Most significantly his close emotional ties with his pupil Shaykh Niẓām al-Dīn Muḥammad Badauni (636/1238–725/1325) are being focused. It was noted that he was an extraordinary ascetic who maintained an austere self-discipline marked by poverty and the renunciation of worldly pursuits. Shaykh Farīd al-Dīn's brother and formal disciple, Shaykh Najib al-din Mutawakkil (d. 671/1272–3) is also included in the list of eminent saints who lived and preached in the capital city Delhi. Shaykh Niẓām al-Dīn Muḥammad Badauni, also called Sultan al-*mashāyikh*, is portrayed as the chief saint of Delhi, a refined intellectual endowed with a vocation of a mystic and talent of a spiritual preceptor. The Awadh-born Shaykh al-mashāyikh Naṣīr al-Dīn Maḥmūd 'Chirāgh-i Dilhī' (d. 757/1356) is described as the most distinguished successor of Niẓām al-Dīn Awliyā of Delhi, foremost saint of his generation in the sultanate capital, which is also the shaykh's eternal abode. A full chapter is devoted to Sayyid Jalal al-din Bukhari, called Makhdum-i-Jahaniyan (1308–81) of Ucch, narrating details of his transnational travels, most of the places also visited by the author who found many relics of the saint being preserved wherever he stayed.

The biographies of Shaykh Bahā 'al-Dīn Zakariyyā (d. between 661/1262 and 666/1267–68), and his son and most important disciple Sadr al-Din ʿĀrif (d. 684/1286), and his grandson Shaykh Rukn al-Din Abū l-Fatḥ (d. 735/1334–5) are refreshing and also have a strong and impressively personal touch. For Shaykh Bahā 'al-Dīn Zakariyyā it was noted that after initial education and having memorised the Holy Qur'ān he left his native place Kot Karor, a mountain village located north of Multan, for Khurasan and, having spent seven years in studies, he left for Bukhara where he acquired fame. Thereafter, he left for Hijaz with the intent of performing Ḥajj and lived as a *mujāwir* – scholar-sojourner – at the tomb of the Holy Prophet for five years. There he attached himself to the traditionist Kamal al-Din Muḥammad al-Yamini who granted him *ijāza* to teach. Eventually he left Arabia for Jerusalem where he paid visits to the tombs of the Prophets and from there he arrived in Baghdad. At Baghdad, he studied under Sufi Abū Ḥafṣ ʿUmar al-Suhrawardī (d. 632/1234) invariably called Hazrat Shaykh al-Shuyukh by the author. He paid visits to the holy shrines of the city. It was at Baghdad that he was invested with the *khirqa* (the cloak of initiation) by Shaikh Shihab al-Din. Thereafter, he travelled towards India and up to Khwarazm with his co-Khalifa Abul Qasim Shaykh Jalal al-Din Tabrizi (d. 1244–45), one of the earliest known Sufis who later settled in Bengal. It is noted that the latter served Shaykh Shihab al-din Suhrawardi at Baghdad for more than seven years and accompanied him on annual pilgrimages to Mecca and Medina. He enjoyed close association with Shaykh Bahā 'al-Dīn Zakariyyā too, therefore both left Baghdad together parting company at Nishapur. Shaykh Jalal al-Din Tabrizi reached Delhi but later shifted to a place called Devtalla near Pandua in Northern Bengal where he constructed a *Khānaqāh*.

Muḥammad b. ʿAṭā Allāh Maḥmūd (d. 643/1246), popularly known as Shaykh Ḥamīd al-Dīn Qāḍī Nāgawrī (d.1246), who came to India with his father ʿAṭā Allāh Maḥmūd from Bukhara and served as Qazi of Nagaur for three years before he left for Baghdad where he spent a year and sought discipleship of Shaykh al-Shuyukh Shihab al-Din Suhrawardi who also bestowed *khirqat-i-khilāfa* (the cloak of initiation) upon him. At Baghdad, he also met Sufi shaykh Qutb al-Din Bakhtiyar and thence he travelled to the two holy cities of Hijaz where he lived as a *mujawir* of the Holy Prophet's tomb for one year, eight months and eight days and spent three years at Mecca before returning to Delhi where he died in 1246 and was buried near his cherished mentor Qutb al-Din Bakhtiyar.

Jamali also mentions his visits to Sufi shrines in India. He mentions a visit to the tomb of Shaykh Muʿin al-Dīn Ḥasan Sijzī, the Grand Shaykh of Ajmer. He also mentions that, in the company of Shaikh Nasīr al-Dīn Dehlawi (son of his mentor Shaykh Sama al-Din, and Shaykhul Islam of Delhi during the reigns of

Afghan sultans Sikandar Lodi and Ibrahim Lodi and Mughal Emperor Babur), he visited the dargah of the regional master Abū Aḥmad Ḥamīd al-Millat wa-l-Dīn (d. Rabiʿ II 677/September 1278), popularly known as Shaykh Ḥamīd al-Dīn Ṣūfī l-Saʿīd Nāgawrī Sivālī, (1192–1274) also called *Sultan al-tarikin* (king of those who leave everything which is other than God).[28] He had also visited the celebrated shrine, at Sarkhej, near Ahmadabad, of Shaykh Aḥmad Khattū (b. Delhi, 737/1336; d. Sarkhej, 10 Shawwal 849/9 January 1446), popularly known as Ganjbakhsh (bestower of treasures). Jamali narrated Shaykh Aḥmad Khattū's early life and his relations with his own preceptor Shaykh Samaʾ al-Din on the basis of the information he obtained from Abdullah Biyabani, the eldest son of Samaʾ al-Din. He described Shaykh Aḥmad Khattū, a son of Malik Ikhtiyar al-Din Muḥammad, a noble of Fīrūz Shāh Tughluq, an aristocrat by birth, but preferred the life of a Sufi after undergoing a mystical trance and became a disciple of Baba Ishaq Maghribī who initiated him on the path. Jamali specifically highlighted that many kings of Hindustan were disciples of Shaykh Aḥmad Khattū and he was also spiritual preceptor and advisor of the rulers of Gujarat and specifically mentioned Aḥmad Shāh I (reigned 813–46/1411–42), the founder of the city, among his devoted disciples.

Shaykh Samā al-din, affectionately addressed as Shaykh al-*mashāyikh*, his spiritual mentor is the last of all in the chain of great Indian shaykhs. He remarked that his preceptor was the most modern of all the saints but in knowledge and erudition of esoteric and exoteric sciences he showed signs of early mystics Abu-l-Qāsim al-Junayd (835–910) and Bāyazīd Basṭāmī, (Abū Yazīd Ṭayfūr) (d. 234/848 or 261/875), major figures in the early history of Sufism. Jamali venerated his teacher immensely and paid homage to him in his poems and odes (*qasidahs*), and one of his poetic compositions Mathnawi *Mihr wa Mah* is dedicated to his mentor. He is said to have been endowed with excellent qualities such as patience, endurance and forbearance. He was a venerable spiritual preceptor who could preach as well as recite the lyrical verses of the Persian poet Shams al-Dīn Muḥammad Ḥāfiẓ of Shiraz to guide those who came to seek his blessings. 'Hamakas talib-e yar and che hushiyar che mast; Hama ja khana-e ishq ast che masjid che kunisht.'

> Everyone is longing for God – consciously or unconsciously;
> Everywhere is the abode of Love – whether it be a mosque or a church.

Shaykh Samāʾ al-Din had also written an erudite *Sharh* (commentary) on Iraqi's *Lamaʿāt* and *Miftah al-Asrar*, the latter being a treatise written on the pattern of the mystical writings of ʿAzīz al-Dīn al-Nasafi, a student of Ṣaʿd al-Dīn

---

28 Maksud Ahmad Khan, 1991.

Ḥammūya (d. 650/1252), who was an affiliate of the Kubrawiyya Sufi order, founded in Khwārazm by Najm al-Dīn Kubrā (d. 618/1221). When Samā' al-Din died on 17 Jumādā I 901/2 February 1496 at his residence in Delhi, he was laid to rest in the northern side of the Hauz-i-Shamsi where he lived during his lifetime, a place indicated for him in a dream by Sulṭān Shams al-Dīn Iltutmish (r. 1211–1236), the first ruler of Indo-Turkish state. On the same place Shaykh Jamali built a mosque for his revered teacher, guide and spiritual preceptor. The mosque, built in 901/1495–6, is described by the Delhi archaeologist Maulvi Zafar Hasan. The tomb of Makhdum Samā' al-Din is dated 901/1495–6, is in close proximity to that of Jamali.[29]

Organised Sufism of Islamic religious orders/spiritual sometimes called ṭarīqa (plural ṭuruq) Sufi path, often had its origins in the travels of individuals driven by an intensely personal desire to acquire knowledge and to fulfil religious duties. Development of Sufism in South Asia could be viewed as part of the milieux of the wider Islamic world. Scholars have emphasised international connections of the Sufi movements and significance of Hijaz in the exchange of knowledge and ideas. Staying in Hijaz was important as it served as a meeting point of Sufis from as far afield as Spain, Central Asia and South Asia. The city of Mecca also 'functioned as a cosmopolitan space in which new doctrines, texts, allegiances, and mystical teachings were possessed of a potential for trans-regional diffusion of a type not always afforded to Ṣūfī s in other urban centres'.[30] Residence in Hijaz apart from performing the annual pilgrimage was an important way for acquiring knowledge, talab al-ilm, pursuit of knowledge either through formal learning as well as interaction with the learned scholars and Sufi shaykhs. Many pilgrims took up temporary pious residence (mujawara) in Mecca and Medina for the purpose of religious devotion, learning and piety.

Jamali travelled widely in Islamic lands, meeting with scholars, mystics and religious figures with whom he formed friendship. Visits to shrines (ziyārah) was the other motive of his travels and consequently the trend-setting centres of Multan, Baghdad, Herat, Damascus, Cairo and Shiraz are part of his locales and geography of his wanderings. Jamali moved from one sacred tomb to the other in quest of spiritual fulfilment and knowledge. Cosmopolitan institutions of Islam, mainly the mosques, madrasahs and Sufi Khānaqāhs, constituted his worldview as well as eventual destinations. It seems that early in his youth, he had mastered the qualities of social polish expected of an urban scholar and gentleman. This would have facilitated his varied social intercourse in the elite academic and mystical circles. He enjoyed hospitality purely on the strength of his social status, earnest piety and bright personality. Apart from

---

[29] Dehlawi, 1988, p. 105; Hasan, 1913, vol. III, pp. 95–6.
[30] Ohlander, 2012, p. 34.

meeting and conversations with numerous shaykhs he visited tombs for the general purpose of meditation, called *muraqaba*, as well as *ziyārat*, the lesser pilgrimage. He depended upon the hospitality and generosity of his hosts, who happened to be mostly the keepers of the mosques, custodians of Sufi shrines and urban notables. Sometimes he was entertained by state officials and bureaucrats such as in Timurid Herat and in the city of poets, Shiraz. In *Siyar al-'arifin* he recounted his meetings, interactions and lively conversations with religious divines and mystics, some of whom were well known personalities of his time and therefore are identified. He carefully recorded his visits to various tombs. The account is particularly replete with his vivid reminiscences of three places, Multan, Baghdad and Herat. He began his journey in spiritual quest by visiting Multan, the emerging headquarters of the Suhrawardi order. Sufi institutions had become a norm in most regions of the vast Muslim states which catered to the needs of ever proliferating Sufi communities and it seems that they were supported both conceptually and financially by the governments and philanthropists. The Sufi hospices known as *buqa*, *ribat* and *Khānaqāhs* had performed significant socio-cultural roles in the process of urbanisation and social change throughout the entire Islamicate world. *Khānaqāh* were a regular and prominent feature of Islamic urbanism, a complex and multipurpose institution catering to the exigencies of the growing and increasingly sophisticated Sufi fraternities. *'Awārif al-Ma'ārif*, a normative manual and now a classic of Sufism that was read by Jamali and which he received as a gift in Baghdad, specifically addresses issues relating to Sufi communal life including *ribat* residence. In most cases, the *Khānaqāhs*, in addition to being caravanserai and rest houses for the comfort of travellers, also functioned as seats of higher studies. Some of the sacred buildings had well-equipped libraries and *madrasahs* attached to them and, in due course, they emerged as international centres of learning, Islamic scholarship and dissemination of ideas. Not only did the free kitchen (*langar*) attached to the *Khānaqāh* provide free food to the poor, but the students and renowned teachers studied and taught, from all around the world. In most of the shrines the senior Sufi masters delivered lectures on Sufism, exegesis (*tafsir*), jurisprudence (*fiqh*) and hadith attended by the commoners as well as the elite.[31]

Shaykh Jamali's first visit was at the tomb of Shaykh Bahā' al-Dīn Zakariyyā, the spiritual sovereign of Multan, to whom he devoted a solicitously written chapter in his account. The city of Multan, a strategic commercial centre in Punjab, which he called the pole of Islam (*qubbat al-Islam*), had become the centre of the Suhrawardi order. He took lodgings in the hospice of *Rauzah* where he was generously treated by Sadr al-din Shahr Allah (d. 1514) who was his institutional heir, a successor (*Sahib-i-Sajjadah*) – literally, those who sit on the

---

[31] Khan, 2004.

prayer rug and live off the income from the land grant and pilgrim revenues of the shrines. There he stayed at the thirteenth-century shrine for forty days and prayed in the same chamber (*hujra*) that was occupied by the founder-saint and received illuminations. Thereafter, he resided at the fourteenth-century tomb of Shaykh Rukn al-Din Abū l-Fatḥ known as Shah Rukn-i-Alam (1251–1335), the grand Shaykh of brotherhood which was within 'arrow reaching distance' from his grandfather Shaykh Bahā 'al-Dīn's *Khānaqāh*. He graphically described the pleasant location of the shrine, considered to be a universally recognised masterpiece of sultanate architecture, and noted that the river (Chenab, a tributary of the Indus) flowed only one *farsang* (a distance of 12,000 cubits) away from the main city centre.

Two important figures served as the central character and source of inspiration with whom he shared ritual practices, a common conception of spiritual genealogy and formal transmission of religious authority. Shihab al-Din Abū Ḥafṣ 'Umar al-Suhrawardī (d. 632/1234) the renowned Sufi intellectual, a mystic and scholar, and Shaykh Bahā' al-Dīn Zakariyyā are represented as pivotal figures of the mystics and mystical tradition and both are invariably addressed with their honorific titles, Shaykh al-Shuyukh and Shaykh al-Islam respectively. In a personal conversation with his host Shaykh Shihab al-Din Ahmad, Jamali claimed his illustrious ancestry from the same shaykh through Shaykh Bahā' al-Dīn Zakariyyā. During his sojourn in Baghdad, upon being questioned by the same Shaykh Shihab al-Din Ahmad, institutional heir (a spiritual/biological descendent) of Shaykh Shihab al-Din Umar Suhrawardi, about the *silsila* affiliation (spiritual lineage or initiatic genealogy) and family background of his Indian host. Jamali is said to have replied that he belonged to the *silsila* of Shihab al-Din Suhrawardi. Upon being questioned further, as through which of the successors of the shaykh he traced his family pedigree or initiatic descent, Jamali remarked that he precisely explained his lineage to Shaykh Shaykh Bahā' al-Dīn Zakariyyā as it existed. It is interesting to note that Jamali claimed spiritual descent from one of the founders of Suhrawardi *silsila* in India, and a central figure in the spiritual lineage of many Sufi shaykhs, but in his self-perception existing differences among various Sufi orders and their ritual practices were of little significance.[32] But his own journey mirrored that of Shaykh Bahā' al-Dīn, for whom he had utmost devotion, and who is said to have travelled far and wide to complete his religious education and spiritual fulfilment. At the holy city of Medina too, where Jamali lived as a *mujawir* or the scholar-sojourner, he was lodged in the same chamber (*qubba*) that was occupied by Shaykh Bahā' al-Dīn Zakariyyā. It was located on the right side of the sacred precincts of the tomb of the Holy Prophet (PBUH). Jamali recalled his stay at

---

[32] *Siyar al-'ārifin* folio 14

Baghdad where he visited the tomb of 'Abd al-Qādir al-Jīlānī (470–561/1077 or 1078–1166), a Ḥanbalī scholar, theologian, preacher and Sufi located in the New Baghdad. The nights were mostly spent at the tomb of Abū Ḥanīfa al-Nuʿmān b. Thābit, the eighth-century theologian and jurist and the eponym of the Ḥanafī law school, which was located in Old Baghdad, on the banks of River Tigris. The distance between the two was just two *kuroh* (a road measure of about two miles). At the shrine of Shihab al-Din Suhrawardi, where he spent two months, he enjoyed the rare privilege of staying in the same cell of the blessed shrine where Shaykh Bahā' al-Dīn Zakariyyā, his spiritual ancestor, had prayed more than two centuries earlier. There, as a pilgrim in residence, he led a placid life of prayer, devotion, fellowship and learning. Shaykh Shihab al-Din the *Sahib-i-Sajjada* presented him with an original manuscript copy of *'Awārif al-Maʿārif* (The Benefits of Knowledge/Gifts of Knowledge), which belonged to the personal collection of its distinguished author. Later the same comprehensive handbook of Sufis was brought to India where it formed part of the collections of the personal library of Shaykh Jamali when he was compiling his Sufi *tazkira*. *'Awārif al-Maʿārif*, a masterpiece, contains a set of rules for life in Sufi lodges, 'literature of embodied morals' in Sufism, constituted a normative manual of Chishtis and Suhrawardiyya both. The text was very well known among the Sufis of South Asia. Indian saint Farid al-Din taught *'Awārif al-Maʿārif* with great devotion.[33]

Jamali also stayed at Tabriz and went to Shiraz, where he also acquired some valuable biographical information about Shaykh Bahā' al-Dīn Zakariyyā from Sayyid Nizam al-Din Mahmud, a disciple of Nimatullah Wali (who died in 1431 in Kirman), the then Shaykh al-Islam of Shiraz and father of Shah Taj al-Din Hasan Tabadikani (d. 1549/51). He met Sayyid Nizam al-Din in Shiraz and Baghdad both. Nain was also on his itinerary, described as a small township located between Yazd and Ardistan, where he paid a visit to the shrine of Sayyid Abd al-Quddus of Mosul, a formal disciple of Shaykh Bahā' al-Dīn Zakariyyā.[34] On his way to Astarabad he paid a visit to the shrine of Hazrat Shaikh Nasir al-Din. He visited Bastam and paid a visit to the tomb of Abū Yazīd Ṭayfūr b. 'Īsā b. Surūshān al-Bisṭāmī (al-Basṭāmī) (d. 261/874–5 or 234/848–9), commonly known as Bāyazīd Bisṭāmī, an early ecstatic Sufi from north-central Iran and went to Kharqan (a city twenty kilometres north of Bastam) to visit the tomb of Shaykh Abul Hasan Kharqani (963–1033) and visited Mihna/Meana in what is today Turkmenistan, where he paid a visit to the shrine of Abū Saʿīd b. Abī l-Khayr (357–440/967–1049).[35]

---

[33] *Siyar al-'ārifīn*, folio 14
[34] *Siyar al-'ārifīn*, folio 27.
[35] Harrow, 2005.

He also mentions Andalus, a city of the Maghreb, where he spent five months. He visited Syria and paid visits to the tombs of prophets and saints who are resting there. Thence he proceeded to (Dar al-Islam) Egypt, and spent more than seven months in Egypt at a place called Dumyat (Damietta in Lower Egypt) at the resting place (takya) of a certain Ahmad Juwaliqposh who was a serving at the shrine of Shaykh Jamal Mujarrad Sawji (d. 1232–3), and lived at Dumyat close to the shrine. From there Jamali visited the cloister (buqʿa) of Shaykh Jamal Mujarrad, alleged founder of Qalandars, an order known for asceticism and renunciation. Jamali also related several popular anecdotes about Shaykh Jamal Mujarrad Sawji which he heard from the local notables and also cited several stories about him from Khayr al-majālis (The Best of Assemblies), an Indo-Persian malfūẓ (lit., conversation, pl. malfūẓāt), which records the assemblies of the renowned Chishtī Sufi Naṣīr al-Dīn Maḥmūd 'Chirāgh-i Dilhī' (d. 757/1356), composed by Ḥamīd Qalandar (Ḥamīd al-Dīn Dihlavī, d. 768/1366–7).[36]

VIEWS OF TIMURID HERAT: SOME RECOLLECTIONS

Timurid-period Herat was the brilliant centre of Perso-Islamic culture when Jamali lived there during the last decade of the fifteenth century. Under Sultan Husayn bin Mansur bin Bayqara (r. 1469–1506), to give him his full name, it was witnessing a cultural efflorescence described by Eva Subtelny as 'a glorious fin de siècle flowering of a culture and the arts during the fifteenth century'.[37] The Timurid court's intellectual life had many facets and Sufism was one of them, overlapping with other pursuits, notably poetry, calligraphy, painting, manuscript illumination as well as architecture on the one hand and Islamic sciences on the other. The duration of Jamali's stay in Herat is uncertain but he lived there before the death of Jami in 1492. During his sojourn at the cultured court of Herat he met with some highly educated and erudite individuals whose memories he continued to cherish until old age when he wrote the present tazkira. Sultan Husayn of Herat, the last notable Timurid prince to rule in Iran, himself was a poet. But Jamali did not mention the Timurid prince in his account nor did he include the name of his famous portraitist Bihzad. Niẓām al-Dīn 'Alī Shīr Navā'ī (844–906/1441–1501), also known as Mīr 'Alī Shīr, the great Uzbek poet, statesman and litterateur is also not mentioned by him. He was an honoured guest of the famous poet-intellectual Jami and met many poets, men of letters and learning. Jamali's visit to Herat is noted in relation to

---

[36] Siyar al-ʿārifin folios 26–27
[37] Subtelny,1997. For overviews of Herat under Timurid rule, see Allen, 1983; Golombek and Subtelny, 1992.

Jami. It is recorded that Jami welcomed into his circle in Herat a certain Shaykh Hamid Jamal Kanboh Dihlavi (d. 942/1535), with the pen name 'Jamali' and flatteringly called him 'the second Khusraw', by way of allusion to Amir Khusraw Dehlawi.'[38]

Jamali was occupied in making acquaintance with the Sufi shaykhs and learned men residing in the city and its environs. He also cultivated close association with some of the prominent bureaucratic intellectuals and religious scholars of Husayn Bayqara's court. Among the prominent persons, poets, men of letters and learning mentioned by Shaykh Jamali was Hazrat Shaykh Sufi (Shaykh Ali), a disciple (*murid*) of Shaikh Zain al-din Khwafi (838/1435).[39] Hazrat Shaykh Muḥammad Ruji d. 904/1499 (original name was Maulana Shams al-din Muḥammad), a former disciple of Jami, was the other notable whom Jamali mentioned. Shaykh Abd al-Aziz Jami (d. 1497), a descendent of Ahmad-i-Jam (d. 1149), is the other distinguished Sufi shaykh who is portrayed as a unique combination of prestigious descent and talent. He mentioned Maulana Nur al-Din Abd al-Rahman Jami (1414–92) as a towering figure calling him 'scholar of the age' and lauded him as the most distinguished amongst the mystics, who had attained a degree of perfection, unrivalled in his day for esoteric and exoteric knowledge. He also commented on Jami's high stature as a poet and wrote that famous indeed are his poems, he was the Sadi of his age.

Next among his acquaintances he mentioned Hazrat Maulana Masud Sherwani (Kamal al-Din d. 905/1500, also known as Masud of Sherwan) for whom the author wrote that he possessed scholarship in various disciplines, and was a luminary of the age. The other savant mentioned is Hazrat Maulana Husain Waiz (Kamal al-Din Husain Waiz Kashifi of Sabzawar d. 1504–5), described as a renowned personality of his time. Maulana Abd al-Ghafur Lari (d. 5 Shaʿbān 912/21 December 1506) was the other illustrious person mentioned by Shaykh Jamali. All of the above-mentioned personalities of Herat were his personal acquaintances, thus claimed the author, but during the period of his sojourn in the city he preferred to stay in the personal apartments (*Khana*) of Maulana Nur al-Din Abd al-Rahman Jami.

At this juncture while discussing the famous courtly figures and spiritual personalities of Herat Shaykh Jamali recalled an interesting discussion that took place in Jami's personal apartment. The discussion centred on the excellence of *Lamʿāt* (divine flashes), a famous treatise on mystical love of Persian Sufi mystic, poet Fakhr al-Dīn Ibrāhīm Hamadānī, called ʿIraqi (b. 610/1213–688/1289 in Damascus). Jamali narrated that Jami sought to ascribe a pivotal role in the

---

[38] Algar, 2013, p. 130
[39] Shaykh Ali died at the end of Sultan Husayn Bayqara's rule in 908/1503. He was, according to Khwandamir, one of the eminent disciples of Shaikh Zain al-din Khwafi (838/1434–5), the founder of Zaini order in fifteenth century Herat. Gross and Urunbaev, 2002 p. 89.

conceptualisation of *Lam'āt* to Sadr al-Din Qunawi (d.673/1274), an influential thinker in Sufi philosophy and a spiritual disciple of Muḥyī l-Dīn Ibn al-'Arabī. Jami proposed that *Lam'āt* are surely the elaboration of mystical and intellectual insights of Sadr al-Din Qunawi. Jami attributed the excellence of the above work to the chief disciple of Ibn 'Arabī (d. 638/1240).[40] Jamali knew that Fakhr al-Din was a sister's son and also a son-in-law of Shaykh Bahā' al-Dīn. He remained in Multan as a disciple of Shaykh Bahā' al-Dīn where he spent some twenty-five years under his tutelage at the *Khānaqāh* in Multan. After the death of Shaykh Bahā' al-Dīn, Iraqi left Multan and first paid a visit to Mecca and from there eventually reaching Konya in Anatolia where he met Sadr al-Din Qunawi. Iraqi left Konya as well after the death of Jalal al-Din Mohammad Balkhi Rumi and came to Damascus where he died. Therefore, Jamali disagreed with Jami and later recalled the discussion and sought to explain the background of the composition of *Lam'āt* which lays down the aesthetic principles of Islamic mysticism. He wrote that Iraqi composed the work at Konya and he studied *Fusûs al-hikam* (The Ringstones of the Wisdoms) under the guidance of Qunawi when he began the composition of *Lam'āt*. Iraqi's short mixed prose and poetry classic, *Lam'āt* was thus inspired by Qunawi's lectures on Ibn al-Arabi. Perhaps he meant that the work was influenced by the (Arabic-speaking speculative) Sufism of the visionary mystic Ibn 'Arabī as embodied in his works but as expounded by Qunawi. Jamali also pointed out a formal resemblance between *Fusûs al-hikam* and *Lam'āt* that both contain twenty-eight chapters. Finally, Jamali maintained that it was surely inspired by the charisma of the persona of Shaykh Bahā' al-Dīn Zakariyyā for whom Iraqi has also composed odes contained in his *dīwān* which comprises about 5,800 bayts (verses), mainly *ghazals*. Perhaps Jamali had studied *Lam'āt* thoroughly and his teacher and mentor Sama' al-Din had also written an erudite commentary (*Sharh*) on it. Hence he had a nuanced understanding of the work and of the intellectual factors which lay in its composition.[41]

He also visited the tomb of the mystic-poet located in Damascus in a district called al-Salhiyeh (Salihiyah cemetery) to the far northwest of the old city on the slopes of Jabal Qasiyun. He wrote that the poet Fakhr al-Din 'Iraqi is buried alongside Muhy al-Din Ibn al-'Arabi's tomb. So great was their influence in the region that people called Ibn al-'Arabi (d. 1240) an ocean of divine verities, 'Sea of Arab', and Iraqi they called the 'Ocean of al-Ajam'. Perhaps he meant the popular saying, 'That [Iraqi] is the Persian Gulf and this [Ibn al-'Arabi] is the Arabian Sea'. Jamali came to know that this was also the final place of

---

[40] *Siyar al-'ārifīn*, folio 80.
[41] *Siyar al-'ārifīn*, folios 17–19, 80.

rest of Shaykh Awhad al-Din Kirmani (d. 1238), which was also visited by him.[42]

While in Herat, which he called the abode of Islam, in the blessed company of Maulana Nur al-Din Jami and Maulana 'Abd al-Ghafur Lari he visited the tomb of Amīr Fakhr al-Sādāt Sayyid Rukn al-Dīn Ḥusayn b. 'Ālim b. Ḥasan Ḥusaynī Ghūrī Haravī (1272–1318) a lesser-known Persian Sufi poet of the thirteenth–fourteenth centuries, popularly known as Amīr Ḥusaynī or Mīr Ḥusaynī (with the *takhalluth* or pen name, Ḥusaynī), who was born in the village of Ghuziv, a village in Ghūr, a mountainous area near Herat. He also spent time in Multan and sought spiritual guidance from Rukn al-Din Abū l-Fatḥ before he went back to Herat. Here Jamali offered his *al-ẓuhr* (midday), *al-'aṣr* (afternoon) prayers and experienced inner peace. He described Sayyid Rukn al-Dīn as a renowned Sufi and famous author of *Nuzhat al-arwah* (Spirits' Delight), a work on Sufism in mixed prose and verse in which the rules of spiritual life are explained and illustrated by anecdotes and sayings of holy men. He also mentioned his other writings entitled *Zad al-Musafirin* (Nourishment of the Wayfarers) and *Sinama Tarb al-muslimin* which he calls *Tarb al-majalis* (Congregations' Delight). Husaini completed his collection of poetry (*diwan*) entitled *Kanz-ul-Rumuz* during his stay at the shrine of Shaykh Shaykh Bahā' al-Dīn Zakariyyā. It was in response to the questions raised by Husaini that Mahmud Tustari composed his *mathnawi* entitled *Gulshan-i-Raz*.[43]

After Jamali's visit to Herat and before his compilation of his memoir-cum-travelogue, Khurasan witnessed tumultuous political events. The Safavid and Uzbek occupation of the region during the first three decades of the sixteenth century witnessed a ruthless persecution of the scholars and Sufis and destruction of tombs he had known. But our author did not comment on these political upheavals. He recalls Sayf al-Din Ahmad, a great scholar and a highly revered spiritual figure, who was martyred at the hands of the Shah of Iran, Ismail I (1501–24), when the Safavid monarch unleashed his reign of terror, yet he remained steadfast in his pious beliefs until the end of his life. Perhaps Jamali would have read the memoirs of Emperor Babur who wrote a brief biographical account of Sayf al-Din Ahmad, the Shaykh al-Islam, a descendant of polymath Mulla Sad al-Din Taftazani (1322–90).

of whose family there have been many Shaykhul Islams in Herat and Khurasan. He was a scholarly person and knew Arabic sciences and traditional disciplines as well. He was pious and religious, an adherent of Shafai School of jurisprudence, who respected all others. They say that for seventy

---

[42] *Siyar al-'ārifīn*, folios 17–19.
[43] *Siyar al-'ārifīn*, folio 19; Hadi, 1995, pp 79–80.

years he never missed a congregational prayer. When Shah Ismail took Herat he martyred him. No one remains of his line.[44]

The 'City of Peace' Madīnat al-Salām Baghdad had also witnessed destruction of the popular shrines and desecration of tombs in the wake of conflict between the rival powers. The tomb of 'Abd al-Qādir al-Jīlānī, one of the oldest shrines of city, had been destroyed while that of Abu Ḥanifa, where he used to spend his peaceful nights vigils, and which he so fondly remembered in his old age as the defining moments of his travels, had also been desecrated. But that perhaps he did not know.[45]

CONCLUSION

The multifaceted personality of Shaykh Jamali Dehlavi and his multifarious contributions as a mystical writer, poet, musician and author of one of the earliest biographical compendiums of Indian Sufi blessed personalities is yet to be appreciated. Shaykh Jamali was a polymath, a trailblazer of many ideas that became standard fare in the subsequent period such as the compilation of Sufi *tazkira*-cum-autobiographical memoirs containing 'holy geographies and sacred narratives' as well as personal narrative and actual life experiences of people and places. For his diverse contribution in the field of art, architecture, aesthetics, literature, Persian poetics and production of memoir-cum-travelogue, he stands as a significant figure whose writings constitute bridges in the transition period from sultanate to Mughal era in Indian history. His rich literary legacy is yet to be explored in a meaningful manner as the bulk of his poetical and literary oeuvre remains unedited and unstudied. Though his fame as a litterateur and widely travelled scholar is largely posthumous, he was a gifted poet and a popular musician whose multilingual Persian verses with Arabic and Hindawi words and phrases composed with Indian music continued to enjoy great popularity during the reign of Emperor Akbar. This literary and poetic fame is testified by 'Abd al-Qādir Badā'ūnī who remains the only near contemporary to have criticised his biographical memoirs, perhaps rightly so, for a number of factual inaccuracies.

A study of his biographical account as presented reveals a highly mobile world of multilingual Sufis and religious savants and learned men across the Indian Ocean. The culture of migration was a reflection of a wide peripatetic tradition of Muslim scholarship as well as the existence of a broadly shared religious culture aided by Arabic and Persian lingua franca which sustained transregional Arabo-Persianate culture. Ḥajj, the annual pilgrimage, remained

---

[44] *The Baburnama*, 1996, p. 221.
[45] Arjomand, 2005, pp. 44–65.

an unbroken permanent link with the Arabic contact zone in this multilingual world of interregional and transnational travels. Following the established routes Sufi and blessed men as well as merchants moved widely between the urban centres of different regions in search of teachers, students and joined networks of knowledge and caravans. Surely in this multicultural, multiethnic transnational world the Sufi shrines served to tie the pre-modern geography of South Asia to that of other regions of Dal al-Islam. Such travel and mobility became possible because of the high rate of urbanisation, trade and a cultural standardisation of a widespread written and spoken Persian language. A member of the Persianate intelligentsia, he remained well connected due to a common lingua franca, Persian being the preeminent language across a vast region connecting Arabia, Iran, Central Asia and India. Physical travel and transnational migrations as a means of acquiring learning among mystics and scholarly circles had been a major characteristic feature of Muslim history throughout the Islamicate world. The transregional and interregional Sufi networks were a widespread phenomenon of the South Asian landscape where multilingual Sufi and religious men moved back and forth in search of knowledge and mentors. Such a movement was greatly facilitated due to the existence of the cosmopolitan culture of *madrasahs*, an essential as well as enduring Islamic institution. Along with Sufi lodges called *Khānqāh*, *ribāt*, *zāwiyā*, the monumental and multipurpose buildings were scholarly-cum-religious centres where multilingual Sufis moved and exchanged ideas on mystical and worldly aspects of life without any distinction between the courtly sphere and spiritual sphere. Moreover, his fascinating portrayal of the sophisticated cultural and intellectual life of Herat, the magnificent capital of the Timurid Empire, which he visited at the time of its greatest flowering of art and architecture under the patronage of Sultan Husayn Bayqara, the last powerful Timurid ruler, is significant. The court culture of the Timurid capital, from poetry to landscape practices, came to be widely emulated in the realms of the Safavid, Ottoman and Mughal empires. The prominent religious and mystical circles of Herat with whom he interacted and formed lasting associations, particularly the mystical figure and hagiographer Jami, exercised a profound influence on the Safavid, Ottoman and Mughal bureaucratic intellectual elite as well as mystics.

Bibliography

Primary sources

Badauni, Abd al-Qadir. 1868. *Muntakhab al-tawārīkh* ('Selection from History'), Maulavi Ahmad Ali and Maulavi Kabir al Din Ahmad, eds. Calcutta, Bibliotheca Indica, Asiatic Society of Bengal, vol. 1.

The Baburnama: Memoirs of Babur, Prince and Emperor. 1996. W. M. Thackston, trans. New York and Oxford: Freer Gallery of Art, Arthur M. Sackler Gallery, Smithsonian Institution and Oxford University Press.

Dehlawi, Abd al-Haqq Muhaddith. 1914. *Akhbar al-Akhyar fi asrar al-abrar*. New Delhi: Mujtabai Press.

Dehlawi, Shaikh Jamali. 1974. *Mathnawi-yi Mihr-u-Mah*, Sayyid Husam al-Din Rashidi, ed. Rawalpindi: Iran Pakistan Institute of Persian Studies.

Dehlawi, Jamali Mawlana Shaikh. 1893. *Siyar al-'ārifīn* [The Feats of the Gnostics]. New Delhi: Matba'a-ye-Rizawi.

Dehlawi, Jamali-yi. 2002. *The Mirror of Meanings (Mir'āt al-ma'ānī): A Parallel English-Persian Text*, A. A. Seyed-Gohrab, trans, and a critical Persian text by N. Pourjavady. Bibliotheca Iranica: Intellectual Tradition Series 8. Costa Mesa: Mazda.

Dehlawi Amir Khusrau, Muḥammad Ismail Meeruthi (ed.). 1918. *Qiran al-Sadayn*. Aligarh: Aligarh College Press.

Dehlawi, Sadiq Hamadani Kashmiri. 2013. *Tabaqat-e-Shahjahani*, Ghulam Ashraf Qadiri and M. Ehteshamuddin, eds. 2 vols. Aligarh: Institute of Persian Research, Aligarh Muslim University.

Dehlawi, Sadiq Hamadani Kashmiri. 1988. *Kalimat al-Sadiqin*, Muhammad Saleem Akhtar, ed. Islamabad: Iran Pakistan Research Centre.

Mushtaqi, Shaykh Rizq Allah. 2002. *Waqi'āt-i-Mushtāqi*, I. H. Siddiqui and Waqar-ul-Hasan Siddiqui, eds. Rampur (UP).

Harawi, Khwaja Nimatullah. 1960–62. *Tarikh-i-Khan-i-Jahani wa Makhzan-i-Afghani* (The Khan Jahan's History and the Afghan Coffers), S. M. Imamuddin, ed., 2 vols. Dacca: Asiatic Society of Pakistan.

Khwurd, Mir. 1884–5. *Siyar al-Awliya*. Lithograph. Delhi: Matba-i-Muhibb-i-Hind.

Kulliyat-i-Jamali Dehlawi of Shaikh Jamali Dehlawi, manuscript Reza Library, Rampur.

Mathnawi Mir'āt al-ma'ānī of Shaikh Jamali Dehlawi, Habib Ganj Collection, 21/137, Maulana Azad Library, Aligarh Muslim University.

Qalandar, Hamid. 1959. *Khayr al-Majalis: mulfuzat -i- hazrat-i- Shaykh Nasir al-Din Mahmud Chiragh-i-Dihli*, K. A. Nizami, ed. Aligarh: Department of History, Muslim University.

Roy, Nirodbhusan, trans. 1958. *Niamatullah's History of the Afghans: Part 1 Lodi Period*, Translated with variorum notes. West Bengal: Shantiniketan Press.

Siddiqui, I. H. 1993. *Waqiat-e-Mushtaqui of Shaikh Rizq Ullah Mushtaqui: A Source of Information on the Life and Conditions in Pre-Mughal India*. New Delhi: Indian Council of Historical Research/Northern Book Centre.

Siyar al-'ārifīn of Shaikh Jamali Dehlawi, Habib Ganj Collection, *Farsiya Tazkirat al-Awliya*, 22/11. Maulana Azad Library: Aligarh Muslim University. Rotorograph Number 173: of Manuscript Number, 115 dated 964 A.H./dated 1556–7, John Rylands University Library, University of Manchester, UK, Seminar Library, Department of History, Aligarh Muslim University.

Mathnawi Mir'āt al-ma'ānī, 21/137. Manuscript: Habib Ganj Collection, Maulana Azad Library, Aligarh Muslim University, Aligarh.

Qadiri, M. A. and H. S. Rashidi. 1976. *Ḥāmid b. Faḍl Allāh, Dehlawi, Jamali, Siyar al-'ārifīn*. Persian edition with Urdu translation by M. Ayyub Qadiri with an introduction by H. S. Rashidi. Lahore: Markazi Urdu Board.

Yadgar, Ahmad. 1939. *Tarikh-i-Shahi*, or *Tarikh-i-Salatin-i-Afaghina* (The Royal History of the Afghan Sultans), M. Hidayat Husain, ed. Calcutta: Baptist Mission Press.

Secondary sources

Ahmad, Aziz. 1965. 'Djamali Ḥāmid b. Faḍl Allāh', in *The Encyclopaedia of Islam*. Leiden: Brill, new edition, pp. 420–1.

Algar, Hamid. 2013. *Jami, Makers of Islamic Civilization*. Oxford: Oxford University Press.

Allen, Terry. 1983. *Timurid Herat*. Wiesbaden: Ludwig Riechert.

Aquil, Raziuddin. 2008. 'Hazrat-i-Dehli: The Making of the Chishti Sufi Centre and the Stronghold of Islam', *South Asia Research*, 28 (1), pp. 23–48.

Aquil, Raziuddin. 2007. *Sufism: Culture and Politics: Afghans and Islam in Medieval North India*. New Delhi: Oxford University Press.

Arjomand, Said Amir. 2005. 'Rise of Shah Ismaʿil as a Mahdist Revolution', *Studies in Persianate Societies*, vol. 3, pp. 44–65.

Asher, Catherine B. 2017. *Delhi's Qutb Complex: The Minar, Mosque and Mehrauli*. Mumbai: Marg Foundation.

Brown, Percy. 1968. *Indian Architecture, Islamic Period*. Bombay: D. B. Taraporewala Sons & Co. Private, 5th edition.

Digby, Simon. 2001. 'The Indo-Persian Historiography of the Lodi Sultans', in F. Grimal (ed.), *Les Sources et le Tems*. Pondicherry: Institut Français de Pondichery, pp. 243–64.

Digby Simon. 1975. The Tomb of Buhlūl Lōdī, *Bulletin of the School of Oriental and African Studies*, vol. 38, no. 3, pp. 550–61.

Digby, Simon. 1965. 'Dreams and Reminiscences of Dattu Sarwani, a Sixteenth Century Indo-Afghan soldier', *Indian Economic and Social History Review* 2.1, pp. 52 80.

Golombek, Lisa and Maria Subtelny (eds). 1992. *Timurid Art and Culture: Iran and Central Asia in the Fifteenth Century*. Leiden: Brill.

Green, Nile. 2008. 'Tribe, Diaspora and Sainthood in Afghan History,' *Journal of Asian Studies* 67.1, pp. 171–211.

Green, Nile. 2006. 'Blessed Men and Tribal Politics: Notes on Political Culture in the Indo-Afghan World', *Journal of the Economic and Social History of the Orient* 49.3, pp. 344–60.

Gross, Jo-Ann and Asom Urunbaev. 2002. *The Letters of Khwaja Ubayd Allah Ahrar and his Associates*. Leiden: Brill.

Hadi, Nabi. 1995. *Dictionary of Indo-Persian Literature*. Ajmer: Indira Gandhi National Centre of Arts, Abhinav Publication.

Hameed ud-Din. 1962. 'Historians of Afghan Rule in India', *Journal of the American Oriental Society*, 82, 1, pp. 45–51.

Harrow, Leonard. 2005. 'The Tomb Complex of Abū Saʿid Faḍl Allāh b. Abīʾl-Khair at Mihna', *Iran*, 43, pp. 197–215.

Hasan, Maulvi Zafar. 1916. *Monuments of Delhi: Lasting Splendour of the Great Mughals and Others*. Mehrauli New Dehli: Aryan Books International, New Delhi (reprint 1997).

Hermansen, Marcia K. and Bruce B. Lawrence. 2002. 'Indo-Persian Tazkiras as Memorative Communications', in David Gilmartin and Bruce Lawrence (eds), *Beyond Turk and Hindu: Rethinking Religious identities in Islamicate South Asia*. New Delhi: India Research Press.

Husaini, S. B. F. 1988. *A Critical Study of the Indo-Persian Literature during Sayyid and Lodi Period, 1414–1526 A.D.* Delhi: MS Publications.

Khan, Gulfishan. 2017a. '*Kalimat al-Sadiqain*: A Sufi Biographical Account', in N. R. Khan (ed.), *Sufism: In India and Central Asia*. New Delhi: Manakin Press Pvt. Ltd., pp. 85–99.

Khan, Gulfishan. 2017b. 'Shaikh Jamali Dehlawi: The Indo-Persian Sufi Poet', in Meenakshi Sundriyal and Juan Manuel E. Baztan (eds), *Lo divino y lo humano: poetas misticos de India y de Espana en la modernidad temprana*. New Delhi: Jawaharlal Nehru University, pp. 41–56.

Khan, Gulfishan. 2016. 'Indo-Persian Sufi-Poets and the landscape of Hazrat-i-Dihli', in Emili Rumi S. K. Sarkar (ed.), *Sufism in India, Interpretive Essays*. Kolkata: Ashadeep, pp. 41–52.

Khan, Maksud Ahmad. 2004. 'Khanqahs: Centres of Learning', in M. Haidar (ed.), *Sufis, Sultans, and Feudal Orders*. New Delhi: Manohar.

Khan, Maksud Ahmad. 1991. 'Shaikh Hamid-u'd-Din Nagauri', *Proceedings of Indian History Congress*, vol. 52, pp. 242–4.

Latif, S. A. 1977. 'Jamali's Relations with the Rulers of Delhi.' in *Medieval India: A Miscellany*. New York: Asia Publishing House.

Lawrence, Bruce, trans. 1992. *Morals for the Heart: Conversations of Shaykh Nizam ad-din Awliya recorded by Amir Hasan Sijzi*. New York: Paulist Press.

Ninomiya, Ayako. 2005–6. 'History of the House of Baha al-Din Zakariya during the period of Delhi Sultanate', *Indian History Congress*, 66, pp. 346–54.

Ohlander, Erik S. 2012. 'Mecca real and imagined: Texts, transregional networks, and the curious case of Baha al-Din Zakariyya of Multan' in John J. Curry and Erik S. Ohlander (eds), *Sufism and Society Arrangements of the Mystical in the Muslim world, 1200–1800*. Routledge Sufi Series. London: Routledge.

Pello, Stefano. 2014. 'Local Lexis? Provincializing Persian in Fifteenth-Century North India', in Francesca Orsini and Samira Sheikh (eds), *After Timur Left Culture and Circulation in Fifteenth-Century North India*. London: Oxford University Press.

Siddiqui, Iqtidar Husain. 2012. *Composite Culture under the Sultanate of Delhi*. New Delhi: Primus Books.

Storey, C. A. 1953. *Persian Literature: A Bio-bibliographical Survey*. vol. I, Part II. London: Luzac & Co. Ltd.

Subtelny, Maria Eva. 1997. 'The Timurid Legacy: A Reaffirmation and a Reassessment', in *Cahiers d'Asie central*, vol. 3, no. 4, pp. 9–19

Suvorova, Anna. 2004. *Muslim Saints of South Asia: The Eleventh to Fifteenth Centuries*. London: Routledge Curzon Sufi Series.

Topsfield, Andrew. 2012. 'Images of Love and Devotion: Illustrated Mughal Manuscripts and Albums in the Bodleian Library', in Susan Scollay (ed.), *Love and Devotion: from Persia and Beyond*. Oxford and Melbourne: Bodleian Library and State Library of Victoria.

Wahid, M. Mirza. 1974. *Life and Works of Amir Khusrau*, Delhi.

Yürekli, Zeynep. 2012. 'Writing down the feats and setting up the scene: hagiographies and architectural patrons in the age of Empires', in John J. Curry and Erik S. Ohlander (eds), *Sufism and Society: Arrangements of Mystical in the Muslim world, 1200–1800*. London and New York: Routledge, pp. 94–119.

Zaweed, Salim. 2015. 'Medieval Monuments of Mehrauli: Reality and Myth', *Proceedings of Indian History Congress* 76, pp. 748–58.

CHAPTER 7

A Persian View of the Maritime Muslim Frontier in Southeast Asia: The Jāmiʿ al-barr waʾl-baḥr

ROGHAYEH EBRAHIMI

INTRODUCTION

With the rise of the Safavid state in Iran and the expansion of Muslim trade through India, networks of Persian merchants became increasingly active in the eastern Indian Ocean maritime trade over the sixteenth and seventeenth centuries. As a window onto this world, this paper explores a previously unpublished Persian text of the period: The *Jāmiʿ al-barr waʾl-baḥr* (Compendium of the land and the sea) by Maḥmūd ibn ʿAbdullah Nīshābūrī. He was a Persian author and traveller with a life-long interest in commerce, trade and navigation in India and beyond. In his account of the Indonesian archipelago, he presents a hierarchical view of civilisation in which Muslim merchants are cast in the role of 'civilising agents' among the expanding Muslim communities of Southeast Asia. This included both the extension of participation in prosperous networks of exchange and the introduction of new cultural and literary traditions to local populations as part of their incorporation into a wider world of Islam. In this, it presents a striking comparative perspective on the accelerating processes of social transformation taking place during a period that was also marked by the arrival and intervention of new European powers in the region.

FROM NĪSHĀBŪR TO NEW GUINEA: AN HISTORICAL ENQUIRY INTO NĪSHĀBŪRĪ'S ITINERARY

While the history of contacts between Persia and Southeast Asia dates back to ancient times, commercial and cultural connections between these two regions took on new dynamics after the rise of Islam, with an increasingly pronounced period of expansion through the eleventh century. By the fourteenth century, Persian literary models were playing a formative role in the development of new Islamicate textual traditions of vernacular Malay literature.[1]

With the rise of the Safavid state in Iran in the sixteenth century and the expansion of Muslim trade through India, networks of Persian merchants became increasingly active in the eastern Indian Ocean maritime trade.[2] As a new window onto this world, my research explores a previously unpublished Persian text of the period: the *Jāmiʿ al-barr wa ʾl-baḥr* by Maḥmūd ibn ʿAbdullah Nīshābūrī (died after 1038/1628). From the fragmentary information in this text, we are told that the author was a voyager from Nīshābūr, with wide-ranging commercial and geographical interests in India and beyond. In 996/1587, as a result of Uzbek attacks on Nīshābūr, he embarked on a ship to set out to India, and arrived at the court of the of Sulṭān Muḥammad Qulī Quṭb Shāh in Golconda where he found a job in military service as an army scribe and then as a functionary of Kunpūr. Finally, after thirty years of adventure and experience, in 1027/1617 he made his way back home to Nīshābūr by way of the holy cities of the Ḥijāz.[3]

Over the course of his Indian sojourn from 996/1587 to 1027/1618, Nīshābūrī assembled a collection of reports, seafaring anecdotes and tall-tales heard from other Muslims, including many Iranians with experience in Southeast Asia. These were incorporated into the text that is at the centre of this study, the *Jāmiʿ al-barr wa ʾl-baḥr*. I have to date managed to locate two manuscript witnesses to this work, one in Iran, Yazd, the Kāẓimīnī Library, Iran (cat.nr.514/53) and another in Pakistan, Islamabad, in The Ganj Bakhsh Library (cat.nr. 4035). This text has gone unnoticed in previous studies of Indo-Persian accounts of Southeast Asia, but in fact it appears to have been a source for Maḥmūd ibn Amīr Walī Balkhī's[4] *Baḥr al-asrār fī manāqib al-akhyār* (the Ocean of Secrets in the accounts of the Nobles), which Muzaffar Alam and Sanjay Subrahmanyam have discussed extensively in their studies of *Indo-Persian Travels in the Age*

---

[1] Marrison, 1955, pp. 52, 67; Colless, 1969, pp. 11–14; Brakel, 1970, p. 2; Marcinkowski, 2002, p. 24.

[2] Baker and Phongpaichit, 2017, p. 125; Marcinkowski, 2002, p. 24.

[3] Nīshābūrī, *Maāt̠ir-i Quṭbshāhī Maḥmūdī*, fol.5a.

[4] Maḥmūd ibn Amīr Walī Balkhī was born at Balkh 1004/1595–96 to a well-to-do family. At the beginning of Shawwal, 1034/1625, he joined a commercial caravan to set out for India and Sri Lanka with the intention of 'surveying the wonders and marvels [of those lands] with the eyes of wisdom'. In India and Sri Lanka, he spent six years in all, from Muḥarram, 1034/1624, when he arrived in Lahore to 20 Muḥarram, 1041/1631, when he returned to Balkh. It is believed he visited Delhi, Agra, Allāhābād, Benāre, Patna, Calcutta, Rājmahāl, Danapur, Hyderabad, Bijapur, Vijayanagar, Sri Lanka, Katak and other cities of India, and collected invaluable information about them (Akhmedov, 1991, pp. 164–5). An important point to note here is that while Balkhī enriched his travelogue by his own descriptions and reflections on many of the places he visited, when treating the realms of the ʿAdil Shāhīs, the Niẓām Shāhīs, the Quṭb Shāhīs and Vijayanagar he mostly repeated the information presented by Nīshābūrī in his treatments of those Indian kingdoms.

of *Discoveries*.[5] In this paper, I would like to present material from one aspect of *Jāmiʿ al-barr wa ʾl-baḥr* that might contribute some new perspective on the extent of Persian networks across and beyond the eastern edge of the Indian Ocean World.[6]

In his own accounts of the Indonesian archipelago, Nīshābūrī informs us that he benefited considerably from information that he found in a manuscript of another Persian-language work describing the lands below the winds (*Zīrbād*) which he used as a basis for a new compilation of geographic and anthropological information. Its writer identified as 'Bukhārī': a well-travelled writer from eastern Iran who had spent many years of his life outside of Persian-speaking lands, reportedly visiting China, India and Ethiopia – as well as Southeast Asia. Bukhārī provided the author of our text with a wealth of information of the region, including reports on the manners, customs and the physical characteristics of local populations, as well as information on their religious beliefs and local flora and fauna, and so on.[7] Bukhārī's information came from his own diverse experiences travelling across the maritime world of Southeast Asia – and it is possible that this Bukhārī may even be the same 'Bukhārī al-Jūhurī', the author of the important Malay literary work composed at Aceh in 1603: the *Tāj al-Salātīn* (mirror for princes), which is a manual of advice to kings that draws heavily upon Persian works in this genre.[8]

THE COMMERCIAL NETWORK OF NĪSHĀBŪRĪ'S ERA

Before developing any further investigation, we need to survey the context in which our text was compiled, and it would be a good idea to start with a short introduction on the commercial network of the Indian Ocean in Nīshābūrī's era. Luckily, Nīshābūrī provided some helpful information himself in the early pages of his work. His text depicts an interconnected chain of entrepôts as hubs of Muslim merchant networks across the Indian Ocean. The most critical entrepôt was Hormuz, where traders from Iran, Central Asia, Anatolia, Syria and Iraq brought their shipments of fabric and other commodities to exchange for tropical luxuries such as aloe wood, ambergris, camphor, cloves, mace and nutmeg – all of which were gathered from the ports of the eastern littoral of the Indian Ocean and beyond into the Indonesian archipelago, the South China Sea and the western reaches of the Pacific.[9] In this paper, I focus on what this text tells us about Persian knowledge of, and interactions with these 'Spice

---

[5] Alam, 2007, pp. 130–74.
[6] Balkhī, 1984, pp. 131–2.
[7] Balkhī, 1984, pp. 131–2.
[8] Bukhair Al-Jauhari, 1966, p. 2; Marrison, 1955, p. 61.
[9] Masashi, 2017, pp. 263–4; McPherson, 2004, pp. 4–5, 16.

Islands' and the surrounding waters of Makassar, the Philippines and coastal New Guinea.[10]

Previous studies of Persian connections to Southeast Asia in the sixteenth and seventeenth centuries have highlighted the importance of ports including Aceh and Ayutthaya along the eastern reaches of the Bay of Bengal, and Nīshābūrī's text further adds to our available information for this with, for example, extensive discussions of the political and military contestations involving Ayutthaya, Tenasserim and Pegu.[11] What is more remarkable, however, is the information that this work provides for areas of Southeast Asia that have not previously been recognised or discussed in relation to Persian maritime networks. Nīshābūrī's text is striking in this regard, particularly for its inclusion of reports on the geography, populations and commodities of islands in the easternmost regions of Indonesia and areas of the Philippines.

THE 'SPICE ISLANDS' OF MALUKU AND BEYOND

While our manuscript does reiterate marvellous accounts of exotic islands drawing on the lore of earlier Arabic texts, including the mythical island of Wāq (with its trees of vocal human-head fruit), there is relatively little such material in comparison to the more sober accounts of the geography of identifiable islands of the east. Examples of the latter, for example, are abundant in Nīshābūrī's treatment of the region that Leonard Andaya has referred to as *The World of Maluku*.[12] There, for example, Nīshābūrī gives remarkably accurate accounts of the more profitable produce of the clove trees of the island of Bacan:

> The clove clusters hang over its tree branches. When it ripens, it turns red in colour, but if it dries up on the top of the tree, it becomes black. At the time of perfect ripeness, the inhabitants cut the clove's fruit off of the branches of trees and harvest them; those on the very high branches and not accessible to the islanders would remain there and turn black. It would consequently develop a different taste devoid of its typical hotness and spiciness. Clove fruit picked at the time of ripeness is very pungent, spicy and enjoyable.[13]

Nīshābūrī also describes the features of and sources of collection for nutmeg and mace, as well as of birds of paradise – though he also uses the latter as a narrative device to introduce a moralising lesson on the virtues of loyal subjects to a noble sovereign:

---

[10] *Jāmiʿ al-barr waʾl-baḥr*, pp. 7–9.

[11] Marcinkowski, 2000, pp. 186–94; Marcinkowski 2002, pp. 23–46; *Jāmiʿ al-barr waʾl-baḥr*, p. 9.

[12] Andaya, 1993, pp. 55–6.

[13] *Jāmiʿ al-barr waʾl-baḥr*: p. 86, all translations from the *Jami* are by the author.

Glory be to God, a little animal and weak creature has such knowledge and power to realize that their lives should be given for their king and home, however, humans with all their dignity, wisdom and reason, follow their lust and whims and close their eyes to reality. They do not sacrifice their lives for their king in order to achieve superior blessings in the eternal world.[14]

While descriptions and reports of export commodities such as aromatic spices and the feathers of 'birds of paradise' may have circulated widely across the maritime Muslim networks of Nīshābūrī's day, his text also includes strikingly detailed descriptions of other aspects of life in the eastern reaches of the Indonesian archipelago that would most likely have been known only to local inhabitants and those travellers that had actually spent some time there: for example, the processing and consumption of sago as a staple starch:

They put the wood in water and then bring it out and desiccate it to create flour. Then, they place it in a mold and make it into [something like a] brick. Later, they put the prepared bricks on top of each other and bind them together to store for use in times of need.[15]

The sphere of Nīshābūrī's knowledge of the easternmost portions of the Indonesian archipelago also included parts of coastal New Guinea, with geographical identifications of the Onin Peninsula and its inhabitants – whom he refers to as 'Fafu' or 'Papu' and describes as 'Cannibal tribe is there; naked and black like Ethiopians with perforated ears and skilful in archery. They live in caves and eat the flesh of all animals ranging from snakes to mice.'[16]

MANILA

Further north from Maluku, Nīshābūrī also related an account of Manila as a prosperous port, with the historical note that 'it had previously been included among the realms of the sultan of Brunei, but at the time when Bukhārī reached it, it was under the control of the Franks'.[17] This last note connects to a pronounced theme that recurs regularly throughout Nīshābūrī's text: that of a sense of competition between the Muslim merchants active in Southeast Asia and the incursions of Iberian Christians into the region.[18] While he notes in the closing line of his account of Maluku 'now . . . the Franks have dominated this island

---

[14] *Jāmiʿ al-barr waʾl-baḥr*: 94.
[15] *Jāmiʿ al-barr waʾl-baḥr*: 93.
[16] *Jāmiʿ al-barr waʾl-baḥr*, p. 103.
[17] *Jāmiʿ al-barr waʾl-baḥr*, p. 105.
[18] Reid, 1993, pp. 151–79.

and taken most of its produce to their lands'. He also notes that the Shāfiʿī Muslim inhabitants of the Banda Islands 'are able to keep themselves safe from Frankish invaders'.[19]

Moreover, Nīshābūrī provided a rigourously researched and detailed anthropological and political description of the way in which Spain colonised Manila. Nevertheless, before proceeding further, we should note that the material quoted in this section emanated from his observations of Bukhārī, who presumably was present in Manila in the early years of the Spanish colonisation there around 1571. He stated:

> When the Franks (Europeans) heard the news of this populated port and its profits and advantages, they sent a number of their big ships with armaments and resourceful people there and told them, 'don't miss that island.' As they realized their strategies of war and fights wouldn't be fruitful in order to capture the island, they proceeded along the path of buying and selling.[20]

He went on to shed light on the variety of early efforts of the Spanish to dominate this era:

> They debased the great and wise persons of the port and aggrandized the shallow-minded people of the island, and proselytized Christianity to the islanders with tricks and enticements. They dressed the islanders in Frankish clothes and taught them the Frankish language, and provided them with many commodities from Rūm until they built lots of fencing around this big island and took the island under their control; once they had gained control of this island, they started thinking about other islands.[21]

MAKASSAR

A narrative of the Islamisation of Makassar is another significant highlight of our manuscript. Nīshābūrī's account presents a number of interesting elements that differentiate it from other written texts on this subject, particularly in its markedly Shiʿite colouring. Nīshābūrī not only framed the Islamisation narrative of Makassar in a distinctively Shiʿite way, but he also used this chance to express his oppositional stance toward European Christians by challenging the principles and beliefs of their religion. In this regard, he portrayed the competition of the Franks and Muslims with these words:

---

[19] *Jāmiʿ al-barr wa ʾl-bahr*, p. 89.
[20] *Jāmiʿ al-barr wa ʾl-bahr*, p. 112.
[21] Ibid.

Simultaneously, a ship from the Frankish lands came to Makassar and offered many gifts to the king of Makassar and presented their religion to him. They gave him a picture of Jesus Christ and told him of the Bible. They built a church and embellished this edifice with lots of figures and ornaments. Then, they asked the king to come there. When the king went there, a number of clergymen and friars started to read the Bible and the Franks did the same, and bowed down to the picture of Jesus and asked the king to do the same. However, as the king was a very wise and thoughtful person, he responded, to whom should I bow down, the crucified person with many arrows on his back and sides and running blood from his sores? Then, he said, tell me the truth about all of this. The monks said Jesus is the Son of God. Afterwards, he asked them who his mother was. They answered Maria, daughter of ʿImrān, who died. How it can be reasonable that such an oppressed person that should have had a nurse remained in this situation but his father, who is God of the heavens and the earth, did not protect his son and release him from the oppression? All your actions and words are far from knowledge and reason, and my actions is a hundred times better than yours.[22]

As we investigated, this text opens up a new view on how the process of the spread of Islam encountered European maritime expansion in the early modern period. In this connection, Reid has argued that the conflict between Muslims and Christians grew intense in the sixteenth century as a result of the establishment of direct commercial and diplomatic relations between Turkey and Aceh in 1560, which blew a fresh spirit into the concept of pan-Islamic resistance against the Portuguese in Southeast Asia.[23] The short-lived Turkish intervention further stimulated the spirit of pan-Islamic solidarity in the Indian Ocean. In 1566 Sultan ʿAlā ud-dīn Riʾayat al-Qahhār (c. 1538–71) of Aceh addressed the Ottoman sultan as khalīfa of universal Islam and asked him to aid the oppressed Muslims of the Indian Ocean and not to leave them alone to face the unbelievers.[24]

Then, Nīshābūrī went on to explain the way in which the Shiʿite School penetrated into the Makassar society. In this regard, he related to us the arrival of a group from Mecca and the dream of the king of Makassar, which were the main reasons of the latter's conversion to Islam. In this respect, he stated:

Another night, he saw, Amīr al-Muʾminīn 'Commander of the Believers' or 'Prince of the Believers' ʿAlī ibn Abī Ṭālib appealing to him more gently,

---

[22] Jāmiʿ al-barr wa ʾl-baḥr, pp. 96–7.
[23] Reid, 1993, p. 165.
[24] Reid, 1993, pp. 164–5; Reid, 2015, p. 65.

'accept Islam and do not worry about this group [the Franks] that I am your assistant and supporter and all of this island will be your obedient servants.' When the king heard that promise from Amīr al-Muminīn, in the early morning, he invited his uncles, brothers and relatives and told them the truth about his dream. So, they invited all Muslims who were/on that island to join them, and as result, the governor of Makassar, his relatives and followers, all renounced idolatry. So, because of this deed, many pagans were fortunate enough to become Muslim and to be the followers of the right religion. The king was named Muḥammad Hidāyat Allāh.[25]

Although unearthing the details of this account will be the subject of further research, here we should state this narrative does not seem to connect to any episode known in Makassarese tradition. The name of the young king, however, might be a mis-heard echo of the name of an earlier Muslim sovereign from one of the earlier Islamised areas of the archipelago. Hidāyat Allāh was the Arabic name of the founder of the sultanate of Banten, more commonly referred to by his Javanese saintly title, Sunan Gunung Jati. An even earlier namesake comes from eastern Indonesia: Sultan Johan Pahlawan Hidayatullah of Ternate (r. 1529–33), whom Ridzali mentioned as the powerful and influential king of Ternate who spread Islam to the Malukan islands of Ambon and Hitu.[26] This is a particularly intriguing potential identification, given the extensive attention to Maluku given in the Jāmiʿ al-barr waʾl-baḥr. The possible influence of Persian scholars at the Ternate court during this period may be reflected in the inclusion of loanwords in some of the Malay-language royal correspondence of Sultan Abu Hayat (r. 1522–9) with Lisbon.[27]

The reason for the confusing identification of the setting of this episode of royal conversion by Nīshābūrī is not clear. It clearly contrasts to much more familiar local accounts of the Islamisation of Makassar,[28] which in any event occurred so late (that is, during the first decade of the seventeenth century), that it would likely have not had sufficient time to be recorded by Bukhārī and then to be incorporated by Nīshābūrī in 1620. There are no apparent matches of the same narrative from the histories of Banten or Ternate either.

Ternate does, however, present a tradition thick with its own ʿAlid resonances, which a Shiʿite of Nīshābūrī's conviction would not have failed to appreciate. The royal lines of traditional rulers of the islands of Ternate, Tidore, Jailolo and Bacan go back to Jaʿfar al-Ṣādiq. This is, of course, the name of the sixth Shiʿite Imām, and a figure who is venerated broadly both within

---

[25] Jāmiʿ al-barr waʾl-baḥr, 103.
[26] Ridzali, 1977: p. 189.
[27] Blagden, 1930, p. 92.
[28] Noorduyn, 1987.

and beyond Shiʿīte communities. His name, for example, appears in the 1549 foundation inscription of the Al-Aqṣa, as well as in the seventeenth-century text of the *Sajarah Banten*.[29] In Ternate the purported arrival of Jaʿfar Ṣādiq to Ternate in 643/5 June 1245 is narrated in a number of local Malay manuscripts, and his stature as the founder of the royal lineage has resonated well into the twenty-first century.[30] The place and nature of ʿAlid elements in the history of Islam in Maluku is a complex subject, and one that I will be developing in a future study.

Taken together then, this material from Nīshābūrī's text presents us with new views of the extent of Indo-Persian networks to the eastern edge of the maritime Muslim world in the early modern period. As such this text not only helps us to comprehend a larger, more complex map of interconnections across an expanding maritime Muslim world, but also provides a striking comparative perspective on the accelerating processes of social transformation taking place in Southeast Asia during a period that was also marked by the arrival and intervention of new European powers in the region.[31]

BIBLIOGRAPHY

Alam, Muzzafar. 2007. 'An Ocean of Wonders', in Sanjay Subrahmanyam and Muzaffar Alam (eds), *Indo-Persian Travels in the Age of Discoveries, 1400–1800*. Cambridge: Cambridge University Press, pp. 130–74.

Andaya, Leonard. 1993. *The World of Maluku: Eastern Indonesia in the Early Modern Period*. Honolulu: University of Hawaiʾi Press.

Balkhī, Maḥmūd Ibn Amīr Walī. 1984. *Baḥr Al-Asrār Fī Manāqib Al-Akhyār*. Karachi: Pakistan Historical Society.

Baker, Chris and Pasuk Phongpaichit. 2017. *A History of Ayutthaya Siam in the Early Modern World*. Cambridge: Cambridge University Press.

Blagden, C. O. 1930. 'Two Malay Letters from Ternate in the Moluccas, Written in 1521 and 1522', *Bulletin of the School of Oriental Studies, University of London* 6.1, pp. 87–101.

Brakel, L. F. 1970. 'Persian Influence on Malay Literature', *Abr Nahrain* 9, pp. 1–16.

Bukhari Al-Jauhari. 1966. *Tāj al-salātīn*, Hussan Kalid, ed. Kuala Lumpur: Dewan Bahasa dan Pustaka, Kementerian Pendidikan Malaysia.

Colless, E. Brian. 1969. 'Persian Merchants and Missionaries in Medieval Malaya', *Journal of the Malaysian Branch of the Royal Asiatic Society*, 42, pp. 10–47.

Ludvik, Kalu and Claude Guillot. n.d. 'La Jerusalem Javanaise et Sa Mosquee Al-Aqsa: Texte de Fondation de La Mosquee de Kudus Date 956/1549', *Archipel* 63, pp. 27–56.

---

[29] *Sejarah Banten* (History of Banten) is a Javanese text containing conversion stories. Most manuscripts of this chronicle are late-nineteenth century, but two are copies of originals written in the 1730s and 1740s. Ricklefs, 1993, p. 10. Kalus and Guillot, 2002, p. 45.

[30] Song, 2019, pp. 117–18.

[31] This article was originally part of my thesis, which was supervised by Professor Michael Feener and Arlo Griffiths. My sincere thanks go out to them for their comments and corrections.

McPherson, Kenneth. 2004. *The Indian Ocean: A History of People and the Sea*. New Delhi: Oxford University Press.

Marcinkowski, M. Ismail. 2002. 'The Iranian-Siamese Connection: An Iranian Community in the Thai Kingdom of Ayutthaya', *Iranian Studies*, 35 (1–3), pp. 23–46.

Marcinkowski, M. Ismail. 2000. 'Persian Religious and Cultural Influence in Siam/Thailand and Maritime Southeast Asia in Historical Perspective: A Plea for a Concerted Interdisciplinary Approach', *Journal of the Siam Society*, 88.1 & 2, pp. 186–94.

Marrison, G. E. 1955. 'Persian Influences in Malay Life (1280–1650)', *Journal of the Malayan Branch of the Royal Asiatic Society*, 28, pp. 52–69.

Masashi, Hirosue. 2017. 'The Rise of Muslim Coastal in North Sumatra: Coastal Rulers and Powers over Hinterland Fertility', in Karashima Noboru and Hirosue Masashi (eds), *State Formation and Social Integration in Pre-Modern South and Southeast Asia*. Tokyo: The Toyo Bunko, pp. 263–84.

Nīshābūrī, Maḥmūd ibn ʿAbdullah. n.d. *Jāmiʿ al-Barr wa ʾl-baḥr*. Islamabad: The Ganj Bakhsh Library MS, 4035.

Nīshābūrī, Maḥmūd ibn ʿAbdullah. n.d. *Maātir-i Quṭbshāhī-i Maḥmūdī*. London: British Library MS IO Islamic, 841.

Reid, Anthony. 2015. *A History of Southeast Asia: Critical Crossroads*. Chichester: Wiley Blackwell.

Reid, Anthony. 1999. *Charting the Shape of Early Modern Southeast Asia*. Chiang Mai: Silkworm Books.

Reid, Anthony. 1993. 'Islamisation and Christianization in Southeast Asia: The Critical Phase, 1550–1650', in Anthony Reid (ed.), *Southeast Asia in the Early Modern Era: Trade, Power, and Belief*. New York: Cornell University Press, pp. 151–79.

Ridjali. 1977. *Hikayat Tanah Hitu*, Z. J. Manusama, ed. Leiden: Leiden University.

Seung-Won, Song. 2020. 'A Heavenly Nymph Married to an Arab Sayyid', *Indonesia and the Malay World* 48, 140, pp. 116–35.

CHAPTER 8

'Sword of the Two Sanctuaries': Islam of and in the Modern Indian Ocean

M. REZA PIRBHAI

INTRODUCTION

This article discusses the relevance of the Barelvi-Deobandi schism in South Asian Sunnism to Islam and Muslims about the modern Indian Ocean. Anchored by a consideration of Wahhabism's place in early Barelvi and Deobandi *fatwa* and polemical literature, the trans-oceanic connections revealed are long-standing and extend well beyond littoral societies. They represent a history *in* the Indian Ocean as part of a global realm dominated by Europe, though the universalisms and cosmopolitanisms they uphold are *of* the Indian Ocean. That is to say, European influence impacted the definition of Islam globally, discursively shaping a thoroughly modern variant in the nineteenth century, represented in South Asia by Barelvis and Deobandis. However, this is not just an Islam in dialogue with Europe. Modern Islam also explicitly rejects pre-modern Islam – the latter in a manner analogous with Wahhabism and in keeping with eighteenth-century reformers more generally. In the light of the Barelvi-Deobandi schism, therefore, a history *of* the modern Indian Ocean as a discreet region remains tenable, but modern forms of Islamic universalism and cosmopolitanism arising in the region and connecting its constituent societies since the nineteenth century shape them differently than under the influence of pre-modern Islam. The consequences for inter- and intra-faith relations are particularly significant.

In 1905, the founder of the Barelvi school of Sunnism in South Asia, Ahmad Raza Khan (d. 1921), travelled to Mecca to perform his second Hajj. While there he presented a group of illustrious Sunni colleagues with a tract arguing that his South Asian rivals of the Deobandi school – also founded in the late nineteenth century – were 'Wahhabis' deserving of being declared apostates (*murtadds*) and infidels (*kafirs*). He returned to South Asia in 1906 armed with thirty-three supportive endorsements (*tasdiqat*) from those colleagues met in the Hijaz. Of course, upon the publication of these *tasdiqat* in a work titled *Hussam al-Haramayn 'ala Manhar al-Kufr wa 'l-Mayn* (The Sword of the Two Sanctuaries at the Throat of Infidelity and Falsehood), Ahmad Raza's opponents were not too reserved to publish works of their own refuting his accusations and charging that he is, in fact, a transgressor of the faith like Wahhabis. One of the earliest such refutations was Khalil Ahmad Shaharanpuri's (d. 1927) *Al-Muhannad 'ala 'l-Mufannad* (The Sword Against the Disproved).

With the above two texts began what historians of the Barelvi-Deobandi schism refer to as a 'Fatwa War', adherents of both schools of thought continuing to pronounce *takfir* (excommunication) against each other into the present.[1] In Pakistan, the schism has even led to the pen quite literally being forsaken for the sword on various occasions. Aside from targeting Shi'a and Ahmadi places of worship, Deobandi religio-political outfits like the Tehrik-i Taliban Pakistan and Lashkar-i Janghvi have bombed and strafed Barelvi gatherings, mosques and affiliated Sufi shrines.[2] Although Barelvi adherents have not resorted to such extremes, they too have been radicalised, often scuffling with Deobandis, attacking Ahmadis and their mosques, as well as most infamously refusing to condemn the murder, by one of their ranks, of the Punjab's Sunni governor for criticising Pakistan's blasphemy laws.[3] The South Asian diaspora has extended their rivalry across the globe – both schools are represented by prominent madrasas in the UK, the USA, the Caribbean and, of course, the Indian Ocean. In all these states and regions, both Barelvi and Deobandi clerics are overwhelmingly influential among South Asian populations. They also proselytise among non-South Asians.[4] The basis of their schism, therefore, cannot be ignored in assessing the nature of Islam currently practised in their spheres of influence.

The task of charting Islamic currents about the modern Indian Ocean is tackled by first outlining the intellectual pedigree of the Barelvi and Deobandi schools, placing them in the socio-political context of the eighteenth and nineteenth centuries. The second section focuses on the literature associated with the early twentieth-century incident mentioned above, including the composition and attitudes of the non-South Asian scholars resident in the Hijaz, when the

[1] Metcalf, 1982; Sanyal, 1996.
[2] See, for example, Behuria, 2008; Jackson, 2013.
[3] Khan, 2011. Also, see such press reports on current events as: 'Pakistan's Barelvis: Transformation from Peaceful to Violent?' DW [https://www.dw.com/en/pakistans-barelvis-transformation-from-peaceful-to-violent/a-41744277; accessed on 23/1/2019].
[4] For the global outreach of Deobandis and Barelvis, including in the Indian Ocean region, see for example, Ingram, 2018. As Sufis, the spread of these movements can also be placed within the context of Sufi networks as studied in Bang, 2014.

opening salvos of the Barelvi-Deobandi 'Fatwa War' were fired. By focusing on the place each school ascribes Wahhabism in their literature, one observation made abundantly clear is that although Wahhabism is considered a legitimate form of Sunni Islam today – largely thanks to Saudi Arabian patronage since the 1930s – only a century ago it existed under the widespread charge of infidelity even in Arabia.[5] However, it must be added that the intellectual trends commonly associated with Wahhabism were already impacting social relations well before Saudi funds came into play. With the rise of Barelvism and Deobandism, in fact, South Asia witnessed the advent of a modern form of Islam not unlike Wahhabism in one crucial manner.

As Itzchak Weismann explains, modern Islamic movements can be defined as forms of a 'Modernity from Within' – participants in a 'discourse . . . accomplished in the course of the twentieth century over against two Others: the external Other of the West and the internal Other of tradition'.[6] In the latter regard, Ahmad Dallal clarifies that tradition, or more accurately 'pre-modern Islamic thought', is not in fact forsaken by most late movements, as it was and is in Wahhabism, but is 'appropriated' and 'reconstructed' under European influence.[7] Barelvis and Deobandis are approached here through this lens on modern Islam. Their appropriation of the past is evidenced by their claims to practise *taqlid* (imitation) in the Hanafi school of law, despite obvious divergences from the past and each other. Their reconstructions of Islam, however, are commonly driven to dismiss the authority of the past, approaching tradition as Other, with much the same implications as Wahhabism.

The Barelvi-Deobandi schism within modern Islam, including its relationship with Wahhabism, is a window on the manner in which Islam should be seen in the post-1800 Indian Ocean context – the very context in which these movements arose. In particular, this complex of Sunni thought problematises certain generalisations found in such widely read and influential works on the Indian Ocean as those of Michael Pearson and Sugata Bose. The first sets the stage by arguing for a historical site of exchange transformed by European intervention particularly since the 1800s, most succinctly described as a shift from the history *of* the Indian Ocean as a distinct space to one *in* the Indian Ocean as part of a global realm.[8] And as Markus P. M. Vink has pointed out, '[t]hese sentiments are widely shared among scholars of the Indian Ocean and "the new thalassology"'.[9] Sugata Bose, however, counters that under the rule of the 'modernizing colonial

---

[5] Much has been written on the spread of Wahhabism under Saudi Arabian patronage. For example, see Ayoob and Kosebalaban, 2009; Commins, 2006; DeLong-Bas, 2004; El Fadl, 2005.
[6] Weismann, 2011.
[7] Dallal, 2000.
[8] Pearson, 2003.
[9] Vink, 2007.

state' and despite the wider influences originating beyond the Indian Ocean, an 'interregional arena' and forms of vernacular 'cosmopolitism' and 'universalism' endured and developed.[10]

No doubt the example of the Barelvi-Deobandi schism adds to the veracity of Bose's intervention, at least so far as an interregional arena exhibiting its own forms of cosmopolitanism and universalism is concerned. But the manner in which their appropriation of the past differs from each other, not to mention shifts noted to have occurred over the twentieth century including the legitimation of Wahhabism, is further indicative of the veracity of John M. Willis' caution, directed at both Pearson and Bose, that vernacular modes of universalism must be understood to arise 'from within particular discursive traditions and makes possible particular cosmopolitan subjects'.[11] Thus, by highlighting an example of exclusionary politics among South Asian Muslims already evident at the turn of the twentieth century – the works of the Indian National Congressman Abul Kalam Azad (d. 1958) – Willis problematises the 'Indian cosmopolitanism' and 'Islamic universalism' that Bose presents as general. The Barelvi-Deobandi schism, in fact, further cramps the room for Bose's timeless dichotomy between an inclusive 'Indian Muslim sensibility' and 'Islamic universalism' on the one hand, and an exclusive Wahhabi 'bigotry' on the other.[12] The connections between Islam and Muslims of the modern Indian Ocean post-1800 certainly reflect vernacular universalisms and cosmopolitanisms obscured by Pearson's emphasis on European activity, but they are far more dynamic, diverse and linked beyond the Indian Ocean than Bose's generalisations express.

Intellectual Pedigrees

The eighteenth and nineteenth centuries ushered momentous changes in both South and West Asia. Mughal, Safavid and Ottoman states not only dwindled in strength, but in the Safavid and Mughal cases collapsed entirely, giving way to a host of successor states in the eighteenth century. Most scholars agree that the decentralisation of power was driven by such economic realities as the rise across regions of capital-holding classes (entrepreneurs, petty landlords, tribal chiefs, and so on) who often allied with former governors to prompt the formation of more local successor states. These successor states in turn played their part in the eventual ascendancy of colonial states in the nineteenth century by forming alliances with colonial institutions such as the array of East India Companies.[13] Thus, from the perspective of the British Empire, as Bose points out, by the late

---

[10] Bose, 2009.
[11] Willis, 2014.
[12] Bose, 2009, pp. 224–32.
[13] Bayly, 1988.

nineteenth century 'an interregional strategic and political link had been forged' from Arabia to the Bay of Bengal – 'an increasingly centralized and modern state', distinct from the mere 'repository of the highest level of sovereignty' that were Mughal, Safavid and Ottoman predecessors.[14] The scholastic reflection of these developments, on which Pearson and Bose do not reflect, is evinced in Arabia and South Asia by such eighteenth-century reform movements as that led by the Wahhabis and Wali Allahis during the period of decentralisation, followed in the nineteenth century by the works of intellectual heirs also reacting to colonial ascendancy. The latter includes, but is not restricted to, the Barelvis and Deobandis.

Although eighteenth- and nineteenth-century reform movements are responses to different socio-political realities, it is important to begin consideration of nineteenth-century movements in the earlier phase as late scholars and schools roundly reference eighteenth-century thinkers as their precursors.[15] In South Asia, Shah Wali Allah (d. 1763), a scholar of primarily Naqshbandi Sufi and Hanafi lineage, is a prime point of reference for Barelvis and Deobandis. He witnessed the decline of Mughal authority and the rise of multiple successor states, Muslim and non-Muslim. Although late scholarship largely considers this to have been a century of economic and cultural effervescence, Wali Allah greeted Mughal decay as a sign of more general decline at least partly brought about by the doctrines of past authorities among the Ulama and Sufis to which his contemporaries adhered unquestioningly.[16] *Taqlid* (imitation), he argued, had distorted Islam, particularly given that even the greatest scholars of the past reflected their times and were fallible, even though he recommended adherence when there was no other choice.[17] Thus, he assumed (at least for himself) the right to *ijtihad* (independent reasoning) as a means by which to embark on a reformist agenda evident in all his dozens of works covering jurisprudence, theology, mysticism and philosophy. It is well beyond the scope of this study to delve into the broad spectrum of fields on which Wali Allah commented, but his legal thought provides a convenient point of focus and measure of influence among later South Asian Hanafis.

---

[14] Bose, 2009, pp. 41–8.
[15] Whereas most scholars agree that eighteenth-century reformers echo each other's interest in hadith study and law, debate rages over the extent to which parallels can be drawn and influence on latter-day thinkers/movements can be asserted. At one extreme, scholars such as John Voll argue that eighteenth-century thinkers and their nineteenth-century heirs are not merely linked by doctrinal orientation, but that they are also bound by scholarly networks that extend from West Africa to Southeast Asia. Others, such as Ahmad Dallal, argue that parallels and scholarly networks are undermined by the particulars of their thought, while latter-day thinkers/movements do not reflect the breath of eighteenth-century forbearers, nor adhere to the same impetus, working under European hegemony. See the articles in Levtzion and Voll, 1987; and, Dallal 2000 and 2018.
[16] See, for example, Baljon 1986.
[17] Wali Allah, 1996, p. 351.

With regard to the *shari'a*, Wali Allah's *ijtihad* applied the principle of *talfiq* (piecing together) to Hanafi and Shafi'i rulings when explicit passages in the Qur'ān and hadith were not available.[18] Furthermore, he did not acknowledge all opinions as equally valid when there was difference between them even within one school (*ikhtilaf*), as had a great variety of foundational Hanafis and others. In Wali Allah's estimation, which he attributed to the Shafi'i school's lead, only that opinion which 'hits the target' of Qur'ānic meaning and/or the support of a sound hadith should be followed.[19] In addition, the authority of opinions dependent on *ijma'* should be restricted to those decided upon by the companions of the Prophet, not later scholars, while those employing *qiyas* should not include the tools of *istislah* (public utility) and *istihsan* (juristic preference) – staples of Hanafi jurisprudence.[20] The implication is a return to the textual sources and emphasis on Prophetic practice, as much as possible unadulterated by the formulae of past scholars.

Wali Allah's contemporary, Muhammad ibn Abd al-Wahhab, was born in 1703 into a family of Hanbali jurists in Najd. As young man, he performed the Hajj and it was while in the Hijaz, particularly in Medina, that his ideas are said to have taken shape under the tutelage of various old school and reformist scholars, including South Asians.[21] He travelled further from there, to Basra, and on his return to Najd sought reform by means of *ijtihad*, acknowledging only Hanbali rulings that did not contradict his readings of Qur'ān and hadith. This does not mean that Abd al-Wahhab was following precedents from South Asia, nor vice versa, but it is certainly the case that his approach to past scholarship was not unique. The drive to emphasise Prophetic practice, in fact, very much echoes Wali Allah's legal thought, despite the fact that Abd al-Wahhab professed Hanbalism and rejected Sufism outright, while the former was a Hanafi and Naqshbandi Sufi. In Abd al-Wahhab's *Kitab al-Tawhid* (The Book of Divine Unity), like his South Asian contemporary's *Tuhfat al-Muwahiddun* (The Wonder of Monotheism), the author places greatest emphasis on a return to scriptural texts, defining all outside of them as *shirk* (associationism) and *bid'a* (innovation).[22] Thus, the implication in both cases, expressed here in Abd al-Wahhab's call, is that such practices as the use of amulets and talismans, sacrifice in the name of any but Allah, saintly or any other form of intercession, the visitation of graves, and so on – all legitimate by past scholarly criteria – stand uniformly condemned.[23]

[18] Wali Allah, 1955, pp. 346–58.
[19] Ibid., pp. 350–4.
[20] Wali Allah, 1996, pp. 349, 435–6.
[21] Commins, 2006; Crawford, 2014; Voll, 1980; Wagemakers, 2012.
[22] See, for example, Pirbhai, 2009.
[23] Abd al-Wahhab, 1996, pp. 32–4, 46–57, 71–82.

Moving into the nineteenth century, the general urge to emphasise Prophetic practice and reevaluate the worth of past scholarship evident in the works of both Wali Allah and Abd al-Wahhab is easily recognisable in South Asian movements now responding to colonial intervention. One such thinker was Shah Muhammad Ismail (d. 1831) – Wali Allah's grandson, a student of his sons and a Naqshbandi Sufi – whose Tariqa-i Muhammadiyya movement claimed Wali Allah's inspiration in assuming the authority of *ijtihad*. But operating in an environment overrun by British and Sikh ascendancy, Muhammad Ismail responded to the latest threats by narrowing the field of legal opinion to acknowledge only Abu Hanifa's (d. 767) rulings when primary textual sources were not specific. As outlined in Muhammad Ismail's *Taqwiyyat al-Iman* (The Strengthening of the Faith), authored after returning from a visit to the Hijaz for Hajj, the effect is that past and current scholars are accused of promoting various forms of *shirk* and *bid'a*, just as in the aforementioned works of Wali Allah and Abd al-Wahhab. Consequently, although a Naqshbandi Sufi like his forefathers, doctrines such as those acknowledging the Prophet's and various *pirs*' (Sufi saints) ability to see the unseen (*'alam ghayr*) beyond the glimpse granted by revelation (*wahy*), as well as prophetic or saintly intercession (*shafa'a*), and such broadly legitimate practices as pilgrimages to Sufi shrines, the tombs of holy figures and even family graves are condemned as *shirk* and *bid'a*.[24] Such similarities between Muhammad Ismail's work and that of Abd al-Wahhab has long led some historians (including the British colonial authorities of the day) to consider him to have come under the influence of Wahhabis while travelling in Arabia, though the issue is debated, particularly given Wali Allah's precedent.

At any rate, the founders of the Deobandi movement – named for the town in which their first madrasa was established in 1867, about a decade after the formal British Raj had taken hold – were students of both Wali Allah's descendants and Tariqa-i Muhammadiyya scholars, from whom they drew much inspiration. Yet, they officially denied *ijtihad*, proclaiming *taqlid* in the Hanafi School. Upon closer inspection, however, Deobandis continued exactly the jurisprudential methods of their professed forbearers. The Deobandi founder Rashid Ahmad Gangohi's (d. 1905) *Fatawa-i Rashidiyya* (The Legal Opinions of Rashid) explicitly endorses Muhammad Ismail's approach to law, describing his method as that which Deobandis follow; that is, to appeal to Qur'ān and hadith first, and if no answer is found, to turn to the opinions of Hanafism alone. Furthermore, if there are differences of opinion between Hanafi scholars, the one reflecting a Deobandi scholar's reading of Qur'ān and hadith is given precedence.[25] The only point on which Deobandis differ with the Tariqa-i

---

[24] Ismail, 1958, 35–74; Metcalf, 2009, pp. 201–11.
[25] Gangohi, 1967, pp. 219–26, 292.

Muhammadiyya, therefore, is the resort to more than Abu Hanifa's opinion, bringing them more into line with Wali Allah.[26] Otherwise, the Deobandis' *taqlid* is virtually identical to Wali Allah and the Tariqa-i Muhammadiyya's *ijtihad*. Thus, just like Muhammad Ismail, one of Rashid Ahmad's *fatwas* declares any who believe in the Prophet's ability to see the unseen (*'alam ghayb*) to be *kafirs* – a point of major contention with Barelvis as discussed below.[27] As well, despite Naqshbandi Sufi bonds, Deobandi attitudes towards Sufism more generally echo the Tariqa-i Muhammadiyya. Along with remonstrations against the visitation of tombs, and so on, such staples of Sufi ritual to date as the *'urs* (death anniversaries) of *pirs* – let alone regional festivals like *Shab-i Barat*, Shia *Muharram* festivals and even Sunni celebrations of *milad al-nabi* (the Prophet's birthday) – are declared beyond the *shari'a*.[28]

Further reflecting Wali Allah's and the Tariqa-i Muhammahiyya's influence, although Deobandi founders included works from the influential eighteenth-century *Dars-i Nizamiyya* 'curriculum' in their madrasa, they placed greatest stress on hadith.[29] The number of works of hadith – the prime source of Prophetic practice – jumped from one in the *Dars-i Nizamiyya* to twelve at Deoband, while those on logic dropped from eleven to six and the five works on mathematics and astronomy were entirely deleted.[30] And in the realm of practice, second generation Deobandis like Ashraf Ali Thanavi (d. 1943) also went further than his predecessors, seeking to stay the influence of European customs. In his widely read *Bihishti Zewar*, Thanavi argues that what is not mentioned in scriptural texts is either wasteful, unnecessary or distracting, and so must be considered sinful. In this light, mere participation in song or dance, in the keeping of dogs as pets, the decorating of one's home with pictures, playing card games or chess, and flying kites or setting off fireworks, is identified as *bid'a*.[31] According to the Deobandi version of the *shari'a*, therefore, doctrines, rituals and customs not regarded as *shirk* or *bid'a* even by Wali Allah in the eighteenth century, let alone that of the earlier Hanafi thought, were added to the list of the un-*shar'i* in the late nineteenth century.

---

[26] At times, Deobandis also used Wali Allah's approach to *ijtihad*; namely, *talfiq*. See, Masud, 1996. In the same volume see Metcalf, 1996.

[27] Gangohi, 1967, p. 228.

[28] Also, Imdad Allah, 1960.

[29] The *Dars-i Nizamiyya* 'curriculum', articulated in the early eighteenth century by a scholar at the eminent 'Madrasa-i Farangi Mahall' in Lucknow, places equal emphasis on religious and rational sciences. Thus, it includes the study of multiple works in Arabic grammar and syntax, Quranic exegesis, jurisprudence, the principles of jurisprudence, theology, philosophy, hadith, logic, astronomy and mathematics. For two versions of the *Dars-i Nizamiyya* and the context in which it was articulated, see, Robinson 2001.

[30] Siddiqi, 1972, p. 121. Also, 'The System of Education' at: [http://www.darululoom-deoband.com/english/sys_of_edu/index.htm; accessed on 13/11/2016].

[31] Thanavi, 1914, pp. 3–7.

Ahmad Raza Barelvi was born into the same colonial environment as the founding Deobandis.[32] Descended from a family once in the employ of the Mughals as soldiers, his grandfather, Raza Ali, had switched to scholarship as opportunities for martial employment diminished with the fortunes of Muslim polity. Raza Ali and his son, Naqi Ali (d. 1880) – Ahmad Raza's father – gained reputations as learned Sufis and 'alims in their locality near Delhi and Ahmad Raza's primary instructor in all the works listed in the *Dars-i Nizamiyya* 'curriculum' was his father, from whom he received several *sanads* (certificates of study) and *ijazas* (permission to teach). By age fourteen, his father had also granted Ahmad Raza the authority to issue *fatwas* – a great responsibility seldom afforded so young a scholar. At twenty-one years of age, Ahmad Raza began his formal initiation as a Sufi under the tutelage of a prominent exponent of the Qadiri order. A year later, in 1878, Ahmad Raza accompanied his father to the Hijaz on his first Hajj. In Mecca, a prominent Sufi no less significantly certified him in the ways of the Qadiri order. The *muftis* (jurist consults) of the Hanafi and Shafi'i schools of law also extended Ahmad Raza their *sanads* and *ijazas* in hadith, *tafsir* (exegesis), *fiqh* (jurisprudence) and *usul al-fiqh* (principles of jurisprudence), even allowing him to use their names when teaching these subjects. And most meaningfully, so far as the depth of the familiarity between South Asian and Hijaz-based Ulama and Sufis is concerned, all this occurred based on the latter's knowledge of his father's reputation, rather than as a result of Ahmad Raza's studying under them. His biographers, both partisan and scholarly, further note that aside from the *sanads* and *ijazas* from his father and other South Asian scholars, those issued in the Hijaz played a significant role in establishing his credentials, even contributing to his proclamation as *Mujaddid* (Renewer of Faith) by followers about the turn of the twentieth century – the merit (*fada'il*) accorded Mecca and Medina extending to scholars learning and teaching there, particularly in South and Southeast Asia.[33]

Like Deobandis, Ahmad Raza and later Barelvis also acknowledged the influence of Wali Allah in seeking to emphasise Prophetic practice. Like Deobandis, they also proclaimed that their school of thought upheld Hanafi *taqlid*. Unlike the Deobandis, however, when the Barelvis spoke of *taqlid*, they allowed for far more latitude in drawing from the spectrum of doctrines, rituals and customary rites past Hanafi jurists had legitimated, such as the idea that the Prophet and *pirs* could glimpse the unseen beyond revelation, or the legitimacy of *milad al-nabi* celebrations. Barelvis also more thoroughly allowed for Sufi norms, including belief in the intercession of *pirs*. As such, it should come as no surprise that from his grandfather's day, scholars of Ahmad Raza's ilk were

---

[32] Bihari, 1938.
[33] Basri, 2008.

engaged in pitched intellectual battles with those of Deobandi lineage. For example, when Muhammad Ismail of the Tariqa-i Muhammadiyya published his *Taqwiyyat al-Iman*, scholarly associates of Ahmad Raza's grandfather, followed by Ahmad Raza's father himself, were at the forefront of the rebuttal around Delhi, and Ahmad Raza carried forward their mantle, including their use of the term Wahhabi in reference to opponents. It is worth noting, therefore, that the use of the term for the Tariqa-i Muhammadiyya is not an adoption of British terminology. Rather, the British appear to have adopted the term from indigenous rhetoric. In fact, it is Usha Sanyal's opinion that Ahmad Raza's representation of the Deobandis as Wahhabis follows from his ultimately tracing their ideals back to the Arabian Wahhabis by means of the intermediacy of the Tariqa-i Muhammadiyya.[34] Whether or not such transregional influences were directly established is debatable, as previously mentioned. However, it is readily apparent that Ahmad Raza would associate the Deobandis with Wahhabis due to his recognition of their doctrinal acceptance of Wali Allah and the Tariqa-i Muhammadiyya's form of *ijtihad* – one that thoroughly rejected past authority – despite their claims of *taqlid* in Hanafism.

Considered collectively, as even this brief narrative suggests, Wali Allah and Abd al-Wahhab, as well as Tariqa-i Muhammadiyya, Deobandi and Barelvi movements, are responses to regionally and temporally different political and economic factors, as well as divided along doctrinal lines (that is, forms of *ijtihad* versus forms of *taqlid*, Sufi versus anti-Sufi, Hanafi versus Hanbali, and so on). Their practical implications also vary, none going as far as Wahhabis with regard to Sufism. Even if only speaking of Barelvis and Deobandis, the former's *taqlid* allowed for such practices as the visitation of tombs, saintly intercession and so forth, while the latter's *taqlid* sought to severely restrict the same but did not invalidate Sufism altogether as in Wahhabism. Both nineteenth-century movements, however, fall into the modern camp, for although they explicitly acknowledge the authority of the past by means of *taqlid*, they appropriate mostly eighteenth-century reformist attitudes towards the past – particularly the explicit want to accentuate scriptural sources and Prophetic practice – when reconstructing Islam in a nineteenth century dominated by Europeans. A closer consideration of the turn of the twentieth century debacle between Barelvis and Deobandis, in fact, adds to the definition of both as modern in the sense of Othering the Islamic past in ways common to Wali Allah and Abd al-Wahhab, with obvious repercussions on the complex of vernacular universalisms defining the societal contours of the modern Indian Ocean.

---

[34] Sanyal, 1996, pp. 204–13.

BARELVIS, DEOBANDIS AND THE HIJAZI ULAMA

It was during a period of open conflict between the Hijazi Sharifs, backed by the Ottomans, and the Najd-based Saudi-Wahhabis – hostilities followed closely by the British for political and economic reasons – that Ahmad Raza visited the Hijaz in 1905–6. Not being under Saudi-Wahhabi rule at the turn of the twentieth century, Mecca and Medina were still, as they long had been, host to a multitude of Ulama and Sufis representative of various sects and schools of thought. Madrasas, *ribats* (Sufi hospices) and the sacred mosques of both Mecca and Medina had long served as sites of teaching and learning, most often funded by non-Hijazi states and potentates (including a long list from South Asia), and one of their most distinctive features was the cosmopolitanism of the resident Ulama and Sufis. From South Asia in particular, scholars of great note visited, resided and taught in Mecca and Medina, and by so doing they joined others from various other parts of the Muslim world, east and west. The cosmopolitanism of the scholars in Mecca and Medina at any given time was, of course, also reflected in the diversity of subjects taught from the perspectives of various theological, legal and mystical schools.[35]

This reality contributes a great deal to appreciating Ahmad Raza's relationship with the scholars resident in the Hijaz, beginning with the support they had afforded him since his first visit in 1878. Indeed, it adds further context (beyond the disparaging opinions of Wahhabism already present in both regions) to his use of the term Wahhabi in reference to his South Asian opponents. This is documented in 1900, when one of his *fatwas* against another of his South Asian adversaries labelled Wahhabi – the Nadwat al-Ulama; a conglomerate of Sunni scholars that sought to reform madrasas by emphasising Qur'ān and hadith at the expense of broader scholasticism – was published with the endorsements (*tasdiqat*) of sixteen scholars based in Mecca and seven in Medina.[36] But it is Ahmad Raza's visit in 1905–6 that best illumines the relevance of the Deobandi-Barelvi divide to the broader complex of universalisms at play across regions.

By the time of Ahmad Raza's second arrival in 1905, his reputation among resident scholars was high enough for some to visit his abode and seek his legal opinions on such practicalities as the legitimacy of paper money and doctrinal considerations related to the extent of Prophet Muhammad's knowledge.[37] The example of Ahmad Raza, therefore, reconfirms the reputation attained by certain South Asian scholars beyond their home region and their influence in the Muslim world beyond. It also implies that a variety of perspectives represented

---

[35] Hurgronje, 1970; Ochsenwald, 1984; Voll, 1980.
[36] Sanyal, 2005, p. 65.
[37] Sanyal, 2005, p. 73.

by South Asians would travel abroad, and this too is validated by the fact that, seeing one of his Deobandi opponents – Khalil Ahmad Shaharanpuri – already in Mecca swaying a judgement against a scholar who shared Ahmad Raza's views on the Prophet's knowledge of the unseen, the latter now took it upon himself to defend the accused and his opinion won broad favour. Sanyal concludes, this success 'appears to have prompted him to seek their confirmation' of his earlier *fatwa* against a Deobandi on the issue of the extent of the Prophet's knowledge.[38]

To accomplish the task, Ahmad Raza penned a polemical work titled *Al-Mu'tamad al-Mustanad* (The Reliable Supports), drawing from his earlier *fatwa*, but expanded to outline his perspective on a number of South Asian scholars representative of Ahmadi, Ahl-i Hadith and Deobandi movements, which he presented to the Ulama and Sufis in the Hijaz.[39] Here, he first outlined the dissolute state of Sunnism in South Asia, a situation in which the 'fundamentals of the faith' (*dharuriyyat-i din*) – which he defines by means of a list of prominent works by past scholars, ranging from *Al-Hidaya* (The Guidance) of Burhan al-Din Ali al-Marghinani (d. 1196) to the seventeenth-century *Fatawa-i Alamgiri* (The Legal Opinions of Alamgir) – are denied by the aforementioned 'Wahhabis'. All are, therefore, declared apostates (*murtadds*) and infidels (*kafirs*) on the authority of the aforementioned works.[40] Although his attack is not restricted to Deobandis, three of the scholars he terms *Wahhabiyya Amthaliyya* (Likeness Wahhabis) and *Wahhabiyya Khawatimiyya* (Finality Wahhabis), whom he argues deny the uniqueness and finality of Prophet Muhammad, are Deobandis, while the others mentioned are Ahl-i Hadith. It is only Deobandis, however, led by Rashid Ahmad Gangohi, that Ahmad Raza calls *Wahhabiyya Kadhdhabiyya* (Lying Wahhabis), who teach that God could lie, thus bringing into question the truth of even the *shahada* (profession of faith). Also purportedly led by Rashid Ahmad of Deoband are the *Wahhabiyya Shaytaniyya* (Satanic Wahhabis), whom Ahmad Raza accuses of teaching that Satan's knowledge exceeds that of the Prophet's, for the former can see the unseen, while the Prophet cannot.[41] The same format is used to make his case throughout the work, shown here by focusing on the last category: the *Wahhabiyya Shaytaniyya*. Ahmad begins by quoting an illustratively offensive passage from a representative work, in this case Khalil Ahmad Shaharanpuri's *Barahin al-Qati'ah* (Certain

---

[38] Sanyal, 1996, p. 207.

[39] The Arabic and Urdu version consulted here is contained in: Khan, 2013. For background on Ahmadis, see Friedmann, 1989. For an introduction to the Ahl-i Hadith see Metcalf 1982, pp. 268–96. Suffice it to say, both the Ahmadi and Ahl-i Hadith creeds differ from Deobandis and Wahhabis in their particulars, but conform to the definition of the 'modern' more generally, eschewing the authority of the past – the first by claiming the insight of revelation (*wahy*), the latter by insisting on *ijtihad*.

[40] Khan, 2013, pp. 74–6.

[41] Ibid., pp. 79–92.

Proofs). This is followed, amid a flurry of admonition, with a rebuttal made up of the contrary statements of past scholars, here consisting of Imam al-Khafaji (d. 1658/9), Shaykh Abd al-Haq Dehlawi (d. 1642) and Ibn Hajar al-Asqalani (d. 1449).[42]

The first point to be taken from the work is that the charges that Ahmad Raza specifically laid at the doorstep of Deobandis were not new for him (for example, the recurrent issue of the Prophet's ability to see the unseen), nor was his use of the term Wahhabi to describe them. But what requires further note is that throughout the *Hussam al-Haramayn*, Ahmad Raza's perspective is legitimated by the selective use of pre-modern scholars of great repute, himself quoting Qur'ān and hadith most sparingly. As well, in keeping with pre-modern attitudes toward *takfir*, before now he had not gone as far as to collectively declare Deobandis apostates and infidels. Sanyal speculates that his attitude had changed by the time he travelled to the Hijaz in 1905–6, because his followers had since acknowledged him as the *Mujaddid*, leading his opponents to cry foul and elevate some of their own to that rank.[43] However, it seems as likely that the decision was influenced by the fact that Rashid Ahmad had indirectly declared Ahmad Raza and his followers' *kufr* in the earlier *fatwa* mentioned, which very much like Muhammad Ismail of the Tariqa-i Muhammadiyya and Khalil Ahmad's *Barahin al-Qati'ah*, limits the Prophet's power to see the unseen. Yet, it is again by appealing to the works of pre-modern scholars that Ahmad Raza argues *takfir* is necessary.[44] Thus, such factors now likely combined to prompt Ahmad Raza to ask leading colleagues in Mecca and Medina to provide endorsements (*tasdiqat*) for his larger arguments and thirty-three were forthcoming.

Ahmad Raza's perspective was endorsed by Shafi'i, Maliki and Hanafi *muftis* (jurist consults) and *qadis* (judges) of the highest rank and reputation then resident in the Hijaz.[45] As well, some were individually specialists in Quranic exegesis, hadith, theology, jurisprudence, the principles of jurisprudence and Sufism (belonging to various orders), which subjects they also taught. Poetry and astronomy has also been noted as the forte of some. Further regarding composition, there were some with local roots, but many were recent immigrants to Mecca and Medina, having been born, lived and studied in various other places beforehand. For example, Shaykh Umar ibn Hamdan al-Mahrasi (d. 1949) was

---

[42] Ibid., pp. 82–7.
[43] Sanyal 2005, p. 108.
[44] Khan, 2013, pp. 90–2.
[45] For the scholastic backgrounds of those who endorsed the *Hussam al-Haramayn* in Mecca and Medina, based largely on Arabic biographical dictionaries (*tabaqat*), see Ensari, n.d., pp. 10–42. Ensari's work has also been double-checked here by means of biographies of various scholars mentioned online, such Shaykh Abd al-Qadir Tawfiq a-Shalabi al-Tarablusi at: [http://www.taibanet.com/showthread.php?t=2745]; and, Shaykh Umar ibn Hamdan al-Mahrasi at: [http://www.daralhadith.org.uk/?p=594; both accessed on 13/11/2016].

born in Tunisia and resided in Cairo before moving to the Hijaz. Others were also from North Africa, such as Shaykh Muhammad ibn Ahmad al-Umari al-Wasti (d. 1946). Shaykh Abdul Qadir Tawfiq al-Shalabi al-Tarabulsi (d. 1950) was born in modern-day Lebanon, Shaykh Umar ibn Abu Bakr (d. 1935) and Shaykh Muhammad Said ibn Muhammad (d. 1936) were born in Yemen, Shah Muhammad Abd al-Haq Allahabadi (d. 1917) in South Asia, and Shaykh Abd al-Karim ibn Hamza (d. 1920) in Daghistan, Russia.[46] Even some of those known to have been born in the Hijaz were the descendants of migrants, such as Shaykh Sayyid Ahmad ibn Ismail al-Barzanji (d. 1916), whose scholarly fore-father was from Iraqi Kurdistan and settled in Medina in the early eighteenth century, and Shaykh Uthman ibn Abd al-Salam (d. 1907), whose forefather migrated from Russian Daghistan about the same time.[47] Nor were such figures necessarily bound to Mecca and Medina, whether from there, having been born there or only present when Ahmad Raza visited in 1905–6. Shaykh Sayyid Ismail ibn Khalil (d. 1911) died in Istanbul, Shaykh Sayyid Ahmad ibn Ismail al-Barzanji died in Damascus, Shaykh Muhammad ibn Yusuf (d. unknown) died in Indonesia, and Mawlana Ahmad bin Muhammad Zia al-Din (d. unknown) is known to have toured South Asia before his death.[48] As expressed in their *tasqidat*, their contributions to Ahmad Raza's charges do not go beyond praising his uprightness and erudition, while confirming his judgement of the accused as *murtadds* and *kafirs*. But further illustrating the seriousness of the transgression in the opinions of the Ulama and Sufis in the Hijaz, six of those who endorsed Ahmad Raza's *Al-Mu'tamad al-Mustanad* even declare it incumbent on the Muslim ruler of the day (*Imam*) to execute the accused if they do not repent.[49] Needless to say, the Deobandi in town was forced to cut short his stay.[50] And upon Ahmad Raza's return to South Asia in 1906, he was now confident enough to publish an abridged version of *Al-Mu'tamad al-Mustanad* together with the thirty-three *tasdiqat* obtained under the title *Hussam al-Haramayn 'ala Manhar al-Kufr wa 'l-Mayn*.

Deobandis are not Wahhabis. Nor is the issue here whether they or Wahhabis are guilty of transgressing the fundamentals of the faith as defined by Ahmad Raza. Rather, the fundamentals he outlines illustrate his own appropriation of pre-modern Islam, while his use of the term Wahhabi to reference Nadwat al-Ulama, Ahl-i Hadith, Ahmadi and Deobandi movements (all known to be divergent schools) makes explicit his use to reference all he thought trans-gressed his limits of *taqlid*, rather than to say that they collectively follow the

[46] Ensari, n.d., pp. 16–17, 22–7.
[47] Ibid., pp. 23–6.
[48] Ibid., pp. 21–2, 25–8.
[49] Khan, 2013, pp. 139–47, 150–1, 153–7, 174–5, 193–206.
[50] Sanyal, 2005, p. 109.

creed of Abd al-Wahhab in particular. Clearly, those of such high erudition in Mecca and Medina who supported Ahmad Raza were also aware of the fact that the charge of Wahhabism did not reference specifically Wahhabi doctrines, but the general demeanour of Wahhabism toward the authority of the past. Furthermore, Sanyal argues that the positive response to Ahmad Raza's entreaty was not made in answer to 'an immediate Wahhabi threat' in the Hijaz, nor does it imply 'an expression of direct political interest in Indian Wahhabis'.[51] Why, then, did such a diverse body step forward? I suggest that the only answer is that they, like Ahmad Raza, understood the term Wahhabi to refer to more than just Abd al-Wahhab's movement. They understood that it referred more generally to movements that challenged the authority of past scholarship in a particular way echoed in Wahhabism, even if originating outside Arabia and responding to colonial intervention. Indeed, only real fears of this modern trend identified with Wahhabism, at least as real as those felt by the like-minded and well-known Barelvis of South Asia, explains the Hijazi scholars not thoroughly checking whether the charges Ahmad Raza placed at his Deobandi opponents' doorstep were actually applicable to them. Rather, the verdict was decided based on Ahmad Khan's representation and reputation alone. It was decided, in other words, on the basis of a pre-existing, cosmopolitan network of scholars cognizant of the menace posed by a stream of modern movements that challenged the form of Islamic universalism represented by Ahmad Raza and others in this network.

The immediate result is that the door was left open for Deobandis to defend themselves, pleading misrepresentation, and their response is no less instructive of the divides and allegiances, existing and sought, across regions. The Deobandi founder Rashid Ahmad most heavily criticised by Ahmad Raza had died in 1905, but his colleagues and students now presented his *fatwas* on the issues, the proceedings best encapsulated in Khalil Ahmad Shaharanpuri's *Al-Muhannad 'ala 'l-Mufannad* – the very scholar who had previously been run out of town.[52] He now returned to Mecca and Medina and was posed twenty-six detailed questions by some of the Ulama who had endorsed Ahmad Raza's anti-Deobandi tract, covering every aspect of his accusations, in response to which Khalil Ahmad systematically presented Deobandi opinion as wholly in keeping with past opinion. The crux of the matter is that Khalil Ahmad emphasised the not entirely accurate perspective that Deobandis practice *taqlid*, not *ijtihad*, in the Hanafi School.[53] Two questions specifically dealing with the extent of the

---

[51] Sanyal, 1996, pp. 207–8.
[52] Shaharanpuri, n.d.. Another of Rashid Ahmad's students, Husayn Ahmad Madani, was also then residing in Medina and, as Metcalf writes, given that Ahmad Raza's 'success was potentially devastating' for him, 'both personally and professionally', he immediately 'sought out signers', some of whom 'he was able to convince . . . of the merit of his own and his elders' teachings'. See Metcalf, 2009, p. 67.
[53] Shaharanpuri, n.d., p. 23.

Prophet's knowledge of the unseen are illustrative. When Khalil Ahmad was asked (question 18) whether Deobandis assert that the Prophet's knowledge is limited to the *shariʿa*, not extending to the 'hidden secrets' (*al-asraf al-khafiyya*) and the 'divine judgement' (*al-hukm al-ilahiyya*) behind it, he quotes two verses from the Qurʾān which Deobandis are said to interpret to mean that the Prophet not only possessed such extensive knowledge, but that no one, not even angels and other prophets, match him.[54] Furthermore, when asked (question 19) if Deobandis asserted that Satan has greater knowledge, in absolute terms, than the Prophet – a charge Ahmad Raza made based on a passage from Khalil Ahmad's own *Barahin al-Qatiʿah* – the author categorically denies any such assertion. He explains that the supposedly offending work only states that the Prophet was unaware of some 'temporal particulars' in relation to Satan, but that his absolute knowledge outweighs that of Satan.[55]

Regarding attitudes toward Wahhabism, Khalil Ahmad accuses Ahmad Raza of being more akin to Wahhabis than Deobandis on the grounds that he 'conceals hopes of being the *Mujaddid*', and declares the infidelity of the Ulama of the *umma*, just as the followers of Muhammad ibn Abd al-Wahhab declared the infidelity of the *umma*.[56] Indeed, he refers to Ahmad Raza as the true innovator throughout and accuses him of contempt, envy, malice and hatred for Muslims and their highest authorities.[57] That is to say, Deobandis responded by distancing themselves from Wahhabis proper, rather than defending them, and by associating Ahmad Raza with Wahhabis reiterated the basic divides between those supposedly accepting the authority of the past and those who do not. And it worked. Although not unanimously, direct contact with Deobandis led a number of scholars who had endorsed Ahmad Raza to issue retractions. The controversy was also brought to the attention of prominent scholars in Cairo and Damascus, who further confirmed the Deobandis as mainstream Sunnis and not 'Wahhabis'.[58]

Reading between the lines of Khalil Ahmad's *Al-Muhannad ʿala ʾl-Mufannad*, however, reveals that unlike Ahmad Raza and the scholars he had convinced to side with him, including some of those who eventually issued retractions, Deobandis did not go as far as to declare Wahhabism proper to be apostasy and infidelity, just as Rashid Ahmad had not gone so far when dealing with the Ahl-i Hadith in South Asia.[59] In one response, Khalil Ahmad explains that there are various meanings attached to the term Wahhabi in South Asia,

---

[54] Ibid., pp. 46–7.
[55] Ibid., pp. 48–9.
[56] Ibid., p. 62.
[57] Ibid., p. 42.
[58] Ibid., pp. 75–126.
[59] Metcalf, 1996, p. 188.

from those who abandon *taqlid*, earning derision in the process, to those who are upright Sunnis.[60] Furthermore, regarding the Wahhabi condemnation of such rites as *milad al-nabi*, Khalil Ahmad does not declare the acknowledgement of the Prophet's birthday a form of *shirk*, as did Abd al-Wahhab, but like the Wahhabis does not consider it obligatory and condemns such customs as decorating mosques, and so forth, on the occasion – all broadly accepted forms of practice at the time.[61] And as for the Wahhabi condemnation of the *salaf* in particular, he asserts that Deobandis do not do this as it is considered 'denial' (*rafd*) of the creed and *bid'a*.[62] Crucially, however, even here he avoids any direct declaration of the Wahhabis as apostates and infidels based on their stated creed and acts.

The reluctance to pronounce *takfir* against Wahhabism proper can be read as purposefully meant to reflect pre-modern tolerance toward difference of opinion (*ikhtilaf*). In fact, when specifically asked about the actions of the Wahhabis in Arabia, Khalil Ahmad quotes one of the very pre-modern works used by Ahmad Raza to legitimate *takfir* to make the counter-argument that even in the case of the 'Khawarij' (Seceders) of old pre-modern scholars opined that there is no need to declare them *kafirs* for theirs is a type of interpretation – a principle he claims Deobandis uphold.[63] This is said in the context of the question of Abd al-Wahhab accusing 'all of *shirk*', thus insulting the companions of the Prophet (*salaf*) and legitimating the spilling of Muslim blood and looting of Muslim property. Khalil Ahmad continues that as the Wahhabis are not from the line of Deobandi scholars, the right or wrong of their reasons for spilling the blood of Muslims, and so forth, must yet be judged by Deobandis in light of the *shari'a*, thus evading the opportunity to state his judgement of Wahhabi actions in Arabia. He only says that if their victims are found to be transgressors of the faith, the action is right, whereas if they are not, the action is wrong. But there is a certain dishonesty in Khalil Ahmad's implication of unfamiliarity with Wahhabism proper, considering that when asked about Abd al-Wahhab's teachings, his teacher Rashid Ahmad had long before issued a *fatwa* clearly stating that the former was a Hanbali who strictly followed hadith injunctions and avoided *shirk*, adding that he also thought him a 'good man'.[64] Furthermore, the pre-modern respect and lenience for those with alternative perspectives that Khalil Ahmad exhibited in the Hijaz, stands in sharp contrast with Deobandi attitudes toward certain South Asian rivals back home. This includes Rashid Ahmad's previously mentioned indirect declaration of Ahmad

---

[60] Shaharanpuri, n.d., pp. 24–6.
[61] Ibid., pp. 52–5.
[62] Ibid., pp. 36–8.
[63] Ibid., p. 37.
[64] Gangohi, 1967, p. 292.

Raza's *kufr* for belief in the Prophet's power to see the unseen and, in the wake of the publication of *Hussam al-Haramayn*, the Deobandi Sayyid Muhammad Murtaza Hasan's (d. 1951) denunciation of Ahmad Raza as 'a *murtadd*, a *dajjal* (Anti-Christ) of the century and a great *kafir*'.[65]

It is clear from this exchange that to the Ulama and Sufis of Mecca and Medina, the root of Wahhabi apostasy was their outright rejection of past opinion (including that of earlier Hanbalis), on which basis the latter forsook past authority to reinterpret the status of the *salaf*, and so forth. Furthermore, although Ahmad Raza had long referred to Deobandis as Wahhabis primarily on the same general basis (denial of the authority of past opinion), the specifics of the charges he laid at the Deobandis' doorstep was not necessarily reflexive of the doctrines of Wahhabis. Thus, Deobandis could easily redeem themselves by distancing themselves from the broader doctrines and acts of actual Wahhabis, while also refuting the charges lodged against them by Ahmad Raza. However, this does not mean Deobandis were not, in fact, representative of the modern trend of reconstructing the past in a manner analogous with Wahhabism, particularly relative to the Barelvis and the Hijaz-based Ulama and Sufis with whom he was most closely associated. Indeed, it is for this very reason that all divides and overlaps are once again illustrated when the Saudi-Wahhabi regime established its grip on the Hijaz in 1924, at which point in time leading Deobandis like Shabbir Ahmad Uthmani (d. 1949) responded to Wahhabism's latest round of destroying tombs in Mecca and Medina and the want to destroy the dome above the Prophet's grave. He was part of a delegation representing the Deobandi-led Jamaat-i Ulama-i Hind, which travelled with representatives of the Khilafat Movement (headed by non-Deobandis) to a meeting of representatives from around the Muslim world convened by Ibn Saud in 1926.[66] Significantly, Shabbir Ahmad argued that Wahhabis were right to say that building over graves was not permissible, but the dome over the Prophet's grave should not be destroyed in order to avoid spreading disunity among Muslims – a line Willis has shown Abul Kalam Azad to have delivered in his own writings.[67] In other words, the Wahhabi position on the destruction of tombs was not condemned by the Deobandis on doctrinal grounds. Indeed, it was validated, but practicality was invoked to stay the act of iconoclasm. Meanwhile, it was scholars

---

[65] The quote is from the *Radd al-Takfir 'ala al-Fahash al-Tanzir*, originally cited in an article published in the journal *Tulu'-i Islam*, since reproduced at: [https://sites.google.com/site/basharatustad/fatwasagain steachother?tmpl=%2Fsystem%2Fapp%2Ftemplates%2Fprint%2F&showPrintDialog=1; accessed on 18/1/2018].

[66] Kramer 1986, pp. 106–217.

[67] For the full text of the speech, see Uthmani, n.d. As well, Ahl-i Hadith scholars were part of the delegation and fully supported the destruction of tombs. Since the 1970s they have also been major recipients of Saudi-Wahhabi largesse, along with Deobandis. See, Yoginder Sikand, 'Wahabi/Ahl-i Hadith, Deobandi and Saudi Connection', [https://sunninews.wordpress.com/2010/04/14/wahabiahle -hadith-deobandi-and-saudi-connection/; accessed on 11/2/2018].

like Abd al-Bari (d. 1926), leader of the Khilafat Movement and scion of the Madrasa-i Farangi Mahall in Lucknow – the very institution from which the eighteenth-century *Dars-i Nizamiyya* issued – who broke with Shabbir Ahmad and Azad to publish multiple tracks chastising the Saudi-Wahhabis outright for the demolitions on the basis of Qur'ān, hadith and Hanafi *fiqh*.[68] In fact, he went as far to write that South Asian Muslims should forego the Hajj so long as the Saudi-Wahhabis, who restricted pluralistic expressions of ritual and prayer, ruled the Hijaz. To which the Saudi-Wahhabis responded by declaring him a *kafir*.[69]

CONCLUSION

About the dawn of the twentieth century, South Asian Ulama and Sufis who visited or were resident in the Hijaz, and those from other parts of the Muslim world who did the same, were not just in contact, but many were well known to each other. They taught and studied together, issued *ijazas*, *sanads* and *tasdiqat* for each other, and consulted on scholarly questions and legal opinions. That very moment in time, however, was also a turning point. Focus on the Barelvi-Deobandi schism and the manner in which the term Wahhabi was used reveals that up until that moment, Wahhabism was broadly considered *kufr* and its adherents seen as *murtadds*. Indeed, the term Wahhabism was itself a catch-all for any who wished to argue that their opponents had abandoned the authority of the past. This would, of course, change after the establishment of Saudi Arabia in 1932. However, the intellectual legitimation of that change was already in place when Ahmad Raza and Khalil Ahmad Shaharanpuri sparred in 1906, for the very Barelvis and Deobandis seeking to establish their own credentials as representative of longstanding Sunnism by measuring themselves against Wahhabi innovation were themselves reflections of nineteenth-century scholarship that resembled Wahhabism in one significant manner. Both, most succinctly put, were modern in so far as each not only defined itself against the external Other of the West. They also constructed an internal Other out of pre-modern Islam in ways that reflect the very eighteenth-century trends that echo through both Wali Allah's and Abd al-Wahhab's works; particularly, the rejection of past scholarship in favour of an emphasis on Prophetic practice rooted in scriptural sources.

The outlines of these intellectual currents and scholarly alignments have significant implications for the manner in which the Indian Ocean must be conceived as a discreet space post-1800. First of all, the very networks of scholars make plain the fact that by the turn of the twentieth century, a history *in* the

---

[68] Willis, 2014, p. 579.
[69] Kramer, 1986, pp. 116, 121.

Indian Ocean, rather than *of* the region, is being written. After all, the case of Ahmad Raza's supporters has been shown to include men connected to places as far afield as North Africa, Anatolia and the Caucasus, not just the Indian Ocean region. However, the globalisation of the Indian Ocean initiated with European expansion also facilitated non-colonial networks not explored in Pearson's view. Indeed, Muslim connections are deeper and broad, including intellectual exchanges that shaped regions further afield, well represented by the nineteenth-century Barelvis and Deobandis. The Hijaz, in this sense, played a more significant role in maintaining Muslim bonds than is represented by the annual Hajj alone.

Bose, like Pearson before him, also considers the Hajj to be the primary factor connecting Muslims across regions, fostering communal and/or cosmopolitan identification by means of the occasional gathering. But Bose ventures further than Pearson to identify the Hajj as a 'crucial Indian Ocean activity' that reflects the continuance of an inclusive 'Indian Muslim sensibility' and a cosmopolitan 'Islam universalism' despite the advent of a 'modernising colonial state' and the Saudi-Wahhabi state he considers 'an ultra-orthodox Islamic one'.[70] Certainly, the examples of pilgrims he chooses to emphasise renders it so and convincingly establishes the continuance of vernacular cosmopolitanisms and universalisms after 1800. However, he makes nothing of Wahhabism renouncing the authority of the past, rather than harking back to an established orthodoxy, even of a Hanbali variety. Nor does he consider that many of the Ulama and Sufis of South Asia were essentially doing the same after 1800, resulting in a variety of schools whose doctrinal and practical outlooks differed from the past and each other. On one side were those like Ahmad Raza whose conception of *taqlid* in the Hanafi school of law sought the legitimacy of the past, but reflected a particular degree of scholastic variety and latitude in terms of practice in the present. And on the other were those like Deobandis who also claimed to be practising *taqlid* in the same legal school, but whose own scholasticism and ideal praxis represents a significantly different vision. In relation to Wahhabism, this is reflected by Barelvis upholding a far more inclusive understanding of the past than Wahhabis, whereas Deobandis undermined that past scholastic variety and the practices it legitimised much more like Wahhabis. As such, Barelvis explicitly declared Wahhabism and all who resembled it to have transgressed Islam, while Deobandis did not. The impression created in Bose's work, therefore, of a timeless dichotomy between 'Indian Muslim sensibility' and 'Wahhabi doctrine', or between 'Islamic universalism' and 'Indian cosmopolitanism' on the one hand, and Wahhabi 'bigotry' on the other, is highly problematic.[71] Indeed,

---

[70] Bose, 2009, p. 195.
[71] Bose, 2009, pp. 224, 232.

such stark divisions have already been questioned by Willis with the example of Abul Kalam Azad. What the featured exchange between Barelvis and Deobandi adds is the further sharpening of contours, revealing not just the rise of modern Islam post-1800, but more than one form of even modern Sunni universalism to have hence defined Indian Muslim sensibilities.

Clearly, the neat assumption of *an* Indian Muslim sensibility and *an* Islamic universalism is untenable. Rather, what resolves out of the Barelvi-Deobandi schism is multiple sensibilities and universalisms, each participating in transregional networks of scholars and believers, reflexive of differing degrees of inclusiveness and exclusiveness. Among these complexities, too, is a profound shift from pre-modern to modern Islam in Arabia and South Asia – one already initiated in the eighteenth century, outside of European influence, so far as the Othering of the pre-modern. This not only separates the universalisms of the Indian Ocean in the colonial nineteenth century from those past, but increasingly defines that which follows into the present.

Considering, in conclusion, the Hajj today as an indicator of all the above shifts into the modern and its effect. Yes, a variety of Muslims, even Shi'as and Sufis, still perform the pilgrimage. Cosmopolitanism, including various forms of association between Muslims with non-Muslims, even thrives. But no longer does the Hajj allow a contemporary Muslim to encounter pre-modern forms of Islamic universalism in the formal sense, for example hearing the sermons of a variety of professors in the mosques of the two sanctuaries or witnessing the variety of customary practices previously exhibited by pilgrims. And no longer does the Hajj facilitate Islamic scholars seeking and receiving *sanads*, *ijazas* and *tasdiqat* from any but Wahhabis and the modern schools that recognise them, such as Deobandis, thus fragmenting and weakening the bonds between all but Wahhabis and modern corollaries from elsewhere. But even more significantly, Islamic universalisms other than those nestled in the modern have been indelibly reduced, the inclusions and exclusions of the pre-modern sidelined in the Muslim imagination, not just in Saudi Arabia, but across the Arabian Sea in South Asia, whether represented by Barelvis or Deobandis. Given the spread of Barelvi and Deobandi influence in parts of Africa and Southeast Asia, alongside that of Saudi-funded Wahhabism, it is not a great stretch to consider the same to be the case across the Indian Ocean more generally. An interregional arena still survives, but overrun by such schools of thought as Wahhabism, Deobandism and Barelvism, its constituent Muslim societies are not defined on the same terms as in the pre-modern era. Indeed, considering the preponderant calls of *takfir* by all such movements, the greatest indication of the decline of the pre-modern relative to modern Islamic universalisms is the pen so often and so widely being forsaken for the sword.

Bibliography

Ayoob, M. and H. Kosebalaban (eds). 2009. *Religion and Politics in Saudi Arabia*. Boulder, CO: Lynne Rienner.

Baljon, J. M. S. 1986. *Religion and Thought of Shah Wali Allah Dihlawi*. Leiden: Brill.

Bang, Anne K. 2014. *Islamic Sufi Networks in the Western Indian Ocean (c. 1880–1940): Ripples of Reform*. Leiden: Brill.

Basri, Basri. 2008. *Indonesian Ulama in the Haramayn and the Transmission of Reformist Islam in Indonesia (1800–1900)*. University of Arkansas, PhD Dissertation, 2008.

Bayly, Christopher A. 1988. *Indian Society and the Making of the British Empire*. Cambridge: Cambridge University Press.

Behuria, Ashok K. 2008. 'Sects Within Sect: The Case of Deobandi–Barelvi. Encounter in Pakistan', *Strategic Analysis* 32:1, pp. 57–80.

Bihari, Zafar al-Din. 1938. *Hayat-i 'Ala Hazrat*. Karachi: Maktaba Rizwiyya.

Bose, Sugata. 2009. *A Hundred Horizons: The Indian Ocean in the Age of Global Empire*. Cambridge, MA: Harvard University Press.

Commins, David. 2006. *The Wahhabi Mission and Saudi Arabia*. London: I. B. Tauris.

Crawford, Michael. 2014. *Ibn 'Abd al-Wahhab*. London: Oneworld.

Dallal, Ahmad. 2018. *Islam without Europe: Traditions of Reform in Eighteenth-Century Islamic Thought*. Chapel Hill, NC: University of North Carolina Press.

Dallal, Ahmad. 2000. 'Appropriating the Past: Twentieth-Century Reconstruction of Pre-Modern Islamic Thought Author(s)', *Islamic Law and Society* 7:3, pp. 325–58.

DeLong-Bas, Natana. 2004. *Wahhabi Islam: From Revival and Reform to Global Jihad*. New York: Oxford University Press.

El Fadl, Khaled Abou. 2005 *The Great Theft: Wrestling Islam from the Extremists*. New York: Harper.

Ensari, Abdul Haq. n.d. 'Supporters of Hussam al Haramain', in Ahmad Raza Bareily (ed.) and Alhaaj Bashir Hussain Nazim (trans.), *Hussam-ul-Haramain*. Karachi: n.p.

Friedmann, Yohanan. 1989. *Prophecy Continuous: Aspects of Ahmadi Religious Thought and its Medieval Background*. Berkeley: University of California Press.

Gaeffke, P. and D. A. Utz (eds). 1988. *The Countries of South Asia: Boundaries, Extension, and Interrelations*. Philadelphia: University of Pennsylvania.

Gangohi, Rashid Ahmad. 1967. *Fatawa-i Rashidiyya*. Karachi: Saeed Company.

Hasan, Mahmud. 1921. *Hazrat Shaykh al-Hind Mawlana Mahmud al-Hasan ka Ek Zaruri Khatt*. Azamgarh: Khilafat Committee.

Hurgronje, C. Snouck. 1970. *Mekka in the Latter Part of the 19th Century*, J. H. Monahan, trans. Leiden: Brill.

Ingram, Brannon D. 2018. *Revival from Below: The Deoband Movement and Global Islam*. Oakland: University of California Press.

Jackson, W. Kesler. 2013. *A Subcontinent's Sunni Schism: The Deobandi-Barelvi Dynamic and the Creation of Modern South Asia*. Syracuse University, PhD Dissertation.

Khan, Ahmad Raza. 2013. *Hussan al-Haramayn 'ala Manhar al-Kufr wa 'l-Mayn* (Arabic and Urdu), Muhammad Hussayn Khan Barelvi, trans. Lahore: Dar al-Nur.

Khan, Ahmad Raza. 1977. *Do Ahamm Fatwe*. Lahore: Maktaba Rizwiyya.

Khan, Ismail. 2011. 'The Assertion of Barelvi Extremism', *Current Trends in Islamic Ideology* 12, pp. 51–72.

Kramer, Martin. 1986. *Islam Assembled: The Advent of the Muslim Congresses*. New York: Columbia University Press.

Levtzion, Nehemia and John O. Voll (eds). 1987. *Eighteenth Century Renewal and Reform in Islam*. Syracuse, NY: Syracuse University Press.

Masud, Muhammad Khalid. 1996. 'Apostasy and Judicial Separation', in Muhammad Khalid Masud et al. (eds), *Islamic Legal Interpretation: Muftis and their Fatwa*. Cambridge, MA: Harvard University Press.

Metcalf, Barbara D. 2009a. *Husain Ahmad Madani: The Jihad for Islam and India's Freedom*. London: Oneworld.

Metcalf, Barbara D. 2009b. *Islam in South Asia in Practice*. Princeton: Princeton University Press.

Metcalf, Barbara D. 1996. 'Two Fatwas on Hajj in British India', in Muhammad Khalid Masud et al. (eds) *Islamic Legal Interpretation: Muftis and their Fatwa*. Cambridge, MA: Harvard University Press.

Metcalf, Barbara D. 1982. *Islamic Revival in British India: Deoband 1860–1900*. Princeton: Princeton University Press.

Ochsenwald, William. 1984. *Religion, Society, and the State in Arabia: The Hijaz under Ottoman Control, 1840–1908*. Columbus: Ohio State University Press.

Pearson, Michael. 2003. *The Indian Ocean*. London: Routledge.

Pirbhai, M. Reza. 2009. *Reconsidering Islam in a South Asian Context*. Leiden: Brill.

Robinson, Francis. 2001. *The 'Ulama of Farangi Mahall and Islamic Culture in South Asia*. London: Hurst.

Sanyal, Usha. 2005. *Ahmed Riza Khan Barelwi: In the Path of the Prophet*. Oxford: Oneworld.

Sanyal, Usha. 1996a. *Devotional Islam and Politics in British India: Ahmad Riza Khan Barelwi and His Movement, 1870–1920*. New York: Oxford University Press.

Sanyal, Usha. 1996b. 'Are Wahhabis Kafirs? Ahmad Riza Khan Barelwi and His Sword of the Haramayn', in Muhammad Khalid Masud et al. (eds), *Islamic Legal Interpretation: Muftis and their Fatwa*. Cambridge, MA: Harvard University Press.

Sedgwick, Mark. 1997. 'Saudi Sufis: Compromise in the Hijaz, 1925–40'. *Die Welt des Islams* 37:3, pp. 349–68.

Shaharanpuri, Khalil Ahmad. n.d. *Al-Muhannad 'ala 'l-Mufannad* (Arabic and Urdu). Lahore: Al-Mezan.

Uthmani, Shabbir Ahmad. n.d. *Ma'raka Makka Mukarrama*. Karachi: Sidiqqi Pakistan.

Vink, Markus P. M. 2007. 'Indian Ocean Studies and the "New Thalassology"', *Journal of Global History* 2, pp. 41–62.

Voll, John O. 2010. 'Islam as a Community of Discourse and a World-System', in Akbar S. Ahmed and Tamara Sonn (eds), *The Sage Handbook of Islamic Studies*. London: Sage.

Voll, John O. 1980. 'Hadith Scholars and Tariqahs: An Ulama Group in the 18th Century Haramayn and Their Impact in the Islamic World', *Journal of Asian and African Studies* 15:3–4, pp. 264–73.

Wagemakers, Joas. 2012. 'The Enduring Legacy of the Second Saudi State: Quietist and Radical Wahhabi Contestations of Al-Wala' Wa-l-Bara'', *International Journal of Middle East Studies* 44, pp. 93–110.

Wali Allah, Shah. 1996. *The Conclusive Argument from God: Shah Wali Allah of Delhi's Hujjat al-Baligha*, M. K. Hermansen, trans. Leiden: Brill.

Wali Allah, Shah. 1955. *'Iqd al-Jid fi Ahkam al-Ijtihad wa al-Taqlid*, M. D. Rahbar, ed. and trans., 'Shah Wali Ullah and Ijtihad', *Muslim World* 44, pp. 346–58.

Weismann, Itzchak. 2011. 'Modernity from Within: Islamic Fundamentalism and Sufism', *Der Islam: Journal of the History and Culture of the Middle East* 86:1, pp. 142–70.

Willis, John M. 2014. 'Azad's Mecca: On the Limits of Indian Ocean Cosmopolitanism', *Comparative Studies of South Asia, Africa and the Middle East* 34:3, pp. 574–81.

PART II

Monuments and Heritage in Muslim Contexts

CHAPTER 9

The Indian Ocean as a Maritime Cultural Landscape and Heritage Route[1]

Eric Falt

The importance of the Indian Ocean is multi-dimensional and vast. With at least forty nations bordering it and constituting a significant proportion of the global population, the Indian Ocean and its littoral states represent multiple ways of life, a plurality of traditions and a long history of social, cultural and economic exchange.

As early as the third millennium BC, merchants and sailors navigated the Indian Ocean in dhows, linking the world's earliest civilisations from Africa to East Asia in a complex web of relationships. The richness of contact created a thriving urban heritage across the seascape, consisting of ports and cities that looked *seaward* as much as they did *inland* for their growth. In subsequent millennia, the expansion of Hinduism, Buddhism, Christianity and Islam, and the spread of technology across the Indian Ocean, created a more nuanced and diverse micro-world, with extensive networks of travel and pilgrimage.

The Indian Ocean is one of the world's few regions where the concept of a 'maritime cultural landscape' can be applied and understood. First introduced in the 1950s by the Swedish maritime ethnologist Olof Hasslof, the idea of a maritime cultural landscape has been defined and developed by the Swedish maritime archaeologist Christer Westerdahl[2] in a series of articles beginning in 1978.

---

[1] The text below was adapted from the Keynote Address at the International Conference 'Muslim Cultures in the Indian Ocean: Diversity and Pluralism, Past and Present' held at the Aga Khan University Institute for the Study of Muslim Civilisations in London on 12 September 2018.
[2] Westerdahl, C. 'The maritime cultural landscape', *The International Journal of Nautical Archaeology*, 21:1, 1992, pp. 5–14.

Westerdahl uses the term to signify the unique development of a maritime space by communities in terms of their habitation, mobility and forms of exchange. Indeed, Indian Ocean routes are characterised by unique architectural features and archaeological sites; local traditions of boatbuilding, travel and navigation; and narratives of the trans-local experiences of maritime communities. To put it another way, a maritime cultural landscape is a holistic idea that includes maritime communities' tangible and intangible cultural heritage.

UNESCO approaches the preservation and promotion of Indian Ocean heritage through several interconnected frameworks. UNESCO's 'One Planet One Ocean' is an integrated approach that deploys scientific solutions and interventions related to education, culture and communication in order to help sustain the world's oceans and the lives they support. As part of this initiative, for instance, UNESCO's Intergovernmental Oceanographic Commission works closely with marine institutes across the Indian Ocean region to disseminate scientific knowledge and build citizens' capacity to respond effectively to environmental and man-made changes impacting the Indian Ocean today. In 2001, UNESCO established a critical link between the study of oceans and the preservation of cultural heritage when it adopted the Convention on the Protection of Underwater Cultural Heritage[3]. This international treaty lays down ethical principles for protecting submerged heritage, and provides a detailed system of cooperation for states and practical scientific rules for the treatment of underwater heritage.

UNESCO's World Heritage Convention of 1972, of course, is a major mechanism for protecting heritage sites; and World Heritage is among our organisation's most visible programmes. More than thirty UNESCO World Heritage Sites lie along the coastline of the Indian Ocean littoral states, and their sheer variety testifies to the cultural and natural diversity of the region. The cultural sites are remarkably wide-ranging, displaying a plethora of historical, architectural and religious styles. In keeping with the theme of this conference, allow me to draw your attention to a few outstanding examples of Muslim culture that are UNESCO World Heritage Sites:

- Located on two islands just off the Tanzanian coast are the remains of two port cities, Kilwa Kisiwani and Songo Mnara. The cities reached the peak of their prosperity in the thirteenth and fourteenth centuries as a result of the Indian Ocean trade with Arabia, India and China. Visiting Kilwa in 1331, the traveller Ibn Battouta described it as 'one of the most beautiful cities in the world'. The standing ruins of Kilwa include the magnificent Great

---

[3] https://unesdoc.unesco.org/ark:/48223/pf0000126065.

Mosque built in the eleventh century, five other mosques, a palace complex and domestic dwellings.

- The Stone Town of Zanzibar is a spectacular example of a Swahili trading town, built to manage the Indian Ocean trade. The townscape has fused and homogenised disparate elements of African, Arabian, Indian and European cultures over more than a millennium.
- Lamu Old Town, off the coast of Kenya, represents the oldest and best preserved example of a Swahili settlement in East Africa. Once the most important trade hub in East Africa, Lamu has influenced the entire region through its technological expertise and its role as a centre for Islamic education and Swahili culture.
- Finally, the famous coral stone mosques of the Maldives, on UNESCO's Tentative World Heritage List, represent a glorious fusion of Islamic and Buddhist architecture and Swahili stone carving techniques.

UNESCO adopted the Convention for the Safeguarding of Intangible Cultural Heritage in 2003,[4] and since then numerous inscriptions from Indian Ocean states have been included in UNESCO's Representative List for the Intangible Cultural Heritage of Humanity. These have included a variety of traditional practices and artistic forms.

- For instance, Pinisi, or the art of boatbuilding in South Sulawesi, also refers to the rig and sail of the famed Sulawesi schooner. The construction of these vessels has been central to the millennia-long Indonesian tradition of boatbuilding and navigation across the Indian Ocean.
- Historically, Asir on the Saudi Arabian coast has been renowned for Al-Qatt Al-Asiri, a traditional form of interior wall decoration still practised extensively by the women of the region. The art form has been passed down from generation to generation, and is believed to enhance social bonding and solidarity among community members and to have a therapeutic effect on its practitioners.
- In the sphere of music, Sega Tambour of Mauritius' Rodrigues Island is a vibrant rhythmic performance of music, song and dance with its origins in slave communities. In fact, UNESCO also manages a wider initiative called the Slave Route Project that safeguards the rapidly vanishing oral traditions of the Indian Ocean's southwestern islands (including Mauritius) which have experienced slavery and the slave trade.

---

[4] https://ich.unesco.org/en/convention.

Looking beyond UNESCO's frameworks for a moment, the UN Sustainable Development Goals adopted by the global community in 2016 also urge us to 'conserve and sustainably use the oceans, seas and marine resources for sustainable development' (Goal 14); and to 'strengthen efforts to protect and safeguard the world's cultural and natural heritage' (Goal 11).

As UNESCO continues to identify and preserve heritage across the world, we realise the value of acquiring a broader perspective that embraces cultural landscapes, routes and corridors, rather than discrete cultural and natural sites. The concept and definition of a 'heritage route' was recognised by UNESCO only recently and public awareness about this new category of heritage is still at a nascent stage. We believe the heritage of the Indian Ocean ought to constitute an 'Indian Ocean Maritime Heritage Route' and be studied and promoted as intensively as certain other famous routes such as the Silk Road or the Maritime Silk Route.

Nowadays two projects in India are exploring the notion of heritage routes. First, in collaboration with UNESCO, the state of Kerala in southern India is in the process of reviving the two-millennia-old Spice Route, as a part of which it has convened a culinary festival involving multiple countries bordering the Indian Ocean. Second, Project Mausam, which was launched by the Indian Ministry of Culture with UNESCO's support, seeks to showcase the Indian Ocean both as a 'maritime cultural landscape' and a 'transnational mixed route' by collating archaeological and historical research from numerous Indian Ocean states to document the diversity of cultural, commercial and religious interactions across the ocean.

Perceiving the Indian Ocean as a maritime cultural landscape and heritage route opens up new possibilities for dialogue and international cooperation. The following chapters are not only examples of joint researches but actions to promote heritage development and sustainable tourism across the Indian Ocean region.

CHAPTER 10

Indian Ocean Heritage and Sustainable Conservation, from Zanzibar to Kilwa

Stephen Battle and Pierre Blanchard

Introduction: Experience in Conservation Heritage in Zanzibar Old Town

Zanzibar has always been a place in flux, a place that is the starting point and culmination of countless journeys and a product of those diverse journeys and plurality of voices. I experienced this directly when I was working as site architect on a conservation project at the Old Dispensary building in Zanzibar in the early 1990s.[1] This building is one of the most important monuments in Stone Town (Fig. 10.1). Completed in 1894, it is located on the waterfront and was built by Sir Tharia Topan, who journeyed to Zanzibar from his home village in Kutch in the 1830s and amassed a fortune as the sultan's customs master. The building is a glorious hybrid of architectural styles and motifs.[2]

One day during the conservation project, I was called over by the site foreman who wanted to show me something. One of the workmen had been removing limewash from a wall inside the building and had come across a piece of graffiti on the original plaster. Written in Kutchi 100 years earlier, it recorded the name of the man, his trade and the village he came from, which was in Kutch. And this was when I realised how circular things can be in Zanzibar, because the site foreman who called me over was also from Kutch, the man who uncovered it was from Kutch, and most of the other workers on site that day were from Kutch. They knew the village the graffiti-man was from. One hundred years

---

[1] Siravo, 1996.
[2] Sheriff, 1995.

Figure 10.1 Old Dispensary building in Zanzibar. © Aga Khan Trust for Culture / Gary Otte (photographer).

after the Old Dispensary had been built, after wars, independence, revolution and demographic upheaval, we had come full circle.

Zanzibar is the place I know best in East Africa. It has changed a lot since 1991 but seen through my architect's eyes it still looks like the quintessential Indian Ocean city, with multiple identities jostling around a port. It also illustrates many of the problems we tackle in conservation. As practitioners, we work for a group called the World Monuments Fund, which is the largest international NGO working in the field of heritage preservation. We implement conservation and planning projects at heritage sites around the world. So, what does conservation entail?

First, there is the technical activity of physical conservation at heritage sites. This combines craft skills, aesthetic judgement and a basic knowledge of chemistry. But as difficult as the technical stuff can be, it is actually the easy part, because as long as you look properly the answer to any question is generally in front of your nose.

The second aspect of what we do as conservation people is often much more difficult.[3] Most of what falls under the heading 'official heritage' in East Africa is from another era and was constructed by societies that no longer exist in the

---

[3] Heathcott, 2013, pp. 21–3.

same form. Much of it is neglected. But we find even the most neglected and decayed sites are alive in local imaginations, animated by powerful stories and meanings. But once you travel more than say two villages away from a site, these places are often seen as piles of old stones. The question we are confronted with time and again is how to make heritage relevant? This is the second thing we do as conservation people. We try to make heritage relevant. Because if it's not relevant it doesn't survive. You can spend as much time and money as you like on technical conservation but if it is not relevant it will probably disappear anyway.

In Africa making heritage relevant can be particularly difficult. In the global north we speak a lot about the uses of heritage. Heritage has an important economic use. The term 'heritage industry' has been coined to describe this, and the economic benefits in advanced economies are huge. The work of the Aga Khan Trust for Culture in Zanzibar was recently criticised by Georges Abungu and it was interpretated as a project that attracted developers and promoted uncontrolled tourism[4]. Whereas most of the recent touristic development was managed by local authorities and international developers are coming mainly from Oman. The aspect of the re-Arabisation of Zanzibar was not discussed by Abungu. In much of sub-Saharan Africa a local heritage industry does not exist. Few Tanzanians travel to Kilwa to consume cream teas. The main economic use of heritage in Africa is in the foreign tourism industry, and again the economic benefits can be substantial. Over time, key heritage sites assume an iconic status and come to represent a place. Tourism is an important way to generate revenue, but it can be a double-edged sword. Finally, if the value of a heritage place is calculated only in tourist dollars its fortunes, and by extension its relevance, will fluctuate with the vagaries of the tourism industry.

Heritage has been used through the ages to construct stories of national identity. Heritage sites are selected to give substance and credence to a national story, establishing values and imposing order on the random and contingent process of nation-building. Think of Big Ben. It symbolises Britain's democracy, which British people think of a fundamental part of their national character. But values often obscure facts. In the case of Big Ben, for instance, when this great symbol of democracy was built in 1859 only fifteen per cent of the male population of Britain had the vote, and no women. It could just as easily be interpreted as a symbol of neo-feudalism. But few countries in sub-Saharan Africa are symbolised by a heritage place in the way that Big Ben symbolises Britain. Perhaps it is because 'national identity' is lower down the list of identities in many African societies, coming after ethnic, clan or family identity? Or perhaps it is rooted in a different understanding of modernity? But for whatever reason, heritage seems rarely to be intertwined with stories of national identity.

---

[4] Abungu, Mchulla, Allausy and Ali, 2018, p. 648.

Even when a heritage place is pictured on a national currency neglecting it is not like denying identity. It tends not to be relevant in that way. So how can heritage be made relevant? One way is to recognise that heritage is not something carved in stone, as it were. As Rodney Harrison wrote:

> Heritage is not a passive process of simply preserving things from the past, but an active process of assembling a series of objects, places and practices that we choose to hold up as a mirror to the present, associated with a particular set of values that we wish to take with us into the future.[5]

Heritage is created, not found. It is created in the present and reflects values held to be important in the present. The story of the slave chamber in Zanzibar is an interesting example (Fig. 10.2). The World Monuments Fund (WMF) implemented a conservation project at the Anglican Cathedral in Zanzibar, which was built on the site of the last open slave market in East Africa. The project included the creation of an exhibit telling the story of the slave trade in the region. Early on in the project we stumbled (naively in retrospect) into a row about the so-called slave chamber at the site. It is underneath St Monica's Hostel. You descend underground into a cramped, dark, claustrophobic space, which gives a visceral sense of confinement. It is an emotional experience. Except it never was a slave chamber. There is no way it could have been. The house that stood on the site in the mid-nineteenth century when it was used as a slave market was on the other side of the compound. According to the title deed, St Monica's was built where 'native huts' once stood. And when you look at the space through architect's eyes, the idea that it was a slave chamber seems ridiculous. It was almost certainly built for cool storage, possibly as a morgue.

The argument about how to treat the slave chamber split the Scientific Committee along ethnic and religious lines. The Committee was not fighting about whether slavery happened, or how awful it was. Everyone agreed about that. The fight was about how heritage was being used, or rather misused. Those who objected thought (correctly) that a lie was being peddled to tourists for commercial purposes. The place had an undeniable emotional power; the discomfort made history palpable in a way that text and photos never could. It had been re-created as heritage to tell a story and reflect a set of values. For the tourists it made history more immediate.

If we accept that there is a process of making heritage, then the key question is; where in society does that production take place? Whose meaning counts? There is no simple answer to these questions. So, how do we make heritage relevant? I am not advocating for constructing facsimiles of slave chambers. But

---

[5] Harrison, 2012.

Figure 10.2 Slave chamber, Zanzibar. Courtesy the authors.

I would like to quote my colleague George Abungu about local participation in heritage management: 'not for us without us; if you do it for me without me, you are against me'. Working in conservation in Africa, this is an important admonition. What I take it to mean is that we can't claim to be assisting local actors if we do not directly involve them in decision-making and give them agency over processes and outcomes. As mentioned by Schnepel, two questions guide the study of heritage: 'Who wants to reconstruct the past? and what are their motives?'[6]. Heritage played an essential role in the dynamics of identity and political legitimacy of social groups and nations around the Indian Ocean and in sub-Saharan Africa.

Applied to conservation of heritage, this is both self-evident and very difficult. Involving local custodians in the physical process of conservation is central to the way WMF operates. We always strive to maximise participation of local custodians, both in planning and implementation. During the project at Kilwa Kisiwani and Songo Mnara in southern Tanzania for instance, we wanted to ensure that economic benefits were spread as widely as possible throughout the community. By the conclusion of the project, seventy-five per cent of the adult population on Songo Mnara and thirty per cent on Kilwa Kisiwani had earned an income from the project. But it is one thing including local actors in the physical process of conservation of heritage, and quite another to involve them in defining its meaning. Generally speaking, history is made in academic spaces. And whilst that is correct, it is also not sufficient. If we want heritage to be relevant in the place where it matters most, which is where decisions are taken on a daily basis that affect its survival, about whether to remove stones

---

[6] Schnepel and Sen, 2019.

to build a new wall or whether to demolish an old wall to make way for a field, if we want heritage to be relevant at that moment, then we have to find a way of including and accepting local stories and meanings that create the heritage place. Because if those stories are forgotten or dismissed then the place becomes just a pile of old stones.

This is not to diminish the process of writing history. Rather it is an admonition to broaden the dialogue to include other voices. To encourage other 'unofficial' voices to create and populate historic places, add layers of meaning from traditional beliefs and oral histories. If we want heritage to be relevant, then we have to find a way of giving agency to custodians of historic places to participate and contribute to the production of heritage. We certainly don't have a magic formula and the story of the slave chamber is a cautionary tale. But this is an increasingly important theme in how we think about what we do as conservation people.

I come full circle back to the Kutchi artisan who scrawled his name on the wall of the Old Dispensary. Should we leave it uncovered? Should we preserve it? What should we do? In the end we re-covered it with limewash. The inscription is still there, and re-covering it was one way of preserving it. But now I know that we made a mistake. It is appropriate that the story of the Old Dispensary is the story of Sir Tharia Topan. And it is appropriate that the building is understood through the prism of an extraordinary period in Zanzibar history. But the story of the Kutchi artisan who helped build it is also relevant, and the story of the Kutchi foreman who uncovered it 100 years later is also relevant. All these voices matter. Our job as conservation people is to find a way to make this plurality and diversity of voices heard. It was the sum of these experiences that inspired us for the WMF project in Kilwa.

History of Conservation in Kilwa

The World Heritage site of Kilwa Kisiwani and Songo Mnara is situated in the Kilwa district of Lindi region and is one of the most important heritage sites in Tanzania (Fig. 10.3). The monuments that make up the sites constitute an exceptional oeuvre of 800 years of East African history. At Kilwa Kisiwani impressive remains of major Swahili monuments are preserved, including an Omani fort, two palaces, large houses, several smaller mosques and the largest Swahili mosque still standing with significant parts of its domed roof remaining. Songo Mnara contains the ruins of mosques, cemeteries and forty stone houses dating from the fifteenth century, some of which are better preserved than any comparable domestic historical building in East Africa.[7]

---

[7] Pradines and Blanchard, 2006; Wynne-Jones, 2018, pp. 253–9.

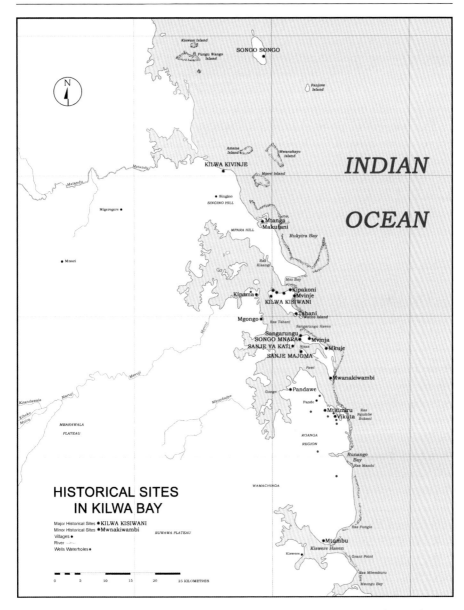

Figure 10.3 Map of Kilwa Kisiwani and Songo Mnara. Courtesy the authors.

The first documented attempt to protect the ruins of Kilwa Kisiwani and Songo Mnara dates from 1900, when Bernhard Perrot, a German settler from Lindi, made a visit to the site and collected a wide variety of items. He collected more than 1,000 copper coins, potteries, beads, inscription stones, architectural elements and woodcarvings. The discovery of Bernhard Perrot was reported in Germany in a newspaper article.[8] The colonial administration, after being informed about the looting, asked Bernhard Perrot to surrender the items he had taken and established zones to protect the ruins from human activities.[9] But these protection zones were only instituted in Kilwa Kisiwani. In 1936, repair work was undertaken at several monuments in Kilwa Kisiwani.

The awareness, protection and knowledge of Kilwa increased due to the efforts of one dynamic archaeologist, Neville Chittick, who was appointed the first conservator of antiquities in Tanganyika.[10] Chittick began archaeological excavations in Kilwa in 1958 and this became extensive from 1960 to 1965.[11] In parallel, from 1958 to 1962, the Department of Antiquities organised conservation works, eventually covering the entire site. The conservation works were done with appropriate techniques and followed established policy:

> the conservation policy on antiquities was to ensure the good condition of the structures, as they were found. Reconstruction was limited to cases of necessity for the safety of the buildings, and when a large share of the materials was available on site, the new work could be guaranteed to respect the original appearance.[12]

After Tanganyika gained independence, the ruins of Kilwa Kisiwani and Songo Mnara were registered as National Monuments under the Antiquities Act in 1964. This act 'protects all monuments built prior to 1863 ... or their remains . . . and includes all adjacent grounds which may be necessary for enclosing and protecting the monuments from deterioration.'[13] But the Department of Antiquities was made part of the Ministry of Education. The country had very few schools and ninety per cent of the population was illiterate. The limited resources of the government were focused on education. The Department of Antiquities was not considered as a priority and was poorly funded. In 1971, the government allotted funds for small works and a major bush clearing at the ruins of Kilwa Kisiwani and Songo Mnara.

In 1981, Kilwa Kisiwani and Songo Mnara were registered on the list of UNESCO World Heritage sites. The listing noted the outstanding attributes of the Kilwa Kisiwani and Songo Mnara ruins complex with respect to their universal value in the East African landscape. In the 1990s the introduction of

---

[8] Kilian, 2006.
[9] Chittick, 1974, pp. 11, 66.
[10] Chittick, 1974.
[11] Chittick, 1974.
[12] United Republic of Tanzania, 1958–1965.
[13] Antiquities Act, 1964 (Tanzania). https://www.tanzania.go.tz/egov_uploads/documents/The_Antiquities_Act,_10-1964.pdf.

IMF policies and the economic crises reduced the government's budget, and the ruins of Kilwa were neglected and left to become overgrown with vegetation.

NEW REHABILITATION AND PROTECTION PROGRAMME IN KILWA, 2002–14

Attention to Kilwa was renewed in 2000 when the Ministry of Tourism and Natural Resources decided to undertake conservation work, to contribute to the site's cultural and touristic attraction and thereby boost development in the region through tourism. The Ministry managed to attract funding from international donors to undertake conservation work. In 2002, a major project 'Kilwa Sites: Rehabilitation and Promotion Programme' worth €400,000 was sponsored mainly by the French and Japanese embassies. The conservation work was conducted as a training worksite to help pass on to local people the necessary know-how in conservation and maintenance techniques. This programme enabled the training of fifteen young workers in masonry and in a basic knowledge of stonecutting.

Project activities were located on the island of Kilwa Kisiwani for logistical reasons. In 2002 and 2003 the Great Mosque, the north wall of the Great House and a tomb in the Malindi Mosque's cemetery were conserved and some emergency work was also carried out on the Gereza Fort (Figs 10.4 and 10.5). In 2004, the work focused on emergency conservation and accessibility at Husuni Kubwa Palace and in the small Domed Mosque (Fig. 10.6). Among other activities, signage was installed to allow a better understanding of the buildings, a jetty was built to facilitate access to the site, and the 'German Rest House' was restored. The project also funded scientific research at Kilwa on geography, anthropology, history, architecture and archaeology: excavations were conducted in Nguruni by Felix Chami and in Songo Mnara by Stéphane Pradines.

With a growing awareness of the poor state of the monuments at Kilwa Kisiwani and Songo Mnara, in 2004 the site was included on the UNESCO list of World Heritage Sites in danger. This attracted other donors, and in October 2005, the UNESCO office in Dar es Salaam and the Antiquities Unit started a project called 'Emergency Conservation of Kilwa Kisiwani and Songo Mnara'. Due to its poor state of conservation, the Songo Mnara site was chosen to be the main beneficiary of the project. The project essentially entailed emergency conservation work, as well as training and capacity building by the Antiquities Unit. It was funded by the UNESCO/Norway Fund in Trust with a total of US$200,000 and it was supervised by a conservation architect and two Antiquities technicians. The project involved up to fifty local workers from the two islands and the Antiquities officers of Kilwa substation. The work carried out included clearing of vegetation and rubble, consolidation and protection

Figure 10.4 The Great Mosque and wall of the Great House, Kilwa Kisiwani. Courtesy the authors.

of the Palace (Fig. 10.7), the Friday Mosque and the Secretary House in Songo Mnara, and creation of structures to protect the Gereza Fort against erosion on Kilwa Kisiwani. All the workers employed came from settlements within the World Heritage site. An important objective of the programme was the training of local workers in conservation techniques to engage local inhabitants in stewardship of their heritage. Creation of a Village Ruins' Committee was facilitated to help create economic opportunities on the island. Five workers were trained to produce high quality lime in a shaft kiln built by the project. Another batch of five workers were trained in stonecutting and ten workers were trained in traditional masonry.

In 2006, the WMF became involved at Kilwa with its first project focused on conservation of the Gereza Fort in Kilwa Kisiwani (Figs 10.8 and 10.9). In 2008, the Kilwa site was included on the World Monuments Fund Watch List. In 2009, through a grant from the Robert Wilson Challenge, WMF devoted a total amount of US$100,000 for the restoration of the Gereza Fort. The project was supervised by the Kilwa Antiquities substation, with a conservation architect for technical advice. The project's objectives were to respond to the urgent conservation needs of the Gereza Fort. In 2002, after the rainy season a major collapse

Figure 10.5 Cemetery of Malindi Mosque, Kilwa Kisiwani.
Courtesy the authors.

occurred in the entrance corridor. The work consisted of vegetation clearance, consolidation and protection of masonry structures, restitution of the flooring on mangrove poles in several rooms, creation of erosion protection structures, as well as installation of a copy of the carved doorway. This monument is the first that visitors see on arriving at the island and it is within the village, thus it plays an important part in the site's significance and identity. Its conservation contributed significantly to the rehabilitation of the World Heritage Site in general.

In 2011, WMF and the Antiquities Unit secured a major grant from the American Ambassadors Fund for Cultural Preservation totalling US$700,000 to implement the project 'Integrated Preservation at Kilwa'. Songo Mnara, which was still the most vulnerable part of the site, was chosen to be of particular concern for preservation activities (Fig. 10.10). The project started with a study to identify areas at greatest risk of coastal erosion and specify interventions. Other objectives included building skills and creating employment opportunities for local craftspeople, strengthening management capacities in the Antiquities Unit and producing an integrated heritage development plan. The project implementation was done by Kilwa Substation of the Antiquities Unit, with consultants from WMF. The team from the local community included six

Figure 10.6 Husuni Kubwa Palace and small Domed Mosque, Kilwa Kisiwani.
Courtesy the authors.

craftsmen, twenty-five skilled workers from Songo Mnara and fifteen from Kilwa
Kisiwani (Fig. 10.11). The conservation work was implemented in coordination
with archaeologists from Rice and Bristol Universities.

Sustainable Conservation in Tanzania, the case of Kilwa

The projects conducted in the Kilwa World Heritage Site since 2002 are not
a juxtaposition of actions following the desiderata and methods of different
donors, but arising from the coordination of the Antiquities Unit and continuity enforced by the persons involved, an initiative for a thorough preservation
process built over time.

After slowly acquiring a detailed understanding and knowledge of the
site and the population close to it, a project methodology was established for
conservation work. The criteria for conservation were not only historical and
aesthetic, but also based on conservation principles: 'the aim of conservation
was to retain the cultural significance of the place'.[14] The project did not impose

---

[14] Burra Charter 1979. https://australia.icomos.org/wp-content/uploads/Burra-Charter_1979.pdf.

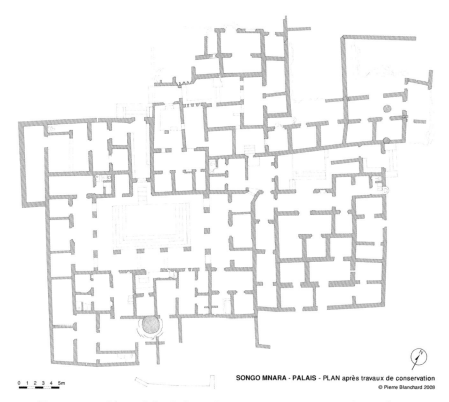

0 1 2 3 4 5m

SONGO MNARA - PALAIS - PLAN après travaux de conservation
© Pierre Blanchard 2008

Figure 10.7 Plan of the Palace, Songo Mnara. Courtesy the authors.

imported theory but adapted its management and philosophy of conservation to the geographical and cultural contexts.

This methodology had the potential to be transformed over time with respect to technological advancement, input from inhabitants and historical knowledge. The project initiated a process that would develop over time. The overarching goals of the project were to create a framework for balanced development on the islands, in which the competing demands of tourism, economic development, social change and heritage preservation could be balanced for the benefit of all, ensuring the survival of the monuments for future generations.

One of the major challenges was to define a project in a local context. Accordingly, the project was implemented by the Antiquities Division using a core team of skilled craftspeople in partnership with a committee of villagers from settlements adjacent to the ruins. The use of foreign experts was limited to missions requiring specific technical skills and training. Project managers and site managers were all civil servants of Antiquities substation in Kilwa Masoko and the technicians and workers were all from the islands.

Fig, 10.8 Insertion of a copy of the door in the Gereza Fort, Kilwa Kisiwani.
Courtesy the authors.

Figure 10.9 Creation of structures to protect against the erosion in the Husuni
Kubwa Palace, Kilwa Kisiwani. Courtesy the authors.

Figure 10.10 View of the ruins at Songo Mnara. Courtesy the authors.

Heritage and development are two faces of the same coin. Sustainable development cannot be achieved without the foundations of education and wealth. People living in poverty focus their resources first on surviving in the present, not preserving the past. For this reason the entire workforce employed by the project was drawn from communities on the islands, thereby maximising benefits to local residents to generate wealth locally. The projects were highly labour-intensive. By providing temporary job opportunities to skilled and semi-skilled labourers, the project contributed to alleviating poverty. To maximise economic benefits for local inhabitants, a system was agreed whereby workers were rotated, thereby ensuring that economic benefits were distributed as widely as possible throughout the communities. By the end of the projects, over 600 people had been employed in various capacities (Fig. 10.12). Seventy-five per cent of the adult population on Songo Mnara had earned some income from the project. Apart from directly improving the economic situation of inhabitants, all of whom survive on very low incomes, this system offered the community a direct return from investment with respect to their heritage.

One principle established was to maximise the participation of women (Fig. 10.13). Statistics have shown that in low-income communities, whenever there is an increase in earnings of women, the result is a significant rise in

Figure 10.11 Skilled craftspeople working with local villagers in the ruins.
Courtesy the authors.

benefits in terms of education for children, family health and women's rights concerning fertility. At Songo Mnara, thirty-seven per cent of the workforce were women. Furthermore, fifty-seven per cent of all adult women on the island were employed at some point. In total, women made up forty-six per cent of the total number of people employed by the project. In addition, fifty-two per cent of participants in the training initiatives were women.

Since 2011, project implementation set out to broaden the impact of the investment by including training and learning opportunities at every step. Close links were forged with two departments of Dar es Salaam University: Architecture and Heritage Management. A total of ninety-seven students and teaching staff participated in field schools and internships during the project (Fig. 10.14). In addition, training courses were implemented in heritage management, masonry, stonecutting, surveying, use of GIS software, and rescue and mitigation archaeology (Fig. 10.15). The training of qualified staff for management and conservation of the monuments was another objective to develop a local operational capacity and to strengthen local management capacities. We consequently opted for a passive learning process under the guidance of technicians or qualified experts, where information was acquired via *in situ* management.

Figure 10.12 Over 600 people had been employed on the project.
Courtesy the authors.

CONSERVATION WORKS

Climatic conditions are harsh due to very high humidity, seasonal torrential rains and strong onshore winds that are high in salinity. As such, physical decay is one of the most severe problems affecting the site. The standing structures are easily affected by water ingress, which propels decay processes by washing away mortar, causing build-up of salts, thereby accelerating deterioration of timber beams and lintels. Decay exacerbates weaknesses inherent in the original construction, which relies on shallow or non-existent foundations, no coursing of stonework and poor bonding between walls, leading to loss of structural integrity and collapse. The monuments in Kilwa were in critical condition and under imminent threat of structural collapse (Fig. 10.16).

The ruins at Kilwa Kisiwani and Songo Mnara are a landmark where decay has achieved a sublime balance and beauty, and where any addition or subtraction of building material could result in a loss of authenticity and aesthetic value. But given their extremely poor condition, intervention was necessary to ensure their survival. Minimum intervention was a key priority to ensure the

Figure 10.13 Group of local women working at the site. Courtesy the authors.

Figure 10.14 Field schools and internships were established during the course of the project. Courtesy the authors.

Figure 10.15 GIS software and rescue and mitigation archaeology were
employed. Courtesy the authors.

survival of the historic structures in their present state whilst reducing the risk
of collapse (Figs 10.17 and 10.18).

One of the complexities of working in Kilwa was the presence of largely
intact archaeological layers just below the surface. For instance, excavations
were undertaken in 2005 before conservation work on the major monuments
commenced.[15] The archaeological aspect of the site was taken into consideration more seriously after 2011, when a specialist in rescue archaeology carried
out salvage excavations and created a risk map (Fig. 10.19). The ruins were
considered a source of documentary evidence to be protected. The project
set out to preserve the authenticity of the site and emphasise the historical meaning and artistic value of the monuments, which are unique historic
records of Swahili architecture. After reviewing the studies and documentation
and analysing the buildings, we chose to use only traditional techniques and
construction materials, while upholding the principle of reversibility of our
contemporary interventions. All the work was documented in drawings, before
and after conservation.

---

[15] Pradines and Blanchard, 2006.

Figure 10.16 Works in progress, Husuni Kubwa, Kilwa Kisiwani.
Courtesy the authors.

According to Elgidius Ichumbaki and Bertram Mapunda, our conservation projects at Kilwa Kisiwani and Songo Mnara destroyed archaeological layers with artefacts being removed without recording and documentation.[16] In 2012, Elgidius Ichumbaki observed that 20–40 cm depth of deposit with mixed up various archaeological materials, including glass beads and both local and imported ceramics, were removed from a small part of Makutani Palace during the conservation works. Between 2005 and 2008 Jeffrey Fleisher and Stephanie Wynne-Jones observed a similar scenario at Songo Mnara, where some rooms in the ruins were cleared of potentially damaging archaeological deposits. According to Jeffrey Fleisher, the rehabilitation of the palace and the so-called 'secretary house' caused irreparable damage to the archaeological integrity of the site. Archaeologists were present on site during this work. The criticisms above were only conceptual, and no attempt was made by the archaeologists to prevent or manage damage to archaeological data. During all conservation work at Songo Mnara carried out in 2012 a foreign rescue and mitigation archaeologist was present on site working under the instruction of Stephanie Wynne-Jones.

---

[16] Ichumbaki and Mapunda, 2017, p. 13.

Figure 10.17 Works in progress, Songo Mnara. Courtesy the authors.

Stephanie Wynne-Jones and Jeffrey Fleisher organised a seminar in Nairobi to talk about this problem, but they didn't adapt their excavations strategies to the challenges of conservation in Songo Mnara. It was like an archaeological excavation in parallel to a conservation project, with no or very little collaboration. If some destruction did occur during the conservation project when archaeologists were on the site, then they are also responsible.

According to our colleague archaeologist Stéphane Pradines who worked in Songo Mnara before the conservation project[17]: 'The criticisms are easy, but actions are always more difficult. The archaeologists working in Kilwa had no experience in rescue and salvage excavations. Most of them were working in East Africa with very little training in field archaeology in their home countries, most of their knowledge was first theoretical and conceptual.'[18] Pradines adds:

First, Fleischer and Wynne-Jones didn't adapt their excavations strategies to the challenges of the conservation project in Songo Mnara and Kilwa Kisiwani, and they stayed on their excavations developing parallel researches

---

[17] Pradines Blanchard, 2006, pp. 25–80.
[18] Pradines, 2017.

Figure 10.18 View of doorway inside the Palace at Songo Mnara.
Courtesy the authors.

linked to their own interests instead of supporting the Tanzanian national project. The archaeologists were working slowly to record a maximum of archaeological data and to avoid any destruction of information. In fact, any archaeological excavation is a destructive process and whereas archaeologists work slowly or quickly it is not linked to the destruction of archaeological data, the most important is to record these data and to record them well. When archaeologists have very little field experience, they are terrified to destroy an object or any archaeological layer. They do not prioritise the scientific importance of artefacts or layers. They will give the same priority and importance to abandonment layers, demolition layers and occupation layers. Then, these archaeologists had no experience in building archaeology that is something crucial on urban Swahili sites such as Kilwa Kisiwani and Songo Mnara. Therefore, Ichumbaki mentioned the destruction of demolition layers in some buildings; he is right, these layers are indeed archaeological layers. Unfortunately, he didn't realise that not all the archaeological layers have the same scientific value; context is extremely important. Superficial layers can be 'polluted' with different archaeological material from late or even

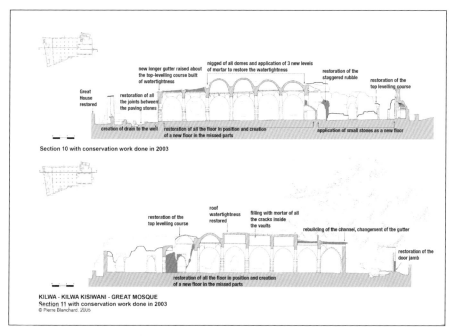

Figure 10.19 Section drawing showing conservation work done on the Great Mosque, Kilwa Kisiwani. Courtesy the authors.

early periods. Many monuments in Kilwa were cleared by previous archaeologists and sometimes restored. Of course, it is possible to do the excavation of previous excavations, but it would have been more constructive to do something in the areas unexcavated to support the conservation project and to add some value to it, by providing a good analysis of the building. Archaeological destructions are not only connected to archaeological layers and objects but also to the integrity of the monument's themselves.

Therefore, Pradines advocates for the development of field schools in building archaeology and rescue archaeology in sub-Saharan Africa to support local researchers, national and international conservation projects and also foreign archaeologists on the model of what he did in Egypt and what we started in Kua in Tanzania.[19]

The ruins are part of an exceptional natural site and are inseparable from their surroundings: island, beaches, village and mangroves. Conservation is not

---

[19] Stéphane Pradines was the director of rescue excavations in Cairo for sixteen years, including twelve years in collaboration with the Aga Khan Trust for Culture and a conservation project on the Walls of Cairo (Pradines, 2018).

only of a physical object but also of its context; we wanted to keep the 'balance' while controlling the balance between the ruins and the natural environment. Considering this principle, we conducted partial restorations leaving some plant growth in the ruins and setting out a protected zone around the monuments. The aim of the project was also to maintain and to revive traditional building techniques, and this was done together with the local population, who underwent technical skills training, because such expertise is often not passed on to the young villagers.

Given that large numbers of ruins and piles of rubble are to be found in a jungle setting, there is a tendency to romanticise their state of decay as something that should not be disturbed. However, our intervention set out to make the ruins more 'readable', so visitors could understand the organisation of the city, function of the buildings, their proportions, the original lighting conditions and the quality of the different spaces. Visitors must be guided, given points of reference and stimulated in their imagination (which can be partly achieved by using signs and markers). In Songo Mnara, we have undertaken clearance and conservation in two buildings in coordination with archaeologists, to expose the ground floor layer and restore the roofing and doors. This is to be able to identify the functions, the initial volume, and thus to better understand the architecture and civilisation that once lived in this damaged building.

Conclusion: Global Warming, Sea Erosion and Land Use Plan

Coastal erosion poses a severe long-term threat to the World Heritage Site. A combination of climate change, which has led to a rise in sea levels, and unsustainable economic use of the marine environment, such as removal of the mangrove forest, excavation of beach sand and destruction of reefs, has exacerbated erosion. The result is severe damage from storm-driven high tides that eat away the coast and undermine foundations of structures adjacent to the shore. The effects of this were graphically illustrated in 2009 when a section of sea wall at Kilwa Kisiwani collapsed into the sea. As the effects of climate change worsen and the pressure on natural resources increases, these problems will get worse. A seminar on Indian Ocean Heritage was organised by the French Ministry of Cultural Affairs in Saint-Denis, La Réunion in 2011. One aspect of the seminar was about the threats and natural risks that Indian Ocean heritage faces, and one major concern was rising ocean levels, higher tides and tsunamis that are putting in danger people and monuments of the coast and islands of the Indian Ocean.[20]

---

[20] Walz and Gupta, 2011, p. 127.

In 2011 our project in Kilwa Kisiwani and Songo Mnara focused on a study of the coastal environment at the site to prepare a risk map which shows areas of greatest vulnerability identifying coastal features that merit protection, such as the mangrove forest area. The study was carried out by Matthew Richmond. In a recent article,[21] Elgidius Ichumbaki and Edward Pollard came back to this concept and insisted on the preservation and management of the mangrove according to archaeological sites. In his report, Matthew Richmond recommended measures to make the site more resilient to the effects of climate change. The study considered the effects of the rise of sea level over a fifty- and ninety-year period, respectively. The concluding remarks were disturbing. In Kilwa Kisiwani, some portions of some monuments (up to about 120 cm) were already below sea level. This will get worse as the sea level rises. The report recommended a range of engineering solutions to combat these threats. Although most solutions were far beyond the scope of our budget, gabions were installed by the Gereza Fort in Kilwa Kisiwani to mitigate the effects of wave action. Diminishing the effects of coastal erosion at the site has been included as a priority in a recent report on 'Investment Prioritisation for Climate-Resilient Livelihoods and Ecosystems in the Coastal Zones of Tanzania'. This was published by the Tanzanian government and World Bank to guide future spending and set priorities in coastal regions of Tanzania.

Both islands that make up the World Heritage Site are protected in their entirety, but both contain modern villages and settlements adjacent to the ruins. There is no formal demarcation between the modern settlements and heritage structures. If encroachment has been limited up until now, it is because development pressure has been low and village inhabitants have respected ad hoc and customary arrangements. Whilst this may continue in the future, population growth is likely to increase development pressure, which in turn could greatly increase the risk of ad hoc arrangements unravelling, with potentially serious consequences for heritage structures. The absence of a Land Use Plan and the need to update the Conservation Management Plan were some of the reasons UNESCO provided for putting Kilwa on the list of Heritage Sites in Danger. Site surveys and Land Use Plans are essential for cultural preservation (Fig. 10.20).[22] The objective of our project was to create appropriate technical and human resources in the Antiquities Division to facilitate sustainable management of the site. Spatial planning enshrined into a formal Land Use Plan (LUP) is an essential tool, defining protected zones where development is prohibited, and identifying other areas where physical or economic development can take place without negatively impacting the site. As a prelude, a

---

[21] Ichumbaki and Pollard, 2019, pp. 243–55.
[22] Wilson and Omar, 1996, pp. 238–40.

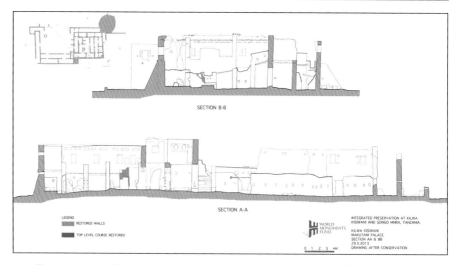

Figure 10.20 Section drawing showing conservation work done on the Makutani Palace, Kilwa Kisiwani. Courtesy the authors.

baseline survey map in GIS format was created. Data collection was carried out by students from the University of Dar es Salaam as part of a summer internship. The planning process started at Songo Mnara. After extensive consultation using participatory planning techniques, a Village LUP was developed and ratified by the District Council. In addition, the Conservation Management Plan for the World Heritage Site, which had become obsolete, was revised and fully updated.

At the completion of our project, all the monuments of Kilwa Kisiwani have been restored and over seventy per cent of standing structures at Songo Mnara had been successfully preserved. Public recognition of the success of the project came in June 2014, when UNESCO removed the World Heritage Site of Kilwa Kisiwani and Songo Mnara from the list of Heritage Sites in Danger. This was achieved by establishing a working methodology that could evolve with technological advancement, respect to the inhabitants of the islands and based on historical knowledge of the site. The goal was to protect the site and support the communities that have inherited this heritage, so the site can endure and the local community can benefit from it.

BIBLIOGRAPHY

Abungu, G., M. Mchulla, A. Allausy and A. Ali. 2018. 'The future of Swahili monuments', in Stephanie Wynne-Jones and Adria LaViolette (eds), *The Swahili World*. Abingdon and New York: Routledge, pp. 642–50.

Bacuez, P. 2008. *Intangible Heritage Tourism and Raising Awareness on Kilwa Kisiwani and Songo Mnara*. Dar-es-Salaam: UNESCO office. https://unesdoc.unesco.org/ark:/482 23/pf0000244385.

Chittick, N. 1974. *Kilwa: an Islamic Trading City on the East African Coast*. Nairobi: British Institute in Eastern Africa, 2 vols.

Garlake, P. 1966. *The Early Islamic Architecture of the East African Coast*. Nairobi and Oxford: British Institute in Eastern Africa.

Halmashauri ya kijiji cha Songo Mnara. 2013. 'Mpango wa matumizi bora ya ardhi kijiji cha Songo Mnara, kata ya Pande, tarafa ya Pande, wilaya ya Kilwa, mkoa wa Lindi (2013–2023)'. Unpublished Land Use Plan for Songo Mnara.

Harrison, Rodney. 2012. *Heritage Critical Approaches*. New York: Routledge.

Heathcott, J. 2013. 'Historic urban landscapes of the Swahili coast new frameworks for conservation' in R. Van Oers and S. Haraguchi (eds), *Swahili Historic Urban Landscapes. Report on the Historic Urban Landscape Workshops and Field Activities on the Swahili Coast in East Africa 2011–2012*. Paris: UNESCO, pp. 20–39.

Ichumbaki, E. and B. Mapunda. 2017. 'Challenges to the retention of the integrity of World Heritage Sites in Africa: the case of Kilwa Kisiwani and Songo Mnara, Tanzania', *Azania: Archaeological Research in Africa*, vol. 52, issue 4.

Ichumbaki, E. and E. Pollard. 2019. 'Valuing the Swahili Cultural Heritage: A Maritime Cultural Ecosystem Services Study from Kilwa, Tanzania', *Conservation and Management of Archaeological Sites*, 21 (4), July, pp. 230–55.

Kilian, K. 2006. *Die Ruinen von Kilwa Kisiwani (Tanzania) und ihre Bedeutung als archäologische Stätte*. Magistra Artium, Philosophischen Fakultät I der Humboldt, Universität zu Berlin.

Mathew, A. G. 1959. 'Songo Mnara', *Tanganyika Notes and Records*, no. 53, pp. 154–60.

Middleton, J. 1992. *The World of the Swahili: an African mercantile civilization*. New Haven and London: Yale University Press.

Nakamura, R. 2006. 'The Religious Attitude concerning the Ruins of the Perished Kilwa Kingdom on the Swahili Coast', *African Kingdoms Studies* 3, pp. 282–306 (in Japanese with English abstract).

Pradines, Stéphane. 2018. 'Redrawing the boundaries: excavating Cairo's Islamic walls', *Egyptian Archaeology Journal* No. 52, pp. 15–19.

Pradines, Stéphane. 2017. 'Swahili past in peril. New archaeology in East Africa', *Journal of Oriental and African studies* 26, pp. 211–36.

Pradines, Stéphane and Pierre Blanchard. 2006. 'Kilwa al-Mulûk. Premier bilan des travaux de conservation-restauration et des fouilles archéologiques dans la baie de Kilwa, Tanzanie', *Annales Islamologiques* 39, pp. 25–80.

Schnepel, B. and T. Sen (eds). 2019. *Travelling Pasts: The Politics of Cultural Heritage in the Indian Ocean World*. Leiden: Brill.

Seppälä, P. and B. Koda (eds). 1998. *The making of a periphery, economic development and cultural encounters in southern Tanzania*, Seminar Proceedings no. 32. Uppsala: Nordiska Afrikainstitutet.

Sheriff, Ed. 1995. *The History and Conservation of Zanzibar Stone Town*. Athens, OH: Ohio State University Press.

Siravo, F. 1996. *Zanzibar: A plan for the Historic Stone Town*. Geneva: The Aga Khan Trust for Culture.

United Republic of Tanzania. 1958–1965. *Annual Report of the Department of Antiquities*. Dar es Salaam: Government Printing Press, 7 issues.

Walz, J. and S. Gupta. 2011. 'Report and Observations on The First Conference on Indian Ocean Heritage: Indian Ocean Heritage, an Emerging Concept organized by the French Ministry of Cultural Affairs and its affiliates in Saint-Denis, Réunion, 2–4 November 2011', *Journal of Indian Ocean Archaeology* 7, pp. 122–8.

Wilson, T. and A. Omar. 1996. 'Preservation of cultural heritage on the East African coast', in P. Schmidt and R. McIntosh (eds), *Plundering Africa's Past*. Bloomington: Indiana University Press, pp. 225–49.

Wynne-Jones, Stephanie and A. LaViolette (eds). 2018. *The Swahili World*. Abingdon and New York: Routledge.

Chapter 11

Early Swahili Mosques: The Role of Ibadi and Ismaili Communities, Ninth to Twelfth Centuries

Stéphane Pradines

Introduction

The role of trade has been crutial in the process of Islamisation in sub-Saharan Africa. Arab, Berber, Persian and Indian merchants spread Islam across the vast geographic areas of the Sahara and the Indian Ocean. The first African converts were among the elite, most often merchants and local leaders. Islamised cities and kingdoms quickly took advantage of this new religion by strengthening their administration and legitimacy through the use of Arabic script. Indeed, Islam was much more than a new religion, it was a revolution which changed eating habits, architecture and also social relations, in particular a system of jurisprudence based on the *shari'a*. The historical mosques built in East Africa can be considered as true pieces of Islamic art and they reflect the diversity and unity of Indian Ocean cultures.

One of the problems of early mosques in East Africa is their identification and chronology. What was the impact of early Muslim communities, especially the Ibadi and the Ismaili, in the Islamisation of the East African coast? Why was the thirteenth century a time of change in mosque architecture and what was the role of Sunni communities in Africa? The responses to these questions must be investigated through the links between migrations, diaspora and trading networks in the Indian Ocean.

There is a common denominator amongst the early mosques in sub-Saharan Africa: it is the preponderant role of what are now called the religious minorities of Islam, notably the Ibadis and the Ismailis. These groups, which emerged from the Shi'ite and Kharijite movements, were at the origin of the Islamisation of sub-Saharan Africa, but also of the introduction of mosque architecture.

Until today sub-Saharan architecture has retained these earliest forms of Islamic architecture.

Kharijism is thus the oldest schism in Islam, which appeared in 657. The Kharijites or 'dissidents' refused to choose between ʿAli and Muʿawiya (the first Umayyad caliph). This Muslim sect was known for its moral and religious rigour. Its members preached an egalitarianism in Muslim society connected with the nomadic origins of the culture. The Ibadis were one of the most tolerant and moderate branches of the Kharijite movement. They were to be found in East Africa and the western Sahara.

As for the Shiʿites, they reassembled around the descendants of ʿAli and Fatima, the Prophet's daughter. They were divided into six branches, of which the main ones in Africa were the Ismailis (who followed the seventh Imam), the Twelvers (who followed the twelfth Imam) and the Zaydis. Various subgroups of the Ismailis were particularly active in East Africa, and included the Qarmatians (who have now disappeared) and the Bohras who were also divided into subgroups. The period from the tenth to the twelfth century was the Golden Age of the Shiʿite dynasties, with the Ismaili Fatimids in Egypt, the Zirids and the Idrisids in North Africa, the Qarmatians in Bahrain and the Buyids in Iran-Iraq.

From the thirteenth century on Sunnism gradually prevailed almost everywhere across the world. The Sunnis experienced a more standardised division with their four legal schools: the Shafiʿites, the Malikites, the Hanbalites and the Hanafites.

The First Muslim Communities in East Africa, from the Ninth to the Twelfth Centuries

Swahili culture extends from Mogadishu in Somalia,[1] down to the bay of Sofala in Mozambique, passing through Kenya, Tanzania and the north of Madagascar – the latter connected to the African continent by the Comoros archipelago (Fig. 11.1). The Swahili civilisation on the periphery of the Muslim and African worlds occupied a position that was highly propitious for the development of an original littoral culture based on commercial relations and the spread of Islam.

According to the *Kitab al-Zanj* and the Chronicles of Pate, the Islamisation of the Swahili coast can be dated back to 696, when the caliph ʿAbd al-Malik b. Marwan is supposed to have built thirty-five towns on the African littoral. The Annals of Oman report facts which are certainly closer to reality:[2] the brothers Sulayman and Saʿid left Oman with their relatives in order to seek refuge in Africa at the time of the conquest of their country by ʿAbd al-Malik

---

[1] Ibn Madjid in Tibbetts, 1971, p. 422; Ibn al-Mugâwir in Ducatez, 2003.
[2] Wilkinson, 1981.

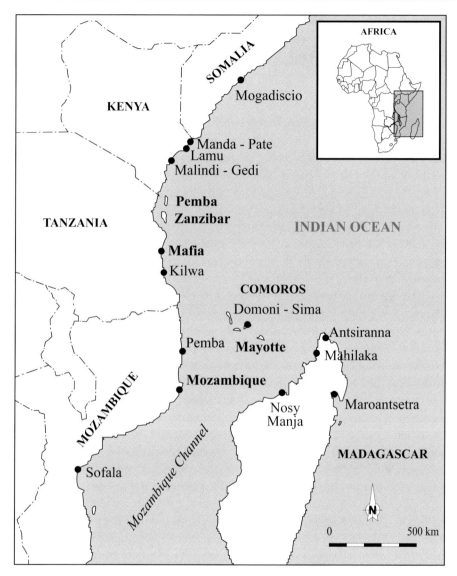

Figure 11.1 Map. Courtesy the author.

in 692. The Ibadis, expelled from the Persian Gulf and southern Arabia, formed one of the first Muslim communities of refugees in Africa.[3] The first Muslims to occupy Pemba and Kilwa were probably Ibadis.[4] The Chronicles of Kilwa state

---

[3] Sheriff, 1995.
[4] Horton and Middleton, 2000, pp. 64–7; Horton, 1996, pp. 421–2.

specifically that two brothers professed the Ibadi doctrine in the city. When the Shirazis arrived in Kilwa in 957, a mosque had already been built on the island and was directed by an infidel. According to the Chronicles of Kilwa, the term infidel does not necessarily mean that that local leader followed African animist practices. It could mean that he simply belonged to a Muslim sect or confession different from that of the newcomers and might have been an Ibadi or a Zaydi.[5]

Shiʿite groups were violently repressed by the Abbasid rulers, particularly from 762 to 799, but as early as 739 a wave of emigrants left the coasts of Iran and Iraq for the south of Somalia. In the following year they were joined by Zaydi Shiʿites from the Yemen.[6] The Zaydis were one of the Shiʿite groups persecuted by the Abbasids who emigrated to the Red Sea and the African coasts. They are reported to have been in Pate in 760[7] and in the Yemen in the tenth century, where they formed a community that exists to this day.[8] João de Barros also mentioned this wave of Zaydi migrants who adapted themselves to the local usages and customs. João de Barros and then Charles Guillain[9] also said that a Shiʿite sect left the port of al-Hasa and founded the cities of Mogadishu, Barawa, Merka and Zanzibar between 887 and 924. These forced migrations show that Africa had been a place of refuge for persecuted Muslim minorities ever since the seventh century. The first Swahili communities were therefore derived from the union of Muslim refugees and merchants with the daughters of local African chieftains. These inter-ethnic marriages constituted a political strategy: the Muslims acquired the protection of the African chieftains, while the latter received in return manufactured products which increased their social status. The acquisition of a new religion, Islam, led to an opening onto the worlds of the Indian Ocean, which reinforced the authority and the prestige of the local chieftains still further. Nevertheless, in the first centuries of Islam the Swahili coast was only feebly Islamised, despite the arrival of political refugees and religious minorities. In the tenth century Ibn Hawkal and al-Masʿudi said that the Zanj adored numerous gods and idols.[10] In the twelfth century the situation had hardly changed, and al-Idrisi declared that most of the Zanj towns, such as Mombasa and Malindi, still had a pagan majority in 1154, and that the inhabitants of Barawa worshipped erected stones.[11] This first 'surface' Islamisation affected above all the ruling classes who adapted themselves to a new culture and a new language of particular use for trade: Arabic.

---

[5] De Barros, *Decadas Da Asia* I, vol. VIII, in Freeman-Grenville, 1962, pp. 32 and 81; Horton and Middleton, 2000, pp. 64–7; Gaube and Al Salimi, 2013, pp. 21–121.

[6] De Barros, 1945, p. 335.

[7] Trimingham, 1964; Horton, 1996, pp. 422–3.

[8] Pouwels, 2000, p. 256.

[9] De Barros, *Decadas Da Asia* in Guillain, 1856, pp. 6–7; Strandes, 1899, p. 73.

[10] Ibn Hawkal, *Kitâb al-Masâlik wa 'l-mamâlik*, 356/967 in Mathew, 1963, p. 105.

[11] Freeman-Grenville, 1962, p. 41.

Between 866 and 883 the great revolt of the Zanj,[12] in the south of Iraq, devastated the most important ports. In this period *Zanj*, an Arabic word taken from the Greek *Zengis*, designated all the black slaves used in Iraq for works of irrigation. After the revolt, Baghdad was cut off from the Persian Gulf and trade with East Africa. The revolt of the Zanj provides abundant information both about the number of African slaves in the Persian Gulf and about their religion. Tens of thousands of black slaves rebelled in the region of Basra (in the south of present-day Iraq). The Dey of Kufa proposed an alliance to the 'prince of the blacks', but the latter, who was an 'Alid (Shi'ite), refused[13] – a fact that also demonstrates a deep division between contemporary Shi'ite groups. After the great revolt of the Zanj, the Persian Gulf again became the scene of dramatic events: in 920 the Qarmatians of Bahrain sacked the port of Basra. The regional antagonisms increased and, in 942, as a reprisal, the ruler of Basra had the Omani fleet set on fire. The Qarmatians, the members of a religious movement based on the messianic ideas of radical Shi'ism, created a powerful and prosperous state independent of the Abbasid caliphate. This state was centred in Bahrain and extended its influence on the east coast of Arabia as far as the south of Iraq. The Qarmatian kingdom was supreme in the Persian Gulf from the tenth to the eleventh century. The Qarmatians possessed the port of al-Hasa. They invaded the Yemen in 883, sacked Mecca in 929 and occupied Oman in 930. In 971, finally, they besieged Cairo, but unsuccessfully. In 1004 they are said to have owned up to 30,000 black slaves from the lands of East Africa. The dynasty ended in 1077, and numerous Qarmatians emigrated to the coasts of Benadir.[14]

The pivotal years between the tenth and the twelfth century were a period of change in the Muslim world. The fall of the Abbasids led to the partitioning of the Muslim empire into a mosaic of rival states that disrupted trade in the Persian Gulf. It was also the golden age of the Shi'ite principalities in the Muslim world.

Between 932 and 1062 the Buyids settled in Baghdad and there was a temporary return of a Shi'ite dynasty. The power of the Abbasids of Baghdad declined to the advantage of a great new Islamic metropolis, Fatimid Cairo. The Egyptian merchants availed themselves of the collapse of the Abbasid Empire since the essential part of African trade was now with the Red Sea. The Sulayhid dynasty in the Yemen was to have close dealings with Fatimid Egypt from 1084 to 1138.[15] An Ismaili dynasty controlled Sindh in Pakistan from 980 and had political and religious relations with the Fatimid caliphs of Egypt. Economically and diplomatically, the Fatimids of Egypt became immensely powerful thanks

---

[12] Talib, 1990, pp. 749–78.
[13] De Goeje, *Mémoire sur les Carmathes du Bahraïn et les Fatimides*. Leiden: Brill, 1886, pp. 9 and 26.
[14] Pradines, 2004, pp. 140–1; Pouwels, 1974, pp. 68–70.
[15] Moncelon, 1995, pp. 29–30.

to trade in the Indian Ocean. Later the Mamluks would pursue the same commercial policy and reinforce their control over the western coast of the Red Sea and the ports of Suakin, Massawa and Assab. The merchants of the Persian Gulf remained active, but other ports were preferred, often on islands such as Kish, Hormuz and Bahrain. The sailors on the island of Kish committed acts of piracy in the whole of the Indian Ocean, attacking Aden in 1135 and making slave raids on the coast of the Zanj.

Numerous African urban centres were created in the tenth and the eleventh centuries and architecture in stone developed, first affecting mosques and the large storehouses of merchants. This period saw the establishment of the Swahili city-states. Between the eleventh and the twelfth centuries the techniques of construction of Swahili mosques became extremely elaborate. The principal characteristic of the mosques of this period was the exclusive use of sea coral cut into little quadrangular blocks with horizontal bedding on lime mortar. This type of masonry was typical of the site of Sanje ya Kati and of the first great mosque of Kilwa Kisiwani.[16] The same technique would be used along the entire Swahili coast during the whole twelfth century. If the collection and utilisation of natural resources such as coral was confined to local populations, the brutal introduction of elaborate techniques of masonry can only have been the result of external influences due mainly to the sailors of the Persian Gulf and the coasts of India.

Al-Masʿudi thus tells us that numerous merchant boats belonged to the Omani sailors and ship owners.[17] He describes the African coastal towns that had not yet been Islamised in 916. The city of Qanbalu was the most important port on the African coast in this period. Al-Masʿudi found that the population consisted of as many Muslims as pagans, but it was a Muslim family that reigned in Qanbalu with a king, the *Mfalme*. Another account by a sailor in the Persian Gulf was written in the middle of the tenth century. Buzurg b. Shahriyar came from the port of Hormuz and wrote the *Kitab ʿAjaʾib al-Hind*.[18] The 'Book of the Marvels of India' was compiled in about 956–957. The Book of Marvels also indicates that the king of an African town had converted his people. This fact is most interesting since it is one of the earliest pieces of evidence of Islamisation in East Africa.[19]

The destruction of Siraf, the port of Shiraz, by an earthquake in 977, followed by the fall of the Buyids in the eleventh century, led to a massive exodus of Persians who emigrated to the islands of Kish and Hormuz in the Persian

---

[16] Chittick, 1974; Pradines, 2009; Pradines, 2010, p. 27.
[17] Al-Masûdi in Freeman-Grenville, 1962, pp. 14–15.
[18] Ibn Hawqal edited by Van der Lith, Sauvaget, *Relation de la Chine et de l'Inde* (1948); Freeman-Grenville, 1962, p. 9; De Planhol, 2000, p. 101; Ducène, 2015.
[19] Pradines, 2009.

Gulf, but also to Jedda on the Red Sea. According to Ibn al-Mugawir the people of Siraf emigrated after the decline of the town at the end of the tenth century.[20] The inhabitants of Siraf reached the Yemen, and then Jedda, from where they were expelled in 1081 by a decree of the religious authorities in Mecca.[21] Their emigration seems to come to an end in the last years of the eleventh century. Wherever they went they appear to have been formidable builders: walls, caravanserais, wells and cisterns.[22] A similar tradition exists on the island of Pemba in Tanzania concerning the populations called Wa-Debuli, said to have originated in Daybul in the Indus Delta (Banbhore). In the Yemen Axelle Rougeulle discovered and excavated an Islamic establishment founded in about 980 and occupied until 1150.[23] The trading post of Sharma, situated on the shores of Hadramawt, was allegedly founded by a diaspora of communities from the Persian Gulf after the decline of Siraf.[24] This exodus of Shirazis appears to have been a phenomenon that affected the whole of the Indian Ocean since numerous oral traditions of Swahili cities claim to have been of Shirazi origin.[25] According to local traditions the first mosques in stone are associated with the Persians, the best known being the one in the town of Kilwa.[26] The Chronicles of Kilwa tell us that the sultan 'Ali ibn Sulayman and his six sons, or his six brothers, fled from their city of Shiraz as a result of persecution and left the country from the port of Siraf in seven ships.[27] At each port of call on the African coast one of the seven individuals founded a town, from north to south: Mandakha, Shaughu, Yanba, Mombasa, Pemba, Kilwa and Hanzuan.[28] The town of Kilwa would have been founded in 957 by Hassan b. 'Ali, one of the sultan's six sons. The father, 'Ali ibn Sulayman, was the last one to stop off in the island of Anjouan in the Comoros archipelago in 985. Other traditions for the Somali towns of Mogadishu, Barawa and Merka mention nine brothers, all Shi'ites, who left on three ships from the port of al-Hasa in the Persian Gulf between 908 and 924, or on two boats which left from the port of Hormuz.[29]

The story of the Shirazi ancestral founders of numerous Swahili towns is obviously a foundaton myth, and yet it would be wrong to deny its historical interest and the permanence of oral traditions on the whole of the East African coast, as Abdul Sheriff has pointed out.[30] From an archaeologcal point of view

---

[20] Ducatez, 2003, pp. 139 and 147, note 65.
[21] Ducatez, 2004, p. 165.
[22] Pradines, 2004, p. 52.
[23] Rougeulle, 2004, pp. 224–5 and 233–4.
[24] Rougeulle, 2017, pp. 145–50.
[25] Spear, 1984.
[26] De Barros, 1945; Chittick, 1974.
[27] Freeman-Grenville, 1962, pp. 45–59; Ducatez, 2003, p. 147.
[28] Freeman-Grenville, 1962, pp. 75.
[29] Guillain, 1856, pp. 6–7; Strandes, 1899, p. 73.
[30] Sheriff, 2001.

there is a collection of archaeological evidence of the role and the impact of the communities of the Persian Gulf on the societies of the Swahili littoral.[31] In fact the term 'Shirazi' designates far more than the town of Shiraz or the Persian port of Siraf. It covers a number of populations from the Persian Gulf who arrived in East Africa at a very early stage and shared common religious values such as Ibadism and Shi'ism (Qarmatians and Ismailis). Consequently the term 'brothers' in the Chronicles of Kilwa could be interpreted as *ikhwan*, 'religious brothers', and the sultan as a spiritual leader.[32] Yakut, for example, reports that in 1116 the leaders of Pemba were Shi'ite refugees from Kufa.

From 957 to 1131 the city of Kilwa, ruled by the Shirazi, launched numerous attacks on neighbouring coastal towns, particularly Shagh (Sanje Ya Kati),[33] Mafia and Zanzibar.[34] Kilwa had difficulty in imposing its sovereignty on these local potentates on the southern stretch of the coast under the reign of Dawud b. Sulayman (1131–70).[35]

A new balance of power emerged in the thirteenth century. The little Shi'ite groups in East Africa were replaced by massive waves of Sunni emigrants, mainly of the Shafi'ite rite.[36] The Shirazi dynasty of Kilwa was replaced in 1277 by the dynasty of the Mahdalis, a Hadhrami clan from the southwest of the Yemen.[37] This new power was connected with the Rasulids of the Yemen, who themselves had close ties with the Mamluks of Egypt, the Seljuks of the Persian Gulf and the Indians of the Indus and Deccan Deltas. The general spread of Sunnism on the east coast could be atrributed to contacts with the merchants of the Hadramawt.[38] In 1331, all the Shi'ite groups seem to have been absorbed by the Sunni, and Ibn Battuta encountered Sunni Shafi'ites on the entire coast.[39]

The thirteenth century was a period of transition in which Swahili masons abandoned the use of blocks of sea coral and preferred ashlar blocks of fossil coral. Swahili masons realised that the cutting of standardised blocks in coral limestone had few advantages in view of the waste of time and manpower. With the expansion of Swahili cities, the builders opted for new building techniques that were both simpler and faster. The walls were built with irregular ashlar blocks of coral limestone held by a framework in coral concrete that completely replaced the earlier bonded walls. The clamping of the corners of the walls was still performed with beautiful, dressed stone. The Swahili masons added gravel

---

[31] Pradines, 2009, pp. 49–53 and 71.
[32] Strandes, 1899, p. 73.
[33] Mathew, 1963, p. 107.
[34] Freeman-Grenville, 1962, pp. 37–9.
[35] Ibid., pp. 86–7.
[36] Wilkinson, 1981.
[37] Wilkinson, 1981; Mathew, 1963, p. 123; Freeman-Grenville, 1962, p. 45.
[38] Al-Malik al-Ashraf (1271) and Abu al-Fidâ (1342) edited by Reinaud, 1848, pp. 206–8; Abu al-Mahâsin (1441) in Guillain, 1856, pp. 299–300; Freeman-Grenville, 1962, pp. 23 and 33.
[39] Ibn Battuta, vol. 2 (1357, ed. 1949), pp. 179–96; Sheriff, op. cit., p. 29.

and fragments of fossil coral to the mortar that thus became more resistant. This veritable coral cement was used during the entire Middle Ages. It was a simple material, easy to install thanks to the technique of coffering. Coffering consisted of pouring concrete between planks of wood where it would be left to dry and then in removing the planks. This made it possible to raise cupolas or even pillars in which rectangular plaques of coral were inserted, as in Kilwa Kisiwani or Songo Mnara.[40]

THE SWAHILI MOSQUES FROM THE NINTH TO THE TWELFTH CENTURY

The Swahili mosques had similarities with the mosques in southern Arabia, Yemen and Oman, with a longitudinal prayer hall, hardly any courtyards, flat terrace roofs and a row of pillars on the axis of the mihrab.[41] The Swahili mosques did not have a central courtyard but were sometimes flanked by small courtyards with a well reserved for ablutions (Fig. 11.2). They did not have a minaret tower. The prayer was called from the roof to which access was gained by way of a little staircase behind the mihrab. The niche of the mihrab formed a quadrangular protuberance jutting out from the mosque. The minaret as a tower from which the muezzin calls the faithful to prayer was almost unknown in East Africa, and indeed, the first mosques had no minaret. In the age of the Prophet the prayer call was uttered from the roof of a house. The so-called ogive or conical minarets made a relatively late appearance on the coast between the seventeenth and the nineteenth centuries. Their morphology is close to the minarets found in the Hadhramawt and the south of the Arabian Peninsula. The masoned minbars multiplied between the thirteenth and the fifteenth centuries. They were little stairways of between three and eight steps in coral stone bounded with mortar and sometimes covered by plaster. They were always situated to the right of the mihrab, perpendicularly to the qibla.

For their masonry, the Swahilis also used an extremely original building material specific to the cultures of the Indian Ocean, especially the Maldives and Sri Lanka – marine coral. The technology of marine coral in architecture appears in East Africa between the ninth and tenth centuries in Shanga in the Lamu Archipelago and in Dembéni in the Comoros Archipelago. At this period, only small blocks of coral were used – they were not cut, they were held by an earth mortar. The small madrepores or porite coral balls were collected at low tide in the lagoon between the beach and the great barrier reef. Large blocks of coral were fished in the sea around the great barrier reef. These blocks can reach several metres in diameter. Marine coral has a very dense fine structure,

---

[40] Pradines and Blanchard, 2005, p. 28; Pradines and Blanchard, 2015.
[41] Costa, 2001, p. 223; Lewcock, 1976.

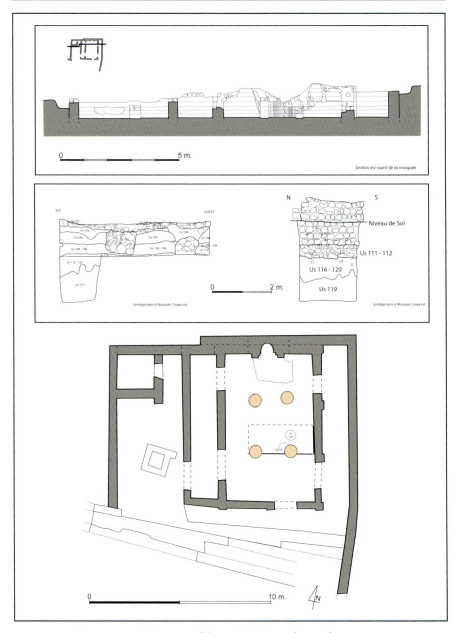

Figure 11.2 Mosque of Sanje Ya Kati, eleventh century.
Courtesy the author.

it is soft and easy to work when it is wet and fresh; it then hardens as it dries. This fine-grained coral was used for making the walls of which it constitutes the ashlars, but it was especially used for mouldings, fine sculptures and decorations of mosques, especially in the mihrab. Each cut coral block is 6 to 10 cm wide; each block sits in a notch in the block behind it, with this joining technique there is no need for mortar.

Between the eleventh and twelfth centuries construction techniques changed dramatically and became extremely elaborate. The main feature of mosques from this period is the exclusive use of well-cut marine coral in small quadrangular blocks with horizontal courses on lime mortars. This type of masonry is characteristic of the site of Sanje Ya Kati or the first great mosque of Kilwa Kisiwani. This technique would be used all over the Swahili coast during the twelfth century. The sudden introduction of elaborate masonry techniques can only be the result of external influences. According to our initial observations, the place of origin of marine coral architecture is located between India and Indonesia. The Maldives and Sri Lanka are located right in the epicentre of this technique and coral architecture possibly originated from this area. Its diffusion by the Abbasid mariners in the western Indian Ocean, and, in particular, in Africa in the ninth century, as well as its globalisation under the Buwayhids and the Fatimids in the eleventh century is very closely linked to the great international maritime trade.

From 1981 to 1989 Mark Horton carried out archaeological research on the site of Shanga in the Lamu Archipelago in the north of Kenya.[42] During his excavation of the great mosque Horton observed nine phases of construction. The first phases do not tell us whether it was a mosque or even a religious building. Islam is attested with certainty in Shanga at the beginning of the ninth century, with a first mosque that covered a rectangular surface of 7.24 by 3.61 metres.[43] It was composed of a square prayer hall preceded by a little vestibule to the south. The main south entrance was demarcated by two square post-holes. A post-hole in the centre of the prayer hall would have had to support a light roof in palm leaves. The walls in wickerwork and cob have left traces in negative: regularly spaced holes of sticks drowned in cob. The mosque rested on a platform of clay, which gave it a dominant position in the centre of the village of Shanga. Two technological innovations were introduced at the end of the ninth century. The first was the use of plaster as a floor coating. The second was the desire to construct a more solid building, different from the traditional private dwelling. The walls were made of wooden poles placed in a foundation trench. The surface of the mosque was then 7.25 by 4.14 metres, but the bipartite plan remained the same. The roofing was always sustained by a

---

[42] Horton, 1991; Horton, 2017, pp. 262–7; Horton, 1994.
[43] Horton, 1996, pp. 209–23.

central column, and a ditch at the centre of the north wall of the mosque might indicate the foundations of a wooden mihrab. The surface of the mosque, finally, had increased considerably to 9.7 by 5.4 metres. Between 1015 and 1035 the mosque of Shanga was reconstructed with foundations 54 cm thick constituted by a double coral facing. The blocks of coral were fished in the sea, carved on their outer face, and bounded with clay. The external faces of the walls were coated with plaster. Horton discovered in Shanga a quadrangular bedrock in coral stone at the centre of the qibla which indicated the presence of a coral mihrab in the eleventh century.[44] The plan of the mosque of Shanga in phase H was identical to that of the mosques in perishable materials of the ninth century. The building formed a rectangle of 10.28 by 7.23 metres, always with a little chamber in the south. To the east of the mosque there was a rectangular water reservoir. The main entrance was probably in the east. The reservoir was used for the ritual ablutions before entering the mosque. The mosque of Shanga was reconstructed between 1160 and 1172. It was built on a platform of white sand, the floor being covered by three layers of plaster. The roofing was supported by two rows of columns connected to the pilasters of the side walls by archways or master beams. The walls were made up of an installation of blocks of worked coral bounded by mortar. The east and west walls were each pierced by three symmetrical doors which corresponded in the inner space of the prayer hall to three bays parallel to the wall of the qibla. The same arrangement can also be seen in the great mosque of Kilwa in the same period. The mihrab of the mosque of Shanga was rebuilt in the middle of the twelfth century and then restored in the fourteenth century.

If a quadrangular bedrock in ashlar blocks of sea coral indicates the presence of a mihrab masoned in Shanga as early as the eleventh century,[45] the earliest Swahili mihrabs that we know, still in elevation, can be dated to the twelfth century. The mihrab of the mosque of Kizimkazi, in the south of the island of Zanzibar, is the earliest known Swahili mihrab still in elevation. It was decorated and bears the date 1107 (Fig. 11.3). The entry of the niche of the mihrab was framed by engaged columns and engaged twisted colonettes. The colonettes carried a trilobal arch. The interior of the niche was interrupted by oblong blind arcades surmounted by a frieze of geometrical motifs, little blind niches, and miniature mihrabs. The salient minbar in coral stone was composed of two steps and a seat, dating, according to J. Schacht, from the twelfth century. The mihrab was decorated with inscriptions in floriated Kufic which ran along each side and in the interior of the niche. These inscriptions were cited by Pearce in 1920,

---

[44] Ibid., pp. 200–8.
[45] Ibid, pp. 203–8.

Figure 11.3 Mihrab of the mosque of Kizimkazi, 1107 AD. Courtesy the author.

and then studied by Flury in 1922.[46] The text to the right of the mihrab was a passage of the Qur'ān dated 1107. Another inscription, however, indicates that the mihrab was restored in 1772. There is some disagreement about the dating of Kizimkazi and particularly about the trilobal arch surmounting the niche of the mihrab. For Peter Garlake, the arch and the frieze of miniature mihrabs date from the restoration of the mosque in the eighteenth century. For Mark Horton, the trilobal arch and its Kufic inscriptions were an integral part of the mihrab of the twelfth century. In my own view the walls with the mini-mihrabs and the inscription are original, but there is nothing to prove that the arch dates back to the twelfth century.

The mihrabs of the style of Kizimkazi are clearly defined morphologically by a niche with trilobal blind arcades surmounted by a frieze of geometrical motifs, small blind niches, or miniature mihrabs.[47] The dating, on the other hand, presents a problem. This group starts in the twelfth century and persists until the fifteenth, notably in Tumbatu, Kisimani Mafia and Songo Mnara (Fig. 11.4).[48] This type of mihrab is situated essentially in the south of the east coast, around the islands of Zanzibar and Mafia, as well as in Madagascar with the mosque of Nosy Manja in the bay of Mahajamba.[49] The style of the mihrab of the Kizimkazi type was recognised by Monik Kervran in an Uyunid mosque in Bahrain, dating from the first half of the twelfth century. The mosque of the Souq al-Khamis had an inscription in floriated Kufic with a dedication to the third emir of the Uyunid dynasty who reigned between 1131 and 1149. It contained the Shi'ite *shahada* and mentions the Twelve Imams. The mosque was also mentioned in the last decades of the Qarmatian Empire towards 1050 and was founded in 1107 at the time when Abu Sinan restored the mosque of the Suq al-Khamis.[50] Mihrab plaques with Kufic characters can also be seen in the Fatimid rearrangements of the mosque of Ibn Tulun in Cairo.

The great mosque of Kilwa Kisiwani is divided into two parts. The northern part corresponds to the earliest mosque, dating from the twelfth century, and the southern part is a later extension. According to the Chronicles of Kilwa, the first mosque was built between 1131 and 1170.[51] It had a rectangular plan measuring 11.8 by 7.8 metres (Fig. 11.5). All that remains are the loadbearing walls whose foundations were composed of a more or less regular arrangement of quadrangular ashlar blocks in coral limestone. This type of arrangement was typical of this period. Three symmetrical vaulted doors opened in the east and

---

[46] Flury, 1922; Lowick, 1985.
[47] Pradines, 2003.
[48] Kervran and Kalus, 1990, pp. 31–45 and 48–9.
[49] Vérin, 1975, pp. 543–4; Poirier, 1954, pp. 71–116.
[50] Kervran and Kalus, 1990, pp. 31 and 48.
[51] Freeman-Grenville, 1962, pp. 122–5; Chittick, 1974, pp. 65–6.

Figure 11.4 Mosque and mihrab of Songo Mnara, fifteenth century.
Courtesy the author.

west walls. The flat roof was supported by nine hexagonal monoxyle columns ordered in three rows, the bases of which, in sandstone in the ground, are still visible.[52] In 1530 the roof collapsed. Judging from the archaeological excavations the debris was thrown into the western antechamber. The roof consisted of coral tiles drowned in mortar. These tiles were engraved with motifs of concentric circles with a diameter between 8.5 and 10.5 cm. Chittick noted traces of red paint on the ceiling, so the mosque may have been painted in bright colours. The mihrab seems more recent than the building of the twelfth century. Its broken arch rests on capitals and pilasters. The niche was decorated with oblong friezes and surmounted by a fluted quarter-sphere vault. Four coral blocks jut out east of the mihrab, indicating the attachment of a fixed minbar, probably in wood. I have also observed traces of oblong niches in the niche of the mihrab. These elements, which recall the mihrabs of Kisimani in Mafia and of Kizimkazi in Zanzibar,[53] were part of the original Shirazi mihrab, but only the upper parts seem to have been refitted in the fifteenth century. The

---

[52] Ibid., pp. 61–5.
[53] Pradines, 2003, pp. 360–1.

Figure 11.5 The Shirazi mosque of Kilwa Kisiwani, built between 1131 and 1170. Courtesy the author.

ablution area of this first mosque was situated in the west. During the restoration Pierre Blanchard discovered an elaborate system of canalisation with tubes of baked clay.

Sanje Ya Kati is a small circular island in the centre of the bay of Kilwa[54] and is occupied by the eponymous archaeological site. It was a fortified trading post protected by a quadrangular wall measuring 100 by 340 metres and flanked by towers.[55] The great mosque was established in the southeast of the site. It was founded in the second half of the eleventh century and renovated in the course of the twelfth century. The building technique is comparable to that of the first Shirazi mosque of Kilwa Kisiwani,[56] with regular bedding and a masonry composed of fresh coral blocks cut in a small square module measuring between 16 and 24 cm and an average of 22 cm (Fig. 11.6). Together with its lateral wings, the mosque of Sanje Ya Kati measures 10.21 by 9.46 metres. The east and west walls of the prayer hall were pierced by two symmetrical doors. The

---

[54] Pradines, 2009, pp. 49–73.
[55] Pradines, 2002.
[56] Chittick, 1974, p. 61.

Figure 11.6 Sanje Ya Kati fresh coral blocks. Courtesy the author.

wall of the mosque was supported by four wooden columns of which I found the foundation bases in ashlar blocks of coral limestone. These supports were placed on the axis of the opening of the mihrab. The floor of the mosque rested on an artificial terrace of several beds of blond sand, which made it possible to raise the level of the building. According to the stratigraphic analysis and the archaeological material associated with it, these levels date from the beginning of the eleventh century. The mihrab was constituted by a semi-circular niche inserted in the wall of the qibla. The entrance was enframed by pilasters on the axis of the columns in the prayer hall. The transition between the pilasters and the niche was ensured by two simple square mouldings. The wall of the qibla was lined on its northern façade by another wall that was in the continuation of the east wall of the eastern wing. The mihrab was not typical of a Swahili mosque since it did not jut out of the building. It was, rather, completely integrated in the wall of the qibla, which was lined for this purpose, and we may wonder which Muslim confession used this type of mihrab. For Mark Horton it is similar to the one of the mosques of Ras Mkumbuu on the island of Pemba, which he dates to the tenth century and attributes to the Ibadi communities.[57]

[57] Laviolette and Fleisher, 2009, pp. 449–52; Horton, 2004, pp. 79–80.

The rectangular prayer hall of the mosque of Sanje was bordered by two lateral wings of the same width. The east wing extended south to incorporate the main entrance of the mosque, and the south side of the building was bordered by a masoned platform preceded by a long step in yellow sandstone, a rock that can also be found in Songo Mnara and Kilwa Kisiwani. A series of three walls was added clumsily against this step at the end of the twelfth century. It was a rustic device completely different from anything in the mosque. The west wing was composed of two cells to the north and a little square courtyard to the southwest with a well in the middle. The little chamber in the northwest corner must have been the area of the latrines. The well is orientated in a different way from the mosque. It is earlier than the mosque visible today and dates from the same period as the dressed blocks discovered in the arrangement of the floor of the prayer hall. These re-used blocks were cut in sea coral and had a stucco coating of excellent craftsmanship. They all came from an earlier building, probably the first mosque of Sanje, built in the middle of the eleventh century.

The site of Gedi is situated in the south of Malindi. Between 1999 and 2003, we discovered and excavated a new great mosque in Gedi, earlier than the one studied by James Kirkman in the 1950s. This mosque had a square plan 26 metres long from north to south and 25 metres wide, in other words 6 metres longer than Kirkman's great mosque dating from the fifteenth century. It was also earlier and radiocarbon dating confirms the construction of the great mosque in the fourteenth century.[58] The mosque was renovated during the same century with the addition of new pillars in stone instead of the columns in wood. It was built on earlier mosques. The first mosque can be dated between 1100 and 1150, with a second phase between 1150 and 1180.[59] Unfortunately it was entirely obliterated when a new mosque was built in the thirteenth century. All that remains are a few bare walls and a floor level in plaster orientated towards Mecca. An ablution area with bosses in sea coral was discovered to the southwest of this mosque (Fig. 11.7). Its north-northwest axis suggests that the building followed the orientation of the so-called Shirazi type of mosques built between the tenth and the twelfth centuries. The earliest layers discovered on top of the geological ground go back to the middle of the eleventh century. We do not have a mosque from this period, but it is very probable that a smaller building was situated just east of the thirteenth-century mosque. A second great mosque was built between 1200 and 1230. It covered completely the earlier building, which was first demolished. The thirteenth-century mosque was about 10 metres long and orientated north-northwest. Unfortunately the

---

[58] Pradines, 2010, pp. 39.
[59] Pradines, 2010, pp. 35–60 and 81–104; Connah, 2016, pp. 233–4.

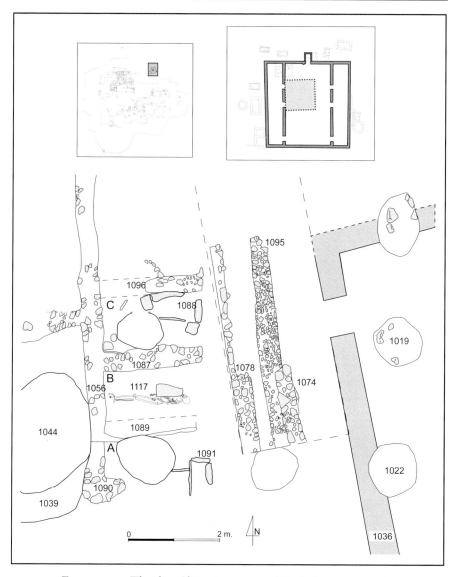

Figure 11.7 The first Shirazi mosque of Gedi (1100–50 AD).
Courtesy the author.

wall of the qibla was re-used for the foundation base of the pillars of the fourteenth-century mosque. All that remains of the almost demolished mosque is a north-south wall, a part of the plaster floor of the prayer hall, and the plaster floor of the lateral east wing. The mosque was shifted slightly to the east. The northwest orientation of the thirteenth-century mosque suggests that the building followed a traditionally Shirazi orientation, like the mosque of the twelfth century. The thirteenth-century mosque was bordered to the west by a series of tombs with sepulchres orientated according to the Muslim rite. The paving covering the grave pits included ritual deposits of black and yellow Yemeni bowls and a Kashan chandelier from the first half of the thirteenth century. The mosque was renovated at the time of the second phase between 1240 and 1280. This mosque, finally, was later completely demolished and covered by an enormous clay terrace that served as a foundation for the great mosque of the fourteenth century. The identical orientation of the mosques of the twelfth and thirteenth centuries could indicate that Gedi did not follow the general change adopted by the majority of Swahili sites with a conversion to the Sunni Shafi'ite rite, a conversion that seems to have been later in Gedi and goes back to the fourteenth century.

Common Features of the First Swahili Mosques

The use of blocks of sea coral was attested in Shanga in Kenya and at Dembeni in the Comoros as early as the ninth century.[60] It was a turning point, with the arrival of new architectural technologies on the east coast of Africa. In my opinion the use of this primary material spread across the Indian Ocean thanks to Abbassid sailors and merchants.[61]

According to Mark Horton the introduction of coral as a building material of the Swahili mosques can be connected with the Fatimid merchants from the Red Sea.[62] He believes that the Fatimids were innovators with respect to their predecessors in their use of stone for imperial and religious architecture rather than the brick commonly used in Egypt since the beginning of the Islamic era. This is wrong since the Fatimids also went in for earthen architecture. In fact stone architecture only really spread with the Ayyubids.[63] In order to prove his point Horton unfortunately takes as his example the town of Suakin, which only reached its apogee in the sixteenth century under the Ottomans. Besides, most of the sites on the Red Sea were built in fossil coral limestone and not in fresh sea coral. According to Horton, finally, the most important proof of Fatimid architectural influence on the east coasts of Africa is the mihrab of the mosque of Kizimkazi on the island of Zanzibar, which, decorated with Kufic inscriptions, can relate to the Fatimids of Egypt.

---

[60] Pradines, Veyssier and Zhao, 2016, pp. 44–6.
[61] De Planhol, 2000, pp. 91–148.
[62] Horton, 1991; Pradines, 2020.
[63] Pradines, 2018.

It was indeed in the eleventh century that Swahili builders started to cut sea coral for the construction of their mosques.[64] This material would be used to build walls until the end of the twelfth century. The first Swahili mihrabs were astonishing because they displayed a great expertise in stonecutting. There was no phase of 'apprenticeship' in the techniques. The mihrabs were constructed independently of the wall of the qibla. They were built first, and the mosque would be integrated around them. And yet this type of mihrab would soon be rejected by the populations of the coast because it required important technical means and no longer corresponded to the demand of the religious movements that would succeed it. The excavations of Sanje Ya Kati allow us to contradict entirely the earlier schemes of urbanisation intended to show a slow and local evolution of Swahili architecture.[65] The houses, the mosque and the fortifications of Sanje Ya Kati form a homogeneous architectural complex, between the eleventh and the twelfth centuries, in their techniques of construction with horizontal bedding, a system consisting of quadrangular ashlar blocks cut in a dense but soft sea coral. The mortars were very thick and deposited in beds. Sanje Ya Kati was a well defined and planned architectural project. The building techniques were remarkably accomplished. In the course of the thirteenth century, we see a degeneration of these techniques with materials of less good quality. With the expansion of the Swahili city-states the dressing of coral stone was abandoned in favour of constructions in coffrage.

Between the eleventh and the twelfth centuries the Swahili mosques adopted a plan which they were to follow until the nineteenth century: a rectangle, crossed by bays parallel to the qibla, a space enframed by two long parallel narrow chambers making up a third of the surface of the prayer hall. The Swahili mosques of the twelfth century seem to have had the same proportions, as we see in the mosque of Shanga[66] which forms a rectangle of 11.22 by 7.21 metres, and in Gedi where the first mosque measured some 10 by 7 metres.[67] In Tanzania the great mosque of Kilwa, built between 1131 and 1170, has a rectangular plan of 11.8 by 7.8 metres.[68] Also in the bay of Kilwa, the mosque of Sanje Ya Kati founded in the second half of the eleventh century measured 10.21 by 9.46 metres.[69] The mosque of Domoni, on the island of Anjouan (Comores) measured 11.8 by 7.4 metres. The first Swahili mosques had a light roof in wood and palm leaves. The supports of the roof were usually in wood and were unable to carry large weights. The roof of the mosque of Tumbatu was supported by nine octagonal columns in

---

[64] Horton, 1991; Wright, 1992.
[65] Horton and Middleton, 2000.
[66] Horton, 1996, pp. 218–23 and 224–9.
[67] Pradines, 2004, p. 27.
[68] Chittick, 1974, pp. 61, 65–6; Freeman-Grenville, 1962, pp. 122–5.
[69] Pradines, 2009, pp. 64–70.

wood, which have left negative traces in the ground. Wooden columns were also used in Kilwa and in the mosque of Gedi.[70] The roof of the mosque of Shanga was apparently supported by columns in wood. The Comorian mosques of Sima and Domoni also had columns in wood in their first phases of the eleventh and twelfth centuries and enframed the niche of the mihrab.[71]

The ancient Swahili mosques had a north-northwest orientation instead of being turned directly north towards Mecca. Mark Horton thought that the north-northwest orientation of the primitive mosque of Shanga was due to a lack of geographical knowledge on the part of the builders.[72] But his hypothesis was only based on the example of Shanga, while we now have more information and have inspected a similar case: the great mosque of Gedi.[73] Judging from their different orientation, the Swahili mosques of the twelfth century may have been Shiʿite. The builders of the first Swahili mosques were certainly of a different ethnic origin and confession. There may have been a change of confession, and a passage to Sunnism connected with a reconstruction of certain places of worship between the thirteenth and the early fourteenth century.[74]

This change must be seen in the global perspective of the Islamic world. At the end of the twelfth century the Yemen was conquered by the Ayyubids, who spread Sunnism in the area. In the thirteenth century the Rasulid princes continued to spread this doctrine in the Yemen and beyond the seas. The spread of Sunnism on the east coast can thus be attributed to contacts with merchants from the Hadramawt. Kilwa would be a perfect illustration, since its inhabitants converted to Sunnism in the thirteenth century with the advent of the Mahdali dynasty of the Shafiʿite confession, and according to Ibn al-Mugawir there was a school that professed this doctrine in Kilwa.[75] As from the fourteenth century all the Shiʿite groups seem to have been absorbed by the Sunnis, for, in 1331, Ibn Battuta met Shafiʿite Sunnites on the whole of the coast.[76]

So, by whom were the first Swahili mosques influenced? Kizimkazi, the earliest Swahili mihrab known in elevation, revealed these transoceanic influences. This architectural example, together with the recent archaeological discoveries, allow us to understand the origin and the role of the communities of the Persian Gulf in the Islamisation and urbanisation of the east coast of Africa. The first mihrabs were erected by master masons who had probably come from the Gulf and the north of India. The populations of the Gulf were generally called

---

[70] Pradines, 2010, pp. 47–8 and 93–5.
[71] Wright, 1992.
[72] Horton, 1996, p. 229.
[73] Pradines, 2010, pp. 31–104.
[74] Horton, 1996, p. 170–208.
[75] Wilkinson, 1981.
[76] Ibn Battuta (1357) in Freeman-Grenville, 1962, pp. 28–30.

'Shirazis' by the Swahilis.[77] Between the beginning of the eleventh and the end of the twelfth century the Shirazis developed an elaborate architecture in East Africa with the introduction of mihrabs and finely carved Kufic inscriptions, such as the mihrabs of Kizimkazi and Tumbatu. By 'Shirazis' we must understand the essentially Shi'ite populations from the Persian Gulf: Iran-Iraq, Bahrain and the Ismailis from the Sindh Delta and the port city of Daybul (Banbhore). In the oral traditions these Shirazis would become the mythical ancestors of numerous Swahili city-states, and particularly of Kilwa. The little mosques of Siraf in the tenth century were fairly similar to the first Swahili mosques. They had an inner space divided by arcades parallel to the qibla and internal dimensions going from 5.4 by 5.5 metres to 9.7 by 10.2 metres.[78] Swahili architecture also presented great stylistic affinities with the decorations and arches of the mihrabs of the northwest of India, which was home to various Ismaili merchants, particularly in the Sindh Delta, the gulfs of Kutch and Cambay, and in Gujarat[79]. According to the Portuguese,[80] Indian communities settled on the entire east coast. Shi'ite Gujarati merhants were thus seen in Mombasa in 1504. The Gujarati Muslims became a minority with the Portuguese domination of the Indian Ocean and the preference for networks of non-Muslim Indians such as the Hindu Banias. The Shi'ite Ismaili traders and the Ibadis would return to Africa from the eighteenth century on with the colonisation of the area by the Omanis.

THE RETURN OF THE SHI'ITE COMMUNITIES TO EAST AFRICA AND THE IBADI REVIVAL, EIGHTEENTH TO NINETEENTH CENTURIES

In 1650 Sayf al-Ya'rubi reconquered Muscat once and for all, thus marking the end of Portuguese hegemony in the Indian Ocean.[81] In 1696 Sayf b. Sultan I decided to send a large expeditionary force to Mombasa and laid siege to Fort Jesus. Despite the reinforcements from Goa, Fort Jesus fell and the Portuguese had to fall back on Goa and Mozambique early in 1698. After the fall of Mombasa, the imam of Oman decided to send governors and garrisons to important cities such as Pate, Lamu, Mombasa, Zanzibar and Kilwa.[82] In 1735 Muhammad b. 'Uthman b. al-Mazrui was appointed governor of Mombasa.[83] He refused to acknowledge the new Omani dynasty of the Al Bu Sa'id and declared his loyalty to the old dynasty of the Ya'rubi, while he himself founded the dynasty of the Mazrui who would rule

---

[77] Pouwels, 1974, pp. 65–4; Pouwels, 1978, pp. 201–26 and 393–409.
[78] Whitehouse, 1984.
[79] Khan, 1988, pp. 158–9.
[80] Pradines, 2004, p. 32.
[81] Le Cour Grandmaison, 1982, pp. 275–6.
[82] Kirkman, 1983, p. 52.
[83] Pate's Chronicles in Stigand, 1913; Mathew, 1963 pp. 52 and 104.

the Kenyan coast. Little by little the sultanate of Oman started to take an interest in the island of Zanzibar which had become a pivot in the slave trade and from where, each year, between six and ten thousand human beings were exported to Muscat, India and the islands of the Indian Ocean. In 1822, the Sultan Sayyid Sa'id sent a war fleet to Africa under the command of Hamid b. Ahmad Al Bu Sa'id and the Mazrui were defeated.[84] The sultan decided to transfer his capital from Muscat to Zanzibar in 1832. In 1837, Sayyid Sa'id b. Sultan (1804–1856), a great manoeuvrer and the founder of the sultanate of Zanzibar, reigned over the coast from Mogadishu to Cape Delgado. The slave caravans were financed by rich Indian merchants, the Banians. In 1873 Sir Bartle Frere observed that all branches of trade, from Cape Guardafui to Madagascar, were in the hands of the Indian community, which exercised a virtual monopoly on the east coast visible to this day. These Indian Muslims, often Shi'ite Bohras, introduced a new style of mosque that broke entirely with the Swahili architectural tradition. The Khoja and the Bohra resumed their control of the maritime trade with the independence of the sultanate of Oman and re-introduced the Ismaili schism into Africa between the eighteenth and the nineteenth centuries.

The seventeen Ibadi mosques of the town of Zanzibar were built in the second half of the nineteenth century and fourteen are in use to this day.[85] It is the largest concentration of Ibadi mosques on the east coast where, however, this particular confession was always in a minority. The most emblematic are the mosques of Laghbari and Mandhiri in the district of Sokomuhogo. The main characteristic of these mosques is their discretion: it is almost impossible to distinguish them from the houses in the dense urban tissue. In contrast to the traditional Swahili mosques, the mihrab does not protrude into the street with a quadrangular aedicule. In the Ibadi mosques the mihrab is built into the thickness of the wall of the qibla. The mosque of Laghbari was raised above the level of the adjacent streets. The foundation base or podium of the mosque was full, and only an ablution area was set up on the ground floor with a stairway leading to the prayer hall (Fig. 11.8). Among the Ibadis there is no Friday mosque. The mosques are small, with a prayer hall divided by rows of columns, a few decorated stucco panels and a minbar that is often concealed. Relations between Omani Ibadis, Indian Bohras and Ismailis, and the Swahili Shafi'ite Sunnis have always been cordial and tolerant.[86]

The Zanzibari-style mosques, or 'Ibadi revival', are characterised by mihrabs with polylobal arches, festooned or twisted, and by decorations carved in the stucco.[87] A new form of moulding appeared, which Garlake called the keyhole

---

[84] Freeman-Grenville, 1962, p. 280.
[85] Siravo, 1996, pp. 45–6.
[86] Sheriff, 1995.
[87] Freeman-Grenville, 1954.

Figure 11.8 Niche minbar of the Sanga Rungu mosque. Courtesy the author.

motif, a semi-circle surmounted by a triangle. Pilasters capped by capitals enframed the entrance of the apse. A simple sloping roof covered the niche of the mihrab and replaced the usual quarter-sphere vault. Joseph Schacht recorded various mosques of this type in Tanzania dating from the nineteenth and early twentieth centuries: Mboamaji of 1856–1870, Bweni Kuu of 1850–1870, the *jamia* of Pangani of 1902, Furdani of 1897 and the mosque of Tambareni of 1907. In Kenya, Mambrui dates from 1880, the *jamia* of Malindi from 1893 and a mosque in Lamu from 1920.[88] Two architectural elements are absolutely characteristic of the Zanzibari-style mosques – the niche minbar and the frieze of mini-mihrabs in the niche of the mihrab.

The frieze of mini-mihrabs inside the quadrangular apse of late mihrabs recalls the tradition of the early mihrabs of Kizimkazi. The mihrab of Kizimkazi seems to have been at the origin of all the Swahili mihrabs decorated with a frieze of mini-mihrabs in the intrados of the niche. A troubling fact is that the mihrabs of the Kizimkazi style appeared when Zanzibar and Pemba had commercial relations with Shiʿite Indian merchants, but also with Omani Ibadis, and it seems to me that the similarity between the early and the later groups reveals the presence

---

[88] Garlake, 1966; Schacht, 1957.

of Ibadis or Ismaili Shi'ites in East Africa,[89] since numerous Omani and Indian mihrabs were produced by this same movement. The mihrab of Chole, off the island of Mafia, has a deep arch of six niches under a frieze of squares; the multi-lobed arch of this mihrab suggests that it dates from the end of the eighteenth century. Sanga Rungu mosque of Songo Mnara, in the north of the island, dates from the end of the nineteenth century. The mosque has a niche minbar and a mihrab niche adorned with mini-mihrabs, characteristics of late Swahili mosques (Fig. 11.9).

The niche minbar, known as 'partitioned', consisted of a masoned stairway placed in a niche to the right of the mihrab, a window or a wooden balustrade, which allowed the khatib to deliver his sermon.[90] According to Garlake the Swahili minbars underwent a local development between the masoned minbar built against the wall of the qibla and the niche minbar built into the wall of the qibla.[91] He appeals to a single case: the minbar of the great mosque of Kua (Fig. 11.10), where a stairway penetrated the wall of the qibla perpendicularly. The minbar, he claims, marked a type of transition between the simple stairway and the niche minbar as in Mboamaji, while in the final stage the minbar was linked to the mihrab as at Kipumbwe. His theory is questionable. Admittedly the medieval Swahili minbars were not in a niche and the site of Kua was indeed a site of transition dating from the sixteenth and seventeenth centuries. The niche minbars, however, were characteristic of the nineteenth century, when the Omanis created new mosques or transformed the old ones, as they did in 1893 with the jamia of Malindi where the protruberant stone minbar was replaced by a niche minbar. The niche minbars seem to have been used indifferently by the Sunni Shafi'ite Swahilis and the Omani Ibadis.

CONCLUSION

The first Africans to be converted formed part of the elites – they were mainly merchants and local leaders. It was a non-uniform and tolerant Islamisation. Early mosques in sub-Saharan Africa were Kharidji and Shi'a, more specifically Ibadi and Ismaili. The dissemination of the mosque architecture was done by the land roads through the Sahara Desert and the sea roads via the Indian Ocean. The legacy of the Ibadi and Ismaili, or more globally the Kharidjites and the Shi'a, is immense in sub-Saharan Africa and they are at the origin of the West African mosques and the Swahili mosques. After the thirteenth

---

[89] Penrad, 1988, pp. 221–35; Berg and Walter, 1968.
[90] Schacht, 1957.
[91] Garlake, 1966, pp. 74–5.

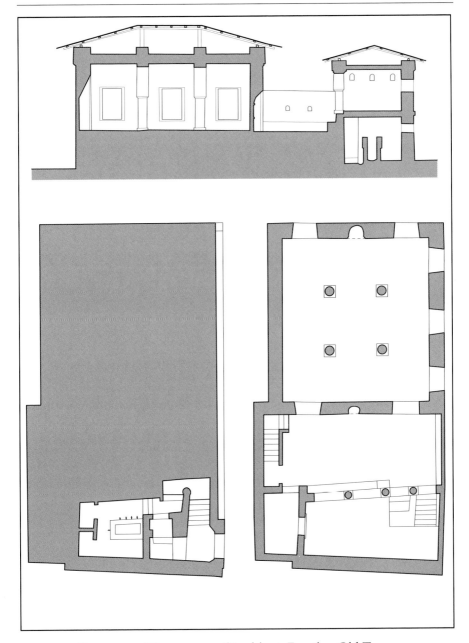

Figure 11.9 The mosque of Laghbari, Zanzibar Old Town.
Courtesy the author.

Figure 11.10 The minbar of the great mosque of Kua, Mafia archipelago.
Courtesy the author.

century, Africans adopted Sunnism en masse – Sunni Shafi'i in East Africa
and Sunni Maliki in West Africa. From this period and onwards the Sufi movements became extremely popular in sub-Saharan Africa and I claim that Sufism
became a philosophical and moral substitute to the previous religious sectarian
movements Ibadi and Ismaili. It is also supported by the permeability between
Sufism and Shi'a spirituality.

BIBLIOGRAPHY

Primary sources, edited and compiled

Abulfida. 1342. *Géographie d'Aboulféda*. De Reinaud M. ed. Paris: Imprimerie nationale,
vol. 2, 1848.

De Barros, J. 1945. *Decadas Da Ásia, dos feitos qie os Portuguezes fizeram no descubrimento,
e conquista dos mares, e terras do Oriente*. Lisbon: Ministério das colonias, 2 vols
(originally published 1552).

Freeman-Grenville, G. S. P. 1962. *The East African Coast (select documents from the first
to the earlier nineteenth century)*. Oxford: Clarendon Press.

Ibn Battuta. 1331. *Voyages d'Ibn Battuta*. Defremery C. and Sanguinetti B. eds. Paris:
Imprimerie Nationale, 1853.

Sauvaget, J. 1948. *Relation de la Chine et de l'Inde* (851), Collection Arabe de l'Association des Belles lettres XLI. Paris: Budé.

Studies and monographs

Berg, F. and B. J. Walter. 1968. 'Mosques, population and urban development in Mombasa', *Hadith* 1, pp. 47–100.

Chittick, N. 1974. *Kilwa: an Islamic Trading City on the East African Coast*. Nairobi: British Institute in Eastern Africa, 2 vols.

Connah, G. 2016. *African Civilizations: an archaeological perspective*. Cambridge: Cambridge University Press, third edition.

Costa, P. 2001. *Historic Mosques and Shrines of Oman*. BAR 938, Oxford: Archaeopress.

De Planhol, Xavier. 2000. *L'Islam et la mer, La mosquée et le matelot VIIe – XXe siècle*. Paris: Perrin.

Ducatez, G. 2004. 'Aden aux XIe et XIIIe siècles selon Ibn al-Mugâwir, son passé légendaire, son histoire sous les zurayîdes et les ayyoubides, son site, ses monuments et ses aménagements', *Annales Islamologiques* 38. Cairo: IFAO, pp. 159–200.

Ducatez, G. 2003. 'Aden et l'océan Indien au XIIIe siècle: navigation et commerce d'après Ibn al-Mugâwir', *Annales Islamologiques* 37, pp. 137–56.

Ducène, J.-C. 2015. 'Une nouvelle source arabe sur l'océan Indien au Xe siècle: le Ṣaḥīḥ min aḫbār al-biḥār wa-ʿağā ʾibihā d'Abū ʿImrān Mūsā ibn Rabāḥ al-Awsī al-Sīrāfī', *Afriques* 6, Paris, DOI: https://doi.org/10.4000/afriques.1746.

Flury, S. 1922. 'The Kufic inscriptions of Kizimkazi Mosque, Zanzibar 1107 A.D.', *J.R.A.S.*, pp. 257–64.

Freeman-Grenville, G. S. P. 1962. *The Medieval History of the Coast of Tanganyika (with special reference to recent archaeological discoveries)*. London: Oxford University Press.

Freeman-Grenville, G. S. P. 1954. 'Some preliminary observations on medieval mosques near Dar es Salaam', *Tanganyika Notes and Records* 36, pp. 64–70.

Garlake, P. 1966. *The Early Islamic Architecture of the East African Coast*. Nairobi: B.I.E.A.

Gaube, H. and A. Al Salimi. 2013. *The Ibadis in the Region of the Indian Ocean. Section one: East Africa*. Olms: Hildesheim.

Goeje, M. J. de. 1886. *Mémoire sur les Carmathes du Bahraïn et les Fatimides*, Leiden: Brill.

Guillain, M. 1856. *Documents sur l'histoire, la géographie et le commerce de l'Afrique Orientale*. Paris: Arthus Bertrand, 3 vols.

Horton, M. 2017. 'Early Islam on the East African Coast,' in F. B. Flood and G. Necipoglu (eds), *A Companion to Islamic Art and Architecture* 1. Oxford: Wiley Blackwell, pp. 250–74.

Horton, M. 2004. 'Islam, archaeology and Swahili identity,' in D. Whitcomb (ed.), *Changing social identity with the spread of Islam. Archaeological perspectives*. Chicago: Oriental Institute, pp. 67–88.

Horton, M. 1996. *Shanga. The archaeology of a Muslim trading community on the coast of East Africa*. London: BIEA.

Horton, M. 1994. 'East Africa', in M. Frishman and H. Uddin Khan (eds), *The Mosque. History, Architectural Development and Regional Diversity*. London: Thames & Hudson, pp. 194–207.

Horton, M. 1991. 'Primitive Islam and architecture in East Africa', *Muqarnas* 8, pp. 103–116.

Horton, M. and J. Middleton. 2000. *The Swahili*. Oxford: Blackwell.

Kervran, M. and L. Kalus. 1990. 'La mosquée al-Khamis à Bahrain: son histoire et ses inscriptions', *Archéologie Islamique* 1, pp. 7–73.

Khan, A. 1988. 'Introduction et propagation du mihrâb dans l'architecture islamique du Pakistan', in A. Papadopoulo (ed.), *Le mihrâb dans l'architecture et la religion musulmanes*. Leiden: Brill, pp. 157–66.

Kirkman, J. 1983. 'The Early History of Oman in East Africa', *Journal of Oman Studies* 6–1, pp. 41–58.

Laviolette, A. and J. Fleisher. 2009. 'The Urban History of a Rural Place: Swahili Archaeology on Pemba Island, Tanzania, 700–1500 AD', *International Journal of African Historical Studies* 42–3, pp. 433–55.

Le Cour Grandmaison, C. 1982. 'Présentation du Sultanat d'Oman', *La Péninsule Arabique d'aujourd'hui*, vol. 2. Paris: CNRS, pp. 263–88.

Lewcock, R. 1976. 'Architectural connections between Africa and parts of the Indian Ocean littoral', *Art and Archaeology Research Paper* 9, pp. 13–23.

Lowick, N. 1985. 'The Coins and Monumental Inscriptions', *Siraf* 15, pp. 84–5.

Mathew, G. 1963. 'The East African coast until the coming of the Portuguese,' in R. Oliver and G. Mathew (eds), *History of East Africa 1*. Oxford: Clarendon Press, pp. 94–127.

Moncelon, J. 1995. 'La Da'wa fatimide au Yémen'. *Chroniques Yéménites* 3. Sanaa: CEFAS, pp. 26–37.

Penrad, J. 1988. 'La présence isma'ilienne en Afrique de l'est', in D. Lomard and J. Aubin (eds), *Marchands et hommes d'affaires asiatiques dans l'Océan Indien et la Mer de Chine, 13e-20e siècles*. Paris: École des Hautes Études en Sciences Sociales, pp. 221–36.

Planhol, X. de. 2005. *L'Islam et la mer, La mosquée et le matelot VIIe–XXe siècle*. Paris: Le Grand Livre du Mois.

Poirier, C. 1954. 'Terre d'Islam en mer Malgache', *B.A.M.* XXXI, pp. 71–116.

Pouwels, R. 2000. 'The East African Coast, c. 780 to 1900' in N. Levtzion and R. Pouwels (eds), *The History of Islam in Africa*. Oxford: James Currey, pp. 251–71.

Pouwels, R. 1978. 'The Medieval Foundations of East African Islam', *International Journal of African Historical Studies* 2–3, pp. 201–26 and 393–409.

Pouwels, R. 1974. 'Tenth-Century Settlement of the East African Coast: The Case for Qarmatian/Isma'ili Connections', *Azania: Archaeological Research in Africa IX*. Nairobi: British Institute in Eastern Africa, pp. 65–74.

Pradines, S. 2020. 'Madagascar, the Source of the Abbasid and Fatimid Rock Crystals: New Evidence from Archaeological Investigations in East Africa', in Avinoam Shalem and Cynthia Hahn (eds), *Seeking Transparency: Rock Crystals across the Medieval Mediterranean*. Berlin: Gebr. Mann, pp. 35–50.

Pradines, S. 2018. 'Ethnicity and architecture. The Fatimid town walls in Cairo', in S. Pradines (ed.), *Earthen Architecture in Muslim Cultures: Historical and Anthropological Perspectives*. Leiden: Brill, pp. 104–45.

Pradines, S. 2010. *Gedi, une cité portuaire swahilie. Islam médiéval en Afrique orientale*. Monographies d'archéologie islamique, Cairo: IFAO.

Pradines, S. 2009. 'L'île de Sanje ya Kati (Kilwa, Tanzanie). Un mythe Shirâzi bien réel', *Azania: Archaeological Research in Africa* 44–1. London: Routledge, pp. 49–73.

Pradines, S. 2004. *Fortifications et urbanisation en Afrique orientale*. Cambridge Monographs in African Archaeology 58, BAR S1216, Oxford: Archaeopress.

Pradines, S. 2003. 'Le mihrab swahili: Évolution d'une architecture islamique en Afrique subsaharienne', *Annales Islamologiques* 37, pp. 355–81.

Pradines S. 2002. 'La bipartition des cités swahili: l'exemple de Gedi (Kenya)', *Southern Africa and the Swahili World, Studies in the African Past* 2, pp. 66–75.

Pradines, S. and P. Blanchard. 2015. 'Songo Mnara. Étude architecturale d'une ville swahilie médiévale', *Taarifa* 5, pp. 9–33.

Pradines S. and P. Blanchard. 2005. 'Kilwa al-Mulûk. Premier bilan des travaux de conservation-restauration et des fouilles archéologiques dans la baie de Kilwa, Tanzanie', *Annales Islamologiques* 39, pp. 25–80.

Pradines, S., H. D. Veyssier Renel and B. Zhao. 2016. 'Irone Be (Dembeni, Mayotte) Rapport de mission 2015', *Nyame Akuma* 85, pp. 44–56.

Rougeulle, A. (ed.). 2017. *Sharma. Un entrepôt de commerce médiéval sur la côte du Hadramawt (Yémen, ca. 980–1180)*. Oxford: BAR.

Rougeulle, A. 2004. 'Le Yémen entre Orient et Afrique: Sharma, un entrepôt du commerce médiéval sur la côte sud de l'Arabie', *Annales Islamologiques* 38, pp. 201–53.

Schacht, J. 1961. 'Further notes on the staircase minaret', *Ars Orientalis* 4, pp. 137–41.

Schacht, J. 1957. 'An unknown type of minbar and its historical signifiance', *Ars Orientalis* 2, 1957, pp. 149–73.

Sheriff, A. 2001. 'The historicity of the Shirâzi tradition along the East African coast', in *Proceedings of the 1st conference on the Historical Role of Iranians (Shirazis) in the East African Coast, Nairobi, 2nd–3rd February 2001*. Nairobi: Embassy of Iran, pp. 21–41.

Sheriff, A. 1995. 'Mosques, Merchants and landowners in Zanzibar Stone Town', in A. Sheriff (ed.), *The History and Conservation of Zanzibar Stone Town*. London: James Currey, pp. 46–66.

Siravo, F. 1996. *Zanzibar: A plan for the Historic Stone Town*. Geneva: The Aga Khan Trust for Culture.

Spear, T. 1984. 'The Shirâzi in Swahili Traditions, Culture and History', *History in Africa* 11, pp. 291–305.

Stigand, H. 1913. *The Land of Zinj, being an Account of British East Africa, its ancient history and present inhabitants*. London: Frank Cass (new edition, 1966).

Strandes, J. 1899. *The Portuguese Period in East Africa*. Nairobi: East African Litterature Bureau (new edition 1971).

Talib, Y. 1990. 'La diaspora africaine en Asie', in Mohammed El Fasi and Ivan Hrbek (eds), *Histoire Générale de l'Afrique*. Paris: UNESCO, pp. 749–78.

Tibbetts, G. R. 1971. *Arab Navigation in the Indian Ocean before the coming of the Portuguese*. London: Royal Asiatic Society of Great Britain and Ireland (new edition 1981).

Trimingham, J. S. 1961. *Islam in East Africa*. Oxford: Clarendon Press.

Vérin, P. 1975. *Les Echelles Anciennes du Commerce sur les côtes nord de Madagascar*. Université de Lille III: PhD, 2 vols.

Whitehouse, D. 1984. 'The smaller mosques at Sirâf (a footnote)', *Iran* XXII, pp. 166–8.

Wilkinson, J.-C. 1981. 'Oman and East Africa: new light on early Kilwa history from the Omani sources', *The International Journal of African Historical Studies* 14–2, pp. 272–304.

Wright, H. 1992. 'Early Islam (Oceanic trade and town development on Nzwani: the Comorian archipelago in the XIth–XVth centuries AD)', *Azania: Archaeological Research in Africa* 27, pp. 81–128.

CHAPTER 12

Traditional Bohra Dwellings of Gujarat, India: Architectural Response to Cultural Ethos

MADHAVI DESAI

Islam, the world's second largest civilisation, is multi-centred, multi-period and multi-regional. The variations of Islamic culture can be found all over the world. Wherever Islam spread, it interacted with the existing traditions and its philosophy influenced the regional architecture to bring about modified expressions, resulting in immense richness in the built environment across time and space. Therefore, architecture was distinctly expressive of the local sub-cultures, either at the micro or the macro level.

Located on the west coast of India, the territorial unit of Gujarat is a political as well as a cultural region. It came under Muslim rule in 1298 when the Delhi Sultan Alauddin Khilji defeated the last Hindu king, Karna Vaghela. Eventually, in 1407, when the Tughluq dynasty had completely weakened in Delhi, the governor Zafar Khan declared independence and established the Sultanate of Gujarat, giving rise to a specific historic architecture called the Indo-Islamic Sultanate style.[1] Under the Delhi Sultanate there was a significant increase in the settled Muslim population.

Of all the states, Gujarat has the longest coastline in India. Its people were well known for being traders, businessmen and financiers since ancient times. Maritime trade via the Indian Ocean was the economic mainstay of the region connecting it with many parts of the world. From the major sea ports of Gujarat, the traders sent their large ships with cotton and silk textiles, indigo, drugs and medicinals to markets in Malacca, the Malabar ports, Aden and Hormuz, and later expanded to the Bay of Bengal, parts of Indonesia and Mozambique. Their imports included European goods, African ivory, Malabar and Sumatra

---

[1] Burton-Page, 1988.

pepper, Chinese gold and Japanese silver.[2] Traditional India was a land of great cities and Gujarat also had a long history of urbanisation. It was characterised by a wide spectrum of distinctive urban lifestyles that generated a rich variety of architectural manifestations. Each epoch of history has affected the urban settlements in the state including the Islamic rule in Gujarat from the beginning of the fourteenth century.[3] Several port towns also rose to prominence in the medieval period, such as Surat, Ghogha, Cambay (Khambhat), Rander, Mundra and Mandvi. These towns developed and declined over the centuries, making Gujarat a mercantile centre, creating great affiliation between ports, hinterlands and trading communities.[4]

One of these prominent communities of traders was that of the Bohras, an Islamic Shi'a sect, who inhabited hinterland settlements as well as port cities. 'There were indigenous communities who had converted to Islam, such as Khojas and Bohras, who were prominent in the trade of Surat.'[5] The Bohras were highly encouraged into maritime trade while, at that time, Hindus were strictly barred by caste restrictions to travel abroad. The Bohras, who were originally upper-caste Hindus, have a distinct identity within the religion of Islam.[6] In Gujarat, the Bohras are largely concentrated in the towns of Siddhpur, Dahod, Godhra, Kapadvanj, Khambhat, Ahmedabad, Kheda, Mehsana, Jamnagar, Bhavnagar and Morbi, to name a few (Fig. 12.1). They have been able to maintain their identity and socio-economic status even in the post–independence period due to their cultural traits and the able organisation of the community under a strong religious leadership.

Within this context, this paper presents their traditional dwellings, which are based on the generic forces of the region and were built within the fortified cities during the medieval period. There is a lacuna in the study of domestic architecture in general and Islamic house form in particular, which this research attempts to bridge. The built-form represents the multiplicity of architectural responses to diverse cultural influences through the process of eclectic adoption. During the 200 years of British rule, the Bohra house form also underwent a social and aesthetic transformation but at a relatively slow pace with minimum impact of external influences. The vibrancy and complexity of façades, the rich

---

[2] Pearson, 1976.
[3] This paper is largely based on the author's book, Desai, 2008.
[4] Kellar and Pearson, 2015.
[5] Arasaratnam, 1987.
[6] 'Conversion to Islam meant the acceptance of Islamic beliefs and rituals and social and political loyalties on the basis of a range of considerations that included purely religious and pragmatic concerns. Moreover, conversion to Islam did not necessarily imply a complete turning from an old life to a totally new life . . . Most converts retained a deep attachment to the cultures and communities from which they came.' Lapidus, 1988, p. 244.

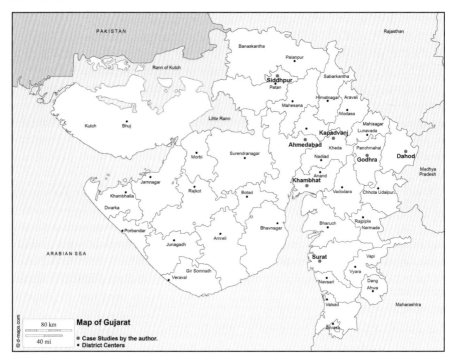

Figure 12.1 Map of Gujarat. Courtesy the author.

elemental variations and the distinct ethos of the interiors combine to express a mature aesthetic language.

THE BOHRA COMMUNITY

In business, the Bohras were thrifty, aggressive and family-centred. Along with a strong influence of their Hindu roots on the social customs, they have remained strictly faithful to the precepts of Islam. During the colonial rule, the Bohras were able to establish a special relationship with the British. They were encouraged to travel through land and sea routes and trade in major cities of India as well as abroad. They still have a pan-Indian presence with Bohra generations found in the cities of Mumbai, Kolkata and Chennai. Apart from India, they also reside in Pakistan, Africa, Sri Lanka, UK, USA, the Middle East and Southast Asia. Trade and travel in the earlier days brought in myriad foreign influences on the traditional dwellings in their native towns.

Designed to accommodate joint-families, these dwellings represent architecture rooted in the regional landscape with vivid and unique characteristics manifested in the settlement morphology, street pattern and the house-form.

Built during the late eighteenth to early twentieth centuries, they evolved to a remarkable level of excellence and sophistication, with the multiplicity of architectural responses to diverse cultural influences (the Hindu, Islamic and Colonial) through the process of eclectic adoption. The architecture and interior attributes of their houses gives the Bohras a strong sense of identity as a community within Islam in India. Though many houses now lie empty, they still represent a living tradition. In fact, not only in terms of the house-form but also in the dress habits, food and language, the regional connection is strongly apparent. They are prime examples of an urbanity where near perfection is achieved in terms of plan organisation, façades, interiors and the overall aesthetic expression within the domestic genre of architecture in India (Fig. 12.2).

Figure 12.2 A typical Bohra house. Courtesy the author.

THE HISTORICAL BACKGROUND

The formal political rule of the Delhi Sultanate began at the end of the thirteenth century in Gujarat. Later, in 1391, the governor of Delhi, Zafar Khan, took on the name Muzzafar Khan and declared independence, beginning the dynasty of the Gujarat Sultanate.[7] As a result, in the early fifteenth century, there arose a new, classical architectural language, termed as the Indo-Islamic Sultanate Architecture of Gujarat that left a distinctive mark on domestic and monumental architecture, urban design and planning as well as culture. This epoch was witness to the long history of harmonious co-existence between Hindus and Muslims.[8]

The great port of Surat in western India dominated accounts of Indian Ocean trade between the late sixteenth and mid-eighteenth century. Consolidated first by an Ottoman noble, it became the Mughal Empire's western window into the worlds of the Red Sea and the Persian Gulf.[9] The urban lifestyle brought about a remarkably homogenous and uniform pattern in these dense, fortified towns while reflecting the social division of the population in its morphology. The settlement was segregated into micro-neighbourhoods locally called *pols* (traditional neighbourhoods), based on well-defined, cohesive communities.[10] Typologically, most houses in the urban *pols* were long, with a narrow frontage that opened onto a street. It was a deep plan with three (or four) sequential rooms and a courtyard at the centre. Within the hierarchical circulation pattern, the main roads, secondary streets and bazaars were public spaces. Open spaces were restricted to small squares. The narrow streets and lanes were essentially integrating spines of movement and also gave shade and thermal comfort in the hot climate. In Gujarat, these micro-neighbourhoods or *pols* still exist today, albeit with more ethnic variations as community/caste rigidity has decreased and occupational variety has increased over the years.

THE BOHRWADS OF GUJARAT

Though the Bohras were engaged in international maritime trade, they belonged to and had great affinity to their native towns in Gujarat. In the nineteenth and early twentieth centuries, when the men travelled abroad for business, they left their families in these towns in the micro-neighbourhoods called Bohrwads (Fig. 12.3). Located in small towns, and in cities like Ahmedabad, Baroda and Surat, they are examples of urban morphology, adapted to fit within the confines of a fortified town. Factors impacting them include climatic conditions of hot-dry

[7] Burgess, 1896.
[8] Shokoohy, 2012.
[9] Subrahmaniyam, 2018.
[10] Desai and Desai, 1991.

Figure 12.3 Part plan of a Bohrwad, Kapadvanj. Courtesy the author.

or hot-humid regions, need for physical security and most importantly, the lack of available space within fort walls, which led to vertical growth.

There are two broad categories of Bohrwads: one has an organic layout while the other is strictly geometrically laid out. Generally, Bohrwads built during the nineteenth century belong to the former category while the later ones built in the early twentieth century belong to the latter. This organic settlement was morphologically well knit, homogeneous and dense. After the houses were built, the residual spaces turned into streets with varying widths and forms. The houses were typically grouped around a street, forming a *mohalla* (a neighbourhood); several *mohallas* formed the Bohrwad. It had a structural unity, orderliness and a sense of visual surprise due to its meandering form. The newer Bohrwads, built in the early twentieth century, outside the inner cities, had rationalised street patterns and standardised plot sizes with regularised planning due to the British influence. Their main streets often had grand mansions lined up in state-of-the-art styles such as Gothic and Art Deco.

The socio–cultural structure of the Bohrwad, being interwoven with religious and social edifices, symbolised the importance of religion and collective activity in an individual's life. Several public buildings formed an inherent part of the Bohrwad depending on its size. A large one contained a mosque, a madrassa (a school for Islamic teaching), a *jamat khana* (a gathering space for community activities and for devotional practice among Muslims), and other buildings for community functions. The neighbourhood mosque was the most important central public space for religious rituals. The public institutions were kept very clean, had regular maintenance, repair and paint as per requirement. In spite of an active community life, the Bohrwads were usually devoid of open and landscaped spaces due to the introverted nature of the community. In general, the settlement unit provided consciousness of social identity and security (Fig. 12.4).

In Islamic culture, a dominant emphasis is on domestic privacy and seclusion as well as on segregation of women. Thus, the minimisation of open spaces such as squares at settlement level was a major contrast to Hindu traditional settlements. There was a sense of enchantment emanating from the urban milieu of these settlements through its overall urban design ambience and cultural homogeneity that integrated its various elements into one composite whole (Fig. 12.5).

STREETS OF BOHRA SETTLEMENTS

From the streets of the Bohrwad, one could observe a gradual notion of urbanism being crystallised as they developed in time. The additive nature of the dwelling units rendered within the streetscape a sense of uniformity and harmony, while the variations in colour, architectural elements, fenestrations and personalisation in ornamentation created an interesting vibrancy. The high density, uniformity of heights and widths as well as the narrowness of the streets portray the notion of medieval urbanity even today. The streets acted as a structuring device and also represented a social contradiction of sorts because in spite of

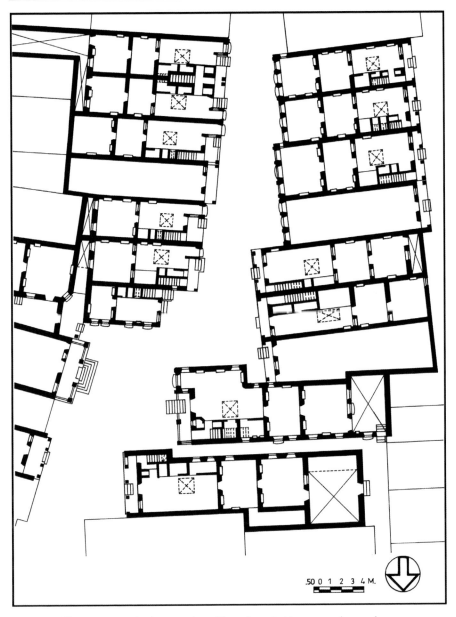

Figure 12.4 A cluster plan, Kapadvanj. Courtesy the author.

being visually and symbolically rich, they were used merely as circulation spines (Fig. 12.6).

A sense of order, extreme cleanliness and a well-designed drainage system also distinguished the Bohrwad streets from those in the traditional Hindu

Figure 12.5 A Gothic mansion, Siddhpur. Courtesy the author.

neighbourhoods. The transition from the street to the house was well defined where, through several physical and psychological pauses such as entrance gates and high plinths, the public interaction was monitored and the private realm was clearly demarcated and secured. Hence, the streets symbolise the homogenous

Figure 12.6 View of a street in the new Bohrwad, Siddhpur.
Courtesy the author.

nature of the community, its strong bend towards beauty and cleanliness, its sense of social self-sufficiency and preference for privacy, including expression of economic well-being.

Spatial Organisation of a Bohra Dwelling[11]

In the organisation of the plan, a typical Bohra dwelling[12] essentially adhered to the regional typology of Gujarat, as it existed in the traditional inner-town fabric. It was an introverted dwelling type, with a strong, internally linear organisation and a multifunctional core. It served as a long, narrow unit between two parallel walls comprising various spaces in a hierarchical sequence. The sense of privacy increased as one went from the street towards the end of the house. However, the notion of privacy was ambiguous, as symmetrically and centrally placed doorways led from one space into another. The significant divisions in

---

[11] The Bohra community, when at its peak glory, was a bustling culture whose liveliness got reflected in its built environment. On the other hand, when we look at these dwellings now, although the physical set-up remains almost the same, its vibrant character has been lost as a result of displacement and migration of a majority of its inhabitants as the towns themselves declined. Hence, past tense has been used to describe the characteristics of its built environment.

[12] Mathew, 1993.

the traditional Bohra house did not follow the functional usages, such as living room, dining room and bedroom. Rather, they evolved from the requirements of private (and public) social responsibility and were interchangeably used for eating, sleeping, recreation and other domestic activities. This flexibility was mainly possible due to the minimum pieces of furniture such as chairs, tables and beds, including there being less rigidity in the definition of interiors and space use patterns (Fig. 12.7). The joint family structure and need for male-female segregation necessitated this flexibility.

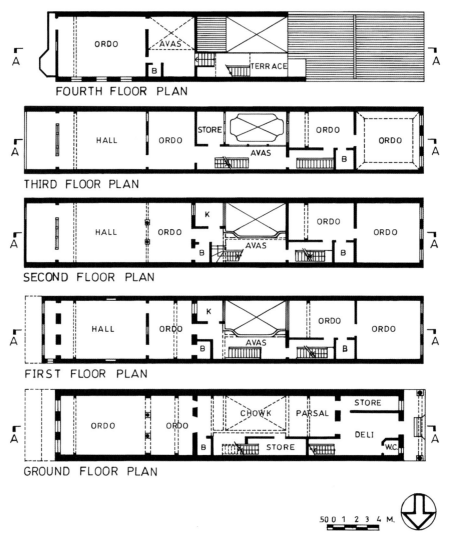

Figure 12.7 Floor plans of a Bohra house, Surat. Courtesy the author.

The major components of the plan organisation include: *otla* (entrance platform), *deli* (arrival space), *avas* (courtyard), *parsali* (ante space to the main room) and the *ordo* (the hall). The *otla* was an open or semi-open space that served as a connection between the dwelling and the street; it was visual and symbolic rather than functional and was occasionally used by women on quiet afternoons. The *deli*, a transitional space at the entrance, was there for indirect control. It signifies the Bohras' need for extreme physical and visual privacy as well as safety for the women. The staircase to the upper floors was always located in the *deli* or *deli*-like spaces. It guarded the privacy of the ground floor by guiding male guests directly to the top floor, to the main hall (Fig. 12.8). During the colonial era, the Bohra businessmen often entertained British officers in the upper hall.

Figure 12.8 An Art Deco staircase, Khambhat. Courtesy the author.

The *avas*, the central courtyard, formed the core of the traditional dwelling and acted as an imaginary divide between the public and the private zones. The kitchen, the water place (*paniara*) and sometimes the store was attached to the courtyard. It was often used as a dining space, a family room or as an extension of the kitchen for food preparation. Next was the *parsali*, which was an ante space to the main room, the *ordo* or hall, and was used for relaxation by women in the afternoon (Fig. 12.9). It also optionally served as a sleeping space.

The *ordo* was the most important space on the ground floor, private and formal in nature, used for entertaining and welcoming family, relatives and friends. It was also sometimes used as a sleeping space at night by the elderly, if necessary. When large (like in Surat), it was partitioned off into living and sleeping areas, sometimes with the help of wardrobes or other furniture, thereby becoming a self-sufficient suite (Fig. 12.10).

On the upper floors, there existed a clear differentiation between the private rooms and the central open cut-out where the vertical circulation terminated. The large sleeping space then became each family's personal domain. There was always a small bathroom attached to each room, as the Bohras follow the religious obligation of ritual ablutions after having sexual intercourse and before saying their prayers. The room was decorated with plaster of Paris niches (often being nine in number, thereby called *naukhanas*) and elaborately made wooden cupboards. These rooms were well-ventilated because of the courtyard on one side and fenestration on the street side. Semi-basements with an independent front entrance were a common feature in the dwellings of certain towns, especially used in the hot summers.

In Surat, it was observed that houses in the entire street were connected by a series of doors on the upper floor, especially if they belonged to families with kinship ties. Here, as mentioned earlier, the hall on the top floor was developed into an elaborate space for social interaction, known as *divankhanu*, an imitation of the aristocratic Mughal practice of designating a male gathering space especially for formal occasions, family celebrations and to receive important guests. Later, with British influence, it was also alternatively called the 'council room' and had Western-style furniture. Formal in nature and the centrepiece of the public realm, it remained the most ornamented and valuable space (Fig. 12.11), separated well away from the women's area.

In the majority of the houses, the top-most floor had only one *ordo* with a pitched roof and the other half was left as a terrace, called *agashi*. It was used for sleeping out in the summers. The aesthetic sense of the community was expressed here through the use of decorative parapets, stairs, pillars and china mosaic flooring.

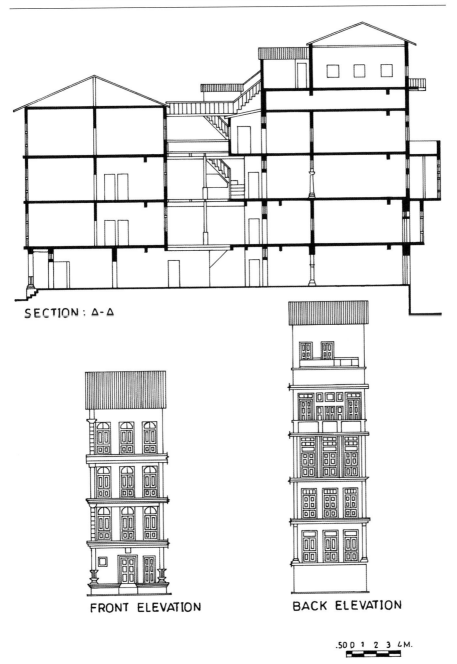

SECTION : Δ-Δ

FRONT ELEVATION   BACK ELEVATION

.50 0 1 2 3 4M.

Figure 12.9 Sectional and elevational views of the Bohra house, Surat.
Courtesy the author.

Figure 12.10 The division in the living/sleeping space. Courtesy the author.

Figure 12.11 The aesthetic richness of some of the interior spaces.
Courtesy the author.

ARTICULATION IN THE FAÇADES

The Bohras had adopted the regional tradition of Gujarat of making façades with intricate details in wood. Originally designed entirely out of wood and later with brick infill, the façades were light, ornate and often exquisite. As illustrated by V. S. Pramar, the woodwork of Gujarat, both in quality and quantity, is by far the most outstanding in India. 'The timber employed was not merely a structural expedient but also a medium of display, as is evident from the profusely and intricately carved doors and windows, balconies, struts and columns, visible in the thousands of houses in urban Gujarat.'[13]

The façades of Bohra houses had an individual physical reality and a visual impact that made them as important as the architectural form. Over time, they accommodated a whole range of styles, building materials and decorative treatments, resulting in attractive façades that became the hallmark of their vernacular architecture. Using textures and patterns, the surface of the façade was visually broken by ornamented columns, brackets and mouldings, at times bringing multicoloured cohesion to the streets. They represented a comprehensive understanding of the elements of design, nature of building materials and versatility of craftsmanship. Careful aesthetic attention was paid to the making of the windows, entrance doors, columns, brackets, grills and other elements. In the embellishments, there was the use of non-figural and abstract geometrical patterns as per the Islamic tradition, which rejects animate objects in carving. The complexity, the use of symmetry and geometry, the positioning of elements and the efforts of personalisation gave the façades an exciting quality. There was a successful blending of Indian features with European ones such as pediments and column capitals, arches, cast-iron grills and balustrades as well as floral motifs. A well developed, state-of-the-art language based on the principles of repetition, harmony and homogeneity could be perceived. In contrast to Islamic philosophy, the Bohras thus strove to represent their ethnic and personal identity through the façades,[14] wherein there was an exterior display of a rich and varied aesthetic expression. Also, as the proportion system was based on human dimensions, the façades reflected the human scale (Fig. 12.12).

The façades were also a symbol of the mercantile community's economic success, an attempt at identifying with the colonial powers through the emulation of their classical as well as popular architecture that existed in the major cities. Apart from Europe, motifs were also adopted from parts of Africa, the Middle East and Southeast Asia, where they travelled for business. This eclecticism

---

[13] Pramar, 1989.
[14] Doshi, 1982.

Figure 12.12 The craftsmanship in wooden façades, Siddhpur.
Courtesy the author.

of the façade is harmonised and controlled by a superior consciousness for the architectural form. Though the façade varied to a great extent, the plan organisation remained constant; hence, the outside was experimental and eclectic while the inside remained conservative (Fig. 12.13).

In the 1940s and 1950s, some Bohras built a new typology of bungalows that were highly influenced by Art Deco and to a lesser extent by Streamline Moderne, which resulted in a new vocabulary of façade-making as well as creating the ambience of the interiors. There happened a reduction and abstraction of ornamentation. This changed notion of style is reflected in the ornamentation of the entire elevation through the making of the pillars, doors, windows, railings and terraces, even extending into the interior spaces.

RICH INTERIORS OF THE HOUSES

It was not only the grandness and intricacies of the façades of the Bohra dwellings but also the making of the interior spaces that set them apart. As rich articulation and focus on enclosed space (a feature common in other forms of Islamic architecture as well) were its most striking features, one can say that the inhabitants' lifestyle was best manifested within the enclosed walls. For the introverted Bohra community, the interior space held a special significance,

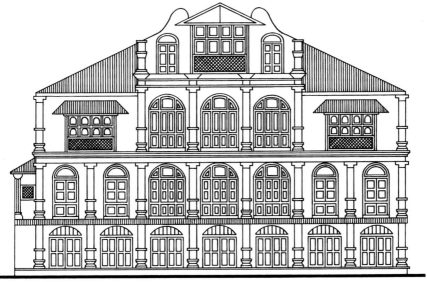

ELEVATION

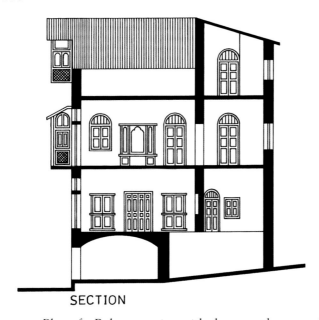

SECTION

Figure 12.13 Plan of a Bohra mansion with shops on the ground floor,
Siddhpur. Courtesy the author.

symbolising their passion for display and decor that was unusual in the region. The niches housed souvenirs from their travels around the world and elaborate cabinets were designed for their storage and display. The extensive use of rugs, carpets and cushions in the interiors allowed for flexible use of space on a daily and seasonal basis. Conspicuous by the absence of furniture, *bichhat* (floor seating on mattresses) was the predominant traditional furniture in the Bohra houses. The aesthetic language of the façades often seemed to be reflected in the intricate details of the wooden cupboards and other display elements in the interiors. Made with the best finishing materials from all over the world and personalised through decorative elements, false ceilings, furniture as well as display objects, the interior space created a personal world for the family within two parallel walls. The wooden cupboards were exquisitely carved and were displayed as permanent fixtures in the interiors. Along with the fenestrations, they created a sense of human scale.

Cleanliness of the body, mind and soul was a dictum of their religion; cleanliness of one's physical environment was a natural extension of this dictum. This religious obligation was strictly adhered to as a philosophy and was also extended to mean aesthetically rich expressions. Persian imitation rugs on the floors, mirrors, painted glass, stained glass windows, glass lamps and chandeliers, upholstered sofas and chairs created a grand interior ambience. The kitchen, bathroom and W.C., though small in size and simple in design, were often enclosed by well-made wooden partitions with panels or ornamentation. It is believed that the Bohras were the first to develop the concept of an attached bathroom in traditional housing due to their regard for ritual purity. Hence, in the interiors of the traditional Bohra house, the cultural ethos of the community was expressed in the most natural way (Fig. 12.14).

Excellent Local Craftsmanship

These traditional dwellings were built through a brick-and-timber constructional system where the structural timber was brought from Konkan and Malabar in southern India by sea. 'Although timber was also an expensive raw material and was not available locally, it could be combined with the brick available locally to maximise its capabilities.'[15] The Hindu craftsmen of Gujarat were some of the most accomplished in medieval India as traditional knowledge was handed down from generation to generation. Being in a hereditary occupation, the artisans achieved the perfection of their art through vigorous apprenticeship and its careful preservation. They designed the dwellings in the accepted vernacular vocabulary within the typological framework of the basic layout. Working with

---

[15] Lambourn, 2006.

Figure 12.14 Example of a very elaborate interior space.
Courtesy the author.

the broad rules of the Hindu building science scriptures, they were allowed creative freedom of expression (Fig. 12.15).

In spite of the standard layout of the plan, the uniqueness of each house depended on the input of the craftsmen in the creation of the interiors and façades. They expressed the acumen of their craft when they easily adopted European motifs. Through their versatile art and creativity, the craftsmen revealed a comprehensive understanding of the elements of design, the nature of the building materials and human expression. The Bohra houses of Gujarat were, thus, first and foremost, a tribute not only to the genius of the craftsmen but also to the great Bohra patronage.

SOCIO-CULTURAL ISSUES OF THE COMMUNITY

The major social determinants of the Bohra house-form were their internalised lifestyle, relative seclusion of women, the importance of the family as the prime social unit and respect for an individual's privacy within the joint family set-up. The inside of the dwelling was considered a relatively secure and predictable inner world in contrast to the potentially alien space outside (Fig. 12.16). The religious tenet of *Taharat* (physical and mental cleanliness) was all-pervasive and had blended with the Bohra lifestyle, extended to include aesthetic ambience. It

Figure 12.15 Craftsmanship in various materials. Courtesy the author.

Figure 12.16 Women's strong association with interior spaces.
Courtesy the author.

was this characteristic that was partly responsible for the special Bohra identity among other Islamic communities in India.

A traditional Bohra house, shaped by several societal forces, created a sense of place in a distinct domestic setting. The ancestral home in the native town was the heart of each family's identity. It is still preferred by many, as these dwellings have a built-in flexibility for future division in case the joint family breaks up into nuclear families (Fig. 12.17).

The high plinths, the half gate, the visually controlled façades, the transition of spaces in a sequential manner from the entrance to the private interiors, the enclosed balconies and screened window-seats were architectural manifestations of the social position of Bohra women within their culture. The Bohras equated the house to one's *ijjat* (prestige) in the community, which is why they have remained well preserved even when they have been empty for years. Externally the traditional house was a projection of one's socio-economic status; at the same time, internally it was laid out with great aesthetic care and finesse due to the spiritual value attached to the act of creation itself. In fact, as the structure and decoration became a unified whole, the Bohras seem to spiritually search for the Islamic concept of inner beauty within the sanctuary of one's own house.

BOHRAS IN OTHER PARTS OF THE WORLD[16]

As mentioned before, the Bohras have been seafaring traders, plying the lucrative trade routes between India, Southeast Asia and the Arab world for centuries. They translated architectural knowledge, up to an extent, in the reconstruction of their early houses in Africa, Singapore and other parts of the world. In the late nineteenth century the British colonial government actively encouraged Indians to settle in East Africa, resulting in a flourishing network of ideas, institutions and movements of people, radiating out from India across the Indian Ocean arena.[17] Indian commerce then grew substantially as a part of a vibrant trade network with Gujarat.

The Bohras, as prominent traders, are among the earliest Asian immigrants to East Africa and are found mainly in the larger urban areas as shopkeepers, landlords, craftsmen, artisans and professionals.[18] Their house form spread as a result of the transregional and transnational forces, where houses are seen as metaphors of a social system. As Linda Donley-Reid discovered in her excellent comparative research in Lamu and Gujarat, there were many similarities in spatial layouts and space use between the Lamu eighteenth- and nineteenth-century

---

[16] Unfortunately, I was not able to find much related research in many parts of the world where the Bohras have migrated.

[17] Metcalf, 2008.

[18] Hatim, 1975.

Figure 12.17 The entrance space with a gate for privacy.
Courtesy the author.

traders' houses and the nineteenth- and twentieth-century Indian shopfront houses (with the domestic quarters on the upper level) found on Lamu's main street. The stairs are located on one side of the house, with an open chowk on the upper level. The front room on the upper level of a Lamu house is also used as the main 'sitting' room of the house, as in the native Bohra houses. They often ordered inscriptions from the Qur'ān to be carved on their door lintels. The craftsmen who worked with stone and wood were, for the most part Hindus, both in India and Africa. It is interesting that the earliest Indian Muslim settlers in eastern Africa were Bohras, converted Hindus, which explains the tendency towards Hindu symbols on doors, both in India and Africa.[19]

CONCLUSION

In the Islamic world, the displacement of regionally specific architectural forms and modes across space and time was often associated with the movement of artisans and patrons.[20] The Bohra dwellings are signifiers of their identity, besides symbolising a great harmony between the local craftsmen and the Bohra patrons, a commonality in the vernacular design process. This process is based on typological models and comprises modifications and variations wherein the individual unit and not the house-type is personalised. There is also an underlying structure within its overall organic attitude, which leaves room for human expression and creativity. Here, the similarity of the parts creates a whole that transcends the quality of the individual. In this method, a great deal of spontaneity and organism emerge, unfiltered by the imposed regulatory controls of the prototypical design. These houses represent a response to the sub-culture, climate, social attitudes and local craftsmanship that existed within the region and the community. They are symbols of modernity and urbanism of the time, while reflecting the bygone era of unparalleled craftsmanship of Gujarat.

In addition, the lifestyle and dwellings of the Bohras reflect the idea of cleanliness and beauty. The intricate design of the façades and interior elements such as rugs, cushions and elaborately carved wooden partitions are a manifestation of the Bohra's prosperity, their reverence for home and religious aspects, their sense of maintenance and exquisite aesthetics. Based on the regional concept and typology, the traditional Bohra dwellings symbolise a process of adaptation as well as a unique and creative transformation generated by layers of decisive cultural influences.

BIBLIOGRAPHY

Arasaratnam S. 1987. 'India and the Indian Ocean in the Seventeenth Century', in Ashin Das Gupta and M. N. Pearson (eds), *India and the Indian Ocean 1500–1800*. Calcutta: Oxford University Press.

Burgess, J. 1896. *On the Muhammadan Architecture of Bharoch, Cambay, Dholka, Champanir, and Mahmudabad in Gujarat*. Archaeological Survey of Western India, vol. VI. London: Griggs & Son.

Burton-Page, John. 1988. 'Historical Context', in George Michell and Snehal Shah (eds), *Ahmadabad*. Bombay: Marg Publications, p. 615.

---

[19] Donley-Reid, 1984.
[20] Flood, 2015.

Desai, Madhavi. 2008. *Traditional Architecture: House Form of the Islamic Community of Bohras in Gujarat*. Pune: The Council of Architecture.

Desai, Miki and Madhavi Desai. 1991. 'Ahmedabad: The City as Palimpest', *Architecture + Design*, no. 3, vol. VIII (May–June).

Donley-Reid, Linda. 1984. *The Social Uses of Swahili Space and Objects*. Unpublished PhD dissertation, Dept. of Archaeology, University of Cambridge. Archaeological Research Facility Stahl Reports. https://escholarship.org/uc/item/73j2m64n.

Doshi, Saryu (ed.). 1982. *The Impulse to Adorn: Studies in Traditional Indian Architecture*. Bombay: Marg Publications.

Flood, Finbarr B. 2015. 'Idea and Idiom: Knowledge as Praxis in South Asian and Islamic Architecture', *ARS Orientalis*, vol. 45, pp. 148–62.

Hatim, Amiji. 1975. 'The Bohras of East Africa', *Journal of Religion in Africa*, vol. 7, issue 1, pp. 27–61.

Kellar, Sara and Michael Pearson (eds). 2015. *Port Towns of Gujarat*, Delhi: Primus Books.

Lambourn, Elizabeth. 2006. 'Brick, Timber and Stone: Building Material and the Construction of Islamic Architectural History in Gujarat', *Muqarnas*, vol. 23, issue 1, pp. 191–217.

Lapidus, Ira M. 1988. *A History of Islamic Societies*, Cambridge: Cambridge University Press.

Mathew, Nisha. 1993. *The Dwellings of Bohra Community in Surat: A Discussion*. Unpublished undergraduate thesis, Faculty of Architecture, CEPT University. http://hdl.handle.net/20.500.12725/12802.

Metcalf, Thomas R. 2008. *Imperial Connections: India in the Indian Ocean Arena, 1860–1920*. Berkeley: University of California Press.

Pearson, Michael. 1976. *Merchants and Rulers in Gujarat: The Response to the Portuguese in the Sixteenth Century*. Berkeley: University of California Press.

Pramar, V. S. 1989. *Haveli: Wooden Houses and Mansions of Gujarat*. Ahmedabad: Mapin Publishing.

Shokoohy, Mehrdada. 2012. 'The Legacy of Islam in Somnath', *Bulletin of the School of Oriental and African Studies, University of London*, vol. 75, no. 2, pp. 297–335. https://www.jstor.org/stable/23259581?seq=1.

Subrahmaniyam, Sanjay. 2018. 'The Hidden Face of Surat: Reflections on a Cosmopolitan Indian Ocean Centre, 1540–1750', *Journal of the Economic and Social History of the Orient*, vol. 61: issue 1–2, March, pp. 205–55.

CHAPTER 13

Regionalism in Religious Architecture of India: A Comparative Study of Mosques in Gujarat and Kerala

Miki Desai

During the propagation of Islam across different regions and cultural traditions, a process of adoption and adaptation from the native architecture occurred, giving rise to varying expressions of its built-form, especially to the religious edifices. These forms became contemporaneous and akin to the architecture of the land where Islam entered. However, Islam as a syncretic religion adhered to the belief of orientation and the principles of plan-organisation of the necessary components of the mosque.

This article focuses upon drawing a comparison between the mosque architecture of Gujarat and Kerala, two distinct regions of India (Fig. 13.1). In this comparison, the location and circumstances are important. Both are coastal regions on the west coast of the country. Gujarat has the longest coastline and a hot-dry climate, with ancient port towns and an entrepreneurial community that exported cotton, silk, fabrics, carpets and quilts, dyes, indigo, agate, beads and tobacco. Kerala has a relatively shorter coastline with important ancient ports but is in the hot-humid region with spices and grains as some of its most valuable export commodities in the past.

Both Gujarat and Kerala had active maritime trade with other Islamic trade centres of Arabia and East Africa via sea and land routes. However, mosques became a ubiquitous feature of India after the establishment of Islamic rule at the end of the twelfth century. The case of comparison majorly stems from the fact that Muslims arrived in Kerala and Gujarat fairly early but not as a domineering power. The intention is therefore to understand the cause of physical and philosophical differences and commonalities that shaped these mosques.

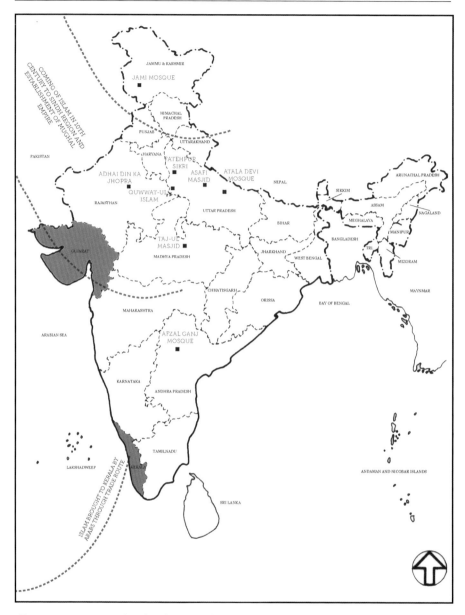

Figure 13.1 Map of India showing location of important mosques and coming
of Islam to Gujarat and Kerala. Courtesy the author.

MOSQUES IN INDIA

The Muslims ruled India for more than six centuries and became the second largest religious group of the country. 'They created an aristocratic confederation and shaped its administrative and legislative processes. They also brought in a new concept of God and a new architecture with them.'[1] Legal and administrative languages remained Farsi/Urdu during the British colonial period and the Gujarati language was fairly influenced by Farsi. As a result, 'mosques' made their presence felt at the beginning of the thirteenth century. Here is seen (Fig. 13.2) one of the early mosques in Ajmer, curiously called Adhai Din Ka Jhonpra. The name literally means 'two-and-a-half day's hut'. Some Sufis claim that the name signifies the temporary life of human beings on the earth. The mosque was commissioned by Qutub-ud-Din-Aibak and built on the remains of an old Sanskrit college, with materials from destroyed Hindu and Jain temples, almost entirely by Hindu masons, under the supervision of Afghan managers. It was designed by Abu Bakr of Herat, an architect who accompanied Muhammad Ghori.

INDO-ISLAMIC MOSQUES: PLANNING PRINCIPLES

'By the seventeenth century, mosques in India had majorly stabilised with big domes, arched gates, prayer halls and high minarets as its essential components . . . Another possible way to look at a mosque could be a building erected over an invisible axis, an axis which is nonetheless the principal determinant of its design.'[2] Asafi Masjid in Lucknow, a good example representing these characteristics, was built by Nawab Asaf-ud-Daulah after the city was declared the capital of Awadh in 1775 (Fig. 13.3). Due to the low cost and limited time, the supposed Iranian architect Kifait-ullah of Delhi chose brick masonry (in place of marble masonry or cladding of Bara Imambara) which was awarded grandness by the masterfully rendered stucco plaster and mouldings.

The orientation of the Indian mosque is east-west as the qibla faces the direction of Kaaba in Mecca. Even as the qibla wall remains blind, the mihrabs are formally and architecturally expressed on it. It may also be punctuated by buttresses depending on the structural requirements.[3] Minbar or mimbar is an equivalent pulpit from where the imam can deliver the sermons. The minaret is an important architectural component that serves the function of identity, a landmark that is useful for calling the devout to prayer (*azan/adhan*). Jami

---

[1] Lang et al., 1997.
[2] Dickie, 1978.
[3] For example, the qibla wall of Ahmedabad is orientated at 273.40 degrees from the geographic north and at Calicut it is at 291 degrees.

Figure 13.2 Adhai Din Ka Jhonpra, Ajmer (1192). Courtesy the author.

Figure 13.3 Asafi Masjid, Bara Imambara, Lucknow (1775).
Courtesy the author.

Figure 13.4 Facade of Jami Mosque at Sarkhej as seen from the large courtyard.
Courtesy the author.

Masjid, the central or city-mosque, has a large *sahn* (courtyard) and often elaborate façades of the prayer hall and minarets. Mosques in Gujarat, by and large, conform to this idealised plan organisation. For example, in the Jami Mosque at Sarkhej, outside of Ahmedabad, despite the absence of a traditional façade (proclaiming the triumph of local trabeated structures over Islamic arched structures), the whole is very convincing (Fig. 13.4).

Thus, these elements led to the establishment of the formal typology of the Indian congregational mosque or *masjid-al-jami* (mosque for *jumma* [Friday] prayers); a space for communal worship and rituals containing symbolic or functional features, each one of which has its own history and significance. All neighbourhood mosques follow the principle of orientation towards Mecca. The majority of the mosques of Gujarat follow the above-mentioned model, however, in forlorn places, and in the settlements with small Muslim populations, even in north India, an open to sky platform, called *Idgah*, with a freestanding qibla-wall, would represent a mosque. There is usually a mihrab on its inside, which is expressed on the outside, at the back of the wall. It is the author's conjecture that where there is not sufficient population to support a mosque, the *Idgah* platform serves as a prayer place (Fig. 13.5). The open space in front of the qibla wall is often used for congregational gathering on Eid and other religious celebrations.

Figure 13.5 An example of *Idgah* in Gujarat. Courtesy the author.

SYNTHESIS FROM OTHER BUILDING TRADITIONS

During the early centuries of Islam, the mosque became more than merely a place for prayer. Mosques were centres of community life and nearly all activities were conducted there. Often schools were attached, as were rooms for travellers, *sarais*. Mosques were also used as courts of justice. The mosque was, in fact, the centre of all religious and secular life.[4]

Indo-Islamic architecture in India is the synthesis of the Hindu, Jain and Islamic building traditions and their expressions in the built-form. The borrowing of Hindu and Jain elements is, therefore, not surprising as Islam of the time constantly absorbed regional elements of the cultures it conquered or converted. The use of Modified Hindu Order of several structural and non–structural elements was often found in their buildings.[5] Trabeated construction and flat roofs/slabs, as well as false arches, were in abundant use. Adhai Din Ka Jhonpra in Ajmer (1192) is a good example of the mosques having been built from the ransacked temples' elements and components. In another example, the Atala

---

[4] Merklinger, 1981.
[5] Ibid.

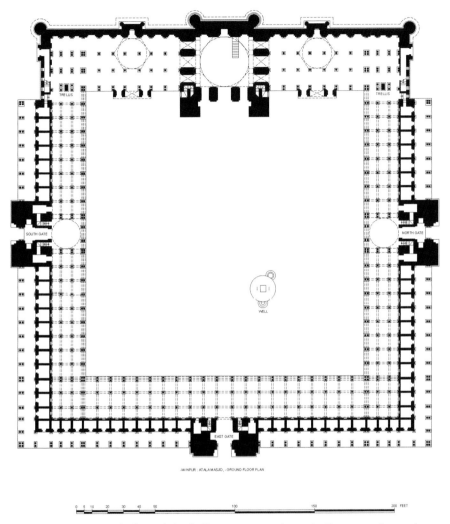

Figure 13.6 Ground plan of Atala Devi mosque (1408). Courtesy the author.

Masjid in Jaunpur, built in 1408, takes its name from the fact that it was built on the site of the Hindu temple of Atala Devi, the materials of which, together with those of other temples in its vicinity, were utilised in its construction. The colonnades surrounding Jaunpur's mosque's courtyard were constructed in a post and lintel style, carrying flat roofs much like the Buddhist cloisters. The other three colonnades, aside from the *Pishtaq*, do not open to the courtyard but to the outside (Fig. 13.6). This is an indication of Indian temperaments to be extrovert in preferring to display. Thus far, the internal four-*iwan*-type mosque had not been established in India. The mosque is outstanding for the flat slab and sloping roofed ceiling along with its handsome and monumental entry with domes and massive walls.

Perhaps the architecture of the Bahmani and Qutub Shahi period are the most impressive traditions of parts of Telangana in south India. The Bahmani sultanate (1347–c. 1527) and the Qutub Shahi (1598–c. 1686) kings built handsome forts, gardened tombs, entrance gates (especially Charminar) and mosques that render a distinct architectural genre. They celebrated the architecture of true arches, domes and vaults. Some of these structural exercises were massive, others were delicate. A great majority of architecture of this region and especially the mosques in this period were built without a strong influence of Hindu architectural principles. They owe much to the Persian tradition. Interestingly, the four-*iwan* courtyard structure of Central Asia and Iran are also evidently seen in the Jamia Mosque in Srinagar, built in 1394, whose construction follows the indigenous Buddhist and Hindu architecture, while the form follows the Persian tradition. In another example, the mosque architecture of the Independent Sultanate period (from the fourteenth to the sixteenth centuries) in Bengal represents the most important evolution of Islamic architecture. This distinctive regional style drew its inspiration from its indigenous vernacular architecture, heavily influenced by Hindu/Buddhist temple architecture.[6] The tomb architecture is much celebrated in north India, where the tombs are, at times, surrounded by Persian gardens. However, in the south, this tradition reaches only to the Deccans, up to Hyderabad and Bijapur (Fig. 13.7). In Kerala, tomb architecture is practically absent signifying the fact that it did not have rulers and dynasties in this region.

ISLAMIC ARCHITECTURE OF GUJARAT

The Arab traders came to the west coast of India as early as the sixth and seventh centuries prior to the establishment of the rule of Islam (twelfth to sixteenth centuries). In Gujarat, they came both by sea and land routes. The region seems to have been well known to them, especially the thriving ports such as Bharuch, Kahmbhat, Rander and others.[7] By necessity and nature, the religion was adaptive in terms of some regional customs and its architecture in general, more specifically for the construction of mosques. When they came to India, the general Indian ethos was of tolerance. The strong nationalistic spirit was absent, both due to its socio-cultural diversity and due to the fact that multiple faiths were followed, some in the conflict of the others. Many sects developed over a period of which Dawoodi Bohra, Sunni Bohra, Sufi, Khoja, Ismaili and Chhipa

---

[6] Hasan, 2007.
[7] Michell, 1988.

Figure 13.7 Tomb at Bijapur. Courtesy the author.

are present in Gujarat. Most of them being converts from the Hindu religion, one can find modified Hindu behavioural patterns in the present practice of Islam or life in general even today. These can be observed as shades or remnants in the language, social customs, rituals, dressing habit and food. However, in Gujarat, all festivals, Eid, Muharram and Urs are celebrated in a full-bodied manner in which people participate wholeheartedly.

In the case of Gujarat, the actual builders of the mosques were local artisans. The stone-artisans of that time were already well versed with architectural elements, were experienced in the construction techniques and the vocabulary of the ornamentation and articulation. Thus, the Gujarati artisans were able to give a 'new form' to an 'alien plan organisation'. Maru-Gurjara craftsmen deployed various elements of this style for both ritual, ceremonial and secular spaces. Therefore, there was no sharp stylistic break after the advent of Islam in Gujarat as the mosques and tombs here exemplify the fluidity and adaptability of the Maru-Gurjara style of architecture.[8] In the example of the Jami Mosque at Ahmedabad, the central dome, in the front, rises high over the roofs of the adjoining areas. The carved balcony forms a stone bench with a sloping back. The domes in Jami Mosque are all constructed in the Maru-Gurjara style of

---

[8] Patel, 2004a.

Figure 13.8 Comparison of Islamic and Hindu dome ceilings.
Courtesy the author.

the Hindu and Jain architecture. In the image above, on the left is the ceiling of the dome of Jami Mosque while on the right is the ceiling in a Jain temple at Ranakpur, Rajasthan (Fig. 13.8). These have converging tiers laid out horizontally, where their interiors and pendants are carved. As part of the Islamic tenet, any anthropomorphic forms or figures were forbidden in the mosque architecture. A new form did emerge and by 1400 there came about an Indo-Islamic genre of Gujarat. During this period, in the rest of the country, a similar process was followed; a variation of a theme or an architectural plurality became evident. Between the twelfth and sixteenth centuries, mosques, *dargahs*, tombs, pleasure gardens and iconic expressions in memory of kings and their relatives dotted north India; as Delhi and Agra became the hotbed of different Mughal rulers.

ISLAMIC ARCHITECTURE IN KERALA

The stylistic development of Islamic architecture in India varies as we move from north two south. Various architectural styles emerge, starting from Tuglaqi/ Qutb Shahi around Delhi, Maru-Gurjara in Gujarat and Rajasthan, Bengal roofs in the eastern regions and Bahmani in parts of Karnataka and Hyderabad. The exploration of architectural styles in the stone architecture of mosques was last seen in Gulbarga mosque (1367) in Karnataka, south of which one finds mosques in timber in the same style as the regional architecture. The maritime traffic on India's southwestern coast was connected to several international communities such as the Chinese, Arabs, Persians, Africans and others. The coastal Malabar region (Kerala of today) also had the Arab traders arriving in the early seventh century exclusively by sea routes. Thus, Islam arrived on the Malabar Coast five centuries before its political domination in northern India. It spread there through migration and the gradual conversion of the native population. Most of the traders depended on monsoon winds for travelling back. This necessitated the need amongst several Arab and Chinese traders to stay in Kerala. The Indian Ocean, thus, left a deep impact on the region's society, culture, religion and politics, making it an exemplary cosmopolitan place.[9]

Small mosques were built in their temporary settlements and, as a duty, they propagated the religion. Islam in Kerala, therefore, has closer links with the Arab system of belief rather than with Islam as practised in the rest of the country. Mosque building in Kerala reached its zenith between the thirteenth and the sixteenth centuries; the period of Arab supremacy in maritime trade with the Malabar.[10] The typical Kerala mosque's identity is unique within the traditional mosques found elsewhere, especially in south India. Architectural precedence of Kerala was in its canonical literature, tectonic aspects as well as its normative typologies that the traditional carpenters practised in. Wood as a construction material did not offer opportunities of embellishment that were amply explored in the stone architecture of Gujarat, defining its pronounced stylistic presence (Fig. 13.9). Broadly speaking, we find different expressions of the built-form in Gujarat and Kerala; this article specifically focuses upon drawing a comparison between the mosques of the two regions.

INDO-ISLAMIC SULTANATE PERIOD MOSQUES OF GUJARAT

Islam had been established in Gujarat well over a century before the political rule of the Delhi sultanate and later as Ahmad Shah's sultanate came into being. As a result, in the early fifteenth century, there arose a new architectural language, termed as the Indo-Islamic Sultanate Architecture of Gujarat. The mosques that developed thereafter were there as an exemplar for Ahmad Shah and his successors.[11] In 1300, the local stone architecture (called Maru-Gurjara

---

[9] Mahmood, 2018.
[10] Dalvi, 2011.
[11] Early Islamic work set precedents for later buildings. The Khirki Mosque in southern Delhi (c. 1380), for instance, became a model for mosques such as the Atala Masjid (1408) and the Jami Masjid

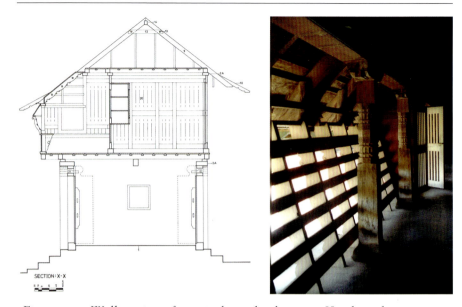

Figure 13.9 Wall section of a typical wooden house in Kerala and an interior image of a slanted lattice (*charupadi*). Courtesy the author.

style from the sixth century) of Hindu and Jain temples and that of the stepwells had crossed its zenith of craftsmanship. The mosques, tombs and city gates of Gujarat, therefore, have a unique position in the Indo-Islamic architectural history of India. They are distinguished for their noble façades, which were enriched by engrailed arches of temple extraction.

Initially, mosques in Gujarat were largely constructed from various elements that were pillaged from destroyed temples. One good example, as described by Dr Alka Patel, is the congregation mosque built by Ahmad Shah in the fifteenth century in the town of Siddhpur in north Gujarat. Siddhpur was famous for the elaborate temple complex of Rudra Mahalaya of the mid-twelfth century, patronised and created by King Siddharaj Jayasinh of the Solanki dynasty. The mosque was partially reconfigured with old components of the Rudra Mahalaya complex. Its fragments and elements were given new contexts and functions that helped in shaping the characteristics of the mosque.[12] Additionally, the craftsmen's repertoire was well equipped with experimentations and iconographic variations in these temples. As a result, a construction system, familiar

(1438–78) at Jaunpur and the Bara Sona Masjid (1526) at Gaur. It is built of quartzite and was coated in a thick plaster with only the portals and beams being built of dressed stone. The arches are of a beam and bracket type and the domes are of a plastered crude concrete. In all, it was an economical way of building. Tadgell, 1990; Taylor and Lang, 2016.

[12] Patel, 2004a.

to the Hindu and Jain temple architectural vocabulary was followed for mosque construction. In another comparison, the architectural order remains the same in the mosque at Champaner, and the mandapa in Adalaj stepwell outside of Ahmedabad (Fig. 13.10). In both the cases, the columns form an octagonal enclosure at the lintel level to carry the dome. However, the expression of the column and lintels in the mosque is devoid of the ornamentation and Hindu iconography. This is also supported by Lambourn's excellent research. Referring to the eighth-century Friday mosque at Cambay, she calls it the fundamental model for the later architecture of the sultanate period of Gujarat during the fifteenth and sixteenth centuries, where 'the design and decoration of many elements throughout the mosque – notably – the doorways, the columns, and the exterior mouldings – are all based in the local Gujarati vocabulary of decoration'.[13] As stated above, Gujarat marvels in its glory of stone architecture. Furthermore, it can be observed that the equivalent of this indigenous distinct architectural language of the sultanate period of Gujarat is the wooden architectural expression of the mosques in Kerala and the two are in complete contrast.

MAPPILA ARCHITECTURE OF KERALA

Islamic influences of northern India did not reach Kerala significantly due to the difficult terrain of the Deccan Plateau. The Arab, Portuguese and even Chinese had maritime trade with this region but this connection did not influence its mosque architecture substantially. In Malabar, the Mappilas may have been the first community to convert to Islam. In Kerala, perhaps, patrons of the mosques of the Muslim community looked for regional precedents more from the viewpoint of construction techniques and systems rather than its formal expression. One can thereby distinguish that Kerala represented a much more modest approach towards the depiction of the built-form of mosques than those in north India. This is also visible in their religious rituals and activities.[14]

'Besides this, geo-climatic forces and Kerala's architectural tradition have resulted in a built-form distinct from that of mosques in other parts of the country, which are based on the design of Prophet Mohammed's house in Medina.'[15] As a result, the architecture of mosques in Kerala is rather distinct. The craftsmen of the residential architecture, who built the mosques, were well versed with the *shastras* of building with wood, largely emulating the construction techniques and systems prevalent to Kerala's (predominantly Hindu) residential

---

[13] Lambourn, 2001.

[14] In north India, the Tajiya procession is a colourful affair where people carry replicas of mosques and tombs. In Kerala however, it is a much more subdued affair without these replicas.

[15] Kuttiammu, 1979, p. 85.

Figure 13.10 Mandapa at Adalaj Stepwell, Ahmedabad (top) and interior of Jami mosque at Champaner (bottom). Courtesy the author.

Figure 13.11 Mishkal Mosque, Kozhikode (14th century).
Courtesy the author.

genre. Consequently, the mosque architecture of Kerala reflects an enlarged
house form.

> The basic plan of the mosque in Kerala comprises a hall and the qibla wall
> which contains the mihrab, the essential component of the mosque. The
> qibla wall is usually on the shorter side in Kerala, facing Mecca. On the
> ground floor, the main hall has arched openings at regular intervals. This hall
> is usually laid out in two parts with a dividing wall that has three openings,
> forming an inner and an outer area of worship. The upper storey is a large,
> single-volume space covered by a roof in the architectural idiom of Kerala.[16]

For example, the architecture and design, both inside and outside, in the
Cheraman Mosque in Kodungallor, built in 629, resemble local Hindu residential influence. It is a double storied structure with a sloping tiled roof. On
the other hand, the Mishkal Mosque, Kozhikode, fourteenth century, was built
entirely in timber by an Arab merchant. It serves as an example of artistic and
architectural finesse that was prevalent at the time it was built (Fig. 13.11).

---

[16] Desai, 2018, p. 97.

Figure 13.12 Cheraman Mosque, Kodungallor (629), showing the old residential style building (left) now masked by the new façade of 1984 (right). Courtesy the author.

In the Thazhathangadi Mosque in Kottayam,[17] the predominantly indigenous architecture influenced the mosque throughout while remaining within the tenets of Islam. It also comprises a *vaju*/ablution pond and a bathing space similar to those in Hindu architecture as a familiar gesture in built-forms.

INFLUENCE OF REGIONAL ARCHITECTURE

The influence of regional architecture is distinctively seen in the mosques of Gujarat and Kerala. While the former is inspired by the temple stone architecture, the latter resembles an elaborate dwelling in wood. For example, the Jami Mosque of Bharuch, constructed in 1322, is entirely built in the indigenous trabeated (beam-and-bracket, pillar-and-lintel) style, with an open prayer hall, its roof supported by richly carved pillars derived directly from the wealth of Hindu and Jain architecture. Similarly, the Jami Masjid of Ahmedabad has an important feature inspired by the temples of the Gurjar at region. On the other hand, the Cheraman Mosque in Kodungallor, Kerala, built in 629 (Fig. 13.12), is believed to be one of the earliest examples based on the residential architecture of the region, wherein its simplicity could be an assimilative gesture. It was built by Malik Deenar, an Arab propagator of Islam. It is believed that this mosque was first renovated and reconstructed in the eleventh century. Since ancient times, trade relations between Arabia and India were active. Even before the days of Muhammad, Arab traders visited the Malabari region, which was a major link between the ports of India and Southeast Asia.

---

[17] Claimed to be more than 1,000 years old.

RESPONSE TO CLIMATE AND NATURE

The differences in geo-climatic forces is one of the major factors distinguishing the mosques of Kerala from those in Gujarat. 'In North India, a mosque has a large *sahn* (courtyard), in which the faithful gather for prayer. The basic difference in Kerala is that the *sahn* is replaced by a one- or two-storey covered hall on a high plinth owing to the heavy rains.'[18] Also, the *Idgah* is a type of place of worship commonly found in many parts of North India, which rarely occurs in Kerala due to its climatic conditions.

Due to the amount of rain that Kerala receives, sloping roofs become mandatory in order to shelter the worshippers. Two-pitch and four-pitch roofs, with or without dormers, thus determine the form of mosque architecture in Kerala. For example, in order to counter the rain, the entire building of the Mishkal Mosque in Kozhikode is raised on a high plinth and a verandah runs on all sides with arched openings.

Often, water is also celebrated in the architecture of the hot and arid region of Gujarat. The large water tank that abuts the Jami Mosque at Sarkhej is flanked by the Queen's pavilion that enjoys the cooled breeze from the waterbody. However, in Kerala's Islamic architecture, such celebrations of water structures are not observed owing to its hot and humid climate. One can thereby assert that climatic conditions form one of the most important criteria in determining the spatial organisation and forms of the mosques.

MATERIALITY AND CONSTRUCTION SYSTEMS

Along with stylistic developments, evolution is observed in the methods of construction in the mosque typology. Brickwork clad by stone was the most common material used in the construction of mosques in Gujarat. However, the Jami Masjid in Bharuch, built in the fourteenth century, is an exception as the walls surrounding the sanctuary are constructed out of stone and are thus the earliest example of original masonry work for the Indo-Islamic Sultanate Architecture. Islamic construction systems differed from the Hindu construction system, as the former was arcuate and had larger spans. Construction by local Hindu craftsmen posed a problem as they did not know the principles of true arch and dome construction (which were the norm in Islamic construction), which they inadequately built through corbelling, finished with mortar and cladded with circular stone elements from inside and plaster from outside, resulting in their eventual collapse.

---

[18] Desai, 2018, p. 95.

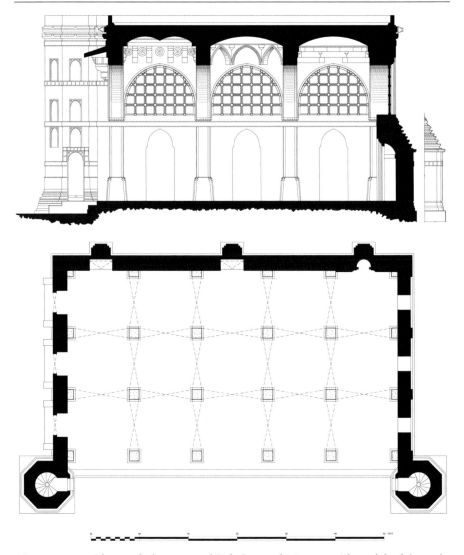

Figure 13.13 Plan and elevation of Sidi Saiyyed Mosque, Ahmedabad (1572). Courtesy the author.

The structural system of Sarkhej Roza complex, built in 1451, in Ahmedabad is predominantly post and beam, with panel arches inserted later. On the other hand, the Sidi Saiyyed Mosque, built by an Abyssinian by the same name, about a century later in 1572, in a similar geography (the old city of Ahmedabad), is composed entirely of arcades of arches with eight square piers supporting the arches from the interior of the mosque, a departure from the conventional mosque design (Fig. 13.13). The flat domes in the interior bays are unique to the

Sidi Saiyyed Mosque. Its façade is opened by five large arches of equal height enclosed within two octagonal buttresses. The most notable part consists of a series of ten arched windows three metres wide and two metres high, four of which are arranged on the far wall and three on the lateral walls. Eight of them are divided into small squares of openwork stone with geometric and floral patterns.

This kind of development of construction methods and therefore expression is not seen in Kerala. Eclecticism that developed in stone did not happen in wood probably owing to the carpenters of Kerala following the rules of the prescribed literature and also because many spatial and formal architectonic gestures that could be made in stone were not possible in wood. Therefore, in Kerala, the roof neither became a dome nor a vault. Instead, there was an elaborate roofing system in timber. The other commonly used traditional building material in Kerala is laterite stone. Considering all these aspects, materials and construction systems have played a pivotal role in shaping the form of the mosque in the two regions.

ARCHITECTURAL AND SPATIAL FEATURES OF THE BUILT-FORM

Although the internal spatial organisation of mosques in both the regions is broadly the same, several incongruities exist in terms of the physical manifestation of the components of the built-form. The introduction of the minarets in the stone-constructed mosques was alien to Gujarati architectural repertoire but purposeful for announcing the *azan* (call to prayer) and a befitting Islamic expression. These were also urban markers in dense cities that rendered the silhouette of the city. Most mosques (built in the fifteenth and sixteenth centuries) in Gujarat, especially Ahmedabad, therefore had minarets before they were destroyed in the 1893 earthquake (Fig. 13.14). On the other hand, Kerala settlements were scattered over a large area and hence the minaret as a device for carrying prayer summons was ineffective and soon discarded. The minarets were also not practical due to the humid weather and the danger of attracting lightning. Instead, the dormers of the roof were enlarged and elaborated (now with loudspeakers) for calling the faithful to prayer.

The Jami Mosque in Ahmedabad, built in 1424, is part of a larger complex and not a stand-alone structure, which comprises two other structures (the king's and the queen's tombs), a ceremonial road and bazaar spaces, thus forming the core of the urbanity of the city. The prayer space in the Jami is a handsome structure with a tripartite arched entry. The middle section has a taller arch signifying a triple height and upper galleries looking into the entrance. This section is flanked by the semi-cylindrical protrusions going up to the top of the mosque. They are the remnants of minarets that fell off during the earthquake

Figure 13.14 Jami Mosque at Champaner where the tall minarets have survived unlike other examples in Gujarat. Courtesy the author.

of 1819. The tripartite entry is flanked by columned façades of five bays each on either side.

Sarkhej Roza, built in 1451 in Ahmedabad, is also a royal complex with a mosque. A large stepped square tank with pavilions on the western and the southern sides and the main complex including the mosque, the royal tombs and *dargah* of the Sufi saint Hazrat Shaikh Ahmed Khattu Ganj Baksh is reminiscent of the social realm of the palace. Today, a large number of people gather at this complex during festivals and other occasions. Royals used the tombs and palaces while common people used the pavilion, water tank and platform. However, this concept of celebrated open spaces is absent in the mosques of Kerala.

Tajiya processions during Muharram (commemorating and mourning the killings of Hussain and his followers) are important public events in most cities of north India, with a sizable population of Sunni Muslims. From different parts of Asia, people make miniature replicas of mosques (called *tajiya*), which can be replicas of actual structures or purely from the imagination, and take them out in a procession in the streets of the cities. Celebrations with such fervour are not a part of Kerala's Islam. This is prevalent in the northern part of the country and is not seen in Kerala owing to the large Shi'a Muslim population, who do not celebrate Muharram. In some regions, however, even the Shi'a sect participates

Figure 13.15 *Tajiyas*. Courtesy the author.

indirectly in the festival with a *tajiya* as an icon to represent and celebrate the Karbala event (Fig. 13.15).

The pitched roofs of the mosque in Kerala differed significantly due to the nature of wood as its material. Its form stood as a contrast to the mosques in the rest of the country because of certain elements like the gable end, ceiling and the slanted lattice (*charupadi*) on its upper floors, including Hindu elements such as square grid false ceilings, well integrated into its architecture. Thus, typical architectural elements, indigenous to each region, became part of the plan of the mosques, thereby transforming them into magnificent spaces of an altered kind.

CONSTRUCTION DETAILS

In the mosque architecture of Gujarat, the anthropomorphic decorative motifs that were disallowed in Islamic architecture were not used while maintaining the architectural order present in the Hindu and Jain architecture. Decorative renderings, as well as the abstraction of iconography, also played an important role in defining the order and the character of various elements such as friezes, brackets, columns, doors, lintels and so on. For example, in the Jami Mosque of Ahmedabad, the dome at the arrival, three large domes in the prayer space and the mihrabs in the western wall are richly decorated (Fig. 13.16). The Nagina Masjid of Champaner (1525) also has a significant amount of embellishment.

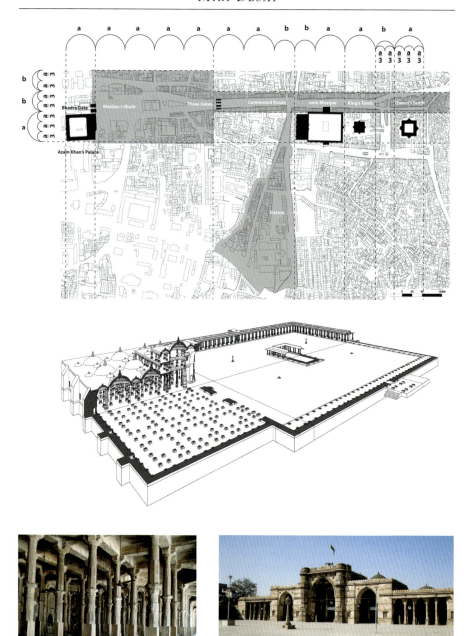

Figure 13.16 Jami Mosque, Ahmedabad (1423). Courtesy the author.

Mosques in northern India often become generators of urban spaces such as plazas and market spaces. The most significant thing to note about Jami Mosque above discussed earlier is that it is not a stand-alone structure. It is purposefully connected to two other structures and faces a ceremonial road with a bazaar around it. This used to take place in a *maidan* (open space) located south of the mosque, in a rich urban context and thus becomes a part of the royal complex comprising the mosque, the king's tomb and the queen's tomb. Sir Thomas Roe, in his memoir of the seventeenth century, notes that Jami Mosque faced a 100-ft wide road, laden with tall trees, leading up to the three gates (*darwaza*). Later analysis by the author shows that there exists certain rhythm-by-dimension in the building and the complex that lead up to the three gates.

The façade of the mosque is broken up into divisions of varying heights; the central, which is the highest, and through which is the principal entrance, was once flanked by minarets (demolished in the great earthquake in June 1819); on each side of this is a lower section; and beyond these are the wings, with open fronts divided by pillars. The interior of the mosque is a columnar space that has 300 sandstone columns in Islamic order that can be seen as a variation of the Hindu and Jain ones. The three domes relieve three spaces within this forest of columns and axially relate to the mihrabs in the western wall of the mosque.

Here are some sectional perspectives and images of the Thazhathangady Mosque in Kottayam (Fig. 13.17). The gable end, ceiling and the slanted periphery on the upper floor are well-integrated Hindu elements found in the mosques of Kerala. The slanted plane is rather bare bones compared to the animated *killivathils* (casement windows) of temples. This is because the animal motifs from the vertical members are disallowed in the mosque's vocabulary of structured and non-structured members. There is also the interior rendering of the perspective of the ground floor, along with the ground floor plan, showing the main space in front of the mihrab, which consists of the three sections for praying. The upper floor plan shows the main area used for prayers, which often functions as a madrasa. In addition, it can be seen that the idea of *poomukham*, or entrance pavilion, is pronounced in the mosque architecture. Decorative carvings are in the form of stylised flowers and complex geometric patterns. The dormers of the roof are enlarged and elaborated (now with loudspeakers) for calling the faithful to prayer.

Thus, in the wooden architecture of Kerala, the appearance was frugal and assimilative with the surrounding residential architecture, reinforcing the tenet of simplicity. Mosques in Kerala are rather purist; devoid of ornamentation or carvings found on the stone façades of mosques in the hot, arid environments of Gujarat. However, some decorative embellishments do appear on windows and doors, cornices, beams, joists and the mihrab, their ceiling designs being similar to those seen in *namaskar mandapas* of Hindu temples of Kerala. The Mishkal

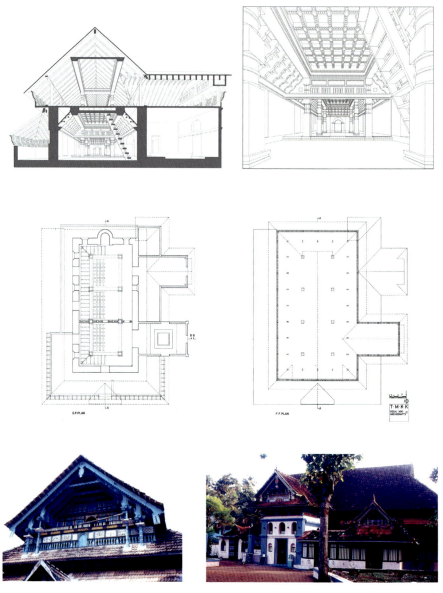

Figure 13.17 Thazhathangady Mosque, Kerala. Courtesy the author.

Mosque (c. 1340) in Kozhikode, for example, has some artistic and architectural features in the form of a beautiful carved wooden minbar. Though rebuilt in 1579 after the fire of 1510, it being a four-storey structure is a statement of the Muslim community's presence in Kozhikode. Traditional lattice (*charupadi*) that surrounds every floor make the interiors habitable (used as a madrasa and resting-place) in the hot-humid weather while giving it a monumental look.

The structural system of the Thazhathangady Mosque in Kottayam is not a daring or enigmatic one, but is rather functional and appropriate for its purpose. However, it is built as per the delineation in the *vastu-shastras* (texts on traditional architecture). It has pronounced dormers and the presence of a stepped-in bathing place/*kund* point towards the semblance with the site of Hindu temples. Idiomatically speaking, in the past couple of decades, north Indian expressions and embellishments such as domes, minarets, pendants, friezes and the use of garish paints have started appearing in the new or renovated (replaced mosques under the guise of renovation) mosques of southern states and in Kerala, in particular. Such examples not only stick out in the local urban scene but also seem rather alien.

CONCLUSION

In art and architecture, both at a monumental scale as in the major mosques and at a domestic scale, Islamic principles of design have had a major influence on the organization of urban and domestic space and on the aesthetic display of and within buildings. The influence is stronger in the north, where the Mughal influence was greater than in southern India.[19]

Historically, local climate, materials, craftsmanship, the community's economic resources and patronage have been the prime modifiers of the mosques' outwardly form.

The design also adhered to most Islamic tenets of directionality, simplicity and cleanliness being followed in the physical and ritualistic aspects of the religion. Thus, a reference to the regional typology was a natural consequence when building mosques on alien lands. Though different in terms of their formal and material aspects, in Gujarat and Kerala most of the Islamic religious practices are kept in place with minor differences in the manner of worship. This is consistent with the fact that usually Islam adopts the regional architecture, keeping the basic spatial organisation of its mosque intact.

The mosques in Gujarat drew inspiration from the well-developed language of the Hindu and Jain religious architectures in brick and stone masonry. The Gujarati construction system and the minimally modified order of architectural elements, tracery, grill/screen work and high-quality construction gave rise to handsome mosques that were markedly different from the form of the Hindu and Jain temple architecture. They also symbolise the talent and versatility of

---

[19] Lang et al., 1997, p. 31.

the craftsmen of the region. In Kerala, the tectonics in wood developed from a set building tradition, the knowledge of which was applied to the architecture of the mosques. There was little scope for ornamentation and elaboration. However, they achieved a well-rehearsed type that offered a large uninterrupted space for a prayer hall.

In both cases, it was the local craftsmen who were constructing for an alien religious philosophy but excelled in their craft. The Islamic tenet of frugality was deeply embedded in the mosque architecture of Kerala. Its scale was non-monumental and it fits quietly into the urban fabric without taking a dominating form. The symbolic value of the religion through the celebration of festivals such as Muharram is not as much in Kerala as in Gujarat, where cities like Ahmedabad celebrate them with great fanfare.

The urban presence of the Gujarati and generally north Indian mosques has a landmark value. They contribute to the urban design aspects and the personality of a city. Bazaars and speciality markets develop around them resulting in the daily congregation of a large number of people. During festivals, the centre of the old city around the Three Gates and the Friday Mosque is teeming with people and it transforms into a truly public domain. Kerala mosques are not a generator of such urban ambiance. Similarly, in north India in general, *dargahs* (shrines) are often gardened special places to visit. Kerala does not seem to have this tradition.

Looking at the outwardly formal transformation (especially of the past decade or so) of the mosques in Kerala (and also elsewhere in Asia, such as Indonesia-Lombok) it is clear that the regional imagery and age-old existence of the mosque do not seem satisfactory or pride-worthy for the followers or patrons of today. The blending and silent image of the past is rejected in favour of a much larger, attractive and even out of place 'modern' image. The use of domes, minarets, opulent materials and colour schemes have a distant referent in the Indian or Middle Eastern mosques, however, for the society, they do manage to create a new symbolism of modernity, power and presence. Kerala's Cheraman Mosque in Kodungallor (629), one of the earliest examples, is now unbelievably transformed with domes, minarets and the colour scheme. Many other important mosques have been transformed by the vocabulary that makes it 'more Islamic' than its otherwise honest local form of Kerala.

The study therefore enables one to perceive that although Islam adhered to certain principles of organisation in the planning of its mosques, regional variations as seen in the examples of Gujarat and Kerala give rise to the cause of physical and philosophical differences in the necessary components of their mosques as Islamic architecture interacted with the existing traditions. The modified expressions brought about immense richness in the built environment across time and space.

BIBLIOGRAPHY

Abu-Lughod, Janet. 1983. 'The Islamic City – Historic Myth, Islamic Essence, and Contemporary Relevance', *International Journal of Middle East Studies*, vol. 19, no. 2, pp. 155–76.

Burgess, J. 1896. *On the Muhammadan Architecture of Bharoch, Cambay, Dholka, Champanir, and Mahmudabad in Gujarat*. Archaeological Survey of Western India, vol. VI. London: Griggs & Son.

Dalvi, Smita. 2011. 'The Architecture of New Mosques in Kerala: Appropriated aesthetics in the aftermath of urbanisation and globalisation'. Research paper presented at the ICIAA 2011, the Department. of Architecture, Jamia Milia Islamia, Delhi. http://103.248.31.52:8080/jspui/bitstream/123456789/578/1/Architecture%20of%20new%20mosques.pdf.

Desai, Miki. 2018. *Wooden Architecture of Kerala*. Ahmedabad: Mapin Publishing.

Dickie, James. 1978. 'Allah and Eternity: Mosques, Madrasas and Tombs', in George Michell (ed.), *Architecture of the Islamic World, Its History and Social Meaning*. London: Thames & Hudson, pp. 154–7.

Grube, Ernst. 1978. 'What is Islamic Architecture?' in George Michell (ed.), *Architecture of the Islamic World, Its History and Social Meaning*. London: Thames & Hudson, pp. 101–4.

Hasan, Perween. 2007. *Sultans and Mosques: The Early Islamic Architecture of Bangladesh*. London: I. B. Tauris.

Hattstein, Markus. 2004. 'Islam – World Religion and Cultural Power', in Markus Hattstein and Peter Delius (eds), *Islam Art and Architecture*. Cologne: Konemann.

Kooria, Mahmood and Michael Pearson (eds). 2018. *Malabar in the Indian Ocean: Cosmopolitanism in a Maritime Historical Region*. New Delhi: Oxford University Press.

Kuttiammu, T. P. 1979. *The Mosques of Kerala: A Study of Adaptation and Re-adaptation of the Islamic Tradition in Splendours of Kerala*. Mumbai: Marg Publications.

Lambourn, Elizabeth. 2001. 'A Collection of Merits . . .': Architectural Influences in the Friday Mosque and Kazaruni Tomb Complex at Cambay in Gujarat', *South Asian Studies*, 17, pp. 117–49.

Lang, Jon, Miki Desai and Madhavi Desai. 1997. *Architecture and Independence, The Search for Identity – India 1880 to 1980*. Delhi: Oxford University Press.

Mahmood, Kooria. 2018. 'Introduction', in M. Kooria and M. N. Pearson (eds), *Malabar in the Indian Ocean: Cosmopolitanism in a Maritime Historical Region*. New Delhi: Oxford University Press, pp. xv–xxvii.

Merklinger, E. S. 1981. *Indian Islamic Architecture: the Deccan 1347–1686*. Warminster: Aris and Phillips.

Michell, George and Helen Philon. 2018. *Islamic Architecture of Deccan India*. Woodbridge: ACC Art Books.

Michell, George and Snehal Shah (eds). 1988. *Ahmadabad*. Mumbai: Marg Publications.

Patel, Alka. 2004a. 'Architectural Histories Entwined: The Rudra-Mahalaya/Congregational Mosque of Siddhpur, Gujarat', *Journal of the Society of Architectural Historians*, 63, 2 (June): 144–63.

Patel, Alka. 2004b. *Building Communities in Gujarat: Architecture and Society during the Twelfth through Fourteenth Centuries*. Leiden: Brill.

Tadgell, Christopher. 1990. *The History of Architecture in India: From the Dawn of Civilization to the end of the Raj*. London: Architecture Design and Technology Press.

Taylor, Joanne and Jon Lang. 2016. *The Great Houses of Calcutta: Their Antecedents, Precedents, Splendour and Portents*. New Delhi: Niyogi Books.

CHAPTER 14

Architecture of Coral Stone Mosques of the Maldives

MOHAMED MAUROOF JAMEEL

INTRODUCTION

Coral stone mosques of the Maldives are tropical mosques built from ornamental Porites coral stone quarried from the reef, using dry construction with carpentry joinery where the structures can be assembled and disassembled. They have features and decorations that illustrate an architecture of fusion and unification from the Indian Ocean regions of South Asia, East Africa, Southeast Asia and the Middle East. This overview of the architecture of the coral stone mosques of the Maldives focuses on its eclectic architecture influenced by the regions of the Indian Ocean. It is based on surveys and studies of the mosques from 2011 to the present by the author.

Maldives is a country that has survived in the middle of Indian Ocean for thousands of years with limited resources such as products of the coconut tree, fish and coral stone. It is a country that is naturally and culturally shaped by the ocean. An archipelago of 1,192 small low-lying coral islands of which 192 are inhabited, only about one per cent of the Maldives is land with an average ground level of 1.5 metres above sea level.[1] Maldives is also an island community that played a crucial role in Indian Ocean travel and became a melting pot of many cultures. The architecture of their coral stone mosques is an excellent example that illustrates the coming together of Indian Ocean cultures at one place.

The following overview based on surveys and studies of the mosques from 2011 to the present describes the eclectic architecture of coral stone mosques of the Maldives and the influences from cultures of the Indian Ocean region. The

---

[1] UNEP-GoM, 2009.

surveys and studies were first made for academic purposes and for an ongoing UNESCO World Heritage Nomination Project. Qualitative research methods were applied with multiple types of empirical data, collected and analysed over many years. The data included historical data, measured surveys, audio and visual observation. This overview presents the history of coral stone construction in the Maldives and carpentry techniques; describes attributes of the traditional mosques leading to coral stone mosques of the Maldives; and finally traces the eclectic architecture that unifies features of the Indian Ocean region.

CORAL STONE CONSTRUCTION

The stony coral family Scleractima, the most important variety that builds the coral reef, is commonly used for construction throughout the coastal settlements wherever it is found in abundance.[2] It is found and used mostly in the tropical regions of the Indian Ocean, Arabian/Persian Gulf, the Red Sea, Pacific and Central America. Coral stone construction thrived in Maldives for more than 1,800 years where its techniques varied, evolving to respond to the means and needs of different historic periods. It varied from simple coral stone blocks set in mortar with little or no surface decoration, to sophisticatedly assembled shaped coral stone blocks with high surface decoration to chipped coral stone and lime/cement masonry with plaster and coral stone concrete.

In Maldives coral stone was first used for construction by the early Buddhists and Hindus of the Maldives. The British archaeologist H. C. P. Bell, in his archaeological expeditions in the Maldives from 1922 to 1935, identified many Buddhist structures using shaped and decorated coral stone blocks set in mortar. He relates his findings in Maldives to Sri Lankan Buddhist origins in Toluvila Monastery in Anuraadhapura.[3]

The Norwegian archaeologist, Professor Mikkelson in his archaeological studies of Kashidhoo site completed in 1998 also revealed that shaped and decorated coral stone blocks set in mortar were used in the construction of the Buddhist monastery. He relates his findings to Buddhist origins in Kanthoradai, Jaffna and the Indian subcontinent. Shell deposits found in the monastery were dated to be between AD 165 and 345.[4] Coral stone structures of the pre-Islamic period were built using shaped coral stone set in mortar and finished with a lime skim coat. They had mouldings and decorative carvings with animal and human motifs (Fig. 14.1). Both Porites coral (*hiriga*) and coral sand stone (*veliga*) were used during this period.

---

[2] Spalding and Green, 2001, p. 34.
[3] Bell, 1940, p. 113.
[4] Mikkelson, 2000, p. 21.

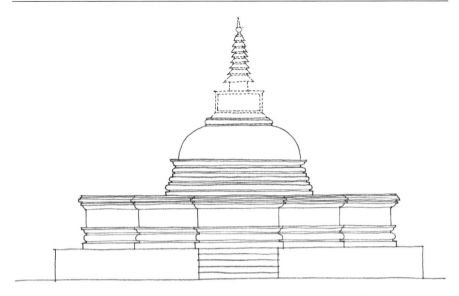

Figure 14.1 Sketch of the stupa in Kuruhinna, Laamu atoll, showing mouldings. Courtesy the author.

In 1153 the Maldives embraced Islam and started the dynastic rule of sultans and sultanas. Arab, Persian and Indian Muslim traders dominated the trade in the Indian Ocean and in 1343 Ibn Battuta, the great Moroccan traveller, describes Maldives society and admired the mosques.[5] During the early Islamic period also, coral stone structures were built using shaped coral stone set in mortar and finished with a lime skim coat. The construction technique was similar to the pre-Islamic period but did not have decorative carvings. Both Porites coral and coral sand stone were used during this period. After the 1500s the Indian Ocean trade dynamics changed, with exposure to emerging European colonial and regional influences like Gujaratis, Malabaris and Mughals. It led to the introduction of new technologies and advancements in arts and crafts. In around 1607 Pyrard de Laval, a French navigator, wrote a detailed account of the Maldives admiring the skills of the Maldivians in building boats and coral stone mosques.[6] This is the golden period of coral stone construction, when the coral stone mosques of the Maldives referred to in this overview were built. This is the period when new construction techniques and fine decoration emerged. The new interlocking construction technique without mortar was called *hirigalu vadaan* by Maldivians, appropriately meaning coral stone carpentry.[7]

---

[5] Mackintosh-Smith, 2002, p. 232.
[6] Pyrard, 2010, pp. 197–227.
[7] Jameel and Ahmad, 2015, pp. 54–5.

After the 1800s coral stone carpentry techniques slowly became extinct giving way to faster masonry techniques using chipped coral rubble with lime mortar and plaster. Porites corals were mined from the sea to be chipped into pieces and corals of the stony coral family were mined to make lime. This type of construction continued in Maldives until cement was introduced in the late twentieth century when coral pieces set in cement and sand mortar became the primary construction method. Faster development after independence in 1965 increased mining of coral stone for construction. Coral debris was being used as aggregate for reinforced concrete and in 1988 the serious biological and physical impact of coral mining was highlighted for the capital Malé region.[8] Coral and sand mining declined after mining from the house reef of the inhabited island was banned in 1992. Today coral stone mining is not possible in Maldives for environmental reasons and many of the traditional techniques are extinct, marking the end of a significant part of cultural history and creativity of Maldivians.[9]

After the increase of maritime activities during the 1500s, European ships such as the Portuguese caravel, along with Arab dhows, Indian bagalas and Chinese junks became common sights along coastal trading ports in the Indian Ocean where Maldivian sailors frequented. The manner of interchange and advancement of maritime skills, technologies and exchange of crafts is still to be investigated but the already famed Maldivian boatbuilders must owe their advancement to these interactions. In 1920, James Hornell, Director of Fisheries of Madras Government, in his study of Indian boat designs admires the superior skills of the Maldivians as boatbuilders, fishermen and sailors.[10] It was during the 1500s that carpentry joinery common to boatbuilding was applied to coral stone building construction resulting in an interlocking construction technique without mortar. Along with the techniques, emerged elaborate coral decorations and carvings of mixed geometric, floral and organic patterns. The builders employed maritime patterns such as the knots and sailing rope, familiar Islamic patterns and familiar South Asian patterns. A complex exchange of artistic ideas and influences within the region is evident by such usage. It is this art of shaping, joining and decoration of Porites coral that defines coral stone carpentry technique.

The process of mining and preparing of coral stone for construction comes through generations of understanding and working with the material. Porites coral heads bigger than one metre in diameter are commonly found in reefs. Three basic types of Porites coral are used in construction: *fuh hiri*, *goh hiri* and *onu hiri*. *Fuh hiri* is the smoothest in grain and easiest to do fine work. *Goh hiri*

[8] Naseer, 1997. p. 76.
[9] Jameel and Ahmad, 2015, p. 57.
[10] Hornell 1920, pp. 59–61.

Figure 14.2 The processing of coral stone construction. Courtesy the author.

is usually knotted in grain and has a harder surface: it is used for areas such as steps and stepping stones. *Onu hiri* is grainy and not used in decorative surfaces and is mostly used in wells, bathing tanks or as rubble fill. Live coral boulders were extracted manually, using rods and ropes on a raft or boat from the shallow parts of the reef where they were available in abundance. They were taken ashore, shaped and dried before usage. The roughly shaped blocks were moved to the sites, trimmed to accuracy and systematically built up layer by layer starting from foundations, plinth and walls (Fig. 14.2). Carpentry joinery such as tongue and groove, mortise and tenon, dado and similar joinery was used to build the mosque. The joints were worked to a precise level of hairline grooves and the wall structures were combined with timber doors, windows, ceiling and roof structure using the same interlocking system that allows disassembly and reassembly. The tools that were used for construction were simple carpentry tools such as adz, chisels, carving knives, gauges, dividers and hand drills.

After construction, most of the structures were decorated with mouldings, carvings and calligraphy. The mouldings have their origins in the pre-Islamic predecessors and can be compared with the mouldings in the structures of Kuruhinna, Laamu atoll excavated by Bell.[11] The surface carvings were combinations of vegetal and geometric patterns. Floral and knot arabesque patterns were common and like many Indian styles such as the Mughal style, as well as East African styles such as those found in the coral grave markers in Kilwa

---

[11] Bell, 1940. p. 112.

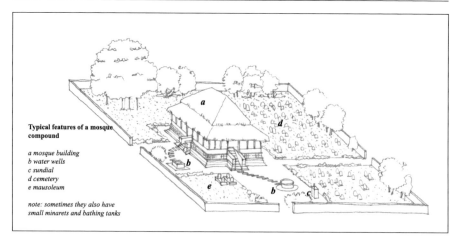

Figure 14.3 Typical features of a mosque compound. Courtesy the author.

mosque complex, Kenya.[12] Some of the geometric patterns can be traced to the pre-Islamic Buddhist structures in Maldives such as the aforementioned structures excavated by Bell. The calligraphic decorations are derived from older Jeli Thuluth from the Arab regions such as those found in Amir Aslam al-Silahdar Funerary Complex Conservation in Cairo.[13]

TYPES OF TRADITIONAL MOSQUES OF THE MALDIVES

Today, four types of traditional mosques using different types of coral stone construction survive in the Maldives, but the term Coral Stone Mosques of the Maldives is given to the specific type built from Porites coral using the 'coral stone carpentry' technique. All traditional mosques have many common features (Figs 14.3 and 14.4). They are located within a mosque compound consisting of the mosque building, water wells for ablution, a sundial to indicate prayer times and a cemetery. Often the compound has mausoleums, minarets and bathing tanks. The space around the mosque building and wells are demarked from the cemetery by a parapet wall called *harimma faaru*. The ablution wells in the mosques are connected to the mosques building through stepping-stones and surrounded by special plants such as jasmine, basil and mint.

The typical traditional mosque building has a symmetric layout with a rectangular prayer hall, mihrab wall and a prominent entrance with rising steps opposite to the mihrab wall. Occasionally they have symmetrically placed side entrances. Mihrab niches are not found among these mosques but they often

[12] Kirkman, 1959, p. 110.
[13] Architect, 2012.

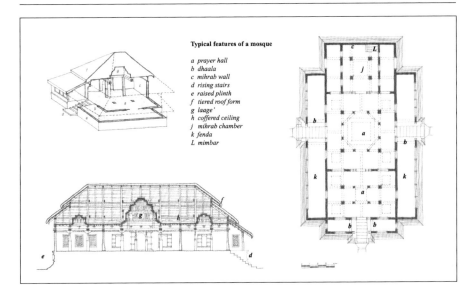

Figure 14.4 Typical features of a mosque. Courtesy the author.

have a mihrab chamber called *mihrab ge'* and verandahs attached to the prayer hall. The side verandahs attached to the rising stairs are called *dhaala* and those that are not attached to the stairs are called *fenda*. The typical traditional mosque building is built on a raised platform with walls, columns supporting a tiered roof and coffered ceilings. The ceiling often has an ornamented central recessed area called *laage'* and, between the roof structure and walls, there would be beams, short posts called *thona* and timber panels dedicated to calligraphic inscriptions called *liya fila*.

Apart from the typical features of the traditional mosque the attributes that define coral stone mosques are the use of shaped Porites coral stone using carpentry assembly technique, intricate coral carvings, decorated mouldings and stairs. Except for one, they all have decorated timber and lacquer works that include turned lacquered posts, ornamented ceilings and calligraphy panels. Individual attributes include mosques with multiple entrances; mosques with and without mihrab chambers, *dhaala* and *fenda*. There are also mosques with multiple, single or no *laage'*. Twenty-three surviving coral stone mosques have been identified so far, out of which six have been included in the World Heritage Tentative List. Illustrated on the next page is a map of the locations of the twenty-three mosques (Fig. 14.5), and seven of the mosques have been selected to represent a cross-section of the mosques in terms of location, size and age.

Fandiyaru Miskiy (c. 1586), located in Koagannu, Hulhumeedhoo, Addu City, is the smallest and oldest surviving coral stone mosque that is in good authentic condition (Fig. 14.6). It is one of many small family mosques in the

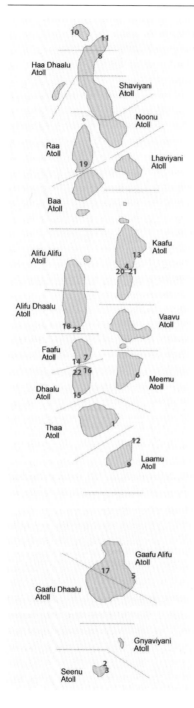

Figure 14.5 Map with locations of the coral stone mosques of the Maldives **1.** Ziyaaraiy Miskiy (c. 1400), Guraidhu, Thaa Atoll. **2.** Boadha Miskiy (c. 1403), Koagannu, Hulhumeedhoo, Addu City. **3.** Fandiyaru Miskiy (c. 1586), Koagannu, Hulhumeedhoo, Addu City. **4.** Malé Hukuru Miskiy (1658), Malé. **5.** Kondey Old Mosque (c. 1687), Kondey, Gaafu Alif Atoll. **6.** Veyvah Old Mosque (c. 1600s), Veyvah, Meemu Atoll. **7.** Bileddhoo Old Mosque (c. 1600s), Bileddhoo, Faafu Atoll. **8.** Nolhivaram Old Friday Mosque (1699), Nolhivaram, Haa Dhaalu Atoll. **9.** Fonadhoo Old Friday Mosque (c. 1700), Fonadhoo, Laamu Atoll. **10.** Ihavandhoo Old Friday Mosque (1701), Ihavandhoo, Haa Alif Atoll. **11.** Kelaa Old Friday Mosque (1701), Kelaa, Haa Alif Atoll. **12.** Isdhoo Old Mosque (1701), Isdhoo, Laamu Atoll. **13.** Huraa Old Mosque (c. 1700s), Huraa, Kaafu Atoll. **14.** Nilandhoo Old Friday Mosque (c. 1701), Nilandhoo, Faafu Atoll. **15.** Kudahuvadhoo Old Friday Mosque (c. 1701), Kudahuvadhoo, Dhaalu Atoll. **16.** Bandidhoo Old Mosque (c. 1701), Bandidhoo, Dhaalu Atoll. **17.** Dhevvadhoo Old Friday Mosque (c. 1701), Dhevvadhoo, Gaafu Alif Atoll. **18.** Fenfushi Friday Mosque (1704), Fenfushi, Alif Dhaal Atoll. **19.** Meedhoo Old Friday Mosque (c.1705), Meedhoo, Raa Atoll. **20.** Malé Kalhuvakaru Mosque (1789), Malé. **21.** Malé Eid Mosque (1815), Malé. **22.** Rimbudhoo Old Friday Mosque (date?), Rimbudhoo, Dhaal Atoll. **23.** Maamigili Old Mosque (date?), Maamigili, Alif Dhaal Atoll. Courtesy the author.

Figure 14.6 Fandiyaru Miskiy. Courtesy the author.

oldest and largest cemetery in Maldives. It was built around 1586 by the noble family of Addu Bodu Fandiyaru Thakurufaanu. The mosque is basic in terms of artistic sophistication with no coral carvings but is an important part of the narrative of coral stone mosque design showing family mosques.

Malé Hukuru Miskiy (1658) and its compound, located in Malé, comprise the most important heritage site in the country and continues to serve as one of the most important places of worship (Fig. 14.7). The present mosque was built in 1658 under the patronage of Sultan Ibrahim Iskandhar I (1648–87). It replaced the original mosque built in 1153 under the patronage of the first Muslim sultan of the Maldives. It is the biggest coral stone mosque and first mosque with intricate carvings and lacquered interiors.

Ihavandhoo Old Friday Mosque (1701), located in Ihavandhoo, Haa Alif Atoll, is a small mosque in the north of the Maldives with high-quality coral stonework and intricate interior details (Fig. 14.8). It still serves its community as a centre for prayer. The mosque was completed on 16 December 1701, under the patronage of Sultan Ibrahim Muzhiruddin (1701–05). The old mosque survives in good condition but unfortunately extensions make it difficult to appreciate its original beauty.

Figure 14.7 Malé Hukuru Miskiy. Courtesy the author.

Figure 14.8 Ihavandhoo Old Friday Mosque. Courtesy the author.

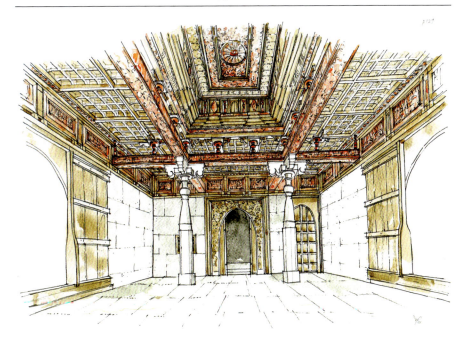

Figure 14.9 Isdhoo Old Mosque. Courtesy the author.

Isdhoo Old Mosque (1701), located on Isdhoo, Laamu Atoll, is the only mosque with an asymmetric floorplan and a special chamber. The mosque is a small coral stone mosque with three entrances (Fig. 14.9). The mosque is historically significant for the special chamber where the ancient royal copper chronicles dating from the twelfth century were kept. The present mosque is likely to have been rebuilt in 1701 under the patronage of Sultan Mohamed of Dhevvadhu (1692–1701) over an older mosque. The coral workmanship of the mosque is simpler and maybe part of the original mosque. It is still used today and has been restored and well maintained with minimal changes.

Fenfushi Friday Mosque (1704), located in Fenfushi, Alif Dhaal Atoll, is part of the best-preserved coral stone mosque compound with a unique coral stone bathing tank, coral stone wells, a sundial and a large cemetery (Fig. 14.10). It is among the best coral stone mosques that have the detailed coral carvings and interior lacquer works. Situated at the center of Fenfushi, it was rebuilt under the patronage of Sultan Mohamed of Dhevvadhu (1692–1701) on the site of an earlier mosque built by Kalhu Kamana, daughter of Ghaazee Hassan Rannabandeyri Kilegefaanu.

Meedhoo Old Friday Mosque (c. 1705), located in Meedhoo, Raa Atoll, is the only surviving coral stone mosque in the north central region of the Maldives and the only one remaining with traditional Indian clay roofing tiles (Fig. 14.11).

Figure 14.10 Fenfushi Friday Mosque. Courtesy the author.

The exact period of construction is unclear, but it was probably built around 1705 over an older mosque. The coral workmanship of the mosque is simpler and may be part of the older mosque. The mosque is well maintained but it has gone through stages of restorations with few changes since the early 1900s.

Malé Eid Mosque (1815), located in Malé, is the last coral stone mosque to be constructed and its coral stone carvings and decoration are the most elegant among all such works (Fig. 14.12). Unfortunately, over time extensions have been added and the mosque compound has been reduced to simply the mosque building and the coral stone well. The old mosque remains in good condition, but the original splendour is no longer apparent because of the extensions and urban congestion around it. The mosque was built in 1815 under the patronage of Sultan Mohamed Muinuddin (1799–1835), at the western end of Malé, to replace an older mosque erected during the reign of Sultan Muzaffar Mohamed Imaduddin (1704–21). Originally built for the Eid prayers, it is no longer the main mosque for Eid, but it still serves as one of the most important mosques in Malé.

Figure 14.11 Meedhoo Old Friday Mosque. Courtesy the author.

Figure 14.12 Malé Eid Mosque. Courtesy the author.

CULTURAL INFLUENCES

The Indian Ocean may not represent a defined civilisation or a single cultural space but due to the multiple exchanges of migration, trade, colonisation and tensions, common characteristics are seen among cultures of its coastal populations. Maldives, located in the centre of the Indian Ocean, represents a community that has a high concentration of mixing of cultures. Its coral stone mosques are typical examples of such a phenomenon and clearly illustrate an eclectic architecture with adaptation of features from the Indian Ocean regions of the South Asia, East Africa, Middle East and Southeast Asia. The architectural features of coral stone mosques were compared with mosques and traditional architecture of the above-mentioned regions to find how they contributed to the coming together of the architecture of the Maldivian mosque.

The comparison reveals the following: Islam was introduced to Maldives as a direct result of the Arab and Persian traders in the Indian Ocean and there is historic evidence of influence of the religious scholars from Yemen, Egypt and Shiraz on the culture of the Maldives. The features of the mosques of the Maldives adopted from Persian and Arabian models include the decorative elements and calligraphy. The calligraphic decorations are similar to the older Jeli Thuluth of the Mamluk period in Egypt and the geometric patterns are influenced from interactions that took place (Fig. 14.13).

Figure 14.13 Thuluth calligraphy from Aslam al-Silahdar Complex, Cairo.
Courtesy the author.

Mosques from East African coastal regions have only a few common characteristics with the mosques of the Maldives even though they use coral stone for construction and have evidence of historical and cultural links. The fact that coral was used in construction was common but coral stone construction in East Africa is different from Maldives; they are comprised mostly of coral rubble set in mortar using masonry techniques while the Maldivian counterpart uses cut blocks shaped to fit and be assembled without using mortar. However, similarities are observed among the decorative iconography and coral carvings. Pillar tombs are not found in Maldives, but carvings and shapes of large grave markers of East Africa are like those in Maldives (Fig. 14.14).

The coastal regions of India had the most to offer to the eclectic architecture of the coral stone mosque. The traditional mosques from Malabar and Coromandel have many features comparable to but not exactly like that of the mosques of the Maldives. The hypostyle prayer hall, verandah-like antechambers, large overhanging tiered roof forms, coffered ceilings and timber decoration are such features. Jami Masjid, first built around 1400 in Calicut and Chembitta Palli, built around 1520s in Cochin respectively are examples of such mosques.[14] Traditional architectural features from Kerala, such as coffered ceilings and woodcarvings also have similarities to the ceilings of the Maldivian mosque, and examples are found in the Sree Padmanabhapuram Palace near Thiruvananthapuram. Common features from the Gujarati region and the Mughal period are also shared among the decorative elements of the mosques of the Maldives. The floral carvings and decorative motifs of this region of India have many similarities to the decorative works found in the mosques of the Maldives. The lacquer work of Kutch and Sankhedar, Gujarat may also have had an influence on that of the Maldives.

Southeast Asian and early Sri Lankan architecture have many features similar to the Maldivian mosque. The raised platform base, rising stairs and exterior decorative stone mouldings of the structures in the monastery complex of the ancient city of Polunnaruwa, Sri Lanka are examples (Fig. 14.15). Maldivians travelled and traded frequently in the port cities of the Bay of Bengal and in the cities of Bangladesh, Myanmar and Thailand. The obvious influence from this region is the lacquer work found in the mosque decoration as well as in the crafts of the Maldives. Lacquer work such as those in the turned lacquered columns and turned pilasters and other lacquer decorations found in the interiors of the coral stone mosques have strong resemblance to the lacquer works of the Myanmar region.

The traditional mosques of the Malacca Straits region have large overhanging and tiered roof forms like those of the mosques of the Maldives. They are also

---

[14] Shokoohy, 2013, pp. 176, 221.

Figure 14.14 Coral stone grave marker from Kilifi, Kenya.
Courtesy the author.

located within mosque compounds consisting of cemeteries. The roof forms and cemeteries of Masjid Kampung Laut, Malaysia, c. 1400s (Fig. 14.16), Masjid Kampung Kling, Malaysia, 1748, and Masjid Agung Demak, Indonesia, c. 1500s are examples that can be compared. There is historic evidence of interactions between the two regions and they share many cultural similarities. But the similarities of roof forms are likely to be responses to the climate rather than a direct architectural influence.

Figure 14.15 Thuparamaya, Polunnaruwa, Sri Lanka. Courtesy the author.

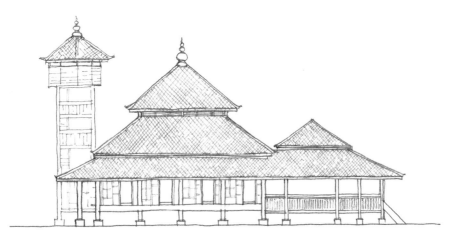

Figure 14.16 Masjid Kampung Laut, Malaysia. Courtesy the author.

CONCLUSION

The attributes that define the Maldivian coral stone mosques are that they are made of shaped Porites coral stone using the coral stone carpentry technique. Coral stone carpentry technique is the technique of shaping, joining, assembling and decorating of Porites corals using carpentry joinery and no mortar. They are built on a decorated raised coral stone platform with coral stone walls, tiered roof form and have coffered ceilings. The ceilings often have an ornamented central recessed area called *laage'* and between the roof structure and walls, there would be beams, posts and timber panels dedicated to calligraphic inscriptions. The mosques also have a symmetric layout with a rectangular prayer hall, a mihrab wall and an entrance with rising steps opposite the mihrab wall. Occasionally they have a mihrab chamber, verandahs and symmetrically placed side entrances. The side verandahs that are attached entrances are called *dhaala*.

The Indian Ocean may not be host to a single culture, but it is an important zone of human civilisation that has shaped countries, cultures and ideologies through its maritime activities. The coral stone mosque is a typical example of such an Indian Ocean cultural phenomenon. Of course, historic and natural influences such as the climate and availability of materials were crucial in the shaping of the mosque, but the mosques clearly illustrate an eclectic architecture with adaptation of features from the Indian Ocean regions of South Asia, East Africa, the Middle East and Southeast Asia.

BIBLIOGRAPHY

Archnet. 'Amir Aslam al-Silahdar Funerary Complex Conservation'. Retrieved 20 July 2012. https://archnet.org/sites/6391/publications/1842.

Bell, H. C. P. 1940. *The Maldives Islands, monograph on the history, archaeology and epigraphy.* Colombo: Ceylon Government Press.

Forbes, A. D. W. 1983. 'The Mosque in the Maldives Islands: A Preliminary Historical Survey', *Archipel*, 26:1, pp. 43–74.

Hornell, J. 1920. *The Origins and Ethnological Significance Of Indian Boat Designs.* Calcutta: Memoirs of the Asiatic Society of Bengal.

Horton, M. 1991. 'Primitive Islam and Architecture in East Africa', *Muqarnas*, vol. 8, pp. 103–16.

Jameel, M. and Y. Ahmad. 2015. *Coral Stone Mosques of the Maldives: A Vanishing Legacy of the Indian Ocean.* California: Gulf Pacific Press.

Jameel, M. M. 2012. *Architectural Typological Study of Coral Stone Mosques of the Maldives.* MSc Thesis, University of Malaya, Malaysia.

Kirkman, J. 1959. 'Mnarani of Kilifi: The Mosques and Tombs', *Ars Orientalis*, vol. 3, pp. 95–112.

McKillop, H., A. Magnoni, R. Warson, S. Ascher, T. Winemiller and B. Tucker. 2004. 'The Coral Foundations of Coastal Maya Architecture: Research Report in Belizean Archaeology'. Proceedings from 2003 Belize Archaeology Symposium, Belize.

Mackintosh-Smith, T. 2002. *The Travels of Ibn Battutah.* London: Picador.

Maloney, C. 1980. *People of the Maldive Islands.* Bombay: Orient Longman.

Mikkelson, P. E. 2000. *Archeological excavation of a monastery in Kashidhoo.* Malé: NCLHR.

Mohamed, N. 2008. *Essays on Early Maldives.* Malé: NCLHR.

Naseer, A. 1997. 'Profile and Status of Coral Reefs In Maldives and Approaches to its Management'. Proceedings from FAO Regional Workshop on the Conservation and Sustainable Management of Coral Reefs.

Pyrard, F. 2010. *The Voyage of Francois Pyrard V1: Of Laval To The East Indies, The Maldives, The Moluccas And Brazil*, A. Gray, trans. Whitefish: Kessinger Publishing LLC.

Shokoohy, M. 2013. *Muslim Architecture of South India (Routledge Studies in South India)*. New York: Routledge.

Silva, R. 1985. *Conservation of the Mogul mosques and the excavations of Maldivian mounds*: UNESCO technical report FMR/CLT/CH/85/119.

Spalding, M., C. Ravilions and E.P. Green. 2001. *World Atlas of Coral Reefs*. California: The University of California Press.

UNEP-GoM. 2009. 'Maldives National Strategy for Sustainable Development', Malé.

UNESCO, W. H. C. 'UNESCO World Heritage Site: Laamu Old Town, Kenya'. Retrieved 10 November 2011. http://whc.unesco.org/en/list/1055.

UNESCO, W. H. C. 'UNESCO World Heritage Site: Old City of Sana'a'. Retrieved 11 April 2011. http://whc.unesco.org/en/list/385.

UNESCO, W. H. C. 'UNESCO World Heritage Site: Ruins of Kilwa Kisiwani and Ruins of Songo Mnara'. Retrieved 10 October 2011. http://whc.unesco.org/en/list/144/.

CHAPTER 15

The Development of Early Islamic Architecture and Decoration in the Malay-Indonesian Archipelago (Nusantara)

BERNARD O'KANE

INTRODUCTION

The moment when Islam is adopted by a new people can be one of the most exciting for Islamic art and architecture. What elements of local culture were adapted to new purposes, and which were borrowed from other Muslim traditions? In the case of Nusantara, where Islam came late and penetrated slowly inwards from the coastal areas, the choices were many, ranging from the decorative exuberance of major cultic buildings of the previously dominant powers in the area, the Javanese Hindu-Buddhist Majapahit empire (1293–early sixteenth century) and its Buddhist and Hindu predecessors, to more soberly constructed vernacular architecture, and to the cultures of Arab, Persian, Indian and Chinese traders, Muslim and non-Muslim, who had been plying their wares through the Malacca Straits for centuries. I will argue that the Nusantara examples' marrying of the grid plan, based primarily on earlier nine-bay examples, to the Chinese frame system, together with the vernacular tiered roofing system, resulted in a style that was one of the most original in the Dar al-Islam.

Unfortunately the lack of authoritative historical sources makes tracing the development of this style difficult, as does another one of its most distinctive features, its dearth of epigraphy. Another drawback to historical analysis is the building material, wood, which in this humid tropical clime rarely lasted more than a few centuries before needing to be replaced.

Historical Background

Early contacts between Arab and Persian traders and Southeast Asia have long been recognised. Imports of Southeast Asia cloves and camphor were readily available to the Romans,[1] suggesting that these contacts also preceded the rise of Islam.[2] Muslim traders had established settlements, in Guangzhou and other sites along the coast of China by the eighth century under the Tang dynasty.[3] The shipwreck of a west Indian Ocean vessel laden with a cargo of treasures from Tang China at Beliting, a small island east of Palembang in Indonesia, testifies to the richness of this trade.[4] However, it was not until much later, in the thirteenth to fifteenth centuries, that Muslim settlements appeared in Sumatra, Java and on the Malay peninsula, notably in Melaka; the area of Aceh in Sumatra had possibly the earliest local Muslim community.

Previous scholarship has tended to emphasise the connections with Arab, Persian and Indian traders, but earlier Lombard and Salamon, and more recently Alexander Wain and John Chaffee, have highlighted the importance of relations with the geographically closer settlements of Chinese Muslims.[5] Wain has shown how the first important Muslim settlement in Java was probably in fourteenth-century Gresik, from where it spread to Demak, founded by a Chinese Muslim merchant named Cu Cu or Jinbun. Together with his son they expanded Muslim power in the surrounding areas on the north coast and even into Sumatra in the fifteenth and early sixteenth centuries.[6]

Demak and Early Mosques

It seems reasonable to begin with the Masjid Agung Demak (Figs 15.1 to 15.3), which has been commonly acknowledged as the earliest surviving mosque on Java whose original date and form can be elucidated from prior documentation, even if it was substantially altered in the twentieth century. Other mosques whose ground plan may have been similar to Demak in their original form, and which also may be late fifteenth or sixteenth century, include the Masjid Agungs of Sendang Duwar[7] and Banten[8] (Figs 15.4 and 15.5) and the Merah

---

[1] Laffan, 2009, pp. 18–19. See also Di Meglio, 1970.
[2] Kersten, 2017, p. 9.
[3] Hartmann and Bosworth, 'al-Ṣīn.'
[4] Krahl, Guy, Wilson and Raby, 2011.
[5] Lombard and Salmon, 1993; Wain, 2017a; Chaffee, 2019.
[6] Wain, 2015. I am grateful to Dr Wain for his numerous perceptive comments on an earlier draft of this paper.
[7] Tjandrasasmita, 1975a, pp. 7–14.
[8] Wahby, 2007, pp. 86–9; Wain, 2015, pp. 401–4 (I am most grateful to Dr Wain for sharing with me his Chapter 8: 'The Origins of the Javanese Mosque').

Figure 15.1 Exterior, Masjid Agung, Demak (the *pendopo* at the front is a
nineteenth-century addition). Photography: Bernard O'Kane.

Panjunan Mosque in Cirebon,[9] together with many later examples such as the
Masjid Agungs of Surakarta and Yogyakarta.[10] The Demak mosque displays
many features that are considered characteristic of the early Javanese mosque: an
enclosure containing a building of square plan with brick walls, and four monumental columns supporting a multi-tiered roof made of shingles (Fig. 15.6 and
also see Figs 15.1 and 15.2). Like most of the mosques associated with the *wali
songo*, nine saints who were active in proselytising in the period c. 1425–1550,
this has an adjacent cemetery with the tomb of the founder that is a centre of
pilgrimage. Instead of a minaret, an exclusively Nusantaran substitute, the drum

---

[9] Brakel and Massarik, 1982, pp. 119–34; Wahby, 2007, pp. 61–3; Wain, 2015, pp. 396–401.
[10] Tajudeen, 2017a, p. 1001. Tajudeen maintains that the assumption that Demak formed the prototype
of the *tajug* mosque with four principal columns supporting the top tier of a three-tiered pyramidal roof
is problematic. However, the examples he gives of other types, principally the Miningkabau examples,
datable to the late sixteenth or early seventeenth century, are significantly later than Demak and its
early copies. It is indeed quite possible, as he notes (p. 1002), that the form appeared in other areas
of Nusantara, but the supposed dating (1380) of the example cited, the Sheikh Karimul Makhdum
mosque in Simunul in the Philippines, is not backed up by any authoritative source. Ironically, the
source he quotes (Lico, 2008, p. 74), classifies it as a 'pagoda-style' mosque (although admittedly Lico
[loc. cit.] equates the former typical form of the Philippines mosque with a multi-tiered bamboo or
wooden structure as being 'reminiscent of a Chinese pagoda or Javanese temple').

Figure 15.2 Interior, Masjid Agung, Demak. Photography: Bernard O'Kane.

(*bedug*) was employed for the call to prayer.[11] Within the mihrab of the mosque is a turtle-shaped outline that has been claimed to be a chronogram equivalent to 1479 CE; but this interpretation is doubtful.[12] A terminus post quem, and probably an indicative date, is provided by the fifteenth-century Vietnamese tiles that are incorporated within the mihrab and on the façade of the mosque on the side opposite the qibla.[13] Tomes Pires mentions that the ruler of Demak, Raden Patah, attended the inauguration of a new mosque in 1506, making it a plausible candidate for its date of foundation.[14]

---

[11] The extraordinarily ugly metal minaret of the Demak mosque dates from 1924. The earliest surviving masonry minaret in Java, at Kudus near Demak, dates from the middle of the sixteenth century, but this is a unique occurrence in early Javanese architecture, leading to the suggestion that the minaret is a reused signal-drum tower from a pre-Islamic temple: Guy, 1989, p. 42. This suggestion had earlier caused consternation in the central Javanese Muslim community, as reported in Kusno, 2003, pp. 58–9.

[12] Behrend, 1984; Wain, 2015, pp. 386–7.

[13] Guy, 1989, pp. 27–46; Takahashi, 2008. Animal motifs are frequently present in the Demak examples. Some fragments excavated at Trowulan, the Majapahit capital, have geometric hexagonal designs reminiscent of tilework further west in the Punjab. For an overview of the latter see O'Kane, 2019, pp. 26–7, 35–6.

[14] Wahby, 2007, p. 63; Wain, 2015, p. 387.

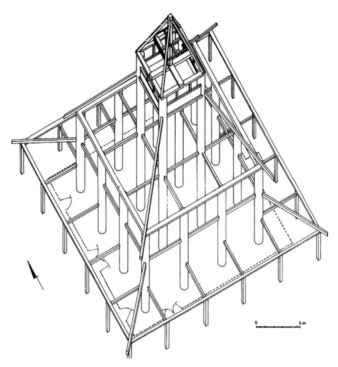

Figure 15.3 Reconstruction of original form, Masjid Agung, Demak (from Dumarçay, 1985). Courtesy École Française d'Extrême-Orient.

The ground plan, like that of many later Javanese mosques, has four massive central columns, surrounded in turn by a column on each side, making a central nine-bay plan, which in turn, in its probable original state (see Fig. 15.3), was enlarged by columns on each side, making a plan of twenty-five equal bays. The walls were arbitrarily fixed between in the middle of the outer circumference of bays.[15] This nine-bay plan is one of the most frequent forms of mosques found in the Islamic world (its twenty-five-bay enlargement was also common).[16] It was also a typical component of Hindu temples,[17] and this may be an additional factor in its predominance in mosques of the Indian littoral, from Gujarat[18] to

---

[15] Dr Alexander Wain (personal communication) has pointed out that the overhang of the roof could have been an advantage with the area's regular heavy precipitation.
[16] O'Kane, 2006.
[17] Ibid., 228; fig. 34. For the possibly similar plan of a structure depicted in the reliefs of Borobudur, see Njoto, 2014, Fig. 21.
[18] Junagadh, al-Iraji mosque (685/1286–7): O'Kane, 2006, fig. 35.

Figure 15.4 Exterior, Masjid Agung, Banten. Photography: Bernard O'Kane.

Tamil Nadu[19] and Bengal,[20] all likely stops on the trade routes from the west to Nusantara. Even beyond these examples, on the trading posts on the west side of the Indian Ocean, many coastal towns also have mosques with the same plan.[21] While the typical three-tiered elevation of the Javanese mosques is radically different from earlier mosques known from any other part of the Islamic world, the ubiquity of the nine-bay plan and variations on it in earlier mosques may well have inclined the builders to adopt it as a standard component of the Islamic architectural heritage.

Most recently, Hélène Njoto has called attention to pre-Islamic buildings in Java that have concentric patterns of columns or piers that may have

---

[19] Ibid., 231; fig 38. A link between the Demak mosque plan and those of south India was previously mooted in Shokoohy, 2003, pp. 238–9.
[20] Ibid., p. 233.
[21] Ibid., pp. 217–19.

Figure 15.5 Interior, Masjid Agung, Banten. Photography: Bernard O'Kane.

supported multiple tiered roofs.[22] The question of tiered roofs of these buildings is somewhat speculative, relying heavily on the reconstructions by Dumarçay of the reliefs from Borobudur.[23] However, although some scholars have tried to link the multi-tiered roofs of the Indonesian mosques with those of the Malabar coast,[24] it is fair to say that the purely non-functional upper tiers of the Javanese examples are quite different in character form the Indian ones, where the upper stories are floored and may have been used as a madrasa or for storage.[25]

---

[22] Njoto, 2014; idem, 2015, pp. 11–27.

[23] Njoto, 2014, figs. 19–24.

[24] De Graaf, 1963, pp. 4–5.

[25] As pointed out forcefully by Wain, 2015, pp. 419–22. The employment of multi-tiers may well reflect the continuing importance even in Islamic times the concept of the holy mountain, Mount Meru: see Wessing, 1991 and idem, 1994. Two depictions of now-vanished mosques from European prints have suggested to some the possibility of Chinese influence. The first is the Aceh great mosque as shown in Peter Mundy's drawing from the 1630s: Mundy, 1919, vol. 3, part 1, p. 122 (fig. 4, top right), whose four-tiered profile has seemingly upturned roofs. These could be related to either Minangkabau or Chinese parallels, but another European engraving of the building c. 1784 (Nationaal Archief, The Hague, inv. nr. VELH0619.22, Atlas Van Stolk, Rotterdam, inv. nr. top1076: https://commons.wikimedia.org/wiki/File:AMH-6875-KB_View_of_Achin.jpg) (fig. 4, bottom right) shows it as having

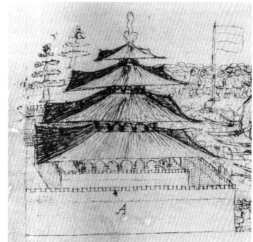

Figure 15.6 Details showing Jepara mosque (top left, from Schouten, 1776),
Aceh mosque (top right, from Mundy, 1919) and Aceh mosque (bottom, from
Atlas Van Stolk, 1784).

But none of the pre-Islamic buildings analysed by Njoto has a central nine-
bay plan surrounded by a bay on all sides, as in the case of Demak and others.
The Masjid Agung of Cirebon, although exceptional among the early Javanese

straight-sloping roofs. The second is the great mosque of Jepara, as drawn by Schouten, 1776, book 1,
p. 38 (fig. 4, left). This looks distinctly pagoda-like, with, implausibly even for pagodas, figures on the
exterior of the upper two-storey tiers. It has been pointed out, with regard to Schouten's drawings, that
'A publisher often gave the engravers who made the printing plates for the book illustrations a free
hand, and they usually had no idea what they were depicting. The famous life-size Mahamuni Buddha
statue Schouten saw in Arakan, for instance, was clumsily depicted with a Western head and a
large beard:' Brommer and Djajasoebrata, 2017, p. 305. Presumably Schouten's drawing of a five-tiered roof,
perhaps originally like that of the Banten great mosque, was similarly transformed.

mosques in having a rectangular plan, also has evenly spaced columns forming regular bays.[26]

The very considerable difference in scale between pre-Islamic wooden frame buildings and the Demak mosque (the latter a square of nearly 25 metres a side[27]), as has been highlighted by Imran bin Tajudeen,[28] is so significant as to make it highly doubtful whether the mosque could have been derived from those earlier buildings.[29] The extensive use of frame buildings, as opposed to those using load-bearing walls, was by this time long-standing practice in Chinese architecture.[30] There, any walls of wood or masonry that surround the building, as in the early Javanese mosques (including Cirebon), are merely screens. The four main central columns (*saka guru*) of the Demak mosque are 16.3 metres tall,[31] vastly in excess of those of any earlier vernacular or cultic buildings from the area. Sadly the insertion of the flat roof (see Fig. 15.2) in the twentieth century has now disguised the massiveness of these piers; their soaring loftiness can be better appreciated in the open ceiling of the Banten mosque (see Fig. 15.5). One explanation that has been given for the unprecedented size of these central piers is the involvement of Chinese shipbuilding techniques. The source that mentions this is the controversial *Chinese Muslims in Java in the 15th and 16th Centuries: The Malay Annals of Semarang and Cirebon*.[32] This, otherwise known as the two *Kronik Tionghua* of Semarang and Cirebon, has long been a source of controversy, but has recently been shown by Alexander Wain to be a fabrication.[33] To mention it at all in this connection may therefore be seen as invidious, but Wain also suggests that the *Annals* may be a hybridisation of earlier indigenous texts.[34] What independent evidence is there to support the possibility that Chinese shipbuilding techniques were used? The first is the unprecedented height of the *saka guru*, unknown in previous Indonesian

---

[26] Wain, 2015, diagram 2.

[27] As noted in Njoto, 2015, pp. 19 and 23, some of the cock-fighting pavilions (*wantilan*) of Bali reach nearly those dimensions and have a plan very similar to Demak, but there is no evidence for any early dating of these, and it may be best to regard them (despite the linkage suggested by earlier scholars) as a later parallel development.

[28] Tajudeen, 2017a, pp. 1001–2.

[29] This has been a common proposal in earlier studies, such as that of Budi, 2004, p. 194, who highlights the connections with earlier communal halls of possibly square plan with multi-tiered roofs that are seen in the stone-carved reliefs of pre-Islamic Javanese temples. However, the discrepancy in scale called for different building techniques.

[30] Boyd, 1962, p. 34; Pirazzoli-T'Serstevens (1972, p. 88) notes that 'the structural framework with its timber beams and pillars in perhaps the most original feature of Chinese architecture.' Another source that argues for the role of Chinese carpentry in the development of mosques in Java is Hartono, 2007.

[31] Wahby, 2007, p. 59. The figure given in O'Neill, 1994, p. 234, of 22 metres is belied by the sectional drawing of the mosque on the same page, whose scale shows that this figure equals the height to the top of the roof finial.

[32] De Graaf and Pigeaud, 1984, p. 28.

[33] Wain, 2017b.

[34] Ibid., p. 194.

architecture. Even in the twelfth century the mainmast and foremast of Chinese ships could be 80–100 feet (25–30 metres) tall.[35] The second is the way in which these heights were frequently obtained on Chinese ships, as in the case of the *saka guru* of Demak and other Javanese mosques, by binding separate pieces of wood together with iron bands.[36] Another point to emphasise again is the abundance of Chinese maritime trading in the area: by the second half of the fifteenth century even private Chinese merchants has built fleets of ocean-going ships.[37] The use of brick for the walls and shingles for the roof are also likely to be features derived from Chinese architecture.[38] And finally, the probability that the foundation of Demak and its subsequent growth into a Muslim power was made by a Chinese merchant and his son[39] increases the likelihood of Chinese cultural influence.

THE DECORATION OF EARLY ISLAMIC JAVANESE MONUMENTS

One of the *wali sanga*, Sunan Kalijaga, reputedly employed the Javanese shadow puppet theatre (*wayang*) as an aid to spreading Islam.[40] It is therefore not surprising, perhaps, that the syncretism that is seen in mosque plans is equally evident in decoration. This syncretism has often been remarked upon,[41] but it is worth revisiting some of the most important early examples to see the extent to which Chinese motifs have an almost equal footing with pre-Islamic Javanese ones.

The twin sets of wooden doors of the Demak mosque are a good place to start (Fig. 15.7). One (Fig. 15.7, left) has makara forms in the centre with what appears to be a winged crown above and a vase-like form on a stand below amidst vegetation, all of pre-Islamic Javanese inspiration.[42] The other (Fig. 15.7, right) set of doors has on each leaf a spiralling scroll with Chinese lotuses. The only other original decoration associated with the mosque is the Vietnamese tiles noted above, which for the most part display motifs common to contemporary Vietnamese ceramics, principally of Yuan and early Ming derivation, including animal motifs such as birds and the *qilin*.[43] At the Masjid Agung of Cirebon original decoration, in carved brick, is confined to the outer wall opposite the qibla and to the mihrab. Interlacing motifs are found

---

[35] Needham, 1971, p. 602.
[36] Ibid., p. 414. Iron bands were also used for reinforcing the *saka guru*: Dumarçay, 1985, pl. 4.
[37] Needham, 1971, pp. 526–7, note f.
[38] As at the fourteenth-century Great Mosque of Xian: Steinhardt, 2015, pp. 120–30.
[39] See n. 8 above.
[40] Al-Attas, 1971.
[41] See, for instance, Lee-Niinioja, 2010. On a more general cultural level see Brakel, 1984 and idem, 2004, and more recently Weiler, 2012.
[42] It has been interpreted as being related to Champa ceramics, but no illustrative parallels have been shown: Bahuruddin, 1998. Another suggestion relates them to stupas: O'Neil, 1998, p. 94.
[43] Guy, 1989, pls 8, 13; Takashi, 2008, figs 1-05, 1-07; 1-19–1-20, 1-26–1-27.

Figure 15.7 Doors, Masjid Agung, Demak. Photography: Bernard O'Kane.

on both; they have been interpreted as being related to traditional Islamic geometric patterns[44] and to the Buddhist Chinese endless knot. The interlacing of the frame with the interior pattern, and the scalloping of the frame in the medallions on either the side of the mihrab[45] relate them more to Chinese originals, as do the quatrefoils containing Chinese lotuses also found on the outer wall. However, balancing these are the Surya Majapahit found at the apex of the mihrab,[46] and the Indian lotuses found both on its engaged columns and suspended from the mihrab vault.

The complex at Mantingan near Jepara contains a mosque and the nearby tomb of Ratu Kali Nyamat, originally built in 1559.[47] These were completely rebuilt in 1927, but still preserve a remarkable variety of original carved stone panels.[48] They are now mostly on the outer wall of the mosque opposite the qibla, with some on the mihrab and on the outside of the qibla wall, and on the exterior of the tomb. Several of the panels display animals: a monkey with a crab,

---

[44] Wahby, 2007, p. 59; Wain, 2015, pp. 393, 396.
[45] Wahby, 2007, figure 2. 32c.
[46] One is also found at the same location at Majid Agung Demak, although its originality there is less certain, given the rebuilding of that portion of the mosque.
[47] Wahby, 2007, p. 105.
[48] These deserve a comprehensive study.

and an elephant, all fascinatingly portrayed through the power of suggestion by outlining in vegetal scrolls.[49] Two of these are in the collection of the Nationaal Museum van Wereldculturen, Amsterdam,[50] but another one of the monkey and the crab, sadly in poor condition, is still on the walls of the mosque (Fig. 15.8, top). Yet another panel, unremarked until now,[51] also contains a figure disguised by whorls; it has the body of a cock with outstretched wings and a dragon-like head on a long neck, presumably a variant of the *garuda* (Fig. 15.8, bottom). Those panels, like many others, are in the shape of horizontally ori-entated cartouches. Two cartouches are vertically orientated. Other shapes, slightly smaller, include medallions, and still smaller squares, frequently with further raised geometrical shapes such as stepped crosses (Fig. 15.9), recalling some of the Vietnamese tiles found at Demak.[52] Most common are yet smaller panels of abstracted wing design (Fig. 15.10). Within the mihrab of this mosque four of these winged shapes are used to frame a medallion; this is more likely their original placement than the isolated rows in which they are mounted at the moment. Closely related forms also frame the square in Figure 15.9.[53] A fascinating variety of motifs appear on these panels. The medallions can include vegetal designs of pure pre-Islamic Javanese scrollwork (Fig. 15.11, top left), chinoiserie blossoms (Fig. 15.11, top right), Chinese endless knot patterns (Fig. 15.11, bottom left), and interlaces with classical Islamic geometric star patterns (Fig. 15.11, bottom right).[54] Two cartouches[55] show a lower wall with a typical Hindu split gate (*candi bentar*) leading to a pyramidal-roofed pavilion. The pavilion, raised on stilts on a platform, is supported by four corner posts and one central one. The scene is set within a mountainous landscape (Fig. 15.12, top right).[56] Other panels display Chinese lotuses and curled-over leaves on long stalks (Fig. 15.13).[57] The smaller square panels are equally varied; one exceptional panel of four levels has Chinese lotuses at the corner of the lowest

---

[49] For a similarly disguised stone-carved elephant on an undated tombstone from the Makam Gunung Jati at Cirebon see Miksic, 2005, p. 124.

[50] The best reproductions are in Njoto, 2018, pp. 2–3.

[51] Possibly because it is mounted upside down in its current position on the outer wall of the mosque.

[52] Takahashi, 2008, figs. 1-18–1-25.

[53] Another close parallel can be seen at the rear of the winged gate at Sendang Duwur, where a row of rosettes in lozenges is flanked by roughly triangular forms similar to the winged panels.

[54] Some blurring between the endless knot and Islamic geometric patterns may be apparent in the attribution in Guy, 1989, fig. 20, to Islamic precedents of what I see more as a Chinese endless knot.

[55] I mentioned above how two panels of the monkey and the crab survive. When the panels were reinstalled in the rebuilt mosque façade some care was taken to align symmetrically to either side of the central entrance of the prayer hall panels with similar designs, of which there are many.

[56] A stylistically very similar carved sixteenth-century (?) wooden panel from the collection of the Kraton Kasepuhan Museum, Cirebon has been classified as exhibiting the Chinese derived *megamend-ung* and *wasadan* (cloud and rocks) pattern: Jessup, 1990, p. 122, fig. 87. The panel is also reproduced (poorly) in Miksic, 2005, p. 137, but is discussed thoroughly by James Bennett in the catalogue entry: ibid., p. 280.

[57] Guy, 1989, p. 36, has also commented on the Yuan influences on these panels.

Figure 15.8 Carved stone panels with figures, Mantingan Mosque.
Photography: Bernard O'Kane.

Figure 15.9 Carved stone panel with stepped design, Mantingan Mosque.
Photography: Bernard O'Kane.

tier and a variant of the surya Majapahit at the centre (Fig. 15.14), similar to that of Figure 15.9.

As Hélène Njoto has suggested, the disguised figural panels can be seen as continuing the Javanese Hindu-Buddhist tradition of figural abstraction.[58] However, it is harder to agree with her suggestion that these patterns 'clearly address a ban on figuration', given the quite explicit use of it in the Vietnamese wall tiles at Demak and at Sendang Duwur and Sunan Drajit examined below. It is also as well to remember that the flouting of the ban on figuration, even in

---

[58] Ibid. Tjandrasasmita, 1975b, pl. 3 lower, shows a similar scalloped cartouche, this time carved in wood, with the figure of a lion amidst foliage, from the Shrine of Sunan Gunung Jati at Cirebon, dated by him to the mid-seventeenth century.

Figure 15.10 Carved stone panels with winged design, Mantingan Mosque.
Photography: Bernard O'Kane.

a religious context, was a regular feature of architecture in many earlier Islamic societies,[59] as in Saljuq Anatolia,[60] throughout the centuries in Iran,[61] and more importantly, closer to hand, in contemporary Chinese mosque architecture.[62]

---

[59] Not to mention, of course, figural imagery in book painting, ceramics and metalwork. For the implications of this in an Islamic context see Ahmed, 2016, pp. 46–57, 121–2.

[60] Perhaps the most cogent discussion of this is in Whelan, 2006, Chapter 4, 'The Search for Sovereign Iconography'.

[61] See, for instance, Pope, 1946; Hillenbrand, 1978; Watson, 1985, pp. 153–6.

[62] See Chen, 2015, pp. 199–219.

Figure 15.11 Carved stone medallions, Mantingan Mosque and tomb.
Photography: Bernard O'Kane.

The shrines at other important early centres of the Pasisir, Ratu Kali Nyamat at
Mantingan (1559), Sendang Duwar (1585), Sunan Jati at Cirebon (late sixteenth
century) and Sunan Drajat at Paciran (early seventeenth century) also have a
considerable amount of original decoration of both carved stone and wood.

The mosque at Sendang Duwur mosque has been completely rebuilt, but
much of the original decoration leading to and at the mausoleum of the *wali*,
Sunan Sendang, remains.[63] The mosque and mausoleum are situated on an elevation, and the pre-Islamic Javanese conception of mountain peaks as sources
of sacred power is echoed here, both in the location and in the sculpture. The
mausoleum is reached by a path skirting the mosque on its north and west sides,
first leading through several split gates, some with figural carvings of peacocks

---

[63] This is one of the few early Islamic buildings to have been the subject of a monograph: Tjandrasasmita,
1975a.

Figure 15.12 Wooden panel, Tomb of Sunan Sendang (left), carved stone panel Mantingan Mosque; (top right), wooden panel on exterior screen, Shrine of Sunan Drajat, Paciran, (bottom right).
Photography: Bernard O'Kane.

and lions, to a masterpiece of exuberant carving,[64] a winged gate (Fig. 15.15), asymmetrical owing to its positioning on the hillside. Its front displays crowned serpents (*nagas*) at the base of the staircase,[65] dragon[66] heads emerging from long necks carved on the jambs, crocodile-like heads at the extremities of the

---

[64] A view not unanimously shared; it has been described by Miksic, 2005, p. 136, as 'decorated to the point of grotesqueness'.
[65] Illustrated in Njoto, 2018, fig. 4.
[66] Described by Tjandrasasmita, 1975a, p. 28, as deer heads, although the long necks and scaly rendering of the ears beside the short horns rather suggest dragons to me.

Figure 15.13 Carved stone panel with chinoiserie designs, Mantingan Mosque.
Photography: Bernard O'Kane.

door frame, and a *makara* at the top of the frame.[67] A mountainous landscape topped by Chinese cloud scrolls like those on the Mantingan panels rises above this. This winged gateway is elongated at the back in the form of a tunnel in order to alert the pilgrim of the holiness of the nearby mausoleum. There are two interesting parallels with this form. One is the normal shape of the mihrab in early Javanese mosques, also an unusually deep recess, rectangular or ending with a semi-circle, and often flanked with winged elements.[68] The concept of the mihrab as gateway is familiar from the tenth-century extension to the Great Mosque of Cordoba; in Java the mihrab surround emphasises the concept of the portal,[69] while its extension as a the corridor adumbrates the concept of a spiritual passage. The presence of Chinese cloud scrolls on the Sendang Duwur portal relates it to another concept (seen also in a secular context, such as the ruler's palace at Cirebon[70]), that of the ascetic's mountain retreat, a particularly apposite parallel for the *wali*'s hillside mausoleum.[71]

---

[67] The lower parts of the head are now obscured by later repairs.
[68] Guillot, 1985, pp. 14–15. Alexander Wain has also pointed to me the resemblance to the tunnel-like entrance to the Merah Panjunan mosque at Cirebon.
[69] See Grabar, 1988 and Subarna, 1988.
[70] Miksic, 2005, p. 126.
[71] Ibid., loc. cit.

Figure 15.14 Carved stone panel, Mantingan tomb.
Photography: Bernard O'Kane.

The mausoleum is datable to 1585, possibly a little later than the mosque.[72] Although small, it has a highly decorated façade. The carved stone base is interrupted by four steps that lead to the level of the tomb; the projecting balustrade flanking it was originally topped by wooden statues of lions.[73] The carved hexagonal cartouches to the left of the staircase (Fig. 15.16) have a central panel with chinoiserie floral pattern on stems, resembling the Mantingan stone panels; they are flanked by landscapes that also resemble those of Mantingan, but with the inclusion of winged elements. The tomb above the

[72] Tjandrasasmita, 1975a, p. 59. The mosque is dated by a chronogram to 1561: ibid., p. 57.
[73] Now in the Jakarta Musuem: Ibid., p. 15, ill. on p. 32; Miksic, 2005, p. 135.

Figure 15.15 Winged gateway, Tomb of Sunan Sendang, Sendang Duwar complex. Photography: Bernard O'Kane.

Figure 15.16 Detail of base of Tomb of Sunan Sendang, Sendang Duwar complex. Photography: Bernard O'Kane.

Figure 15.17 Details of interior screen carving, Tomb of Sunan Drajat, Paciran. Photography: Bernard O'Kane.

stone base has a façade of carved wooden panels, five to the left of the door and one to the right. The door itself is in two leaves. The carving on these (see Fig. 15.12, left) reflects the dichotomy below; both landscapes and scrollwork of Javanese Hindu-Buddhist inspiration, and chinoiserie blossoms and leaves on long stalks.

Even closer to the Mantingan carvings are those in wood of the shrine of Sunan Drajat (1609–22)[74] near Paciran. The mausoleum has an inner and outer façade, the carving on both of which so closely resemble each other that we can be sure of their contemporaneity. Like the Sendang Duwur tomb, the inner façade of Sunan Drajat has an asymmetrical entrance, with the two-leaved doorway positioned to the right of the façade, flanked by four panels on its left and one to the right (Fig. 15.17). Also like Sendang Duwur, lions guard the

74 Wahby, 2007, p. 67.

Figure 15.18 Detail of exterior wooden screen, Tomb of Sunan Drajat,
Paciran. Photography: Bernard O'Kane.

entrance, stone on the inner façade and wooden on the exterior.[75] The exterior
screen has a two-leafed doorway in the middle, flanked by six panels in two tiers
on each side (Fig. 15.18). The lower tier is divided into four groups of three,
each having a central panel showing landscapes with mountains and winged elements (see Fig. 15.12, bottom right) (also present on the doors), and on either
side panels with chinoiserie blossoms on tall stalks (Fig. 15.19).[76] The latter
emerge from the water (indicated by the Chinse convention of overlapping fan
shapes),[77] and on one[78] panel, hiding in plain sight, inconspicuous but, unlike
the Mantingan panels, undisguised, are two small birds. One is top centre, the
other, with its neck bent backwards, one third from the top left – more evidence
for the acceptance of figuration in a religious context.

---

[75] Only one, on the right, now remains on the exterior. Lions were also a common decorative element in
     Chinese architecture, and were also found in Islamic monuments there, such as at the tomb of Baha
     al-Din in Yangzhou, originally founded in 1275: Chen, 2015, pp. 79–81, 216–17, figs. 231, 233.
[76] The same combination is present on the interior panels, with those to the left of the door alternating
     chinoiserie with landscapes, there without the winged elements.
[77] Badly damaged except at the left in Fig. 19, but more clearly visible in other panels.
[78] Unfortunately my photographic coverage is not sufficiently detailed to ascertain whether they were
     present anywhere else; but three of the other similar panels do not contain animals.

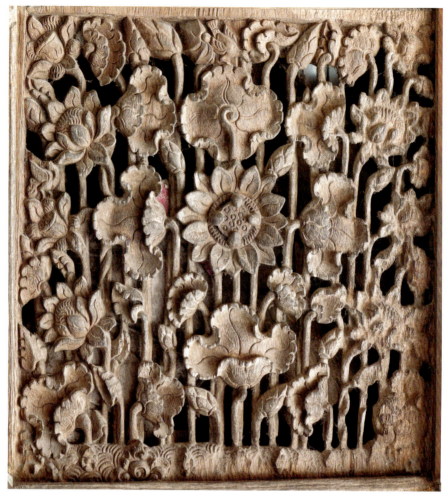

Figure 15.19 Panel of exterior wooden screen, Tomb of Sunan Drajat, Paciran.
Photography: Bernard O'Kane.

CONCLUSION

The predominance of the square plan with four main columns continued in other parts of the Nusantara, such as Malaysia. What is supposedly the earliest mosque in Malaysia, the Masjid Kampung Laut, is similar to Demak and other major Javanese early mosques in having four pillars supporting a three-tiered roof.[79] It is smaller than the examples in Java, perhaps owing to its substructure

---

[79] For the best documentation see now Aziz, 2016, pp. 1–8.

of stilts, which could support less weight.[80] However, it has wooden rather than brick walls, and it has been pointed out that such a timber structure is unlikely to be older than a few centuries.[81] In the eighteenth and nineteenth centuries, as exemplified by a cluster of mosques at Melaka, to the tiered roof was added an elaborate finial, coloured tiles and an upward sweep to the roofs, all indicative of borrowings from Chinese prototypes.[82] This is unsurprising, given the large Chinese presence within the Melakan population.[83]

The syncretistic nature of mosque architecture and decoration in Nusantara has often been remarked on. I have tried to emphasise this, while tilting the balance towards the Indian littoral and the Islamic world further west in general in terms of the origin of the ground plan of many of the important early mosques, and towards China in the mechanics of the construction of the massive central piers of these mosques and their surrounding frame structure, and in the decoration of many early shrines as well as mosques. However, it would be judicious, as has been recently remarked by Imran bin Tajudeen, not to see these overlaps in the reductionist terms of indigenous versus foreign.[84] Continuing up to the present day, when it has been argued that Chinese Muslim identities in Indonesia incorporate various transnational connections, translocal imaginings and local negotiations,[85] pre-modern Islamic architecture in the Nusantara reflects equally complex cross-cultural interactions.

In Nusantara, the process whereby Muslims became the majority took longer than in most other parts of the world where Islam is the dominant religion. This is reflected in the fusions evinced in so much of its Islamic architecture and decoration. But, as usual, the architects and artists involved transcended their eclectic sources to produce works of great originality and power.

BIBLIOGRAPHY

Ahmed, Shihab. 2016. *What is Islam? The Importance of Being Islamic*. Princeton: Princeton University Press.

Al-Attas, S. M. N. 1971. 'Indonesia. History, the Islamic Period,' in *Encyclopaedia of Islam, 2nd edition*, Leiden: Brill. Consulted online on 20 August 2020 http://dx.doi. org.libproxy.aucegypt.edu:2048/10.1163/1573-3912_islam_COM_0374.

Aziz, Azim A. 2016. *Masjid – Selected Mosques and Musollas in Malaysia*. Kuala Lumpur: ATSA Architects.

---

[80] Takahashi, 2016, p. 70.

[81] Bruce, 1996, p. 78. For some other early examples see also Rasdi, 2007.

[82] Best studied in the definitive publication of these buildings: Tajudeen, 2017b. But he notes that their minaret forms, most often previously associated with Chinese pagodas, resemble more those of the Tamil Nadu community in southeast India.

[83] Bruce, 1996, p. 79.

[84] Tajudeen, 2017b.

[85] Weng, 2014 and Wubin, 2011.

Bahuruddin, M. Andy. 1998. 'Masjid Kuno Demak Jawa Tengah,' in Rudy Harisayah Alam (ed), *Sejarah Masjid-Masjid Kuno di Indonesia*. Jakarta: Badan Litbang Agama Departemen Agama, pp. 68–70.

Behrend, Timothy E. 1984. 'Kraton, Taman, Mesjid: A Brief Survey and Bibliographic Review of Islamic Antiquities in Java,' *Indonesia Circle. School of Oriental and African Studies. Newsletter*, 12:35, pp. 29–55 (https://www.academia.edu/34966485/Kraton_taman_mesjid_A_brief_survey_and_bibliographic_review_of_Islamic_antiquities_in_Java).

Brakel, L. F. 2004. 'Islam and Local Traditions: Syncretic Ideas and Practices', *Indonesia and the Malay World* 32, No. 92, pp. 5–20.

Brakel, L. F. 1984. 'Der Islam und lokale Traditionen – synkretistische Ideen und Praktiken. Indonesien', in W. Ende and U. Steinbach (eds), *Der Islam in der Gegenwart. Entwicklung und Ausbreitung, Staat, Politik und Recht, Kultur und Religion*. Munich: Verlag C. H. Beck, pp. 570–82.

Brakel, L. F. and H. Massarik. 1982. 'A Note on the Panjunan Mosque in Cirebon', *Archipel* 23, pp. 119–34.

Brommer, BeaMarijke, Barend-van Haeften and Alit Djajasoebrata. 2017. 'Wouter Schouten's Drawings of Batavia: 1658–64', *The Rijksmuseum Bulletin* 65, pp. 300–10.

Boyd, Andrew. 1962. *Chinese Architecture and Town Planning 1500 B.C–A.D 1911*. London: Alec Tiranti.

Bruce, Allan. 1996. 'Notes on Early Mosques of the Malaysian Peninsula', *Journal of the Malaysian Branch of the Royal Asiatic Society* 69/2, pp. 71–81.

Budi, Bambang Setia. 2004. 'A Study on the History and Development of the Javanese Mosque: Part 1: A Review of Theories on the Origin of the Javanese Mosque', *Journal of Asian Architecture and Building Engineering* 3, pp. 189–95.

Chaffee, John W. 2019. *New Approaches to Asian History: The Muslim Merchants of Premodern China: The History of a Maritime Asian Trade Diaspora, 750–1400*. Cambridge: Cambridge University Press.

Chen, Qing. 2015. *Mosques of the Maritime Muslim Community of China: A Study of Mosques in the South and Southeast Coastal Regions of China*, PhD thesis, SOAS University of London. https://eprints.soas.ac.uk/29805/1/4212_Chen.pdf.

De Graaf, H. J. 1963. 'The Origin of the Javanese Mosque', *Journal of Southeast Asian History* 4, pp. 1–5.

De Graaf, H. J. and Th. G. Th. Pigeaud; translated and commentary, M.C. Ricklefs (ed.). 1984. *Chinese Muslims in Java in the 15th and 16th Centuries: The Malay Annals of Semarang and Cirebon*. Melbourne: Monash University.

Di Meglio, Rita Rose. 1970. 'Arab Trade with Indonesia and the Malay Peninsula from the 8th to the 16th Century', in D. S. Richards (ed.), *Islam and the Trade of Asia*. Oxford: Bruno Cassirer Ltd., pp. 105–35.

Dumarçay, Jacques. 1985. 'La charpenterie des mosquées javanaises', *Archipel* 30, pp. 21–30.

Grabar, Oleg. 1988. 'Notes sur le *mihrab* de la Grand Mosquée de Cordoue', in Alexandre Papadopoulo (ed.), *Le mihrab dans l'architecture et la religion musulmanes*. Leiden: Brill, pp. 115–18.

Guillot, Claude. 1985. 'La symbolique de la mosquée javanaise. À propos de la 'Petite Mosquée' de Jatinom', *Archipel* 30, pp. 3–19.

Guy, John. 1989. 'The Vietnamese Wall Tiles of Majapahit', *Transactions of the Oriental Ceramic Society* 53, pp. 27–46.

Hartmann, M. and C. E. Bosworth. 'al-Ṣīn', *Encyclopaedia of Islam*, 2nd edition. http://dx.doi.org.libproxy.aucegypt.edu:2048/10.1163/1573-3912_islam_COM_1080 (accessed online 1 May 2019).

Hartono, Handinoto dan Samuel. 2007. 'Pengaruh Pertukangan Cina pada Bangunan Masjid Kuno di Jawa Abad 15–16', *Dimensi Teknik Arsitektur* 35, pp. 23–40.

Hillenbrand, Robert. 1978. 'Recent Work on Islamic Iconography', *Oriental Art* N.S. 24, no. 2, pp. 2011–13.

Jessup, Helen. 1990. *Court Arts of Indonesia*. New York: The Asia Society Galleries.

Kersten, Carool. 2017. *A History of Islam in Indonesia*. Edinburgh: Edinburgh University Press.

Krahl, Regina, John Guy, J. Keith Wilson and Julian Raby. 2011. *Shipwrecked: Tang Treasures and Monsoon Winds*. Washington and Singapore: Arthur M. Sackler Gallery, Smithsonian Institution.

Kusno, Abidin. 2003. '"The Reality of One-Which-Is-Two": Mosque Battles and Other Stories: Notes on Architecture, Religion, and Politics in the Javanese World', *Journal of Architectural Education* 57, pp. 57–67.

Laffan, Michael. 2009. 'Finding Java: Muslim Nomenclature of Insular Southeast Asia from Śrîvijaya to Snouck Hurgronje', in Eric Tagliacozzo (ed.), *Southeast Asia and the Middle East: Islam, Movement and the Longue Durée*. Stanford: Stanford University Press, pp. 17–64; also available as National University of Singapore, Asia Research Institute, Working Paper Series, No. 52, 5–6. (https://tengkudhaniiqbal.files.word press.com/2014/09/finding-java-2005-michael-laffan1.pdf) (accessed 1 May 2019).

Lee-Niinioja, Hee Sook. 2010. 'Javanese Muslims' Tolerance and Flexibility through Syncretic Ornamentation', *South and Southeast Asia: Culture and Religion (The SSEASR Journal)* 4, pp. 113–31.

Lico, Gerard. 2008. *Arkitekturang Filipino: A History of Architecture and Urbanism in the Philippines*. Diliman, Quezon City: University of the Philippines Press.

Lombard, Denys and Claudine Salmon. 1993. 'Islam and Chineseness', *Archipel* 57, pp. 115–31.

Mundy, Peter. 1919. *The Travels of Peter Mundy, in Europe and Asia, 1608–1667*, Richard Temple, ed. London: the Hakluyt Society.

Miksic, John. 2005. 'The Art of Cirebon and the Image of the Ascetic in Early Javanese Islam,' in James Bennett (ed.), *Crescent Moon: Islamic Art and Civilization in Southeast Asia*. Adelaide: Art Gallery of South Australia, pp. 120–44.

Needham, Joseph. 1971. *Science and Civilisation in China Volume 4: Physics and Physical Technology: Part III: Civil Engineering and Nautics*. Cambridge: Cambridge University Press.

Njoto, Hélène. 2018. 'What was Islamic about Javanese Art in the Early Islamic period (15th–17th century)?' *NSC Highlights* 7. https://www.iseas.edu.sg/images/pdf/NSC_Highlights_7_v2.pdf.

Njoto, Hélène. 2015. 'On the Origins of the Javanese Mosque', *Newsletter, International Institute for Asian Studies*. https://www.academia.edu/17330622/Helene_Njoto_On_the_Origins_of_the_Javanese_Mosque_IIAS_Newsletter_n.72_Autumn_2015_p._45.

Njoto, Hélène. 2014. 'À propos des origines de la mosquée javanaise', *Bulletin de l'Ecole Française d'Extrême-Orient* 100, pp. 11–37.

O'Kane, Bernard. 2019. 'Mughal Tilework: Derivative or Original?', *South Asian Studies*, 35:1, pp. 25–42.

O'Kane, Bernard. 2006. 'The Nine-Bay Plan in Islamic Architecture: Its Origin, Development and Meaning,' in Abbas Daneshvari (ed.), *Studies in Honor of Arthur Upham Pope*. Survey of Persian Art, vol. XVIII. Costa Mesa: Mazda Publishers, pp. 189–244.

O'Neil, Hugh. 1998. 'The Mosque as a Sacred Space', in Gunawan Tjahjono (ed.), *Indonesian Heritage: Architecture*. Singapore and Jakarta: Archipelago Press, pp. 94–5.

O'Neill, Hugh. 1994. 'South-East Asia', in Martin Frishman and Hasan-Uddin Khan (eds), *The Mosque*. London: Thames and Hudson, pp. 225–40.

Pirazzoli-T'Serstevens, Michèle. 1972. *Living Architecture: Chinese*. London: Macdonald.

Pope, Arthur Upham. 1946. 'Representation of Living Forms in Persian Mosques', *Bulletin of the Iranian Institute* 6/7, pp. 125–9.

Rasdi, Mohamad Tajuddin Mohamed. 2007. 'Mosque Architecture in Malaysia: Classification of Styles and Possible Influence', *Alam Bina* 9, pp. 20–2 (http://eprints.utm.my/id/eprint/1780/).

Robson, S. O. 1981. 'Java at the Crossroads: Aspects of Javanese Cultural History in the 14th and 15th Centuries', *Bijdragen tot de Taal-, Land-en Volkenkunde* 137, pp. 259–92.

Schouten, Wouter. 1648. *Oost-Indische voyagie*. Amsterdam: Voor J. Hartgerts.

Shokoohy, Mehrdad. 2003. *Muslim Architecture of South India: The Sultanate of Ma'bar and the Traditions of the Maritime Settlers on the Malabar and Coromandel Coasts (Tamil Nadu, Kerala and Goa)*. London and New York: Routledge Curzon.

Steinhardt, Nancy Schatzman. 2015. *China's Early Mosques*. Edinburgh: Edinburgh University Press.

Subarna, A. 1988. 'Le *mihrab* de la Grande Mosquée de Kasepuhan (Cirebon-Indonésie)', in Alexandre Papadopoulo (ed.), *Le mihrab dans l'architecture et la religion musulmanes*. Leiden: Brill, pp. 167–73.

Takahashi, Sakai. 2016. 'The Java/Malay Style Mosques Architecture and the Examples in Buton', *Journal of Southeast Asian Archaeology* 36, pp. 61–78.

Takahashi, Sakai. 2008. 'Preliminary Study of Vietnamese Decorated Tiles Found in Java, Indonesia (1)', *Taida Journal of Art History* 25, pp. 131–70 (http://ntur.lib.ntu.edu.tw/bitstream/246246/281796/1/0025_200809_4.pdf).

Tajudeen, Imran bin. 2017a. 'Trade, Politics and Sufi Synthesis in the Formation of Southeast Asian Islamic Architecture', in Finbarr Flood and Gülru Necipoğlu (eds), *A Companion to Islamic Art and Architecture*. Hoboken: Wiley, pp. 996–1022.

Tajudeen, Imran bin. 2017b. 'Mosques and Minarets: Transregional Connections in Eighteenth-Century Southeast Asia', *Journal East-Southeast* 18, Issue 4, http://www.journal18.org/2056. DOI: 10.30610/4.2017.4 (no pagination).

Tjandrasasmita, Uka. 1975a. *Islamic Antiquities of Sendang Duwar*. Jakarta: The Archaeological Foundation.

Tjandrasasmita, Uta. 1975b. 'Art du Mojapahit et art du Pasasir', *Archipel* 9, pp. 93–8.

Wahby, Ahmed. 2007. *The Architecture of the Early Mosques and Shrines of Java: Influences of the Arab Merchants in the 15th and 16th Centuries?*. PhD. dissertation, University of Bamberg, 2007 (available online at http://www.opus-bayern.de/uni-bamberg/volltexte/2008/137/).

Wain, Alexander. 2017a. 'China and the Rise of Islam on Java', in A. C. S. Peacock (ed.), *Islamisation: Comparative Perspectives from History*. Edinburgh: Edinburgh University Press, pp. 419–43.

Wain, Alexander. 2017b. 'The Two *Kronik Tionghua* of Semarang and Cirebon: A Note on Provenance and Reliability', *Journal of Southeast Asian Studies*, 48.2, pp. 179–95.

Wain, Alexander. 2015. *Chinese Muslims and the Conversion of the Nusantara to Islam*. PhD thesis, Oxford University.

Watson, Oliver. 1985. *Persian Lustre Ware*. London: Faber and Faber.

Weiler, Desiree. 2012. *Synkretismen im Sakral- und Profanbau Javas: Eine globalgeschichtliche Perspektive*, MA thesis, University of Vienna (http://othes.univie.ac.at/18983/, accessed 5 May 2019).

Weng, Hew Wai. 2014. 'Beyond "Chinese Diaspora" and "Islamic Ummah": Various Transnational Connections and Local Negotiations of Chinese Muslim Identities in Indonesia', *Sojourn: Journal of Social Issues in Southeast Asia*, 29.3, pp. 627–56.

Wessing, Robert. 1994. 'The Gunongan in Banda Aceh, Indonesia', *Archipel* 35, pp. 157–94.

Wessing, Robert. 1991. 'An Enclosure in the Garden of Love', *Journal of Southeast Asian Studies* 22, pp. 1–15.

Whelan, Estelle. 2006. *The Public Figure: Political Iconography in Medieval Mesopotamia*. London: Melisende Publishing.

Wubin, Zhuang. 2011. *Chinese Muslims in Indonesia*. Singapore: Select Books.

About the Contributors

Stephen Battle is the Principal Project Director responsible for sub-Saharan Africa at the World Monuments Fund.

Pierre Blanchard is Conservation Architect in Tanzania at the World Monuments Fund.

Madhavi Desai was Adjunct, Faculty of Architecture, CEPT University, Ahmedabad from 1986 to 2018.

Miki Desai is a recipient of the EARTHWATCH grant and former head of the Masters Programme in Sustainable Architecture at CEPT University, Ahmedabad.

Roghayeh Ebrahimi is at the Centre Asie du Sud-Est (CASE/UMR 8170), Paris.

Eric Falt was Director of the UNESCO New Delhi Office from May 2018 to September 2022. He is now Director and Representative of UNESCO for the Maghreb region, based in Rabat, Morocco.

Walid Ghali is Associate Professor at the Aga Khan University – Institute for the Study of Muslim Civilisations and the Head Librarian of the Aga Khan Library, London.

Valerie J. Hoffman is Research Professor Emerita of Islamic Studies in the Department of Religion, the University of Illinois, Urbana-Champaign.

Mohamed Mauroof Jameel is an architect and independent researcher on the architectural heritage of the Maldives.

Gulfishan Khan is Professor in Medieval Indian History, Coordinator and Chairperson of the Centre of Advanced Study in the Department of History and Coordinator of the Musa Dakri Museum at the Aligarh Muslim University.

Sana Mirza is Head of Scholarly Programs and Publications at the Freer Gallery of Art and Arthur M. Sackler Gallery, the Smithsonian's National Museum of Asian Art.

Beatrice Nicolini is Professor of History and Institutions of Africa, Faculty of Political and Social Sciences, Catholic University of the Sacred Heart, Milan.

Bernard O'Kane is Professor of Islamic Art and Architecture, the American University in Cairo.

M. Reza Pirbhai is Associate Professor of South Asian and World History, Georgetown University's School of Foreign Service.

Stéphane Pradines is Professor of Islamic Art and Architecture and the founder and Head of the Indian Ocean programme at AKU-ISMC.

Farouk Topan is Professor Emeritus at the Aga Khan University (AKU).

Index